XIN LI XUE
YUAN LI YU YING YONG

心理学原理与应用

主 编◎庄国萍 王 玲 孙慧英
副主编◎孙晓清 赵 嘉 王金素

华东师范大学出版社
·上海·

图书在版编目（CIP）数据

心理学原理与应用/庄国萍，王玲，孙慧英主编
．—上海：华东师范大学出版社，2022
ISBN 978-7-5760-3038-9

Ⅰ.①心… Ⅱ.①庄…②王…③孙… Ⅲ.①心理学
-高等师范院校-教材 Ⅳ.①B84

中国版本图书馆CIP数据核字（2022）第124997号

心理学原理与应用

主　　编	庄国萍　王　玲　孙慧英
项目编辑	范美琳
特约审读	王秋华
责任校对	侯心怡　时东明
装帧设计	庄玉侠

出版发行　华东师范大学出版社
社　　址　上海市中山北路3663号　邮编 200062
网　　址　www.ecnupress.com.cn
电　　话　021-60821666　行政传真 021-62572105
客服电话　021-62865537　门市（邮购）电话 021-62869887
地　　址　上海市中山北路3663号华东师范大学校内先锋路口
网　　店　http://hdsdcbs.tmall.com

印 刷 者　上海昌鑫龙印务有限公司
开　　本　787毫米×1092毫米　1/16
印　　张　23.25
字　　数　561千字
版　　次　2022年8月第1版
印　　次　2025年6月第3次
书　　号　ISBN 978-7-5760-3038-9
定　　价　49.00元

出 版 人　王　焰

（如发现本版图书有印订质量问题,请寄回本社客服中心调换或电话021-62865537联系）

前言

　　心理学的基本素养已经成为未来教师所必须具备的重要素养之一，心理学课程亦成为系列教师教育课程的基础课程之一。2016年12月30日，中宣部、教育部等22部门联合印发的《关于加强心理健康服务的指导意见》中指出："教育类专业要加强心理学理论教学和实践技能培养"。2018年1月20日，中共中央、国务院《关于全面深化新时代教师队伍建设改革的意见》再次明确提出"大力振兴教师教育，不断提升教师专业素质能力"的要求，其中把握心理发展规律，因材施教，促进学生的全面发展已经成为教师专业素养的重要组成部分。心理学课程作为高等院校重要的教师教育类课程，对提升未来教师素质具有重要作用。因此，在新形势下，编撰一部符合新时代教师素质要求、突出心理学原理在教育教学实践中的应用，并利用现代教育技术手段、创新教学方法的教材，已经成为时代的呼唤。

　　本教材是潍坊学院教师教育学院心理学教师长期一线教学的实践与探索，也是他们在此基础上的思考与凝练。本教材共有十五章，前十三章主要选取普通心理学基本理论中与教育教学实践密切相关的心理过程和个性心理等内容，同时根据教学的实际需求，以及学生对教师职业心理与学生心理健康相关内容的迫切需求，增设了后两章学生心理健康教育与辅导、教师职业心理的相关内容。以上教材内容的选取亦为后续学习"发展心理学""教育心理学"等相关课程奠定基础。全书以基本理论为主线，突出心理学在教育教学实践中的应用，为未来教师奠定教育科学素养。

　　本教材的编写特色主要有以下几点：一是可读性强。教材力求文字简练、概念明确、引文详实、图文并茂，比较符合师生们的阅读需求；二是应用性突出。在科学性、基础性的前提下，突出心理学原理的应用，以期帮助学生达到理论与实践的结合；三是实用性显著。本教材既保持学术性，又适合心理学知识零基础的学生学习，教育教学以及生活化案例的结合便于学生活学活用理论，符合本科院校公共心理学课的教学要求和实际；四是立体可视化。立足当代社会的互联网和信息技术优势，扩展教学资源。借助教材中的"结构图"把握教学内容的逻辑构成；通过二维码关联复习思考题，达到对知识点深度学习的目的，提高学生的自学能力；通过扫描二维码获取进一步阅读书目和自测量表，增加学生学习知识的厚度。

在体例编排上，本教材根据心理学原理与应用的教学需要，在每章之前设立本章的导入语、本章应掌握的重点内容以及结构图，每章内容中穿插拓展相关知识的专栏，每章之后提供本章小结、关键术语、讨论与应用、复习思考题、进一步阅读书目等栏目，部分章节还提供了帮助学生了解自我的心理自测量表。受篇幅所限，相关练习题及答案、进一步阅读书目、自测量表等都采取二维码的方式供学生扫描阅读。

本教材适合作为高等院校公共心理学课程教材，也可用作教师资格证培训及教师职后培训教材和自学者参考用书。

党的二十大报告强调，要"加强教材建设和管理"。教材是我国教育中的重要阵地，作为教材编写者，应紧扣时代的脉搏，将党的二十大精神落实到教材中，推动心理学科的建设与创新发展，提高教育教学质量和水平，以满足社会对心理学人才的需求，进一步强化教材在"立德树人"和"教书育人"中的协同作用，使教材更规范、更丰富、更实用，更好地发挥铸魂育人的功能。

本教材编写作者均为长期从事师范专业心理学课程教育教学研究的骨干教师，有着多年心理学本科教学的经历。他们将多年的教学经验和教学研究成果融合到本教材的内容体系中。本教材由庄国萍、王玲、孙慧英任主编，由孙晓清、赵嘉、王金素任副主编。全书各章承担执笔任务的是（以章节先后为序）：庄国萍（前言、第十三、十四、十五章）；王玲（第一、二、三章）；王金素（第四、六章）；孙晓清（第五、七、八章）；赵嘉（第十一、十二章）；孙慧英（第九、十章）。庄国萍、王玲、孙慧英负责本教材的提纲设计、组织协调和统稿定稿工作，赵嘉、孙晓清、王金素协助主编做了部分统稿、校对和整理工作，潍坊学院教师教育学院2017级学生梁晓娟、邓玮健、尹琳、朱红祥、王茜、张艺也为本教材的编写搜集了相关资料。

本教材在编写过程中引证了国内外许多心理学研究者的成果与资料，未能一一致函征询，在此向各位原作者表示歉意和谢忱。

由于编者学识、水平有限，书中缺点和不足在所难免，恳请广大读者批评指正。

编者
2023年12月

目录

第一章　绪论 / 1

第一节　心理学是一门什么样的科学 / 3
第二节　心理学的研究对象 / 9
第三节　心理学的历史发展 / 13
第四节　心理学的研究方法 / 22

第二章　心理的实质 / 29

第一节　心理是脑的机能 / 31
第二节　心理是客观现实的反映 / 43

第三章　感觉和知觉 / 51

第一节　感觉 / 53
第二节　知觉 / 63
第三节　感知觉规律在教育教学中的应用 / 72

第四章　记忆 / 81

第一节　记忆概述 / 83
第二节　记忆过程分析 / 88
第三节　记忆规律在教育教学中的应用 / 99

第五章 想象 / 105

　　第一节　表象概述 / 107
　　第二节　想象概述 / 110
　　第三节　想象的种类 / 115
　　第四节　想象规律在教育教学中的应用 / 118

第六章 思维 / 123

　　第一节　思维概述 / 125
　　第二节　思维的一般过程和形式 / 133
　　第三节　问题解决 / 137
　　第四节　思维规律在教育教学中的应用 / 147

第七章 注意 / 153

　　第一节　注意概述 / 155
　　第二节　注意的规律 / 158
　　第三节　注意规律在教育教学中的应用 / 166

第八章 情绪、情感 / 173

　　第一节　情绪、情感概述 / 175
　　第二节　情绪、情感的规律 / 180
　　第三节　情绪、情感规律在教育教学中的应用 / 186

第九章 意志 / 197

　　第一节　意志概述 / 199
　　第二节　意志行动的过程 / 205
　　第三节　意志规律在教育教学中的应用 / 209

第十章 个性心理与行为动力 / 215

　　第一节　个性概述 / 217
　　第二节　需要 / 220
　　第三节　动机 / 224

第四节 兴趣 / 236

第十一章 能力 / 241

第一节 能力概述 / 243
第二节 能力理论 / 246
第三节 能力测量 / 253
第四节 能力的个别差异 / 258
第五节 能力的影响因素及培养 / 262

第十二章 气质与性格 / 267

第一节 气质 / 269
第二节 性格 / 277

第十三章 自我意识 / 299

第一节 自我意识概述 / 301
第二节 自我意识发展的一般规律 / 307
第三节 自我意识规律在教育中的应用 / 312

第十四章 学生心理健康教育与辅导 / 319

第一节 心理健康概述 / 321
第二节 学校心理健康教育 / 324
第三节 学生心理辅导 / 328

第十五章 教师职业心理 / 339

第一节 教师的职业角色心理 / 341
第二节 教师的职业心理特征 / 346
第三节 教师的职业成长心理 / 350
第四节 教师的职业心理健康 / 355

参考文献 / 360

第一章 绪 论
XULUN

亲爱的同学,当你开始学习这本书的时候,你的内心可能充满了无数的疑问和好奇,心理学是不是可以让自己知道别人在想什么?心理学究竟研究什么?为什么要学习心理学等问题。接下来,就请带着你的疑问和好奇,开始心理学的学习之旅吧!在本章,你将了解到心理学的起源与发展,知晓心理学的研究对象和研究领域,接触到心理学家们的各种理论学说。通过本章的学习,相信你会对心理学产生与以往不同的认识和见解。让我们一起走进心理学的世界吧!

通过本章的学习,你将能够
- 理解和掌握心理学的概念
- 明确心理学的研究对象
- 知晓心理学的前世今生
- 了解心理学的不同理论学说

【本章结构】

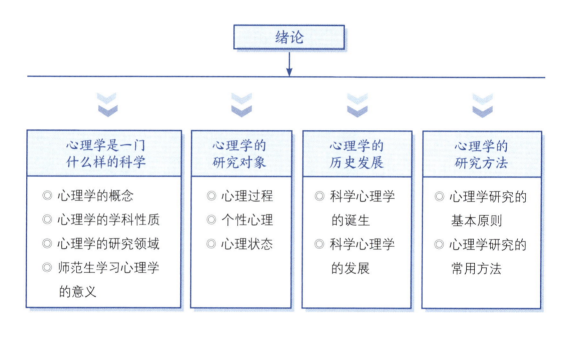

本章主要回答"心理学是什么"的问题,它有助于你掌握心理学的定义、心理学的研究对象和领域,以及心理学研究的原则和方法,并能帮助你了解心理学的前世今生以及学习心理学对师范生的重要意义。

第一节
心理学是一门什么样的科学

一、心理学的概念

当人们初次接触心理学时,往往容易产生某种神秘莫测之感,不知道也不了解心理学究竟是一门什么样的科学,这不足为奇。心理学是一门新兴的学科,它从哲学中分化出来成为一门独立的学科,距今只有一百多年的历史。心理学研究的对象,不是有形的实体,它无法用电子显微镜之类的仪器进行观察。正因为如此,人们不免觉得心理学有些神秘。

那么,心理学究竟是一门什么样的科学呢?我们首先分析一下心理学的英文单词。心理学,英文是"psychology"。这个词源于希腊文,由"psycho"和"logos"两部分组成。"psycho"的意思是"精神""心灵""灵魂",即人的心理,"logos"的意思是"学问""解说",连起来就是"关于心理、精神的学问或解说"。这个解释可以称得上是对心理学最早的定义,然而,这个定义并不能使人们对心理学有全面科学的认识。事实上,因为心理现象的复杂性,人们对心理科学内涵的认识随着不同学科和不同流派的发展也在不停地发生着变化。

19世纪末期,现代心理学创始人之一,美国心理学家詹姆斯(William James)认为,心理学的研究对象是人的意识。这一观点在20世纪20年代受到了新兴的行为主义学派的挑战。行为主义学派的创始人华生(John Watson)认为,人的意识是看不见、摸不着的,心理学应该研究看得见、摸得着的行为,而不是意识,只有研究可以被客观观察和测量的行为,心理学才能成为一门科学。然而,精神分析学派的开山鼻祖弗洛伊德(Sigmund Freud)对以上两种观点均嗤之以鼻。他认为,人的心理活动除了可以被觉察的一小部分外,更庞大的一部分心理活动是不可觉察的,弗洛伊德称之为"潜意识"或"无意识",而这才应该是心理学力图研究的重点。从这些学派之争中,我们可以看出,心理学所涉及到的研究领域是非常广泛的,除了上述的意识、行为、无意识之外,有些研究者对动物心理也很感兴趣。于是,对心理学下一个令所有人都满意的定义就变得非常困难。

学习心理学的人经常会被问到这样一个问题:"你是学心理学的,那你知道我此时此刻心里在想什么吗?"其实,心理学不会研究这个问题。一个人想些什么稍纵即逝,复杂多样,心理学不研究这些捉摸不定的东西,任何一门科学也都不会如此。当我们去研究它时,仅仅是为了揭示隐藏在这些现象后面的本质规律。因此,现在的研究者一般认为,心理学是一门研究人的心理现象产生、发展及变化规律的科学。如,我们知道,人眼可以看,人耳可以听,那么在什么条件下人们可以看得更清楚,听得更明白呢?有哪些因素会影响到我们看和听的效果呢?再深入一些,看和听的过程是如何产生的?人的大脑内部发生了哪些变化等,这就是在探讨人的心理现象产生、发展、变化的规律。

这个定义突出了两点：第一，讲明了心理学研究的主要是人的心理。动物也有心理，例如，猴王能指挥群猴与乌鸦作战，大猩猩和黑猩猩能掌握大量的手势语言等，说明它们的心理是相当高级的。心理学既研究人的心理，也研究动物的心理，主要研究人的心理和行为，研究动物的心理和行为是为了能更好地解释、预测与调控人的行为。第二，讲明了心理学要研究的是人的心理活动的规律。因为人的心理活动同其他事物一样，是有规律可循的，而且任何科学都是研究事物的规律的，没有规律的事物就不能成为科学研究的对象。

二、心理学的学科性质

人的心理现象十分复杂，人的心理的形成和发展会受到许多因素的影响，这些因素有的属于内部因素，如个体自身神经生理的活动特征、躯体特征等；有的属于外部因素，如每个人生存的环境、接受的教育、从事的实践活动等。这就要求我们在研究人的心理现象时，要从不同的角度和层面，采用不同的方法。有时需要从影响个体心理的内部因素入手，探讨个体心理活动的内部规律和内在机制；有时需要分析影响心理活动的外部因素，比如家庭、学校、社会以及人和人之间的相互关系等对个体心理发展的影响。一般说来，侧重于个体心理内在规律和机制的心理学研究具有自然科学的倾向，而侧重于社会对个体心理影响的心理学研究则具有社会科学的倾向。这样，心理学就具有了一种既和自然科学有关、又和社会科学有关的独特性质，也就是说，心理学是一门介于自然科学和社会科学之间的交叉学科。

作为自然科学倾向的心理学分支有实验心理学、生理心理学、医学心理学等，这些心理学分支和生物学、物理学、化学等学科有比较密切的联系。比如，对感知觉的研究就涉及被感知物体的声、光等特性，涉及感知神经的激活和对信息的处理，对神经细胞的研究又涉及细胞膜内外的电位差、细胞内的神经介质等内容。

作为社会科学倾向的心理学分支有社会心理学、发展心理学、管理心理学等，这些心理学分支和社会学、人类学、教育学等学科有比较密切的联系。当我们对人尤其是作为群体的人的某种社会行为进行研究的时候，就离不开历史的、文化的以及经济的观点。

不同倾向的心理学在研究方法上也有所不同，作为自然科学倾向的心理学更多地采用观察、实验等研究方法，在研究中注重条件的控制和变量的关系，研究的结果大多是定量的；作为社会科学倾向的心理学则较多地采用社会调查、个案研究、文献综合等方法，侧重于宏观因素的分析，所得的结果主要是定性的。不过随着统计方法的普遍使用以及计算机逐渐成为研究中不可缺少的工具后，即使是作为社会科学倾向的心理学研究，也有逐步向定量化发展的趋势。

三、心理学的研究领域

随着研究手段和相关学科的发展，心理学在理论上已经建立了自己独立的科学体系，在应用上也与社会实践领域建立了广泛的联系，形成了众多的分支领域，每个分支领域都有自己特定的研究对象、任务和意义。总体来说,可以将心理学的众多分支分为基础研究和应用研究两大领域。

(一) 基础研究

1. 普通心理学

普通心理学(general psychology)研究心理现象的一般规律,它以正常的成年人的心理活动和心理特征为主要的研究对象,同时它也概括各方面研究的成果。它是心理学的主干,心理学的不同分支都是由它分化出来的。

在普通心理学范围内,专门研究心理活动的不同过程和心理特征的不同方面的有:感觉知觉心理学、记忆心理学、思维心理学、言语心理学、情感心理学、意志心理学、个性心理学等。

2. 实验心理学

实验心理学(experimental psychology)是在实验室控制条件下进行研究工作的心理学分支学科。实验心理学的研究主题包括感觉、知觉、动机、情绪等,比如人们如何记忆,是什么导致遗忘,人们如何决策和解决问题等。与专门研究某一方面的心理学不同,它是研究心理学的一种方法学。许多心理学家为实验心理学奉献了科学的方法,并且随着日益精密的实验装置和测量仪器的使用,心理学的实验研究在客观性和准确性方面不断得到提高。

3. 认知心理学

认知心理学(cognitive psychology)是20世纪50年代中期在西方兴起的一种心理学思潮,20世纪70年代成为西方心理学的一个主要研究方向。它采用反应时研究法、计算机模拟和类比、口语记录法等研究方法来研究人的高级心理过程,主要是认知过程,如注意、知觉、记忆、思维和语言等。以信息加工观点研究认知过程是现代认知心理学的主流,可以说,认知心理学在很大程度上相当于信息加工心理学。它将人看作是一个信息加工的系统,认为认知就是信息加工,包括感觉信息的输入、编码、存储和使用的过程。认知心理学的兴起是西方心理学发展中的一个巨大变化。人工智能是现代认知心理学的一个重要研究方向。

4. 生理心理学

生理心理学(physiological psychology)是研究人的心理活动的生理机制的心理学分支学科,它以人脑的形态、结构和功能参数作为研究对象,分析在不同生理状态下个体行为与活动的生理机制,是心理学基础研究的重要组成部分。生理心理学在现代脑科学研究及现代技术的基础上,努力揭示心理现象的大脑解剖机制以及心理现象与脑功能之间的相互关系。

5. 发展心理学

发展心理学(developmental psychology)是研究个体从受精卵开始,到出生、成熟直至衰老的生命全程中心理发生、发展规律的心理学分支学科。其中研究心理种系发展的心理学叫比较心理学,它通过对人的心理与动物心理的比较来确定两者之间的联系和差别。研究个体心理发生、发展的心理学叫毕生发展心理学,分为婴幼儿心理学、儿童心理学、少年心理学、青年心理学、中年心理学和老年心理学。发展心理学是心理学理论体系的重要组成部分,也是对发展中的个体进行教育、培养、训练的心理学理论根据。

6. 人格心理学

人格心理学(personality psychology)是研究人与人之间个体差异,并整合各种影响因素对一个真实的人进行综合描述的心理学分支学科。它主要研究人格特征、人格动力、个体差异以及人格评鉴技术等问题。人格心理学家试图确定是什么原因导致一个人与另外一个人不同?为什么一些人容易忧郁和紧张,而另一些人却感到愉快和放松?为什么一些人稳重、谨慎,而另一些人不安静、好冲动?为什么男、女两性之间存在如此悬殊的差异等问题。

7. 社会心理学

社会心理学(social psychology)研究群体环境中个体心理发生、发展及其变化的规律,包括群体心理现象与行为、个体在所属群体影响下产生的心理现象与行为,以及自我调适行为。例如,个体如何受群体的影响而改变其行为?个体如何受到别人的压力而出现顺从行为?社会心理学在两个水平上进行研究:个体水平和群体水平。在个体水平上进行的研究内容有:个体社会化过程、印象形成、社会动机、社会态度等;在群体水平上进行的研究内容有:群体规范、人际吸引、人际关系、群体心理等。

除此之外,还有理论心理学、心理测量与统计、心理学史等基础学科。这些学科分别从不同的方面为心理学的整体发展做出了贡献,使我们得以从多个角度、多个层面逐步加深对神秘的心理现象的认识。

(二)应用研究

1. 教育心理学

教育心理学(education psychology)研究教育过程中教与学的心理活动规律,揭示教育过程和人的心理活动发展之间的相互关系。教育心理学以教师与学生之间的相互作用为研究对象,包括受教育者知识和技能掌握的心理特点、行为习惯和道德品质的形成规律,家庭、学校、社会等对受教育者的心理影响等。教育心理学包括学科教学心理学和德育心理学。教育心理学的研究直接关系到教育改革、人才培养,因此具有重要的理论和实践意义。

2. 工业心理学

工业心理学(industrial psychology)包括工程心理学和管理心理学。工程心理学研究现代工业中人与机器的关系,例如,设备如何适应人的活动特点,使人减少疲劳、增加安全与舒适度、提高工作效率等。管理心理学主要研究领导与管理风格,在管理活动中如何进行人员选拔、提高与激励员工的工作积极性及潜能发挥,进行员工在职培训,处理工作环境中的人际关系,提高工作效率、经济效益和社会效益等。

3. 临床心理学

临床心理学(clinical psychology)是运用心理学原理诊断和治疗异常心理的心理学分支学科。心理异常的临床表现包括情绪问题、行为怪异、犯罪倾向、智力迟钝、适应困难、人际关系紧张等。临床心理学家不同于精神病医生。临床心理学家以心理学原理和心理测量探索异常者心理方面的问题,并以心理矫正技术使心理异常者恢复正常。精神病医生则以医生的身份,运用医学知识,对病人施以手术或采用药物手段来治愈病人。对尚未发生心理异常但存在心理困扰的人，则需要进行心理咨询。心理咨询是运用心理学原理和心理疏解技术，通过商谈等程序，探讨来访者心理困扰的原因和行为问题症结，寻找摆脱困境的条件、途径和对策，使其自身改变原有的认知结构、负面态度和行为模式，增强自信心，以实现对社会生活的良好适应。

4. 司法与犯罪心理学

司法与犯罪心理学（judicial and criminal psychology）是研究违法行为以及处理违法行为中的心理学问题的学科。司法心理学的研究主要涉及犯罪、侦察、审讯以及改造罪犯等过程，研究内容包括犯罪原因、侦讯技术、改造手段以及侦察和审讯人员应具备的心理素质和心理技能等。犯罪心理学更加具体地研究罪犯形成犯罪心理和发生犯罪行为的原因、过程和规律。它通过对罪犯的知觉、推理、信念、态度和决策的研究，试图解决"是什么导致人犯罪"的问题。另外，它还研究人犯罪后在逃跑过程中或在法庭上的反应。青少年犯罪的心理特点、心理动机、个体人格和情绪特征是当前犯罪心理学研究的热点问题。

随着社会的发展，心理学的应用领域越来越宽广。近年来，健康心理学、军事心理学、航空心理学、市场营销心理学、领导与管理心理学等应用分支在世界范围内取得了迅速的发展。应用心理学家的努力，促进了人类潜能的发展，改善了大众的心理健康，促进了社会问题的解决。但是当今社会的压力、冲突和矛盾使得人们产生了越来越多的心理问题，应用心理学还有很长的路要走。

四、师范生学习心理学的意义

心理学课程是高等院校师范类学生的必修课，心理学课程的学习对师范生的专业成长来说有很大的帮助。

（一）有助于师范生学好教育科学理论

我国高等院校师范类的教学计划中都列出了心理学、教育学、学科教学法和教育实习四门公共必修课。这四门课犹如四级台阶：第一级是心理学，第二级是教育学，第三级是学科教学法，第四级是教育实习。心理学作为先行课，要为其他三门课打好理论基础。如果不学好心理学的基础理论知识，就无法科学地理解教育学和学科教学法的基本概念和基础理论，更无法搞好教育实习。当代教育改革的理论，大部分是心理学家、教育学家根据学生心理发展规律提出来的。不学好心理学的基础理论，就无法理解教育改革理论，更无法参加教改实践。

（二）有助于师范生运用心理学原理提高教学效果

教学是教师工作的核心内容，提高教学质量是每位教师锲而不舍的努力方向，更是学校教学改革的根本目标。而教学是师生双方共同参与的双边活动，是教育者对被教育者施加影响的基本途径，是科学性和艺术性相结合的工作，并不是仅仅掌握某学科的专业知识就能轻松驾驭和胜任的。美国著名教育心理学家盖茨（A. J. Gates）曾说过："当别人向你问及类似'你是教数学的老师吗'的问题时，你最恰当的回答应该是'我不是教数学的老师,我是教学生学数学的老师。'"① 因此,提高教学质量的关键,是教师如何采用最佳的教学手段以优化影响学生学习效果的各种因素,这就需要了解学生进行信息加工的一些主要心理过程、获取知识和发展能力的规律以及有关的非智力因素情况,从而运用心理科学在这些方面所提供的原理,增加教学的科学性和艺术性,切实提高教学质量。

(三) 有助于师范生运用心理学原理提高育人效果

对于一名合格的教师来说,既要教书还要育人,两者缺一不可,这是作为教师的两项重要工作。师范生今后接触的教育对象可能是刚刚迈入校门的小学生,也可能是处于叛逆期的初高中学子,不管是哪个年级的学生,他们都正处于人生中身心发展的重要时期,也是接受外界影响的关键时期。在对他们进行知识传授的同时,还要帮助他们塑造良好的个性,形成优良的个性特征。这样,就需要了解个性的结构和形成的规律、影响因素,以及儿童、青少年发展中的年龄特点,采取恰当的措施对发展中的儿童、青少年施加影响。随着育人工作内涵的丰富,对青少年社会交往的指导、性教育和心理咨询与辅导,也被纳入了育人工作的范畴。这一切都需要师范生——未来的教师从心理学中获得有关的科学知识和相应的操作指导。

(四) 有助于师范生运用心理学原理进行教育科研

未来的教师不只是进行教书育人的工作,还要善于在教书育人的实践中不断探索、不断改革,积极地进行教育科研工作。可以说,在教育理论的指导下,结合自身的教育实践开展教育科研的能力,也是未来教师基本素质的一个组成部分。而在运用教育理论进行教育科研、教育改革的过程中,心理学具有十分重要的作用。如苏联心理学家维果茨基(Lev Vygotsky)提出的"最近发展区"理论、瑞士心理学家皮亚杰(Jean Piaget)提出的"认知发展阶段"理论,在教育领域都有重大影响。因此,师范生学习心理学原理和研究方法,将大大增强其今后开展教育科研的能力。

(五) 有助于师范生运用心理学原理促进自身发展

处于青年期、又正值求学阶段的师范生,也面临自身的发展。心理学这门课程既对师范生从事教育青少年工作有着多方面的意义,也对他们现时的自我教育、自身发展具有同样有效的促进作用。运用心理学原理能优化教书育人的效果,也自然能优化自我教育、促进自身发展的效果,只是对象不同而已。例如,师范生将来要能运用有关记忆、思维方面的规律去指导学生掌握记忆策略和解决问题的思维策略,现时则首先要能运用有关规律来指导自己学习,提高学习效率。而将来如果要运用心理咨询手段去辅导学生,现时则可以此来调节自己的心理,以求健康发展。对于师范生来说,这种促进作用更有特殊的意义,因为师范生自身素质的全面发展不仅仅益在自身,更利在后人,其素质的提高又会进一步促进将来教书育人的工作。

---

① 卢家楣,魏庆安,李其维.心理学:基础理论及其教学应用[M].上海:上海人民出版社,1998:40.

第二节 心理学的研究对象

我们生活在一个五彩缤纷的世界。我们周围存在着各种各样的现象，如日月星辰、山川河流、飞禽走兽、花鸟虫鱼，这些属于自然现象；还有社会现象，如风土人情、社会准则、道德规范、婚姻家庭等。这些现象分别由不同的学科进行研究，构成了人类不同的知识领域。除此之外，还有一种重要的现象即心理现象，对心理现象的研究也构成了独特的学科体系。

心理现象是世界上最复杂、最奇妙的现象之一。它没有形体，看不见，摸不着，因而不易被人们了解。但是心理现象又每时每刻在每一个人的身上发生着，因而又是每一个人都非常熟悉的。心理现象无处不在，可以说，只要有人的地方就有人的心理现象。雨果曾说过："地球上最辽阔的是海洋，比海洋辽阔的是天空，而比天空更辽阔的是人的心灵。"人们的学习、劳动、交往、娱乐、教育、教学、科学发明与艺术创作都与心理现象密不可分。

人的心理现象千姿百态，我们如何具体地认识它呢？这就需要把心理现象作具体的划分，以便分门别类、有条不紊地认识它。现代心理学的一种流行观点是把人的心理现象看作一个复杂的系统。据此，有人把心理现象划分为心理事实与心理规律；有人把心理现象划分为无意识现象与意识现象。我们采取的是多数心理学家的观点，即把心理现象划分为心理过程、个性心理和心理状态三大范畴。

一、心理过程

心理过程指人对客观事物不同方面及相互关系的反映过程。它是心理现象的动态形式，包括认知过程、情绪和情感过程、意志过程。

（一）认知过程

认知过程（cognitive process）是指个人获取知识和运用知识的心智活动，是人的最基本的心理过程，包括感觉、知觉、记忆、思维和想象等过程。

感觉是人脑对客观事物个别属性的反映。比如这里有一个水果，它的颜色是红、青两色或两色混合，形状类似圆柱形，摸起来很光滑，闻起来很清香，吃起来甜润可口，这样，通过我们的各个感官，眼睛、鼻子、舌头，我们了解到了这个水果许多方面的特征，这个过程我们把它称之为感觉。

在感觉的基础上，我们把由各个感觉通道得来的信息综合起来，形成对事物整体的认识，感觉就上升为知觉。通过眼看、手摸、鼻子闻、嘴巴尝，我们知道这是一个苹果，而不是一个桔子。知觉就是人脑对客观事物整体属性的反映。感觉和知觉往往紧密地联系在一起，不能截然分开，一般统称为感知觉。也就是说，在现实生活中，纯粹的感觉是很难找到的，某一种水果，我们一眼看到，就知道是什么水果了，无需再用手摸、用鼻子闻，不用一一了解它的个别属性,就可形成对事物的整体认识,这是因为知觉的产生与人的知识经验密切相关。

一些感知过的事物,虽然已成过去,但在需要的时候或无意中还会浮现在脑海中,这种现象就是记忆。如,游览了杭州西湖,其美丽的景色会在大脑中留下深刻的印象;读了李白的《望庐山瀑布》后,再看到瀑布,又会触景生情,自然地吟诵出诗歌来,这种人脑对过去经历过的事物的反映,叫做记忆。

人不仅能直接地感知事物的表面特征,还能间接地、概括地反映事物的内在的、本质的特征,这个过程就是思维。例如,中医讲究望、闻、问、切,医生根据病人的脉搏、体温、舌苔等的变化,可以推断其体内的疾患;教师根据学生的外部表现和言行,可以了解其内心世界;当看到天空中乌云密布、燕子低飞,我们便能推断出要下雨了等,这都是一个个的思维过程。

人不仅能够在头脑中再现过去事物的形象,还能在此基础上创造事物的新形象。例如,文学艺术家通过对生活的体验和观察,塑造了一个个典型形象,而我们在阅读这些作品的时候,这些人物形象又会一一浮现在我们的脑海中。以及我们在头脑中对未来生活和工作情景的勾画等,这类心理活动叫做想象。

感觉、知觉、记忆、思维和想象都属于人的认知过程。

(二) 情绪和情感过程

情绪和情感过程(affective process)是人对客观事物能否满足其需要而产生的态度体验过程。人在认识客观事物的时候,并不是呆板冷漠的,而总是对它表现出一定的态度,产生这样或那样的感受和体验,例如,我们对祖国名山大川的赞美,对不道德行为的反感,对本职工作的热爱,对取得成绩的喜悦等,这些在认知基础上产生的喜、怒、哀、乐等态度体验,心理学上称之为情绪、情感过程。

(三) 意志过程

人在认识事物、体验情绪和情感的同时,还能在认识的基础上及情绪情感的推动下对客观事物发挥能动作用,有目的、有计划地改造世界。这种自觉的确立目的,克服困难,以实现预定目的的心理过程称为意志过程(will process)。意志过程是人的主观能动性的集中体现。

认知过程、情绪和情感过程、意志过程三者相互联系、相互影响。一般来说,认知过程是情绪和情感过程、意志过程的基础。没有认知,人的情感既不能产生,也不能发展。同样,只有在认知和情感的基础上,人才能自觉地进行意志行动。"知之深,爱之切,行之坚",说的就是这个道理。反过来,情感、意志过程又能巩固和深化人的认知过程。

此外,还有一种特殊的心理现象,它不属于某一种独立的心理过程,但是所有的心理过程都离不开它的参与。这种特殊的心理现象就是注意。我们在感知某一种事物,回忆某一件事情,思考某一个问题,想象某一个形象时,必须伴随着注意才能使我们更好地看清它、听清它、思考它。注意是伴随在心理过程中的一种心理活动,它是人们从事任何活动、获取信息、提高工作效率的必要的心理条件。

二、个性心理

心理过程是人的心理的共性,但在每一个人身上体现时,由于社会生活环境、教育、先天条件等因素的影响,又会表现出特殊性、差异性,并逐步形成人的心理的个性。个性是一个人在活动中所表现出来的比较稳定的心理倾向和心理特征的总和,它是人的心理现象的静态形式。个性心理包括三个方面:个性倾向性、个性心理特征和自我意识。

(一) 个性倾向性

个性倾向性(personality trend)包括需要、动机、兴趣、信念、世界观等,它是人的个性心理结构中最活跃的因素。

需要是人的行为的直接导因,在生活中,人们之所以去从事某一行动是因为人们心中有某种需要。如我们在课堂上认真听讲,是因为我们有求知的需要;下课后我们到餐厅吃饭,是因为我们有饮食的需要。可以说,人的各种活动,从饥择食、渴择饮到从事物质资料的生产、科学技术的发明与创造、文学艺术的创作,都是在需要的推动下进行的。按照马斯洛的理论,人的需要是有不同层次的,有低级需要,也有高级需要,从生理需要、安全需要,到归属和爱的需要、尊重需要、自我实现的需要等,这些不同层次的需要激发了人们不同的行为,成为个性积极性的源泉。

动机也是这样,在实际生活中,我们去做什么,而不去做什么,是由一个人的需要和动机决定的,需要和动机是人们行动的直接导因。

兴趣也是支配人的行动的内部动力因素之一。如有的人喜欢读历史,有的人喜欢学外语,有的人喜欢逻辑思考,有的人喜欢文学创作,由于个人兴趣的不同,导致我们选择学习不同的专业,兴趣也能支配一个人的行动。

除此之外,人还有更高层次的驾驭人的行为的因素,如理想、信念、世界观、价值观等,如有的人热爱生活,有明确的目标,这促使他严格要求自己,认真努力地学习和工作;有的人则百无聊赖,过一天算一天,没有明确的生活目标,最终一事无成。这体现了不同的人生观、世界观对人的行为的影响。这些因素从更高层次约束着人的需要和动机,使之符合一定的社会道德规范。

总之,个性倾向性用一句话来概括就是,它是推动人行动的内部的动力源泉,反映一个人的心理倾向,有时也将其称为个性的动力系统。

(二) 个性心理特征

个性心理特征(psychological characteristic of personality)包括能力、气质和性格,这是人的个性心理的具体表现。个性心理特征体现着人的心理的鲜明的差异性。例如,有的人记得快、记得牢,有的人记得慢、忘得快;有的人善于绘画,有的人有音乐才能;有的人善于形象思维,有的人则善于抽象思维;有的人善于创造性地解决问题,有的人则循规蹈矩,不善开拓,这些都是能力方面的差异。有的人喜欢把注意力指向外部世界,有的人喜欢内省;有的人脾气急,有的人脾气慢;有的人反应快,有的人反应慢,这是气质方面的差异。有的人诚实勤恳,有的人敷衍懒惰;有的人自私虚伪,自我中心,有的人热情大方,肯体谅他人,这是性格方面的差异。"人心不同,各如其面",就是指人的个性心理特征方面存在的差异。

(三) 自我意识

自我意识(self-consciousness)是人对自己及其与周围世界关系的意识,它包括个体对自身的意识和对自身与他人关系的意识两大部分。自我意识是人的意识活动的一种形式，人除了能认识和改造客观世界之外，还能认识和改造人类自身，这是人的心理区别于动物心理的一大特征。自我意识主要通过自我认识、自我体验和自我调控三种形式表现出来。人们常常会问自己"我是谁""我是个什么样的人""我为什么会成为这样的人"等，这些问题涉及的就是自我认识过程。人不仅能认识自己，还能在认识的基础上进行自我体验，"我这个人怎么样""我对自己满意吗""我能接受自己吗"等，这些问题涉及的是自我体验过程。自尊、自爱、自豪、自卑、自惭形秽是常见的自我体验形式。人在自我认识、自我体验的基础上，经常会问自己"我要成为一个什么样的人""我如何改变自己""我怎样闯过难关"等，这些问题涉及的就是人的自我调控过程。因此，自我意识是改造自身主观因素的途径，它能使人不断地进行自我监督、自我修养、自我完善。

心理过程与个性心理是紧密联系在一起的。第一，心理过程在每个人身上表现时，总具有个人的特点。也就是说，个性心理是通过心理过程形成的。第二，个性心理要通过人的心理过程表现出来，并制约着心理过程的发展。正是因为心理过程和个性心理相互融汇，相互制约，才形成一个人完整的心理面貌。

三、心理状态

在日常生活中，我们还会发现这样一种心理现象，有时我们感到情绪激昂，心情愉快，做什么事情都很有劲头；有时我们又感到情绪低落，无精打采，对什么事情都提不起兴趣，这在心理学上称为心理状态。

心理状态是心理活动在一定时间内出现的相对稳定的持续状态。它既有心理过程的暂时性、可变性的特点，又具有个性的持久性、稳定性的特点。所以心理学把心理状态看作介于这二者之间的中间状态。人的心理活动和行为表现都是在一定的心理状态下进行的。要想真正理解一个人的心理活动和行为表现，是不能不了解他此时此刻的心理状态的。学生学习、工人生产、士兵打仗、运动员比赛等，其成效如何，都与心理状态有关。因此，心理状态作为心理学研究对象的一个重要部分，已日益引起人们的重视。心理状态的表现是多方面的，它可以表现在知、情、意的任何一个方面。如好奇、疑惑、沉思，这是认知方面的心理状态；淡泊、焦虑、渴求，这是情绪方面的心理状态；克制、犹豫、镇定，这是意志方面的心理状态。研究、考察人的心理状

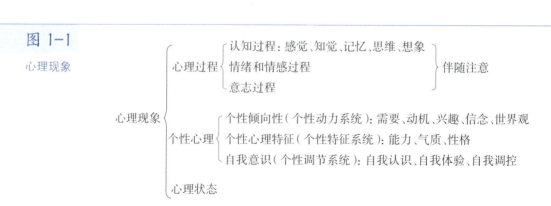

图 1-1　心理现象

态,不仅要描述其表现形态,而且要把握其具体成因,这样才有应用价值。

通过以上阐述,我们知道,心理学的研究对象可以划分为心理过程、个性心理和心理状态三大范畴,而每个范畴又包含着一些不同的方面。这种划分对于了解和研究人的心理是方便的,但必须防止把这种划分绝对化。在现实的人身上,不论哪种心理现象都不会孤立地存在。人的心理具有高度的整体性。心理的各组成部分之间存在着相互联系、相互依存、相互影响的辩证关系。在学习以下各章时,我们必须记住心理学的这个基本观点。

第三节
心理学的历史发展

一、科学心理学的诞生

德国心理学家艾宾浩斯(H. Ebbinghous)曾经说过,心理学有着漫长的过去,但却只有短暂的历史。因此,心理学是一门既古老又年轻的科学。说它古老,是因为心理学源于已有两千多年历史的哲学。说它年轻,是因为心理学从开始独立成为一门科学至今,只有一百多年的时间,是一门正在成长的年轻学科。

在心理学独立成为一门学科以前,有关"知识""观念""心""心灵""意识""欲望"和"人性"等心理学问题,一直是古代哲学家、教育家、文学艺术家和医生们共同关心的问题。

在欧洲,心理学的历史可以追溯到古希腊柏拉图、亚里士多德的时代。亚里士多德(Aristotle)是一位学识渊博的哲学家,他从理论上对灵魂的实质、灵魂与身体的关系、灵魂的种类与功能等问题进行了探讨。他的著作《论灵魂》是历史上第一部论述各种心理现象的著作。亚里士多德把心理功能分为认知功能和动求功能。在他看来,认知功能有感觉、意象、记忆、思维等。外物作用于各种不同的感官产生感觉和感觉意象。简括的意象构成经验,从经验抽象出概念,构成原理,就是思维。在感觉与思维之间,意象具有重要的作用。他说:"灵魂不能无意象而思维",思维所用的概念是由意象产生的。动求功能包括情感、欲望、意志、动作等过程。自由而不受阻碍的活动会产生愉快的情感,这种情感有积极的作用。相反,活动受到阻碍将引起不愉快的情感,它的作用是消极的。亚里士多德的这些思想对后来心理学的发展产生了影响,对当代的心理学思潮也有重要的影响。

在我国,心理学的思想可以追溯到先秦诸子百家时代。如孔子在其教育实践中提出"多见""多闻""多问""学而时习之""温故知新""学而不思则罔,思而不学则殆"等教育心理学思想。孟子主张"人性本善",认为"学不可以已""学至乎殁而后止",倡导终身学习、持之以恒的思想。荀况则主张人性本"恶",注重环境和教育在人性改变中的作用,写下著名的《劝学》,论述了学习的重要性,学习的步骤、内容、途径等有关问题。

但由于心理现象的复杂性,历史上专门针对心理学问题进行探讨的著述甚少。在19世纪70年代之前,心理学一直作为哲学的一个部分而存在,研究心理现象的多数为哲学家、教育家和思想家,研究方法带有极大的主观性和思辨性。随着17世纪至19世纪生理心理学、生物学、心理物理学的发展,心理学才终于脱离哲学的怀抱,成为一门独立的学科。

1879年,冯特(Wilhelm Wundt)在德国莱比锡大学创立了世界上第一个心理实验室,用实验的手段来研究心理现象,这被公认为是心理科学独立的标志。冯特反对用哲学思辨的方式探讨心理现象,坚持用观察、实验以及数理统计等自然科学的方法揭示心理过程的规律,因而取得了丰硕的研究成果,并培养了一批来自世界各地的学生。冯特一生著作很多,其中《生理心理学原理》一书被誉为"心理学独立的宣言书",是心理学史上第一部有系统体系的心理学专著。冯特也因此被誉为"实验心理学之父"和"心理学之父"。

图1-2 威廉·冯特

威廉·冯特(Wilhelm Wundt, 1832—1920),德国生理学家、心理学家、哲学家,构造主义心理学派的创始人,实验心理学之父。为科学心理学的诞生作出了卓越的贡献。他学识渊博,著述甚丰,一生作品达540余篇,研究领域涉及哲学、心理学、生理学、物理学、逻辑学、语言学、伦理学、宗教等。他的《生理心理学原理》是近代心理学史上第一部最重要的著作。主要著作有:《生理心理学原理》《民族心理学》《关于人类和动物心灵的讲演录》等。

专栏1-1

科学心理学产生的历史源头

心理学是在19世纪末独立成为一门学科的。近代心理学的诞生和发展有三个重要的历史源头。

(一)近代哲学思潮的影响

近代哲学主要是指法国17世纪的唯理论和英国17—18世纪的经验论。

唯理论(rationalism)的代表人物是17世纪法国著名哲学家笛卡儿(Rene Descartes)。笛卡儿认为只有理性是真实的,只有理性才是真理的唯一尺度。在身心关系的问题上,笛卡儿承认灵魂与身体有密切的关系。如感知觉、想象、某些情绪活动等心理现象都离不开身体的活动。身体就像一部自动的机械,其活动受力学规律的支配。笛卡儿用反射(reflex)的概念来解释动物的行为和人的某些无意识的简单行为。虽然承认身心的密切关系,但笛卡儿认为,用身体的原因不足以解释全部的心理活动，只有灵魂的参与，才能引起人的心理活动。所以笛卡儿把统一的心理现象分成了两个方面，即一方面心理依赖于身体组织，另一方面心理是独立于身体组织之外的，因而陷入了二元论。笛卡儿持有"天赋观念"的思想，即人的某些观念不是由经验产生的，而是先天所赋予的。笛卡儿关于身心关系的思想推动了解剖学和生理学的研究，这对现代心理学的诞生有直接的影响。他对理性和天赋观念的重视也影响到了现代心理学的理论发展。

经验主义（empiricism）的代表人物是洛克（John Locke），他被认为是经验主义哲学的奠基人。洛克反对笛卡儿的"天赋观念"说。洛克认为人的心灵最初像一张白纸，没有任何观念。一切知识和观念都是后天从经验中获得的。洛克把经验分成外部经验与内部经验两种。外部经验叫感觉，来源于客观的物质世界。人的经验来源于物质世界的属性或特性对外部感官的作用。而内部经验叫做反省，是人们对思维、意愿、好恶等个体的内部活动的观察。洛克的思想摇摆在唯物主义和唯心主义之间，他重视外部经验，承认客观的物质世界是外部感觉的源泉，这是唯物的；但他同时承认反省和外部感觉一样，是观念的独立源泉，这种思想又摇摆到唯心主义的方面去了。

随着经验主义的不断发展，出现了联想主义的哲学思想。代表人物有詹姆士·穆勒（James Mill）、约翰·穆勒（John Mill）、培因（Alexander Bain）等。他们用联想的原则来解释人的全部心理活动。联想主义认为所有复杂的观念都是由简单观念借助联想而形成的。我们有关"砖头"的观念，借助联想的功能就会形成"墙"的观念；"泥灰"的观念借助联想而形成"地面"的观念；"玻璃"和"木条"的观念借助联想会形成"窗户"的观念；"墙壁""地面"和"窗户"的观念借助联想会形成"房屋"的观念等。人的心理世界就是由观念按联想的原则建构起来的。

哲学上唯理论与经验论的斗争一直持续到现代，并表现在现代心理学各种理论派别的斗争中。例如，在个体发展的问题上存在遗传决定论和环境决定论的争论，这种争论实际上反映了唯理论与经验论的斗争。同样，联想主义对现代学习、记忆和思维的理论也产生了深远的影响。巴甫洛夫的条件反射说和华生的行为主义，这些学说和理论都受到了联想主义的影响。

（二）生理学的影响

19世纪30年代，生理学已成为一门独立的实验科学。生理学的发展，特别是神经生理学和感官生理学的发展，对心理学走上独立发展的道路产生了重要的影响。

19世纪，西班牙人卡哈尔（S. R. Cajal）根据前人神经解剖学的知识和自己显微镜内染色切片研究的结果，提出了神经元学说。1819年，法国著名生理学家马戎第（F. Magendie）通过动物实验发现传导感觉信息和运动信息分别由不同的神经所分担。1840年，德国人雷蒙德（Du Bois Reymond）发现了神经冲动的电现象。

1850年，德国著名科学家赫尔姆霍茨（H. Von. Helmholtz）用青蛙的运动神经测量了神经的传导速度，这项研究为在生理学和心理学中应用反应时的测量方法奠定了基础。1861年，法国医生布洛卡（Paul Broca）从尸体解剖中发现，严重的失语症与左侧额叶部分组织的病变有关，从而确定了语言运动区（布洛卡区）的位置。1869年，英国神经学家杰克逊（H. Jackson）提出了大脑皮层的基本机能界限：中央沟前负责运动，中央沟后负责感觉。1870年，德国生理学家弗里茨（G. Fritsch）与希兹（E. Hitzig）用电刺激法研究大脑功能，发现动物的运动性行为是由大脑额叶的某些区域支配的。这些研究不仅加深了人们对大脑机能分区的认识，而且为研究心理现象和行为的生理机制开辟了广阔的前景。这个时期生理学家和物理学家在感官生理学方面的一系列重要发现，也为心理学用实验的方法研究感知觉问题奠定了基础。

（三）物理学的影响

物理学以其严谨精确的研究方法在科学界取得了巨大的成功。19世纪中叶，心理学研究开始借鉴物理学的科学研究方法。1834年，德国生理学家韦伯（Ernst Weber）第一次提出阈限的概念，并提出了著名的韦伯定律（Weber's Law）。另一位贡献巨大的人物为费希纳（Gustav Fechner），费希纳在韦伯定律的基础上提出说明心量和物理量之间关系的定律，即感觉强度与刺激强度的对数成正比，这就是心理学中著名的费希纳定律（Fechner's law）。费希纳把物理学的数量化测量引入心理学，提供了感觉测量和心理实验的方法和理论，为冯特建立实验心理学奠定了基础。

——郑红，樊洁，倪嘉波，等.心理学原理与应用[M].北京：清华大学出版社，2015：14.

二、科学心理学的发展

科学心理学诞生之后，在19世纪末至20世纪初期，由于人们对心理学研究的对象和方法的看法不同，加之各种哲学思潮的影响，心理学领域出现了许多学派，它们研究的重点不同，观点各异，争论不休。直到20世纪30年代以后，各个学派之间才开始形成了相互学习、取长补短、兼收并蓄、积极发展的局面。20世纪50年代以来，认知心理学和人本主义心理学迅速发展，成为当代心理科学发展的新趋势。随着科学技术的发展，在社会实践活动需要的推动下，心理学通过不断改进和完善原有的研究方法和技术，其基础理论研究进一步深入，应用性研究蓬勃发展。据统计，现代心理学已经有20多个学术派别，100多个分支，形成了庞大的心理科学体系。今天，心理学的许多研究成果，不仅应用于教育、医疗、工程技术、航空航天等领域，而且渗透到仿生学、人类学、控制论、人工智能、系统工程等许多尖端科学技术部门，愈来愈显示出科学心理学的价值和强大的生命力。

（一）构造主义心理学（structural psychology）

构造主义心理学的奠基人为冯特，著名代表人物是其学生铁钦纳（E. B. Titchener），构造主义心理学是心理学独立后的第一个心理学流派。其基本观点为：心理学应该研究人的意识（经验）及意识的构造，就像化学把物质分解为各个元素一样，意识的内容也可以被分解为各种基本元素。该学派把人的意识分为感觉、意象和情感三种元素。感觉是知觉的元素，意象是观念的元素，而情感是情绪的元素，所有复杂的心理现象都是由这些元素构成的。在研究方法上，构造主义主张使用实验内省法，这是一种将内省法与实验法结合起来的方法。即研究者控制刺激，使之系统地发生变化，然后让被试直接报告自己体验到的内部经验。在他们看来，了解人们的直接经验，要依靠实验过程中被试对自己经验的观察和描述。

构造主义心理学倡导应用实验室实验法来研究心理学，为后来实验心理学的发展开辟了广阔的道路。但他们只重视对意识结构的研究，不注重心理学在实际中的运用，这一取向受到了心理学家们的批评。到20世纪20年代后，构造主义心理学的影响逐渐衰落。

图1-3　爱德华·布雷福德·铁钦纳

爱德华·布雷福德·铁钦纳（Edward Bradford Titchener，1867—1927）是英籍美国心理学家，实验心理学的代表人物之一。他生于英国奇切斯特，1885年进入牛津大学学习古典文学和哲学，1890年到德国师从威廉·冯特学习心理学。1892年到美国康奈尔大学教授心理学。他继承和发展了冯特的实验心理学，于1898年正式创立构造心理学学派。

（二）机能主义心理学（functional psychology）

机能主义心理学的创始人是美国著名心理学家詹姆斯，其他代表人物还有杜威（John Dewey）和安吉尔（James Angell）等人。机能心理学也主张研究人的意识，但是他们不把意识看成个别心理元素的集合，而看成川流不息的过程。在他们看来，意识是个人的、永远变化的、连续的和有选择性的。意识的作用就是使有机体适应环境。如果说构造主义强调意识的构成成分，那么机能主义则强调意识的作用与功能。以思维为例，构造主义关心什么是思维，而机能主义则关心思维在人类适应行为中的作用。机能主义的这一特点，推动了美国心理学面向实际生活的进程。20世纪以来，美国心理学一直比较重视心理学在教育领域和其他领域的应用，这与机能主义的思潮是分不开的。

图 1-4 威廉·詹姆斯

威廉·詹姆斯（William James，1842—1910），美国本土第一位哲学家和心理学家，也是教育学家、实用主义的倡导者，机能主义心理学派创始人之一。1904年当选为美国心理学会主席，1906年当选为美国国家科学院院士。2006年被美国的权威期刊《大西洋月刊》评为"影响美国的100位人物之一"（第62位）。詹姆斯的著作有：《心理学原理》《对教师讲心理学和对学生讲生活理想》《实用主义》《彻底经验主义论文集》等。

（三）行为主义心理学（behaviorism psychology）

19世纪末20世纪初，正当构造主义和机能主义在一系列问题上发生激烈争论时，美国心理学界出现了另一种思潮：行为主义（behaviorism）。1913年，美国心理学家华生（John Watson）发表了《在行为主义者看来的心理学》，宣告了行为主义的诞生。斯金纳（Burrhus Frederic Skinner）进一步发展了华生的理论，提出了著名的强化理论，成为行为主义学派的重要代表人物。

图 1-5 约翰·华生

约翰·华生（John Broadus Watson，1878—1958）美国心理学家，行为主义心理学的创始人。1915年当选为美国心理学会主席。主要研究领域包括行为主义心理学理论和实践、情绪条件作用和动物心理学。他认为心理学研究的对象不是意识而是行为，心理学的研究方法必须抛弃内省法，而代之以实验法和观察法。他还把行为主义研究方法应用到了动物研究、儿童教养和广告方面。他在使心理学客观化方面发挥了巨大的作用，对心理学的发展产生了重大影响。

图 1-6 伯尔赫斯·弗雷德里克·斯金纳

伯尔赫斯·弗雷德里克·斯金纳（Burrhus Frederic Skinner，1904—1990），美国心理学家，新行为主义学习理论的创始人，也是新行为主义的主要代表。斯金纳提出了操作条件反射原理，用强化理论来解释人类行为的习得。为表彰斯金纳在心理科学方面作出的重大贡献，1990年8月10日美国心理学会授予他"心理学毕生贡献奖"荣誉证书。主要代表作有：《沃尔登第二》《超越自由与尊严》《言语行为》等。

行为主义有两个重要的特点：第一，反对研究意识，主张心理学应当研究行为；第二，反对内省，主张用实验方法。在华生看来，意识是看不见、摸不着的，因而无法对它进行客观的研究。心理学的研究对象不应该是意识，而应该是可以观察的事件，即行为。华生曾经说过，在一本心理学书中，"永远不使用意识、心理状态、心理内容、意志、意象以及诸如此类的名称，是完全可能的……它可以用刺激和反应的字眼，用习惯的形成，习惯的整合以及诸如此类的字眼来加以实现"。行为主义还主张"环境决定论"，认为个体的行为完全是由环境所控制和决定的。行为主义产生后，在世界各国心理学界产生了很大的反响，行为主义强调用客观方法研究可以观察的行为，这对心理学走上科学的道路有积极的作用。但是由于它的主张过于极端，不研究心理的内部结构和过程，否定研究意识的重要性，把人和动物等同起来，因而限制了心理学的健康发展。

（四）格式塔心理学（gestalt psychology）

在美国出现行为主义的同时，德国也涌现出了一个心理学派别——格式塔心理学。格式塔心理学派的代表人物有韦特海默（Max Wertheimer）、柯勒（Wolfgang Kohler）和考夫卡（Kurt Koffka）。

图 1-7　马克斯·韦特海默

马克斯·韦特海默（Max Wertheimer, 1880—1943），德国心理学家，格式塔心理学创始人之一。他早期学习法律和哲学，后转学心理学，在屈尔佩的指导下获得哲学博士学位，然后长期执教并从事心理研究工作。1933年移居美国，受聘于纽约社会研究新学院。虽然韦特海默一生著述不多，但他对格式塔心理学的发展有很大影响。他主张从直观上把握心理现象，并把整体结构的动态属性看作是心理学的本质，认为应从整体到部分去理解心理现象。他还研究了神经活动和知觉的关系、知觉和思维的关系。主要代表作有：《似动现象的实验研究》《创造性思维》等。

图 1-8　库尔特·考夫卡

库尔特·考夫卡（Kurt Koffka, 1886—1941），美籍德裔心理学家，格式塔心理学的代表人物之一。他于1908年获得哲学博士学位，1910年参加了韦特海默进行的似动现象实验，并成为格式塔学派的主要发言人之一。考夫卡最早向美国心理学界介绍了格式塔心理学，对格式塔心理学的对象、方法等问题作了详尽的阐述，使格式塔心理学系统化。主要代表作有：《思维的成长：儿童心理学导论》《格式塔心理学原理》等。

格式塔（gestalt）在德文中的意思是"整体""完形"，所以格式塔心理学也称为完形心理学，它代表了这个学派的基本主张和宗旨。格式塔心理学反对把意识分解为元素，认为整体不等于部分之和，意识经验不等于感觉和情感元素的总和，思维也不是观念的简单联结。所以应该把人的心理作为一个整体来进行研究，这样才能把握心理发展的全貌。

格式塔心理学很重视心理学实验，在知觉、学习、思维等方面开展了大量的实验研究，取得了丰富的研究成果，其思想在文学界、美术界也产生了广泛的影响。

（五）精神分析学派（psycholanalysis）

这是由奥地利维也纳精神病医生弗洛伊德（Sigmund Freud）创立的一个学派。他的理论主要来源于精神病的临床治疗实践经验，如果说构造主义、机能主义和格式塔心理学重视意识经验的研究，行为主义重视正常行为的分析，那么精神分析学派则重视异常行为的分析，并且强调心理学应该研究无意识现象。

精神分析学说认为，人类的一切个体的和社会的行为，都根源于心灵深处的某种欲望或动机，特别是性欲的冲动。欲望以无意识的形式支配人，并且表现在人的正常和异常的行为中。欲望或动机受到压抑，是导致精神疾病的重要原因，所谓精神分析是指一种临床技术，它通过释梦和自由联想等手段，发现病人潜在的动机，使精神得以宣泄（catharsis），从而达到治疗疾病的目的。

精神分析学派重视动机的研究和无意识现象的研究，这是他们的贡献。但是他们过分强调无意识的作用，并且把它与意识的作用对立起来。他们的早期理论具有泛性欲主义的特点，把性欲夸大为支配人类一切行为的动机，这些都是很有争议的。

图1-9 西格蒙德·弗洛伊德

西格蒙德·弗洛伊德（Sigmund Freud，1856—1939），知名医师、精神分析学家，犹太人，精神分析学的创始人。他提出"潜意识""自我""本我""超我""俄狄浦斯情结""力比多""心理防卫机制"等概念。尽管他提出的精神分析学后来被认为并非有效的临床治疗方法，但激发了后人提出各式各样的精神病理学理论，在临床心理学的发展史上具有重要意义。弗洛伊德著有《梦的解析》《精神分析引论》《图腾与禁忌》等。他被世人誉为"精神分析之父""二十世纪最伟大的心理学家之一"。

（六）人本主义心理学派（humanistic psychology）

这是由美国心理学家马斯洛（Abraham H. Maslow）和罗杰斯（Carl Rogers）于20世纪50年代所创建的一个心理学流派。它既反对精神分析学派贬低人性、把意识经验还原为基本驱力，又反对行为主义把意识看作行为的副现象，认为心理学应以正常人为研究对象，研究人类异于动物的一些复杂经验，诸如价值、生活责任、生命意义等真正属于人性各种层面的问题，被称为心理学的第三势力。人本主义心理学强调，人在充分发展自我潜力时，力争实现自我的各种需要，从而建立完善的自我，并追求建立理想的自我，最终达到自我实现。人在争取需要满足的过程中能产生人性的内在幸福感和丰富感，给人以最大的喜悦，这种感受本身就是对人的最高奖赏。人本主义方法论不排除传统的科学方法，而是扩大科学研究的范围,以解决过去一直排除在心理学研究范围之外的人类信念和价值问题。人本主义的兴起,较大地影响了教育心理学、发展心理学、咨询辅导及心理治疗等的发展。人本主义心理学是一门尚处在发展中的学说,其理论体系还不够完备,许多理论观点难以得到验证,但却可能代表着心理学发展的一个新的方向。

图 1-10　亚伯拉罕·哈罗德·马斯洛

亚伯拉罕·哈罗德·马斯洛(Abraham Harold Maslow,1908—1970),美国社会心理学家、比较心理学家,人本主义心理学的主要创建者之一,智商高达194的天才,第三代心理学的开创者。他的主要成就包括提出了人本主义心理学,提出了著名的需要层次理论,代表作品有:《动机和人格》《存在心理学探索》《人性能达到的境界》等。

图 1-11　卡尔·罗杰斯

卡尔·罗杰斯(Carl Ransom Rogers,1902—1987),美国心理学家,人本主义心理学的主要代表人物之一。他从事心理咨询和治疗的实践与研究,主张"以当事人为中心"的心理治疗方法,首创非指导性治疗,强调人具备自我调整以恢复心理健康的能力。罗杰斯于1947年当选为美国心理学会主席,1956年获美国心理学会颁发的杰出科学贡献奖。主要著作有:《咨询和心理治疗:新近的概念和实践》《当事人中心治疗:实践、运用和理论》等。

(七)认知心理学派(cognitive psychology)

认知心理学是探索人们如何获取知识和使用知识的心理学,它自20世纪50年代中期以来,随着信息论和计算机科学与技术、语言学、神经科学等学科的迅速发展而兴起。1967年,美国心理学家奈塞尔(U. Neisser)发表《认知心理学》一书,标志着认知心理学的正式产生。在本书中,奈塞尔第一次使用了认知心理学这个术语,并阐述了认知心理学的基本理论。奈塞尔认为认知心理学主要是研究人类认知的信息加工过程,探讨人对信息的获得、存储、加工和使用的过程。诸如人是如何通过感知觉、注意、记忆、语言、思维与推理等心理活动对信息进行加工、转换,而使其成为知识与经验来解决所面临的问题的;人是如何运用知识来对自己的行为和认知活动做出决定并产生效果的等。认知心理学继承了行为主义客观的研究方法以及格式塔心理学在知觉、思维和问题解决等领域的研究成果,承认在人类信息加工中存在某些(精神分析学派提出的)无意识的过程,并用客观的方法研究这些过程。在此基础上,认知心理学还发展了一些特有的研究方法,如计算机模拟法、发声思维法等。可以说,认知心理学为心理学提供了一种新的研究模式,它的影响遍布现代心理学的整个领域,代表了现代心理学发展的趋势。认知心理学还与计算机科学相结合产生了人工智能。但是人脑不等于计算机,人是一个社会性的复杂的个体,用简单的模拟来推测人及其复杂的认知活动还是需要做进一步探讨的。

第四节

心理学的研究方法

人的心理现象是世界上最复杂和最难认识的现象之一。如果没有正确的指导思想和科学的方法论,就很难使心理学的研究达到科学的地步,取得较大的成效。

一、心理学研究的基本原则

(一)客观性原则

客观性原则要求对任何心理现象,必须以实事求是的态度按照它们的本来面目加以考察,必须在人的生活和活动中客观地进行心理研究。诚然,各门科学的研究都必须遵循客观性原则,但是,由于心理学研究的是人的心理现象,是人的主观世界,更应该反对主观臆想和揣测,强调坚持客观性原则。心理现象就其映象来讲是一种主观存在,但它是由一定的客观现实引起的,并总是通过人的实践活动,以语言、表情和行为等方式表现出来。因此,研究人的心理现象,必须根据其产生、发展的客观条件和外部表现,如实测验作用于被试的刺激强度和反应的客观指标,才能真正揭示心理现象发展的规律。

专栏 1-2

伯 特 事 件

西里尔·伯特(Cyril Lodowick Burt,1883—1971)是英国最有影响力的心理学家之一。他出生于英国伦敦一个医生家庭,以提出心理测验中的因素分析以及研究遗传对智力和行为的影响而闻名。

伯特共发表了300多篇论文。在这些论文中,最著名的是对自小分开抚养的同卵双生子的研究。同卵双生子有相同的基因,如果智力受遗传影响的话,那么即使他们从小生长在不同的环境,他们的智力高低也会非常接近。的确,伯特发现分开抚养的同卵双生子的智商非常相近。伯特在退休后就这个问题发表过3篇论文。

这3篇论文被广泛引用,但在伯特去世后不久却给他的声誉带来了麻烦。1972年,普林斯顿大学的心理学家利昂·卡民在读了伯特的这3篇论文后,注意到虽然这3篇论文涉及的孪生子数目不同,但是最终的数据却一模一样,而且精确到小数点后3位。虽然卡民本人并非智商领域的专家,但是统计学常识却告诉他,这样的巧合是不可能发生的。卡民认为不仅这3篇有关孪生子研究的论文,而且伯特自1909年"出道"以来所有的论文的数据全都是编造出来的。伯特生前好友莱斯利·赫恩肖受命撰写伯特的传记。他对这些指控极为愤怒,呼吁学术界不要忙着下结论。然而,在研究了伯特的私人记录之后,赫恩肖改变了看法,不得不在1979年出版的伯特传记中承认对伯特的指控很可能是成立的。同时,英国心理学学会也正式认定伯特造假。

——李红.心理学基础[M].北京:高等教育出版社,2009:23.

(二)教育性原则

教育性原则要求在进行心理学的研究时,不能损害被试的身心健康,而应从有利于教育、有利于个体身心健康的角度来设计和实施研究。由于心理学的研究对象是人,所以在进行心理学研究时应该遵循教育性原则。心理学研究的初衷是为了更好地了解心理世界,掌握其发生、发展的规律,以便指导人更好地发展。因此,在进行研究时,不仅要在课题选择上考虑教育意义,使其结果有助于被试更好地发展,而且在研究方案的设计上和实际进行的过程中也应考虑对被试的良好教育影响,不能有损于被试的身心健康发展。这一原则在教育教学领域中显得尤为重要。

专栏1-3

"小阿尔伯特"实验

华生与雷纳进行的恐惧性条件反射实验是在一名叫阿尔伯特的11个月大的婴儿身上做的。实验初期,阿尔伯特与小白鼠玩了3天。后来,当阿尔伯特伸手去触摸白鼠时,身后响起了猛烈敲击钢条的声音。这显然是一种令人生厌的声音,小阿尔伯特的反应是惊怕和摔倒。在白鼠与敲击钢条的声音一起出现3次后,光是白鼠就会引起小阿尔伯特害怕和防御的行为反应。在6次条件作用后,当白鼠单独出现时,阿尔伯特也表现出强烈的恐惧情绪和躲避反应。在阿尔伯特1岁以后,华生进行了一系列泛化测验。他们发现阿尔伯特开始惧怕任何有毛的东西，不管是看见了白兔、狗、毛大衣、棉毛甚至圣诞老人面具，他都会哭或焦急，类似于对白鼠的反应。可见阿尔伯特的惧怕已泛化到一切带毛的东西上了（王振宇，2000）。

接下来，华生尝试用各种办法建立新的条件反射以便消除小阿尔伯特的恐惧情绪。但不幸的是小阿尔伯特在接受可能的治疗之前，离开了日托中心，举家迁徙到别的地方去了。

从研究角度来说，小阿尔伯特实验提供了恐惧性条件反射形成的直接证据，具有相当的科学价值。但科学是为人服务的，对人的心理的关怀是心理学研究的初衷，为了取得科学的进步而给一个不到一岁的孩子造成难以愈合的心理伤害显然是不人道的。因此，这个实验遭到了学术界的严厉批评。

——李红.心理学基础[M].北京：高等教育出版社，2009：23.

（三）发展性原则

发展性原则要求在对人的心理现象进行研究时，要坚持发展的观点。唯物辩证法指出，世界上任何事物都处在运动和发展变化之中。心理现象也是这样，总是在不断地变化发展着。就个体的某一心理来看，其在不同年龄阶段的表现方式和水平就有所不同；一种心理品质形成之后，随着环境和实践活动的改变，也会有一定的发展。遵循发展性原则，既有利于预测人的心理发展的前景和方向，也有利于做好当前的教育工作。因此，把心理现象置于发展过程中研究，防止和反对静止、凝固地看待心理现象，也是心理学研究的一个重要原则。

（四）系统性原则

系统性原则要求在对人的心理现象进行研究时，必须考虑各种内、外部因素之间相互联系和制约的作用，注意把某一心理现象放在多层次、多因素的系统之中进行分析。人的心理现象是一个极其复杂的动态系统，它与外部刺激、活动内容、客观环境以及其他各种心理现象之间都有紧密的联系。其中任何一种因素的变化，都可能引起人的心理的变化。因此，对于人的心理现象，必须进行全面的、系统的分析和考察，而决不能把它看作孤立的东西进行简单的研究。

（五）理论联系实际原则

理论联系实际原则要求心理学的研究要联系人们的现实生活，使研究结果有利于提高人们的生活质量。科学研究的成果是为了运用于生活实际，不能为了研究而研究。因此，心理学研究应尽可能提高研究的生态效度，以便研究结果可以在人们的实际生活中得以应用。心理学研究中的生态效度指研究结果推广到具体研究情景以外的可能程度。此外，心理学研究中建立起来的理论和观点，也需在实际情形中验证其正确性，这是一条检验科学研究的基本标准。

二、心理学研究的常用方法

在心理学研究的基本原则指导下，心理学的具体研究方法可以有多种。下面介绍几种主要的常用方法。

（一）观察法

观察法是在日常生活条件下，有目的、有计划地观察和记录被试的外部表现（行为、言语、表情等），了解其内部心理活动特点和规律的方法。观察法是人类认识世界的基本方法，也是心理学研究的主要方法之一。人的各种活动都是在人的心理的支配、调节下进行的，因此，通过对人的外部言行的观察，可以了解人的内部心理活动的特点。如儿童心理学的创始人普莱尔（William Thierry Preyer）对自己的孩子从出生开始到三岁每天都进行系统观察，最后把这些观察记录整理成一部有名的著作《儿童心理》。

观察要取得成效需要注意以下几点：

第一，明确观察的目的，即确定观察的内容。比如要观察学生的攻击行为，首先要确定什么样的行为可算得上是攻击行为，并对攻击行为进行分类，如把攻击行为分为"言语攻击"和"行动攻击"两类。

第二，制定观察计划。确定好观察内容后，就要制定详细的观察计划，什么时间观察，每次观察持续多长时间，采用什么策略进行观察等。

第三，保证观察的可靠性。为保证观察的效果，最好在"单盲"的情况下进行观察，即不让被观察者知晓观察者的存在。

第四，及时做好记录。观察不是一蹴而就的过程，有些观察需要耗费较长的一段时间，所以做好观察记录就非常必要。为了记录的方便，可以先对要观察的行为进行编码，如前面讲到的攻击行为，我们可以对儿童不同的攻击行为进行编码。

观察法可以应用于多种心理现象的研究，尤其适用于教师了解、研究学生的心理特点和规律。观察法是在日常生活条件下使用的，因而简便易行，所得的材料也比较真实。但由于它不能严格控制条件，不易对观察的材料做出比较精确的量化分析和判断，这也是观察法的局限性。观察法常常被用来作为发现问题的一种前期研究方法。

（二）实验法

实验法是有目的地控制或创设一定条件，以引起被试某种心理现象，从而研究其规律的方法。实验法可以分为实验室实验法和自然实验法两种。

1. 实验室实验法

实验室实验法是借助专门的实验设备，在严加控制实验条件的情况下进行的一种研究方法。这种方法的优点是有助于发现事物间的因果联系，并可以进行反复验证；缺点是主试严格控制实验条件，使实验情景带有较大的人为性质，因而实验的结果同日常生活条件下的心理现象往往存在一定的差距。

2. 自然实验法

自然实验法也叫现场实验法，它是在人们实际生活或工作场景中，通过创设或控制一定的条件来研究被试的心理特点或规律的方法。自然实验法消除了实验室实验法的缺点，得到的结果比较真实可靠，结论可以重复验证，因而在心理学研究中被广泛采用。

专栏 1-4

心理学家如何探索人的心理

人的心理，看不见、听不到、摸不着，因而人们常常把心理比喻为"黑箱"。对于这个"黑箱"，作为探索心灵奥秘科学的心理学，是通过哪些途径对它进行探测的呢？

第一条途径是通过言行来探测人的心理。个人的言行总是受其心理支配的，可以根据人的言行表现去了解其心理。"诗言志"，通过一个人写的诗可以了解其志向。又如，一个学生考试考得好与不好，通常会产生不同的心理变化并表现在行为上：考得好感到欢欣鼓舞，而考得不好则行为沮丧。通过这个学生的情绪变化，大致可以推测出其心理上的变化。

第二条途径是通过生理变化来推测人的心理活动。任何心理活动都会有生理变化的线索。有些是很容易观察到的，如人紧张时会出汗、害羞时脸红等，但更多的心理活动则需要借助于精密的仪器来探测。例如，有些人说他们睡觉时从来不做梦。研究者可以使用一种叫做脑电仪的仪器来记录他们睡眠时的脑电波。如果脑电图出现快波时，把那些说自己从来不做梦的人弄醒，他们就会生动地回忆出刚刚做的梦。这说明，运用精密的生理仪器可以检测到人们在睡眠时是否做梦、是否有心理活动。

第三条途径是通过研究者的推论来推测人的心理。比如，学生考试成绩的好坏可能会表现在其言行上，如果进一步了解到这个学生是一个一贯刻苦努力的学生，因而大致可以推断，他（她）这次考得好会进一步增强其学习热情和信心，这次考得不好会激发他（她）加倍努力，以便取得更好的成绩。这种类似的推断在日常生活中是经常出现的。

——黄希庭，郑涌.心理学十五讲[M].北京：北京大学出版社，2005：2.

（三）调查法

调查法是研究者通过被试对所拟定问题的回答，来研究其心理活动特点和规律的方法。调查法可以分为两种，一种是问卷调查，也称问卷法，这种方法要求调查者事先拟好问卷，由被调查者在问卷上根据自己的实际情况做出回答。问卷法中的问卷设计是研究的关键，直接涉及到研究结果的科学性。这就要求研究者提出的问题应该清晰、易懂，不能模棱两可，也不应有暗示。此外，进行问卷调查时还要注意选取代表性样本，所谓代表性样本是指能准确反映总体某一特征的一组人。问卷法能够比较迅速地获得大量资料，便于定量分析。但不便对被试的态度进行控制，获得的材料不够详尽。

另一种方式是访谈调查，也称访谈法，是研究者对被试进行面对面的提问，然后随时记录被试的回答或反应来了解其心理发展的一种方法。运用访谈法，研究者首先要确定访谈目的，拟好访谈提纲；其次，要取得被试的信任，保证访谈在自然的气氛中进行；最后，提出的问题要简单明白，易于回答。访谈法简便易行，但得出的结论有时带有主观片面成分。

（四）测验法

测验法也叫心理测验，它是研究者利用标准化的测验量表来测定人的智力和心理特征等个性差异的方法，包括智力测验、人格测验、能力倾向测验、气质类型测验等。测验量表是通过大量实验而确定的能够反映人的心理发展水平的题目和作业。对测验结果与常模（参照指标）进行比较，即可测出被试的心理发展水平。心理测验的编制和实施都有明确规定和标准化程序，必须严格遵守，否则就会影响测验的结果，甚至使心理测验失败。

（五）个案法

个案法是研究者对一个或几个被试在较长的时间内进行追踪研究，借以发现其心理的发展、变化规律的方法。个案法是对人的心理纵向地、连续地进行研究的一种方法。这种方法易于了解心理发展的趋势，也可以研究人的个性差异。但应用此方法时，设计要周密合理，研究要持之以恒。

（六）活动产品分析法

活动产品分析法是研究者通过对人的作业、作品、日记、手工制作、生产成品等的分析，了解其心理活动特点和规律的方法。活动产品分析法可以了解人的能力水平和认知结构，也可以揭示人对事物的态度和某些个性品质。比如，分析儿童的绘画作品，可以帮助我们在一定程度上判断儿童的认知发展水平。研究表明，智力落后儿童的绘画，其内容通常是原始的，而且惊人地千篇一律。但是，人的活动产品和人的心理活动之间并不是简单的一一对应关系，因此，活动产品分析法应该与其他方法结合使用，以便相互印证，得出科学的结论。

（七）教育经验总结法

教育经验总结法是指教育工作者对自己日常工作中获得的那些行之有效的经验进行整理总结，并从中提炼出所包含的心理活动规律的方法。教育经验总结法的优点是教育工作者可以结合自己的实际工作，随时随地对一些取得较好成效的做法加以总结提升，缺点是应用这种方法进行研究时，对研究者的自身素质和理论修养水平有较高的要求。

总之，心理学的研究方法有很多，每一种方法都有其优缺点。因此在研究一个心理学课题时，不应该只使用一种方法，而是兼用几种方法，相互取长补短，相得益彰，才能得到相对客观准确的研究结论。

本章小结

心理学是研究心理现象的发生、发展及其变化规律的科学，人的心理现象的表现形式有心理过程、个性心理、心理状态。心理学是一门古老而年轻的科学。具体研究的方法有观察法、实验法、调查法、测验法、个案法、活动产品分析法、教育经验总结法等。心理学研究必须遵循客观性原则、教育性原则、发展性原则、系统性原则、理论联系实际的原则。

关键术语

心理现象　心理学的研究领域　心理学的起源与发展　心理学的研究方法

讨论与应用

1. 阅读下面的材料并思考，学习了第一章后，你对心理学有什么新的认识？上述说法正确吗？

有人说，学了心理学后就可以让我知道别人心里在想什么；有人却说，心理学就是心理咨询，心理学家只研究变态的人，心理学家都会催眠；也有人说，心理学就是骗人的东西，心理学成果不过是些常识……

2. 阅读下面的材料，说说你怎么看？

宝宝的爸爸妈妈都是大学教授。在宝宝4岁的时候，有人说："遗传了这么优秀的基因，宝宝以后一定也会非常优秀。"也有人说："宝宝以后的发展关键还是看父母的教育，以及后天环境的影响，和遗传没有什么关系。"听到这些说法，宝宝的爸爸妈妈私下里嘀咕，环境和遗传对于宝宝大约是一半对一半吧。

本章讨论与应用答题
思路与要点
（扫描二维码）

本章复习思考题
（扫描二维码）

本章进一步阅读书目
（扫描二维码）

第二章
心理的实质
XINLIDESHIZHI

亲爱的同学,通过前面一章的学习,你知道了心理学是研究心理现象的科学。对于什么是心理现象已经熟悉了,但它是如何发生的呢?要回答这个问题却不是那么容易。因为人的心理现象是宇宙间最复杂的现象之一,也是人类有史以来就企图认识的重大问题之一。人为什么会有心理活动?为什么人与人的心理活动会有那么大的差异?到底是哪些因素影响了人的心理?接下来就请在本章的学习中找寻它们的答案吧!

通过本章的学习,你能够
- 了解心理的神经生理基础
- 理解心理活动的基本方式——反射
- 明确客观现实在心理产生中的作用

【本章结构】

```
                        心理的实质
                            │
            ┌───────────────┴───────────────┐
            ▼                               ▼
     心理是脑的机能                    心理是客观现实的反映
     ◎ 神经系统的结构与功能            ◎ 客观现实是心理的源泉和内容
     ◎ 条件反射                       ◎ 人的心理是对客观现实的主观反映
                                      ◎ 人的心理是对客观现实的能动反映
                                      ◎ 实践活动对心理形成的影响
```

人类对自身心理的关注催生了一个个理论解释,包括从远古的灵魂说一直到现代的科学心理观,都在努力地揭示人的心理的实质。今天为多数人所接纳的一个观点是:心理是脑的机能,客观现实是心理的源泉和内容。

第一节
心理是脑的机能

在远古时期，受科学发展水平的制约，人们普遍认为人的心脏是产生心理的物质器官，相信"心之官则思"（《孟子·告子上》）。从我国文字的构成中也能看出古人的这一思想认识，汉字中凡与心理活动有关的字，几乎都带有竖心旁或心字底。近代，随着医学和解剖学的发展，尤其是随着认知神经科学对大脑定位与功能研究的深入，人们逐渐认识到脑是产生心理的器官，心理是人脑的机能。

> **专栏2-1**
>
> ### 盖吉再也不是原来的盖吉了
>
> 1848年9月13日，一个名叫菲尼亚斯·盖吉（Phineas P. Gage）的铁路工人，在美国佛蒙特州施工时发生了一起人身伤害事故。在一次意外爆炸中，他不幸被一根3.7英尺的铁棍击穿左侧颅骨，可是他的意识还是清醒的。人们用卡车把他送回旅馆时，他自己走上了楼。随后的2—3周内，他濒临死亡。幸运的是，他活了下来，并且受到的身体伤害不太严重，仅左眼失明和左脸麻痹，运动、言语并没有问题。
>
> 但是，盖吉变了……在性格上发生了相当大的变化，可以说完全变成了另外一个人。
>
> 受伤前，大家都认为他是一个机灵、有毅力、精力充沛、努力工作的人；受伤后，他变得无理、放纵、脾气暴躁、反复无常，常常说粗话。
>
> ——李红.心理学基础[M].北京：高等教育出版社，2009：64.

从上面的事件中我们看到，人的大脑不仅关系到我们对信息的收集和判断，还可能会影响到我们人格的形成。人的心理的方方面面都和人的生理尤其是人脑有着密切的关联。脑是产生人的心理的物质器官。那么为什么人脑有这样一种功能呢？是因为人脑有产生心理的适宜结构——神经系统的存在。

一、神经系统的结构与功能

人的神经系统（nervous system）是由大量神经细胞形成的神经组织与结构的总称，包括中枢神经系统（central nervous system，简称CNS）和周围神经系统（peripheral nervous system，简称PNS）两大系统。

构成神经系统的基本单位是神经细胞,也叫神经元。

(一)神经元的结构和功能

神经元即神经细胞,是构成神经系统的结构和功能的基本单位。神经元是具有细长突起的细胞,它由胞体(cell body or soma)、树突(dendrites)和轴突(axon)三部分组成。如图2-1所示。

图 2-1

神经元的主要结构

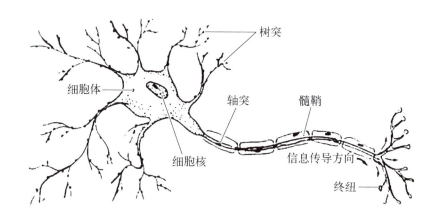

胞体由细胞膜、细胞核、细胞质组成,中央处的细胞核是细胞的能量中心。通过化学反应,胞体为神经活动提供能量,并大量制造用于传递信息的化学物质。自胞体伸出两种突起:树突和轴突。呈树枝状、短而多的是树突,它的主要功能是接受来自其他神经元的信息并传至胞体。一个神经元通常有数百个树突,这就大大增加了其接受信息的能力。轴突是一根细长的突起,最长可达1米,每个神经元只有一个轴突。其作用是传导刺激到它联系的各种细胞。轴突外面包裹着髓鞘,由胶质细胞构成,起保护作用。轴突末梢有许多膨大的细小分支,呈葡萄状,称为突触小体,它是传递信息给另一个神经元的发放端。

神经元的基本功能是接受信息、传递信息。神经元是通过接受和传递神经冲动来进行信息交换的。神经冲动是指当任何一种刺激作用于神经元时,神经元就会由比较静息的状态转化为比较活跃的状态。神经冲动在细胞内的传导是一种电的传导。在细胞的表面,受刺激的部位(兴奋部位)与未受刺激的部位(静息部位)之间出现了一个电位差,在细胞膜外产生了未兴奋部位向兴奋部位的电流,在细胞膜内则产生反方向的电流,构成局部电流回路。神经冲动的传递遵循全或无的规律。即当刺激强度未达到某一阈限值时,神经冲动不会发生,而当刺激强度达到该阈限值时,神经冲动发生并在瞬时达到最大强度,此后刺激强度即使再继续加强或减弱,已诱发的冲动强度也不再发生变化。神经冲动的这种特性使信息在传递途中不会变得越来越弱。

神经元之间则依靠突触来实现信息的接受和传递。突触指一个神经元与另一个神经元相接触的部位。如图2-2所示。突触包含三个部分:突触前成分、突触间隙和突触后成分。突触前成分指轴突末梢的球形小体，里面包含许多突触小泡，其中含有神经递质。神经递质是神经元之间进行信息传递的化学物质。这些化学递质有的是兴奋性递质，如乙酰胆碱、去甲肾上腺素等；有的是抑制性递质，如多巴胺、甘氨酸等。神经递质通过球形小体前方的突触前膜释放出去，进入到突触间隙中。突触间隙指一个神经元末端与一个神经元开始之间的缝隙，其间隔约为200埃（1埃=10^{-8}厘米）。突触后成分指下一个神经元或临近神经元的树突末梢或胞体内的一定部位。它通过突触后膜与外界发生关系。突触后膜含有特殊的分子受体（另一种化学物质），从而引起突触后神经元的电位变化，实现神经兴奋的传递。突触的这种结构保证了神经冲动从一个神经元传递到与它相邻的另一个神经元。

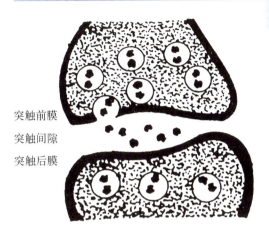

图 2-2

突触的结构

依据神经元的功能可以把神经元分为感觉神经元（传入神经元）、运动神经元（传出神经元）和中间神经元（联络神经元）三大类。感觉神经元的树突的末端分布于身体的外周部，接受来自体内外的刺激，将兴奋传至脊髓和脑。运动神经元的轴突与肌肉和腺体相连，它的兴奋可引起肌肉和腺体的活动。中间神经元介于两者之间，起着神经元之间机能联系的作用，多存在于脑和脊髓里。

（二）中枢神经系统

人类的中枢神经系统（central nervous system，简称CNS）是人体神经系统的主体部分，其主要功能是传递、储存和加工信息，产生人的各种心理活动，支配并控制人的全部行为。中枢神经系统包括脊髓和脑两部分。

1. 脊髓的结构和功能

脊髓（spinal cord）是中枢神经系统的低级部位，位于脊椎管内，略呈圆柱形，上接延髓，下端止于一根细长的终丝，外连周围神经，31对脊神经分布于它的两侧。脊髓由灰质和白质组成，灰质主要由神经元胞体和树突构成，白质由神经元轴突组成。内含中央管，中央管内有脑脊髓液，与大脑第四脑室相通。

脊髓的功能主要表现为两个方面：第一，它是躯体与脑部神经传导的通路。来自躯体和四肢的刺激通过脊髓传导至大脑，而由大脑发出的指令也必须通过脊髓到达效应器。第二，它是一些简单反射活动的中枢。感觉神经元将神经冲动传入脊髓后，中间神经元不把它传入大脑，而是直接传给运动神经元，至效应器直接形成反射，如膝跳反射、跟腱反射、防御反射等。

2. 脑的结构和功能

脑（brain）位于颅骨内，由脑膜所包裹，并悬浮于脑脊液中。脑是中枢神经系统的高级部位，也是中枢神经系统最重要的结构，所有复杂的心理活动都与脑密切相

图 2-3

脑的构造示意图（纵切面）

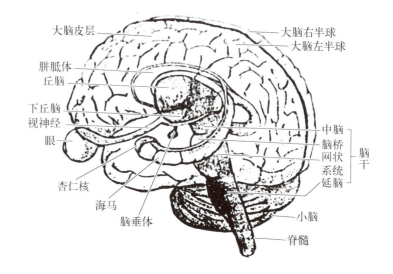

关。人脑中含有人体全部神经细胞的百分之九十，大约为150亿个神经细胞。人脑呈复杂的网状结构，在每一立方厘米的组织内含有约四千万个突触，它们昼夜不停地活动。人脑的结构大体上可以分为脑干、间脑、小脑和大脑这样几个部分，如图2-3所示。

（1）脑干

脑干（brain stem）是位于人脑最深层的神经结构，包括延脑、脑桥和中脑。主要负责人体的心跳、呼吸、消化、体温、睡眠等与生命息息相关的活动。

延脑（medulla）下接脊髓，上接脑桥。来自头部皮肤与肌肉的感觉信息，来自味觉、听觉、平衡觉和躯干的感觉信息要传送到脑必先经过延脑。延脑还有许多对有机体生命十分重要的中枢，如控制肠胃蠕动、呼吸、心跳以及血管舒缩、唾液分泌、汗腺分泌等的神经中枢。所以，延脑也有"生命中枢"之称。

脑桥（pons）介于中脑和延脑之间，有许多传递信息的上行和下行传导神经束。它是维持机体平衡的初级中枢，对睡眠有调控作用。

中脑（midbrain）位于脑桥之上，恰好处在整个脑的中间。它也是上行和下行神经信息的主要通路。这里有视、听的反射中枢，凡是瞳孔、眼球肌肉、虹膜、睫状肌的调节均受中脑的控制。

在脑干各段的广大区域，有一种由白质和灰质交织混杂的结构，叫网状结构（reticular formation，简称RF），主要包括延脑的中央部位、脑桥的被盖和中脑部分。网状结构按功能可分成上行激活系统和下行激活系统两部分。上行激活系统主要控制着机体的觉醒或意识状态，保持大脑皮层的兴奋性，维持注意状态。上行网状结构如果受到破坏，将会使人陷入昏迷状态，不能对刺激做出反应。下行激活系统主要起加强或减弱肌肉活动状态的作用。

（2）间脑

间脑位于大脑两半球之间，连接大脑半球和中脑，主要包括丘脑和下丘脑。丘脑（thalamus）是个中继站，是皮质下较高的感觉中枢。除嗅觉外，所有的感觉信息都先传送到丘脑，在这里进行初步的分析综合，再由丘脑传送至大脑皮质的各感觉中枢。

下丘脑（hypothalamus）是植物性神经系统的主要皮下中枢。它直接与大脑各中枢相联系，又与脑垂体和延脑相联系。它的主要机能是控制内分泌系统，维持正常的代谢，以及调节饥饿、渴、性等生理活动。它也是情绪反应的重要中枢。

（3）小脑

小脑（cerebellum）位于脑干背面，分左右两半球。其功能主要是协调身体的运动，控制身体的姿势并维持平衡。一些复杂的运动，如走路、舞蹈等，一旦学会，似乎就编入小脑，并能自动进行。如果小脑受损伤，会出现痉挛、运动失调，丧失简单运动能力。小脑在出生前三个月才开始发育，出生后一年才完成。近年来的一些研究表明，小脑在某些高级认知功能（如感觉分辨）中有重要作用，小脑功能缺陷还可能导致口吃、阅读困难等。

（4）大脑

人类的大脑（cerebrum）是控制人类全部心理活动的重要结构，它不仅重量占据全部脑重量的2/3，而且作用也远远超过脑的任何其他部分。大脑分为左、右两个半球，由大脑皮层及其履盖着的边缘系统和基底神经节构成。

大脑半球的表面有大量神经细胞和无髓鞘神经纤维覆盖着，呈灰色，叫灰质（gray matter），也就是大脑皮层（cerebral cortex）。大脑皮层是中枢神经系统中最重要的部分，平均厚度为2.5—3.0毫米，可分为六层，面积约为2200平方厘米，上面布满了下凹的沟和凸出的回。分隔左右两半球的深沟称为脑纵裂，脑纵裂底部由胼胝体相连。在大脑半球上主要有三条明显的沟裂。大脑半球外侧面，由顶端起与纵裂垂直的沟称为中央沟。在半球外侧面，由前下方向后上方斜行的沟称为外侧裂，半球内侧面的后部有顶枕裂。这些沟裂将半球分成额叶、顶叶、枕叶和颞叶几个区域。中央沟之前为额叶，中央沟后方、顶枕裂前方、外侧裂上方为顶叶，外侧裂下方为颞叶，顶枕裂后方为枕叶，如图2-4所示。每一个脑叶都有一定的功能区分。例如，枕叶是视觉中枢；颞叶是听觉中枢；顶叶是躯体感觉中枢，负责触觉、痛觉和温度觉；而额叶是运动控制和认知活动的中枢，它与计划、决策、目标设定等功能有关，一旦因意外伤

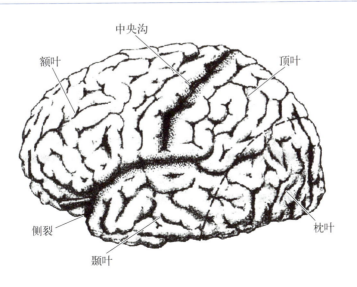

图2-4

大脑左半球

害导致额叶功能的毁坏,将会导致人的行为能力和人格的改变。

大脑半球的内部由大量神经纤维的髓质组成,叫白质(white matter)。它负责大脑回间、叶间、两半球间及皮层与皮下组织间的联系。其中特别重要的横行纤维叫胼胝体(corpus callosum),位于大脑半球底部,对两半球的协同活动有重要作用。一旦切断胼胝体,就会损伤两半球间信息的交流。

边缘系统(limbic system)是位于胼胝体之下包括多种神经组织的复杂神经系统,边缘系统的构造与功能尚不能十分确定,在范围上除包括部分丘脑和下丘脑之外,还包括海马和杏仁核等。海马(hippocampus)是边缘系统中最大的脑结构,在外显记忆获得中具有重要作用。海马损伤的病人能够学到一些新任务,但却不能记住它,也不记得发生了这件事,即它们失去了把新信息存入长时记忆的能力,但并不妨碍获得意识觉知之外的内隐记忆。杏仁核(amygdala)的功能与动机、情绪有关。

基底神经节位于大脑半球深部,主要包括尾状核和豆状核,合称为纹状体。其主要机能是调节肌肉的张力来协调运动。

医学和解剖学的研究已经发现,大脑两半球在机能上存在显著差异。法国医生布洛卡(Pierre Paul Broca)于1861年在解剖尸体时发现,患者大脑左半球某部位损伤,导致了病人的"失语症",这证明脑的左半球与言语活动有关。布洛卡发现的区域在额叶的后下部,被称为"布洛卡区"(Broca area)或运动性言语中枢,这一区域如果受损会引发运动性失语症,病人可以理解句子,但不能流利地表达出来。随后人们又发现了听觉性言语中枢、视觉性言语中枢和书写中枢等相应部位,这些发现使言语中枢的定位更为清晰。

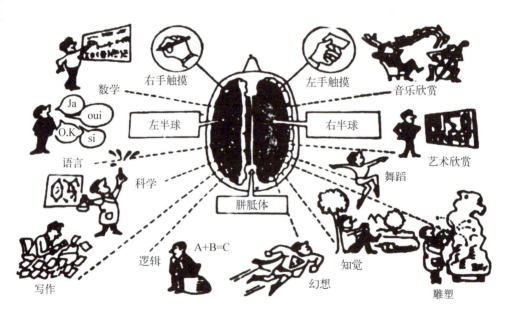

图 2-5
大脑两半球功能的一侧优势

现代脑科学研究认为,大脑左半球在言语、书写、推理等方面具有优势,右半球在空间关系、情绪、欣赏、艺术、音乐等方面具有优势。但是,大脑两半球的功能不是截然分开的,对于正常人而言，左右半球是协同工作的，而且有5%右利手的人和15%左利手的人在大脑两半球都发生言语加工过程。研究还显示，大脑皮层不同区域的功能还具有代偿作用，一些部位受到损伤，其他脑皮层的部位经过训练可以在一定程度上代替原有部位工作。因此，我们既要正视大脑两半球的机能差异，也要重视脑的全面开发。目前，学术界比较流行"全脑开发"的理念，即强调大脑左右半球虽有不同分工，但也有协同功能。要重视全面开发两半球的协同功能，最大限度地发掘大脑的潜能，实现脑功能发展的最优化。

专栏 2-2

如何锻炼人的右脑

日本学者品川嘉也认为：日本人由于接受过统一的、规范的学校教育，导致使用大脑左半球过度，而大脑右半球使用不足。因此，他提出了一套针对大脑右半球使用不足的九种锻炼方法：

① 刺激左半身的感官和神经。即要求人们在日常生活中，经常用左手抓握扶手，多使用左脚，多使用左侧视野和左侧听觉。

② 锻炼类型识别能力。即人脑记忆和识别物体形象的能力。通过锻炼人对物体形象启发识别的能力，可以锻炼大脑右半球。其活动包括：记住棋类布局，用左视野观察颜色；记住人的面孔等。

③ 锻炼图形识别能力。养成用图形而不是用语言表达和记忆的能力。活动包括：做笔记时不用文字而用图形；多做迷宫游戏。

④ 锻炼绘画意识。通过欣赏图画和风景，可以加强右脑功能。日常活动包括：有意识地眺望自然风景；有意识地找出自己喜欢的绘画、摄影作品，多到室外练习写生，观察他人的舞蹈动作，并记在心中。

⑤ 锻炼形象思维能力。通过下列活动，可以促进人的形象思维能力的发展。活动包括：读体育报道时联想其具体的场面；读剧本时联想具体的场景；用珠算法练习心算能力。

⑥ 锻炼空间认识能力。通过下列活动，可以促进人的空间认知能力的发展。活动包括：改变上下班（或上学、放学后）的回家路线；有时仰望天空中的浮云，并在大脑中想像它们的立体形象；玩折纸游戏。

⑦ 锻炼五种感觉。视觉和听觉是左右交叉的，而嗅觉、味觉、触觉则主要是大脑右半球负责。因此，多让自己辨别各种气味、多品尝各种食物的味道，多接触各种触觉刺激，可以提高大脑右半球的功能。

⑧ 多听右脑音乐。研究证实，听日本古典音乐，会激活大脑左半球的活动；而听西方古典音乐，则激活大脑右半球功能。因此，多听西方古典音乐，可以促进大脑右半球功能的发展。此外，听各种动物如鸟和虫子的叫声，也可以提高大脑右半球的功能。

⑨ 想象力训练。研究表明,想象是先由大脑右半球产生,然后由大脑左半球引导而在大脑右半球出现的,能直接转换为创造力。因此,让自己的想象力天马行空地、自由自在地进行,有利于大脑右半球能力的改善和提高。

上述方法的原理是:人体的神经系统在进入大脑之前是左右交叉的。也就是说,大脑左半球支配身体的右半侧,大脑右半球支配身体的左半侧。因此,要想刺激大脑右半球,就应当有意识地使用人的左手、左脚活动左侧肢体,这样就为活化人的大脑右半球创造了条件。长期坚持,就能促进大脑右半球功能的增强。

——郭黎岩.心理学[M].南京:南京大学出版社,2002:61—62.

(三)周围神经系统

周围神经系统(peripheral nervous system,简称PNS)从中枢神经系统发出,导向人体各部分,可分为躯体神经系统和自主神经系统。周围神经系统担负着与身体各部分的联络工作,具有传入和传出信息的作用。

1. 躯体神经系统

躯体神经系统(somatic nervous systen,简称SNS)是调节身体骨骼肌动作的系统,起着使中枢神经系统与外部世界相联系的作用,包括脑神经和脊神经两部分。脊神经发自脊髓,穿椎间孔外出,共31对,主要分布于躯干和四肢,它的主要功能是实现反射过程中神经中枢与运动系统的联系。如图2-6所示。脑神经由脑

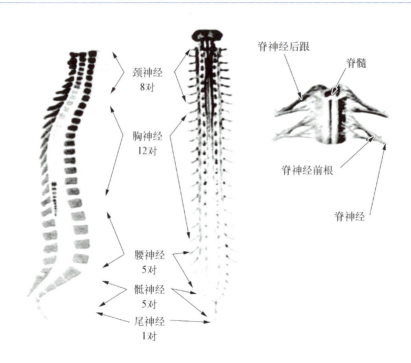

图 2-6 躯体神经示意图

部发出,如图2-7所示,共12对,主要分布于头面部,负责支配眼球运动、面部感觉、面部表情、面部肌肉运动、舌的运动、颈部活动和脏器活动等许多功能。通常认为,躯体神经系统是受意识调节控制的。

2. 自主神经系统

自主神经系统(autonomic nervous system,简称ANS)是维护身体基本生命过程的系统,也称作植物性神经系统,它分布于内脏器官、心血管、腺体及其他平滑肌之中,主要由下丘脑控制。自主神经系统分为交感神经系统(sympathetic nervous system)和副交感神经系统(parasympathetic nervous system)。交感神经的功能主要表现在当机体应付紧急情况时产生兴奋以适应环境的变化,如心跳加快,冠状血管血流量增加,血压增高,血糖升高,呼吸加深变快,瞳孔扩大,消化减慢等一系列反应。副交感神经的作用主要是保持身体安静时的生理平衡,如协助营养消化的进行,保存身体的能量,协助生殖活动等。这两种系统在许多活动中具有拮抗作用,又是相辅相成的。例如,交感神经使心搏加快,而副交感神经则使之减慢;副交感神经使胃的消化功能增加,交感神经就使其降低;交感神经使身体出汗,副交感神经就会抑制出汗等,正是这种活动维持了机体的平衡,一旦这种平衡受到破坏,机体就会出现非自主不良反应。

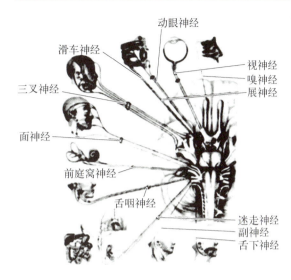

图2-7 脑神经示意图

二、条件反射

现代医学和解剖学以大量无可辩驳的研究事实证明了脑是产生心理的器官,是产生人的心理现象的物质基础。那么人的大脑是如何产生人的心理的呢?现代研究结果认为,人的一切心理活动,从其产生方式上来说都是人脑的反射活动。

(一)反射和反射弧

什么是反射?所谓反射(reflex),就是有机体借助神经系统对来自内外的刺激所作的有规律的应答活动。反射活动在生活中是很常见的,比如受到蚊虫叮咬,我们会用手去拍打,这就是一个简单的反射活动。实现反射活动的神经结构叫反射弧(reflex arc)。它由五部分组成:感受器、传入神经、中枢神经、传出神经、效应器。当外界刺激作用于人的感受器(感觉器官)时,感受器上的神经末梢产生神经冲动,通过传入神经到达中枢神经,中枢神经对这个冲动携带的信息进行分析、整合,下达指令,通过传出神经到达效应器(肌肉、腺体),作出反应,实现一个完整的反射活动。如图2-8所示。

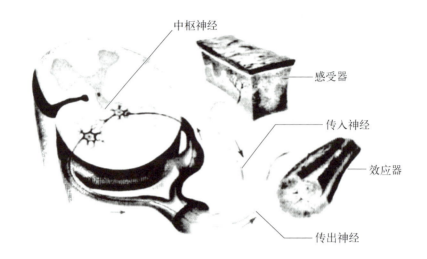

图 2-8
反射弧

当然，人的心理活动绝非这样简单。人的心理活动除受当前刺激影响之外，还要受人的过去经验、当时的心理状态、头脑中储存的价值观念、社会规范等的制约，这使人的心理活动呈现出丰富复杂的特点。而且，从感受器到效应器之间，不仅可以有正向传递，也可以有逆向的信息反馈。反馈是指反射并不中止于效应器的活动，效应器的活动本身又会成为新的刺激，引起新的神经过程，并返回传达到神经中枢的过程。由于反馈的存在，使机体的反射活动得以连续进行，并使神经中枢更好地感知和调节效应器的活动，从而保证人的行为的连续性、完整性和准确性。

（二）反射的种类

反射有两种，一种是无条件反射，一种是条件反射。

1. 无条件反射

无条件反射（unconditioned reflex）是个体在种族发展过程中形成并通过遗传而获得的，不需要任何学习和训练就可以实现的反射。无条件反射的反射弧生来就已联系好，不需要经过后天的学习和训练，它是一种固定的神经联系，而且借助于神经系统的低级部位——脊髓就可以实现，所以无条件发射又被称为本能或种族反射。例如，咳嗽、眨眼、吸吮等反射都是不学而会的无条件反射，它们无需经过大脑来控制。无条件反射是人与动物共有的反射，有助于机体躲避危险和种族延续。

无条件反射只能对少数刺激发生反应，而且具有刻板、固定的性质，不能适应复杂多变的现实环境。为了更好地适应环境，机体就形成了另一种反射——条件反射。

2. 条件反射

条件反射（conditioned reflex）是在无条件反射的基础上逐渐形成的，是在个体生活过程中为适应环境变化而建立起来的反射，如过马路时红灯停绿灯行，学生听见铃声回到座位上准备上课等，这都是条件反射。条件反射的神经联系是暂时的，既可以建立也可以消退。条件反射的形成过程就是在大脑皮层建立暂时神经联系的过程。就条件反射建立的神经过程而言，它是生理现象，而就其揭示的刺激物的意义和信号作用而言，则是心理现象。因此，人的心理活动是与条件反射相联系的。

条件反射可以分为经典性条件反射和操作性条件反射两大类。

（1）经典性条件反射

一个原来不能引起某种无条件反射的中性刺激物，由于总是伴随某个能引起该无条件反射的刺激物出现，重复多次后，该中性刺激物也能引起无条件反射，这种反射称为经典性条件反射。

经典条件反射理论是俄国著名的生理学家巴甫洛夫在一系列动物实验的基础上提出来的。巴甫洛夫用狗作为实验对象。我们知道狗吃食物分泌唾液是一种无条件反射，在这个基础上，可以让狗建立条件反射。实验时，在给狗吃食物之前，先打铃或呈现灯光，这样经过多次结合后，可以看到这样的现象：铃响之后，即使不给狗食物吃，狗也出现了分泌唾液的现象。这样，狗就形成了对铃声的信号反应，即条件反射的形成，它是在无条件反射的基础上形成的。如果这种练习不再强化，狗所建立起来的听到铃声就分泌唾液的反应又会逐渐消退。

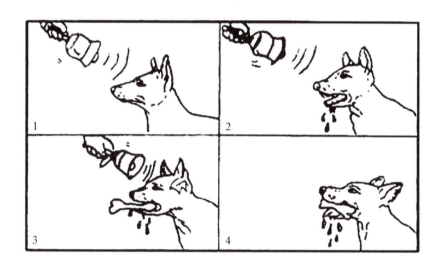

图 2-9

经典条件反射形成示意图

经典条件反射在日常生活中应用较为广泛，"望梅止渴""一朝被蛇咬，十年怕井绳"说的就是条件反射。另外，马戏团里也会利用条件反射原理训练动物进行各种表演，大学生可以利用条件反射原理帮助自己形成良好的生活作息习惯。

（2）操作性条件反射

该理论由美国心理学家斯金纳（B. F. Skinner）提出。斯金纳认为，经典性条件反射原理并不能解释人类所有后天习得的行为，因而提出操作性条件反射理论来解释人类行为习得的过程。他亲手制作了著名的"斯金纳箱"对白鼠和鸽子进行实验。（如图 2-10 所示）

"斯金纳箱"是一种特制的控制箱，箱内隔光、隔音，装有自动控制系统，还有一套杠杆和喂食器。动物在箱内只要按压杠杆，喂食器就会自动提供一粒食物丸。实验时将禁食一段时间的小白鼠放入箱内，开始时小白鼠在箱内四处乱跑，并向四周攀附，偶然有一次，它触压到了杠杆，于是一粒食物丸滚落到箱子里，白鼠吃到了美味的

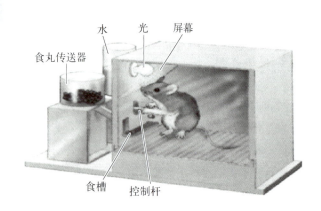

图 2-10
"斯金纳箱"示意图

食物。随着越来越多的偶然现象的发生，白鼠终于明白了这个机关的妙处，所以只要饥饿或者想吃东西了，它就会去按压杠杆，也就是说，白鼠最终习得了按压杠杆这个动作。

斯金纳认为，行为可以分为两类，一类是应答性行为，另一类是操作性行为。应答性行为（respondent behavior）是指经典条件反射中由已知的刺激引起的行为。如听到铃声就知道上课、下课了。操作性行为（operant behavior）是指个体自发出现的行为，发生时看不到刺激，斯金纳认为操作性行为的起因并不重要，重要的是动作发生之后跟随的结果是什么，它对行为出现的频率有重要影响。白鼠作出按压杠杆的动作后即刻得到了食物，这对白鼠再次作出按压杠杆的行为反应起到了重要的强化作用。

斯金纳认为，人的行为大部分是操作性的，行为的习得与及时强化有关。因此，可以通过强化来塑造儿童的行为。个体偶尔发出的动作得到了强化，这个动作后来出现的概率就会大于其他动作。

强化可以分为正强化与负强化两种。正强化是指由于一种刺激的加入增加了一个操作反应发生的概率的作用，如行为之后给予奖励，白鼠作出按压杠杆的动作就得到食物；负强化是指由于某一刺激的排除而加强了某一操作反应发生的概率作用，如行为之后撤消厌恶刺激，给予白鼠轻微的电击，只要按压杠杆，电击就会解除。不管是正强化还是负强化，其作用都是增加反应频率。

对于师范生而言，利用操作性条件反射原理，一方面可以塑造自己良好的行为和心理品质，另一方面也可以从未来教学的角度，学习塑造学生良好行为和心理品质的方法。例如，对于学生的积极行为予以肯定和鼓励，对消极行为则采用消退原理，从而塑造学生良好的品质。

经典性条件反射和操作性条件反射的基本原理是一致的，都是建立在无条件反射的基础上，条件反射建立之后都必须利用强化才能使行为得到巩固，若不强化，建立起的条件反射便会逐渐消退。两者也是有区别的，经典性条件反射更利于原有行为的改造，操作性条件反射更有助于塑造新行为。

（三）两种信号系统

从条件反射的形成可以看出，条件刺激物成了无条件刺激物的信号，从这层意义上说，条件反射实质上就是信号反射。

客观世界存在两种性质不同的信号刺激物，即第一信号和第二信号，与此相应也存在着两种不同的信号系统：第一信号系统和第二信号系统。

第一信号是指现实的、具体的刺激物，如声音、颜色、气味、形状等。由这种具体刺激物为条件刺激形成的条件反射系统属于第一信号系统。如"望梅止渴",吃过梅子的人看到梅子时会产生唾液,就是一种第一信号系统的活动,这是由梅子的视觉映象引起的。第一信号系统是动物和人所共有的,在这种反射系统的基础上,有机体只能形成对现实的直接反映,如感觉等。

第二信号是由语言中的词组成的刺激。它是信号的信号,是一种抽象和概括化的信号,可以代替第一信号而起作用。比如"谈梅生津"就属于这种情况。这里,"梅子"一词代表着具体梅子的形状、颜色、味道等而起信号作用,成为第一信号的信号,所以称为第二信号。由语词作为信号刺激而建立的条件反射系统,称为第二信号系统活动。第二信号系统是人类特有的反射系统,借助于这个系统的活动,人才能间接而概括地反映现实,揭露事物的本质和规律,传递知识和经验,有意识地调节自己的行为。

人的两个信号系统是密切联系、协同活动的。人的活动一般都是第一信号系统与第二信号系统的协同活动,纯粹的第一信号系统活动或纯粹的第二信号系统活动几乎是没有的。第一信号系统的活动是第二信号系统形成的基础;反过来,第二信号系统又对第一信号系统起支配和调节作用。两种信号系统的协同活动,是人类活动自觉性的一个必要条件。人们通过词可以随时对自己发出各种信号,命令自己去进行各种活动。正是词的这种作用,才使人的活动能够相对地脱离各种客观事物的直接制约,形成心理活动的有意性和自觉性,以及一切随意活动和行为。对正常人来说,第二信号系统起着主导作用。

第二节
心理是客观现实的反映

一、客观现实是心理的源泉和内容

心理是脑的机能,这仅说明了心理产生的生理机制,脑自身不会产生心理,它仅是产生心理的物质承载者。就像一个加工厂,我们的大脑是厂房,是机器,要生产出产品来,还必须有原材料,那么要加工的原材料从何而来呢?这就必须依赖于客观现实,客观现实是心理的源泉和内容。人的心理不是无缘无故产生的,人的心理是对客观现实的反映,是人脑与客观现实相互作用的结果。

客观现实是指客观存在的一切事物,可以是被人的意识所反映的客观物质世界,也可以是意识之外存在的客观事物,客观现实不依赖于人的意识而存在。对人类来说,客观现实包括自然环境和社会环境。

自然环境是人类赖以生存和实践的环境,是人的心理的源泉之一。包括天地日月、山川河流、花草树木、飞禽走兽等自然界中的万事万物。社会环境,包括人的社会生活、城市乡村、街道房屋、生产劳动、工具厂房、人际关系等，这是人的心理的最主要的来源。只有当客观现实作用于我们的感觉器官时，我们才能产生感知觉、记忆、思维、想象、情感等各种各样的心理现象，我们才能由不知转化为知。无论是简单还是复杂的心理现象，其内容都来自于客观现实。

社会环境（生活条件）在产生人的心理方面起着决定性的作用。没有人的社会生活，离开人的社会经验，即使具备产生人的心理的物质基础——人脑，也不可能产生人的心理，人将不能成其为人而只是生物的个体。因此可以说，人的心理是客观现实作用于人脑的产物，是客观现实在人脑中的反映，客观现实是人心理活动的内容和源泉。

二、人的心理是对客观现实的主观反映

心理对客观现实的反映都是经过个体的主观世界折射而形成的，是一种主观的反映。正是由于心理对客观世界的反映是一种主观映像，才显示出人的心理的千差万别和丰富多彩。心理反映的主观性主要表现在以下两个方面：

第一，从反映的形式看，心理是主观的。心理与其所反映的客观事物是不同的，客观现实是客观的，以物质的形式存在于现实中，心理是主观的，以观念的形式存在于人的头脑中。心理与其反映的客观事物是相像的，但却不能等同，就像我们在镜子中看到的自己和真实的自己不同一样，心理是物体的映像，是观念性的东西，自己可以操控，而物体是实在的事物，是我们无法用自身的意识来改变的客观存在。

第二，从个体心理反映的差异看，心理是主观的。在现实情境中，不同国家、不同民族、不同个体对同一个事物的反映会不一样，这恰好体现了心理的主观性。每个人的心理都受个人的知识经验、需要、动机、个性特征等因素的影响，而个人内在的差异也使其对同一事物的反映带有个人的特点，呈现出明显的主观特色。如一根电线杆从远处看时，其在视网膜上的映象短，近处看时映像长，但在我们看来，两者是一样长的，这是知识经验在反映中的作用；同样是观察一种现象，严谨细心的人比粗枝大叶的人观察到的东西多，这是性格在反映中的作用；同样上一节语文课，有的学生兴致很高，全神贯注地听老师讲课，有的学生因为一些不愉快的事情心神不宁，上课时不知道老师讲了些什么，这是当时的心理状态对反映的影响。因此，个体不同的内心状态、经验、背景、性格等都会影响到对事物的反映。不同的人对同一事物的反映可以不同，长江的水在关羽看来是英雄的血，红醉霜林在崔莺莺看来是离人的泪。甚至同一个人在不同时期对同一事物的反映也有所不同。如杜甫有两首描绘祖国河山的诗，一首是《城西陂泛舟》，这首诗是"安史之乱"以前的作品，其中"春风自信牙樯动，迟日徐看锦缆牵，鱼吹细浪摇歌扇，燕蹴飞花落舞筵"，所看到的花、鱼、燕，都足以引起诗人的乐趣。但在另一首《春望》里，还是花红鸟啭、莺歌燕舞，在诗里却黯然失色了。"国破山河在，城春草木深，感时花溅泪，恨别鸟惊心"，同样的美景，却没有引起诗人的丝毫乐趣，相反，却勾起绵绵的愁绪。

同样的客观现实可以引起人们不同的心理反映，这说明人的心理反映具有主观性。人的心理具有主观性并不否认人的心理的客观性。只不过要强调人是认识的主体，事物是认识的客体。人的心理反映的主观性归根结底还是来源于客观现实。如一个文科生和一个理科生走进书店所关注的对象可能会不一样，文科生首先注意的是与文科有关的书

籍,理科生首先注意的是与有理科有关的书籍,之所以这样,是由于在实际生活中长期的教育训练形成的结果。人的心理反映的这种主观性绝不是人认识事物的弱点,相反,由于人反映事物的选择性,人的过去经验、个性心理特征参与人的反映过程,才保证了人的认识不断精确与深化。

正是由于人的心理反映具有主观性的特点,因此,在教育教学中就要考虑到学生的个别差异,考虑学生心理反映的主观性,并根据学生的心理特点预测学生的心理反映,因人施教,才能发挥教育的积极作用。

三、人的心理是对客观现实的能动反映

人对客观现实的反映,不像镜子和照相底片那样简单和刻板,人对客观现实的反映不是消极的、被动的,而是积极主动的,是人和周围世界相互作用的结果。人在生活实践的要求下,积极参与社会实践活动,获得关于周围事物的认识,把握事物发展变化的规律。人在认识世界的基础上,又会自觉地确定目的,制定活动计划,并运用意志努力,通过实际行动去改造客观事物。正是在这个从客观到主观,又从主观到客观的过程中,体现了人的能动性。

人的心理的能动性,除表现在人能认识世界和改造客观世界外,还表现在人有自我意识,能对自己有比较明确的认识、评价,并在认识自我的基础上,实现对自我的改造。人的自我认识、自我改造、自我完善也体现了人的能动性。

四、实践活动对心理形成的影响

心理是脑的机能,是对客观现实的反映。有了正常的大脑,有了客观现实并不一定产生心理现象,这是因为心理是在人认识和改造世界的社会实践中实现的。

专栏 2-3

生活经历如何影响你的脑

初次接触现代神经科学的学生们经常感到奇怪,生活经历怎么会影响脑呢?

罗本格及其同事完成的一项经典研究结果表明,养在恶劣和优越环境下的大白鼠脑发育不同。恶劣环境是指把大白鼠单笼饲养,只是一个小小的笼子,除了食物和水没有什么别的玩具。优越环境是指几只大白鼠生活在宽大笼内,多种玩具每天轮流放在笼中,让这些大白鼠共享。经不同时期,从数天到数月后,实验者分别检查两种环境下鼠脑的不同,结果非常显著。生活在优越环境中的鼠脑,平均大脑皮层重量和厚度均大于恶劣环境生活的鼠,这种测量差异十分显著,甚至生活在优越环境下仅数天的鼠也不同。超过儿童期的鼠也会出现这种差异,这就是说,即使老年鼠也会在改变为优越环境的生活中受益。虽然这一研究是用大白鼠进行的,但研究者们相信,这一结果可以很好地用于人类被试。优越的生活环境对脑的发育和脑功能的维护会

有好的影响。

利用脑成像技术，可以测量出与个体生活经验相关的很特殊的脑差异。想象一下，一位钢琴演奏家需要十分精确地控制左手指的力。脑扫描发现，钢琴演奏家左手指的皮层代表区比非钢界演奏者明显增大（Elbertetal, 1995）。而右手指由于在钢琴演奏中不需要太多感觉作用，他的大脑皮层代表区也没有明显增大。对于12岁以前就学习弹钢琴的演奏家，其左手指的大脑皮层代表区格外增大。可能你已猜到，一些生活经验对脑功能的影响是不良的，前面已经说过，脑内海马对于外显记忆的获得是重要的结构。研究家们发现，慢性应激引起海马神经元树突明显萎缩（McEwen, 1999; Sapolsky, 1996），慢性应激状态是一种机体的生理和心理资源持久性耗竭状态，它不仅造成海马细胞树突萎缩，记忆能力也受损。例如，大白鼠在慢性应激之后，丧失了成功习得的迷津导航能力（Conrad et al., 1990）。神经科学现代研究的重要目标，是设计一些方法对抗不良生活经验对脑的影响后果。我们大家都会从这类研究中受益。

——理查德·格里格（Richard J. Gerrig），菲利普·津巴多（Philip G. Zimbardo）. 心理学与生活［M］. 王垒，王甦，等，译. 北京：人民邮电出版社，2003：69.

1. 社会实践是人的心理产生和发展的唯一途径

人的心理不是自发产生的，只有作为心理源泉的客观现实和作为反映器官的脑两者相互作用，才能产生正常的心理，而这种相互作用是通过人的实践活动实现的。人所有的心理现象都是在各种实践活动中，在人们彼此交往过程中产生和发展起来的。人的心理是对一个人整个生活经历的真实写照。人从出生那天起，就从事着各种各样的活动、游戏、学习，成年后又从事着各种社会实践，人通过各种实践活动去感知周围的事物，并不断改造着客观世界，正是在丰富多彩的实践活动中，产生了人对事物的认识，使人的认识和知识逐渐丰富起来，并形成了人的兴趣、动机、情感、愿望等，表现出人们克服困难的意志行动。同时，由于社会实践活动的多样性和复杂性，也形成了人们不同的能力和性格。因此人们在实践活动中，在改造周围世界的同时，也改变着自身，改变着人对客观事物的反映，丰富和发展着人的心理。相反，如果没有人的社会生活实践，即使具备了人脑，仍然不能产生人的心理。"狼孩"的事实充分说明社会生活实践对人的心理的产生与发展起着决定性作用。

1920年，人们在印度发现两个在狼群里生活的孩子，大的叫卡玛拉，发现时约8岁，小的叫阿玛拉，只有2岁，但她很快就死去了。卡玛拉不会讲话，用四肢行走，不穿衣服，不吃人手里拿的肉，只吃扔在地上的生肉，用舌头舔食物吃，她既怕火又怕水，从不让洗澡。即使天气寒冷，她也要撕掉衣服。她怕强光，白天缩在墙角，夜间出来活动，夜间视觉敏锐，深夜发出狼一样的嚎叫，经过辛格博士及其夫人的悉心照料与教育，2年后，卡玛拉学会了站立，4年后，学会了6个单词，6年后，学会了走路，7年后，学会了45个单词，同时会用手吃饭、用杯子喝水。但是到17岁临死时，她也只有相当于4岁儿童的心理发展水平。卡玛拉是人的后代,具有人脑这块高度发达的物质,但为什么只有动物的本性,而没有人的心理呢?其根本原因就是她很小就被狼叼走,从小脱离了人类的社会生活,无法进行社会实践活动,不能学习人类的语言,不能进行人际交往和接受人类的知识经验等。在她的头脑中只有狼群生活的反映,而没有人类社会生活的内容,所以不能产生人的心理。

除了"狼孩",世界各地还陆续发现了被野兽哺养长大的以及离开人类社会而长大的野生儿。所有这些孩子都只能发出不清楚、不连贯的声音,不能直立行走,活动敏捷,跑得很快,跳跃攀登很出色。他们有发展得很好的听觉、视觉和嗅觉,然而即使经过很长时间的学习也没能学会说话,无法适应人类的生活。可见,从小脱离人的社会生活条件便不能形成人的心理。

那么,一个成人已具备正常人的心理,如果长期脱离人的社会生活,离开丰富的外界刺激,其心理会产生怎样的变化呢?抗日战争时期被日本侵略者抓到北海道做劳工的刘连仁的经历可以说明这个问题。

专栏 2-4

劳工刘连仁的故事

1944年9月2日,山东省高密县井沟镇草泊村村民、31岁的刘连仁被日本兵强行绑架,押送至日本北海道,在矿井里做苦工。在这里,劳工们遭受着非人的对待。黑暗的矿洞里没有光明,更没有安全设备,空气弥漫着脏臭味。每天干16小时就算幸运了。完不成定量,不但不让吃饭、休息,还要挨皮鞭抽、皮鞋踢,劳工们经常被打得皮开肉绽,鲜血直流。许多人就这样被活活折磨死了。身高1.81米的刘连仁在家时体重90公斤,到了这里很快就变成了50公斤。在地狱般的井下被奴役了近一年之后,1945年7月31日的晚上,不堪折磨的刘连仁和另外4名难友从厕所里钻坑逃了出去,但其他4位伙伴都被日本人抓了回去,只有刘连仁侥幸逃脱,躲到了北海道人迹罕见的深山野林中。夏天,山里的野韭菜、野蒜、野梨、野葡萄、榆树皮,都是他赖以充饥的食物。有时他到山脚下的海边弄来一些海带,那就算是珍贵的食品了。冬天,这些海带就是他一个季节的食粮。寒冷的北海道,6月才化完雪,9月又飞起雪花来,冬天的温度常在零下40℃以下,连树木也冻裂了皮。在如此恶劣的环境下,如何生存?归国无望的刘连仁就地挖了一个洞,洞穴仅能容身,他双手抱膝蹲坐在里面,浑身蜷缩,像动物那样,处于半昏迷的"冬眠"状态,饿极了吃几口海带、舔几口雪水……就这样过着与世隔绝的孤独、凄惨的野人生活,每年在洞中靠一捆海带过六七个月,等到春天出来,他都是先在地上爬,过了几天以后才会走路。其实就在刘连仁进山以后不到一个月,日本就宣布战败投降了。可他哪里知道?他在山中度过了13个难熬的冬天。1958年2月8日,刘连仁被上山打猎的猎人发现了。当刘连仁出现在日本人面前时,他们都被这个"野人"吓得倒退了几步。

当时北海道华侨总会事务局长席占明先生得知消息后,前往探望刘连仁。席占明问了他很多问题,可表情焦灼的刘连仁就是发不出音来,原来,多年的孤独生活,他没和任何人有过语言交往,舌头已经僵硬,几乎不会说话了。后来,席先生灵机一动对他说:"我问你话,你若认为对了就点头,不对就摇头。"席先生问他是不是中国人,刘连仁点头,席先生又问他是什么地方人,刘连仁终于费劲地说出一个"山"字,几经猜测,席先生说出了"山东"两个字,刘连仁泪如泉涌⋯⋯随后,席先生每天教他说话,刘连仁的口齿慢慢恢复了正常。1958年4月15日,飘零异国14年的"穴居野人"刘连仁终于回到祖国的怀抱。

——郑红,樊洁,倪嘉波.心理学原理与应用[M].北京:清华大学出版社,2011:44.

刘连仁的经历说明,长期脱离正常人的实践活动,会对人的心理产生严重影响。

这些案例也充分说明,人类的社会实践活动对人的心理产生和发展起着决定性作用,是人的心理产生和发展的基础。人正因为通过社会实践活动,接触各种事物,完成各种活动,与人交往,形成复杂的人际关系,人的心理才能形成,才能认识事物的本质和发展规律。

2. 社会实践是检验心理反映是否正确的标准

人的心理、意识是否正确地反映了客观现实,必须在社会现实中加以检验。当人们根据对事物的反映进行活动时,实践的结果就能证明哪些反映是正确的,哪些反映是错误的。人不断地纠正着自己的认识和行动,使心理反映更正确,更符合于客观实际。这就进一步促进了心理的发展,使心理反映达到深刻化和完善化的程度。

综上所述,人的心理是人脑的机能,是客观现实的反映。这种反映既是客观的,又是主观能动的,并且是在社会实践活动中发生发展、通过社会实践活动加以检验的。由于人在实践中所接触到、感受到的客观事物日新月异地变化着,人的心理也随之而发展变化。所以,人的心理对于客观世界的反映是永远不会完结的。

本章小结

心理是脑的功能,是对客观现实的反映。脑是产生心理的物质器官。神经元是神经系统的基本构成单位,神经系统的结构和功能是心理产生的生理基础,反射是神经系统的基本活动方式,实现反射活动的神经结构叫反射弧。反射有无条件反射和条件反射两种。心理是客观现实的反映。客观现实是心理的源泉和内容,心理是人脑对客观现实的主观映像,心理在实践活动中发生发展并通过实践活动得以验证。

关键术语

心理的实质　神经生理　反射　反射弧　客观现实

讨论与应用

1. 请阅读下面这段材料，然后用本章学习的知识分析：为什么裂脑人会出现这么奇异的现象？它说明人类大脑两半球与我们的心理现象有什么关系？

奇异的裂脑人

人体大脑的两个半球中间是由被称为"胼胝体"的神经纤维束连接起来的，这样可以保证左右两半球在功能上的统一。历史上，把因割裂大脑两半球联合部分而使其成为具有"两个独立脑半球"的病人称为"裂脑人"。美国著名脑科学家斯佩里（S. U. Sperry）博士长期潜心于"裂脑人"的实验研究，并于1981年获得了诺贝尔医学生理学奖。

斯佩里通过一系列特殊的实验，发现了"裂脑人"的许多新奇现象。例如，让"裂脑人用左眼注视着一个美元符号，而用右眼注视着一个问号，当要他用左手画出他看到的东西时，他很快地画出美元符号；但当问他看到什么时，他却立即回答说"一个问号"。

同样，斯佩里博士在测试"裂脑人"用触觉再认物体的能力的实验中，也发现病人的反应十分有趣。在实验中，斯佩里博士给病人某个物体，当病人把物体握在右手时，能叫出物体的名称并描述物体；而当物体被放在左手时，他却不能用语言描述物体，但能够在非语言的测验中确认它。例如，病人可以将左手中的物品与各种物品组合中的同样物品相匹配，如果让病人左手拿着积木，他虽然不能说出物体的名称，但可以根据积木的颜色把积木排列成某种图形。

2. 阅读下面的材料，思考这一实例说明了什么？

美国学者丹尼曾做过一个惨无人道的实验。他从孤儿院里选了40名婴儿，将其分别放入被严格控制隔离的笼内，不与任何人交往，经过几年的喂养，这40名婴儿全部变成了痴呆儿。后来这个实验被揭露出来，引起了社会舆论的强烈谴责，丹尼不得不停止实验。实验虽然停了，但是被害的40名儿童经社会多方资助，极力挽救，收效却甚微。40名儿童中除少数儿童能掌握基本的生活能力外，大部分儿童终生痴呆。

3. 试用心理学的有关理论加以分析。

一天，王老师讲了一个寓言故事，课后让全班同学谈谈其含义和现实意义。结果全班几十位同学你说东，我说西，很难找到两个相同的看法。全班几十位同学都是同一时间内听的同一节课，为什么会引起不同的看法呢？

4. 试分析该现象的原因。

同看一部电影，人们的评价却大不相同。有的人认为非常精彩，有的人认为一般，有的人却认为不怎么样。

本章讨论与应用答题思路与要点 （扫描二维码）	本章复习思考题 （扫描二维码）	本章进一步阅读书目 （扫描二维码）

第三章
感觉和知觉
GANJUEHEZHIJUE

  大千世界丰富多彩、变化万端。我们每时每刻都在适应身边的环境，努力地认识和探索着它们的奥秘。我们能看见缤纷的世界，能听到美妙的声音，能尝到甜美的滋味，也能闻到芬芳的花香。我们尽自己所能来认识客观世界，大到宇宙天体，小到具体事物，无不始于感觉和知觉。感觉和知觉是人类认识世界的开端，也是我们一切知识的来源，是人的心理活动的基础。本章将带你进入奇妙的感知觉研究领域，了解感知觉的主要研究和基本知识。

通过本章的学习,你能够
- 理解和掌握感觉、知觉的概念及种类
- 明了感觉和知觉的规律
- 了解感觉和知觉在实践领域的应用

【本章结构】

```
                    感觉和知觉
        ┌──────────────┼──────────────┐
        ▼              ▼              ▼
      感觉            知觉       感知觉规律在教育教学中的应用
 ◎ 感觉的含义及其分类  ◎ 知觉概述      ◎ 了解直观教学的手段
 ◎ 感觉的一般规律      ◎ 知觉的特性    ◎ 根据感知规律组织教学,
                     ◎ 知觉的信息       提高教学质量
                        加工过程      ◎ 学生观察力的培养
                     ◎ 知觉的种类
```

从本章开始,我们要学习心理现象中的认识过程,而人们对世界的认识是从感知觉开始的。通过感觉,我们将了解外界事物的光、声、色、温湿度等物理、化学的特性,通过知觉我们将知道事物的名称和意义。感觉和知觉是我们认识世界的开端和基础。

第一节 感觉

一、感觉的含义及其分类

(一) 感觉的概念

感觉(sensation)是人脑对直接作用于感觉器官的客观事物的个别属性的反映。例如,看到的颜色、听到的声音、嗅到的气味等都是感觉。人类生存于物质世界中,物质世界的一切事物都具有光、声、色、味、温度、湿度、光洁度等各种物理的、化学的特性,当这些属性直接作用于人的眼、耳、鼻、舌和皮肤等感觉器官时,就会在头脑中引起相应的视、听、嗅、味、触等感觉。可见,感觉是人脑对客观现实的反映,客观现实是感觉产生的源泉和内容。如果没有作用于感觉器官的客观事物,便不会产生任何感觉。感觉是客观的,又是主观的。人们的任何感觉都受他的情绪状态及身体状况的影响。因此,感觉又是客观世界的主观映象。感觉不仅反映事物的外部属性,还反映有机体的变化和内部器官的状况。例如,人体的运动姿势、饥饿、疼痛等。

作为一种心理现象,感觉与其他心理现象相比具有两个明显的特点:第一,感觉所反映的是当前直接作用于感官的客观事物,而不是过去的或间接的事物;第二,感觉所反映的是客观事物的个别属性,而不是事物的整体和全貌。它对客观事物的反映,只局限在"个别属性"的范围之内。

(二) 感觉的生理机制

感觉的产生是分析器活动的结果。分析器是有机体感受和分析某种刺激的神经装置。它由外周感受器、传入神经、大脑皮层感觉中枢三部分构成。人体有许多种分析器,如视觉分析器、听觉分析器、嗅觉分析器、味觉分析器、触觉分析器等。

感觉的产生首先要有刺激物作用于感受器(receptor)。刺激物对感受器的作用叫刺激(stimulus)。一般来说,每一种感受器都有其适宜刺激,即它们仅对某一种形式的能量变化特别敏感。例如,可见光波是眼球内视网膜的适宜刺激,声波是内耳柯蒂氏器官的适宜刺激,温度变化是温度感受器的适宜刺激。感受器接受一定强度的刺激产生兴奋,刺激的能量就转化为神经细胞上的电活动(即神经冲动)。分析器的外周感受器实质上是一种能量转换器。环境的各种刺激经过感受器的转能作用,以神经冲动的形式传向中枢。来自各种感受器的神经冲动分别经各自的感受传导通路传向各级神经中枢,最后传至分析器的高级中枢——大脑皮层的感觉代表区。大脑皮质各感觉代表区的活动是产生各种感觉的主要生理基础。皮质的各感觉代表区的临近部位是它们的相应联络区,联络区的功能是辅助感觉区,使感觉区获得的信息更加准确。

(三) 感觉的分类

根据刺激的来源不同,可以把感觉分为外部感觉和内部感觉。

1. 外部感觉

外部感觉是由机体以外的客观刺激引起、反映外界事物个别属性的感觉。它包括视觉、听觉、嗅觉、味觉和肤觉。

（1）视觉

视觉（visual sense）是可见光波作用于视觉分析器而产生的一种感觉。产生视觉的适宜刺激是波长为380—780纳米的电磁波,即可见光。光是具有一定频率和波长的电波。宇宙中存在各种电磁波,而其中只有一小部分才是可见光。接受光波刺激的感受器是眼睛视网膜上的感光细胞。当适宜的光刺激透过眼睛到达视网膜时,将引起视网膜中的感光细胞产生神经冲动,神经冲动沿视神经传导到大脑皮质的中枢时,视觉就产生了。通过视觉,我们可以辨别外界物体的明暗、颜色、大小、形状等特性,视觉是人们获得外界信息的主要感觉通道,80%以上的信息都是通过视觉获得的。

图 3-1
可见光波长

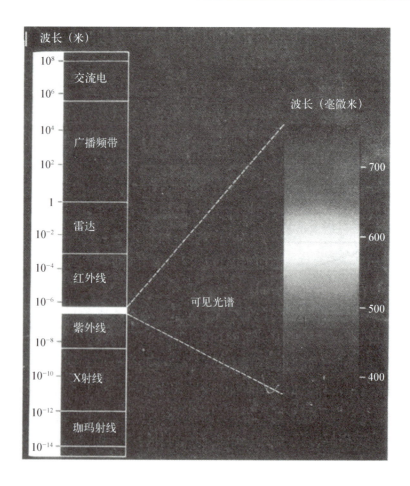

（2）听觉

声波作用于听觉分析器所产生的感觉就是听觉（auditory sense）。引起听觉的适宜刺激是频率（发声物体每秒钟振动的次数）为16—20000赫兹的声波。低于16赫兹的振动是次声波，高于20000赫兹的振动是超声波，都是人耳不能接受的。接受声波刺激的感受器是内耳的柯蒂氏器官内的毛细胞。当声音刺激经过耳朵传达到内耳的柯蒂氏器官内的毛细胞时，引起毛细胞兴奋，毛细胞的兴奋沿听神经传达到脑的听觉中枢，就产生了听觉。

（3）嗅觉

某些物质的气体分子作用于嗅觉分析器时产生的感觉叫做嗅觉（sense of smell）。引起嗅觉的适宜刺激是有气味的挥发性物质，接受嗅觉刺激的感受器是鼻腔黏膜的嗅细胞。有气味的气体物质作用于嗅细胞，嗅细胞产生兴奋，经嗅束传至嗅觉的皮层部位（位于颞叶区），因而产生嗅觉。

（4）味觉

可溶性物质作用于味觉分析器而产生的感觉叫做味觉（sense of taste）。引起味觉的适宜刺激是可溶于水或液体的物质，接受味觉刺激的感受器是位于舌表面、咽后部和腭上的味蕾。人类基本的味觉有酸、甜、苦、咸四种，其他味觉都是由这四种基本味觉混合而产生的。但近年的研究发现，除传统的四种味觉外，人还有对"鲜味"的感觉，也叫"味精觉"[①]。味觉的产生往往需要借助嗅觉的协同作用，感冒时鼻子堵塞会影响人的味觉。味觉的适应和对比现象都比较明显。

（5）肤觉

物体的不同特性作用于相应的外周感受器所引起的各种各样的感觉叫做肤觉（skin sense）。引起肤觉的适宜刺激是物体机械的、温度的作用或伤害性刺激，接受肤觉刺激的感受器位于皮肤、口腔黏膜、鼻黏膜和眼角膜上（如皮肤内的游离神经末梢、触觉小体、触盘、环层小体、棱形末梢等），呈点状分布。

肤觉的基本形态包括触压觉、温度觉、痛觉。其他各种肤觉是由这几种基本形态构成的复合体。

专栏3-1

催眠与疼痛

1829年，一位法国外科医生克劳奎特（Cloquet）在法国医学科学院报告了一例对一位患有右侧乳腺癌的妇女所做的不同寻常的手术。在手术前，只给病人进行了催眠，而没有注射任何麻醉药物，结果在切开病人乳腺至腋窝并去掉肿瘤和腋窝腺体的整个手术期间，病人没有一点疼痛的感觉。此报告一时引起了极大的反响，人们甚至指责克劳奎特是骗子。然而在随后的几年中，就有很多人报告说也用催眠术进行

[①] 彭聃龄.普通心理学[M].北京：北京师范大学出版社，2012：143.

了无痛手术，这些报告唤起了人们对催眠术可以缓解疼痛的心理学机制的研究兴趣。在大多数学者看来，催眠术缓解的只是病人对手术的焦虑、恐惧和担忧，而疼痛作为感觉是否也得以缓解，至今还是一个有争议的问题。也许，在催眠状态下疼痛可能达到某些较低的水平，只是没有达到意识水平而已。关于这一点，希尔加德（Hilgard）的实验也许可以说明。

希尔加德用循环冰水作疼痛刺激。他请被试把一只手放进冰水里，另一只手则放在一个指示疼痛感受的按键上，并请被试用1—10级报告感受到的疼痛强度。在催眠状态下希尔加德惊奇地发现，被试说不痛，而且全然不理会放在冰水中的那只手，但放在按键上的手却按下按键报告疼痛的感觉，表现得和没有受到催眠时一样，这一发现说明，在人们的意识中存在不同水平的认识机能，疼痛可以达到意识的某一水平，但仍可能达不到被意识到的水平。

——崔丽娟.心理学是什么[M].北京：北京大学出版社，2002：113—114.

2. 内部感觉

（1）运动觉

反映身体各部分运动和位置的感觉叫运动觉（kinesthesia）。引起运动觉的适宜刺激是身体运动和姿势的变化，接受运动觉刺激的感受器位于肌肉、韧带、关节等的神经末梢。凭借运动觉，我们可以行走、劳动，还可以进行各种体育活动，完成各种复杂的运动技能；凭借运动觉与触觉、压觉等的结合，我们可以认识物体的软硬、弹性、远近、大小、滑涩等特性。

（2）平衡觉

反映头部位置和身体平衡状态的感觉叫平衡觉（equilibratory sensation）。引起平衡觉的适宜刺激是身体运动时速度和方向的变化，以及旋转、震颤等，接受平衡觉刺激的感受器位于内耳的前庭器官，即椭圆囊、球囊和三个半规管。平衡觉的作用在于调节机体运动、维持身体的平衡。平衡觉与视觉、机体觉有联系，当前庭器官受到刺激时，视野中的物体仿佛在移动，我们会产生眩晕、恶心、呕吐等反应。

（3）机体觉

机体内部器官受到刺激时产生的感觉叫机体觉（organic sensation）。引起机体觉的适宜刺激是机体内部器官的活动和变化，接受机体觉刺激的感受器分布于人体各脏器的内壁。机体觉在调节内部器官的活动中具有重要作用，它能及时地反映机体内部环境的变化、内部器官的工作状态。当人体的内部器官处于健康、正常的工作状态时，一般不会产生机体觉。机体觉的表现形式有饥、渴、气闷、恶心、窒息、便意、性、胀、痛等。

（四）感觉的意义

感觉虽然是最简单的心理过程，但在人们的生活和工作中却有重要意义。

第一，感觉提供了内外环境的信息。通过感觉，人们能够知晓外界事物的颜色、明度、气味、软硬等各种属性，为进一步认识外界事物提供了前提；感觉又是一切认识的开端，是获得知识的基础。离开了感觉，人们既不可能有记忆，也不可能有思维和想象，认识便成了无源之水，无本之木。通过感觉，我们还能认识机体内部的各种状态，获得自身的位置、运动、姿势、饥饱、劳逸、心跳等种种信息，这为自我调节提供了前提，如饥择食、渴择饮。因此，没有感觉提供的信息，人们就不可能根据自己机体的状态来调节自己的行为。

第二，感觉保证了机体与环境的平衡。人们要正常生活，必须与环境保持平衡。比如，人们必须从周围环境获得必要的光、声、色、温度、湿度等的刺激，保持能量的平衡，以便激活大脑皮层，使大脑保持清醒，维持正常的心理活动。又如，人们总要通过各种感觉获得一定的信息，与外在环境保持平衡，如果信息严重超载或严重不足，都会破坏信息的平衡，给机体带来严重不良的影响。国外"感觉剥夺"的实验就证明了这一点。

> **专栏 3-2**
>
> ### 感觉剥夺实验
>
> 当今世界，常常让我们感到嘈杂、纷扰，我们有时是多么渴望有片刻的宁静。但心理学研究表明，当与外界处于高度隔绝的状态时，人的正常心理活动会发生奇异的变化。
>
> 1954年，加拿大心理学家贝克斯顿（W. H. Bexton）、赫伦（W Heron）和斯科特（T. H. Scott）等首次以人为被试进行了"感觉剥夺"实验。被试是自愿报名的大学生，每天的报酬是20美元，所有的被试要做的事是每天24小时躺在一张小床上，时间尽可能长（只要他愿意）。为了营造出极端的感觉剥夺状态，实验者让被试进入一个有隔音装置的小房间里，让他们戴上半透明的塑料眼罩，可以透进散射光，但没有图形视觉；手和胳膊戴上纸板做的套袖和棉手套，限制他们的触觉；头枕在用U形泡沫橡胶做的枕头上，同时用空气调节器的单调嗡嗡声限制他们的听觉。实验前，大多数被试以为能利用这个机会好好睡一觉，或者考虑论文、课程计划。但后来他们报告说，对任何事情都不能进行清晰的思考，哪怕是在很短的时间内。他们不能集中注意力，思维活动似乎是"跳来跳去"的。感觉剥夺实验停止后，这种影响仍在持续。（如图3-2所示）
>
> 结果，尽管报酬很高，但几乎没有人能在这项实验中忍耐三天以上。最初的8个小时好歹还能撑住，之后，有的被试吹起了口哨，有的自言自语，显得有点烦躁不安。对于那些8小时后结束实验的被试，让他们做一些简单的事情，他们都频频出错，注意力难以集中。
>
> 实验持续数日后，50%的被试报告有幻觉，其中大多数是视幻觉，也有被试报告有听幻觉或触幻觉。视幻觉大多在感觉剥夺的第三天出现，幻觉经验大多是简单的，

如光的闪烁,没有形状,常常出现于视野的边缘。听幻觉包括狗的狂吠声、警钟声、打字声、警笛声、滴水声等。触幻觉的例子有,感到冰冷的钢块压在前额和面颊,感到有人从身体下面把床垫抽走等。当实验进行到第四天时,一些被试出现了双手发抖、不能笔直走路、反应速度迟缓以及对疼痛敏感等症状。

被试参与完实验后,实验者对他们进行追踪调查,发现他们在实验结束后,需要3天以上的时间才能恢复到原来的状态。

感觉剥夺实验说明,感觉的丧失会严重影响人的认知过程,特别是思维过程,并涉及人的情绪和意志,造成心理的紊乱乃至病态。可见,人们在日常生活中"漫不经心"接受的刺激以及由此而产生的感觉是多么重要。

——李红.心理学基础[M].北京:高等教育出版社,2009:95—96.

图 3-2
感觉剥夺实验

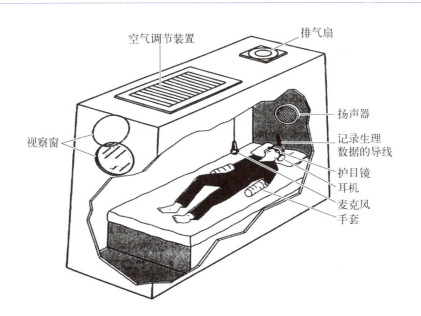

二、感觉的一般规律

我们知道,感觉是因为刺激作用于我们的感官而引起的,但这并不是说任何刺激都能引起我们的感觉。空气中漂浮的灰尘时刻都落在我们的皮肤上,但是人并没有任何感觉,而当灰尘积聚成较大的灰尘颗粒落到我们皮肤上时,就会有感觉了,这说明刺激必须达到一定的强度才能引起感觉。这就涉及人的感受性和感觉阈限的问题。

(一)感受性和感觉阈限

感受性(sensitivity)是人对适宜刺激的感觉能力,即感觉的灵敏程度。每个人对同一种刺激的感受性是有差异的,同样强度的刺激,有的人能感受到,有的人则感受不到,这说明人的感受性是有差异的。感受性的大小用感觉阈限的值来度量。感觉阈限(sensory threshold)是指人能感到某个刺激的存在或刺激发生变化所需的强度的临界值。任何一种感觉都存在着两种感受性:绝对感受性和差别感受性。

1. 绝对感受性和绝对感觉阈限

绝对感受性(absolute sensitivity)是指刚刚能察觉出最小刺激量的能力。绝对感觉阈限(absolute sensory threshold)则是指刚刚能引起感觉的最小刺激量,也叫感觉的下阈。绝对感受性和绝对感觉阈限成反比关系:绝对感觉阈限越小,也就是引起感觉所需要的刺激量越小,绝对感受性越强;反之,绝对感觉阈限越大,则绝对感受性越弱。例如,一个人能比别人听见弱的声音,人们就说这个人的听觉感受性比别人高。

绝对感觉阈限因刺激物的性质和机体的状况而不同。在适当的条件下,人的感觉阈限是很低的。一般,人感受的强度是由刺激的强度决定的。刺激强度越大,感觉越强。虽然低于绝对感觉阈限的刺激人们感觉不到,但却能引起一定的生理效应。如低于听觉阈限的声音刺激能引起脑电波的变化和瞳孔的扩大。但若刺激强度超过了一定限度,就不再增加感觉强度,而是产生痛觉。人们把那种刚刚引起痛觉的刺激量叫做感觉的上阈。超过上阈的刺激强度,就会使感觉器官受到损伤,严重的还会造成感觉的丧失。绝对感觉阈限的大小因有机体内部和外部条件的影响而有所不同。如表3-1所示。

表 3-1
几种重要感觉的绝对感觉阈限

感觉种类	绝对感觉阈限
视觉	看到晴朗夜空下30英里外的1只烛光
听觉	安静环境下听到20英尺以外表的滴答声
味觉	可尝出两加仑水加入一茶匙糖的甜味
嗅觉	闻到散布于3个居室中洒一滴香水的气味
触觉	感觉从1厘米高处落到脸颊上蜜蜂的翅膀

2. 差别感受性和差别感觉阈限

在刺激物引起感觉之后,如果刺激在数量上发生变化,并不是所有的变化都能被人们觉察出来。例如,用两脚圆规的两个针尖,距离2毫米刺激手臂,人感受到的是一点,增加到3.3—4毫米时,我们才能感觉到是两点。这种刚刚能引起差别感觉的最小刺激量叫差别阈限(difference threshold),这种刚刚能觉察出最小差别量的感觉能力叫差别感受性(difference sensitivity)。二者也呈反比例关系,即差别感觉阈限越大,差别感受性就越小。反之亦然。

1834年,德国生理学家韦伯(E. H. Weber)在系列实验中发现,能够被机体感觉到的刺激强度变化（即差别感觉阈限）与原刺激强度（即标准强度）之间的比值是一个常数。例如，他在研究重量感觉时发现，100克重量要增加3克时，才能被我们感觉到比100克稍重一些，如果200克则要增加6克，300克需要增加9克，才会感到重量的变化。可见，差别阈限值是刺激重量的同一分数：3/100=6/200=9/300≈1/33，这个分数表示，必须在原有重量上的基础上增加它的1/33，才能觉察出重量有了变化。韦伯将上述关系用公式表示为：△I/I=K。式中：I为标准刺激强度或原刺激强度；△I为引起差别感觉所需要的刺激增量，即最小可觉差；K为常数（韦伯分数或韦伯比率）。这个公式后来被称为韦伯定律（Weber's law）。韦伯定律指出，对刺激的差别感觉，不取决于刺激增加的绝对量，而取决于刺激增量与原刺激量的比值。韦伯发现对于每一种刺激，这个比率的数值是不同的。不同感觉的韦伯分数（即K值）越小，表示该感觉对差异越敏感。研究表明，韦伯定律仅适用于中等强度的刺激，对于过弱或过强的刺激，韦伯分数会发生变化。如表3-2所示。

表 3-2 不同刺激的韦伯常数值

刺　激	韦伯常数（K）
气味浓度	0.07
光　强	0.01
声音频率	0.003
压　强	0.14
声　强	0.15
味道浓度	0.20

（二）感觉现象

感觉随着刺激的不同而有所变化，这种变化一方面由刺激的时间因素和空间因素决定，另一方面也由感觉之间的相互作用引起，刺激引起的感觉变化是各种感觉所共有的特性。

1. 感觉适应

感觉适应（sensory adaptation）是指由于刺激物对同一感受器的持续作用从而使感受性发生变化的现象。感觉适应可以引起感受性的提高，也可以引起感受性的降低。在生活中，感觉适应现象是很普遍的。我们从明亮的阳光下走进黑暗的电影放映大厅，开始时什么也看不清，过了一段时间以后才分辨出物体的轮廓，这叫暗适应。暗适应的全程约为40—60分钟，对光的感受性可提高20万倍。当从黑暗的电影院内走到阳光下，最初感觉阳光耀眼，发眩，看不清外面的物体，但只要稍过一会儿就能看清周围的事物，这叫明适应。明适应的过程比较短暂，一般5分钟左右就可以完成。又比如，人在一个乱哄哄的房间内待一段时间后，出来到院子里会感到很安静，这是因为在那个房间里人的听觉感受性降低，对院子里本来的声音也听不见了，这是听觉的适应。下水游泳，开始感到很凉，过一会儿就不再觉得凉了，这是冷觉适应。"入芝兰之室，久而不闻其香；入鲍鱼之肆，久而不闻其臭"，这是嗅觉适应。戴着眼镜找眼镜，拿着橡皮找橡皮，这是触觉的适应等。在所有的感觉中，唯独痛觉没有适应或很难适应。因为痛觉是伤害性刺激的信号，如果痛觉能够适应，将危及机体的生存。

2. 感觉后像

感觉后像（sensory aftermage）是指感受器的视觉刺激作用停止后，在视网膜上仍暂时保留了这种刺激引起的感觉印象。视觉后像分正后像和负后像两种,正后像是指视网膜上暂时保留的感觉印象与原刺激物相同。例如,注视日光灯30秒钟,然后关灯,此时仍可看见亮着的白色灯管。电影正是利用了这个原理,制成前后不同的静止画面,每秒放映24片,连续放映,于是就成了活动的电影。负后像是指视网膜上暂时保留的感觉印象与原刺激物相反。

应该说明的是,不仅视觉有后像,其他很多感觉也有后像现象。例如,当触压刺激已经消失后,我们仍会感到皮肤上有短暂的触压的感觉,这就是触压觉后像。"余音绕梁,三日不绝",说的是听觉后像。后像的产生是由于神经兴奋滞后作用,是感觉的暂留现象,这种暂留的时间一般约为0.1秒,但持续的时间与刺激强度和作用的时间成正相关。

3. 感觉对比

感觉对比(sensory contrast)是指同一感受器接受不同的刺激而使感受性发生变化的现象。它分为同时对比和先后对比。

同时对比是指几个刺激物同时作用于同一感受器而产生的对某种刺激物的感受性的变化。例如,同样一个图形,放在黑色的背景上显示得亮些,而在白色的背景上则显得暗些,彩色对比在背景的影响下,向着背景色的补色方面变化,而且两色的交界附近,对比也特别明显。例如,若把一个灰色的小方块放在绿色的背景上就显得红些,放在红色的背景上就显得绿些。(如图3-3所示)。

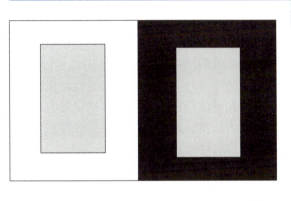

图 3-3
感觉对比

先后对比是指几个刺激物先后作用于同一感受器而产生的对某种刺激物的感受性的变化。例如,吃糖后马上吃桔子,会觉得桔子很酸。这是因为吃糖降低了对甜的感受性。反之,先吃桔子后吃糖,会觉得糖更甜,这是因为吃桔子提高了对甜的感受性。

4. 不同感觉的相互补偿与协作

感觉的补偿作用是指某种感觉缺失以后可以由其他感觉的发展来加以弥补。例如盲人缺失了视觉后,其听觉能力往往得到很好的发展,所以盲人可以借助听觉分辨道路的平坦情况,判断前方是否有障碍物,从而可以灵巧地避开等。另外,盲人还可以通过发展触觉来阅读盲文,聋人可以凭借振动觉来欣赏音乐等。在日常生活中,不同的感官常是特定的相互协作和互为补充的关系。例如,尝出美味需要依赖味觉和嗅觉感受器的合作。

5. 联觉

一种感觉兼而引起另一种感觉的现象叫联觉。

联觉的形式有很多,比较常见的是色觉所引起的其他感觉。例如,色觉会引起人的温度觉。红、橙、黄这些颜色让人感觉温暖,蓝、青、绿则让人感觉清冷,所以前者被称为暖色，后者被称为冷色。色觉还会引起轻重感和远近感的不同。同样大小的两个箱子，白色让人感觉轻快，黑色让人感觉沉重。淡颜色能起到扩展空间的作用，深颜色则能起到收敛空间的作用。

听觉和视觉之间也有联觉现象。在听觉的刺激下会出现视觉形象，这是音乐欣赏的心理基础。听觉和皮肤觉之间的联觉现象也很明显，如听到可怕的事情，毛骨悚然，浑身起鸡皮疙瘩。

日常生活中，人们说的一些话语如"甜蜜的声音""酸溜溜的语调""冰冷的脸色"等，反映的也是人的联觉现象。

（三）实践活动与感受性的发展

人的感受性与实践有着密切的关系。个体间感受性之间的差别与实践活动有关。专门从事某种职业的人，由于长期使用某一感官，使得相应的感受性也逐渐提高。如黑色织造工能分辨出40种深浅不同的黑色，而普通工人只能区分出两三种。有经验的飞行员能辨别1300转/分和1340转/分的差别。由此可见，人的感受能力并非天生固有的，是可以经后天练习得到提高的。

感受性的发展就是个体感受性在实践活动中获得提高的过程。一般而言，制约感受性发展的条件主要有个体感觉器官自身具有的潜能、相关的实践活动和个体的意志努力程度。这三个条件在感受性发展过程中缺一不可，只有健康的感觉器官才具有发展的可能，个体有意识的意志努力和实践锻炼可以把可能性变为现实性，感受性才能获得永久性的提高。

为什么感受性可以通过努力和实践训练得以提高？这是因为人的感受器本身的结构具有较大的可塑性。感觉器官的感受性遵循"用进废退"的规律，某一感官有缺陷的人可以发展另一些感官的感受性来加以补偿。研究发现，盲人出生时手指皮肤中的触觉小体与正常人相同，由于他们在后天生活实践中比正常人更多地使用触觉来接受外界信息，因此，他们的触觉感受性就得到了发展。

专栏 3-3

在太空中的感觉是怎样的

在电视上，人们看到宇航员们在失重条件下飘来飘去，显得挺自在。实际上，对太空生活的适应并不像人们想象的那么轻松，当飞行器进入空间轨道时，有大约70%的人的第一个感觉是被抛了起来，一半以上的宇航员都曾经因太空适应综合征（space adaptation syndrome）或称"太空病"而感到不适应。

（1）太空病的感觉像晕船吗

太空病是运动疾病的一种。与晕船、晕车和晕机一样，人最初的感觉是头和轻微的空间方位混乱。所不同的是，人在太空中通常没有脸色苍白、出冷汗和恶心的现象。在地球上，人在呕吐前会先感到恶心，但在太空中，呕吐是突然的和没有先兆的。

当人们看见另外一名宇航员上下颠倒地飘动，或从某个特别的角度看了地球一眼，都可能使人呕吐不止。由于失重会改变大脑对头部、肌肉和关节发送来的信号的感觉，所以，太空病比晕船要难受得多。

（2）需要多长时间才能适应失重

太空病的不适应现象通常在2—3天后消失。最近的研究表明，伴随适应过程的是，宇航员完全使用视觉线索，而不再使用平衡系统的信息。但是，在长期执行太空任务之后，一些宇航员返回地球的短时间内会出现"地球病"——头晕和恶心，在回地球后的头一两天，让宇航员闭着眼睛站在地上是相当困难的，这时，他们需要经历一次与进入太空时相反的适应过程。

——丹尼斯·库恩（Dennis Coon）.心理学导论——思想与行为的认识之路［M］.郑刚，等，译.北京：中国轻工业出版社，2003：217—218.

第二节 知觉

一、知觉概述

（一）知觉的定义

知觉（perception）是人脑对当前直接作用于感觉器官的客观事物的整体属性的反映。

知觉是比感觉更复杂的心理活动过程，它在经验的参与下，反映客观事物的整体。任何事物都是包含着许多个别属性的综合体。这些个别属性并不是各自孤立的，而是结合成一个整体同时或相继作用于人的感官，于是在人的头脑中，就产生了对事物整体的映像，这就是知觉。比如，我们看到一种水果，看到它的颜色和形状时，不仅会产生相应的感觉，同时也马上会产生对这种水果的知觉，知道这是哪一种水果，叫什么名字等。因此，脱离知觉的感觉是很少的，除了新生儿，人们一般是以知觉的形式来反映世界的。由于感觉和知觉密不可分，所以统称为感知觉。

知觉是在感觉的基础上产生的，但它不是个别感觉成分的简单相加。例如，我们看到一个正方形的成分是四条相等直线，把对四条相等直线的感觉相加在一起，若没有知识经验的帮助（比如，不知道正方形的定义），就不能确认这是一个正方形。所以感觉的简单相加不能构成对事物的知觉,而必须在经验的参与下,即知道它是什么事物,叫出它的名称,并能用词来标志它,才能综合个别感觉成分,形成对事物整体的认识,成为知觉。

因此,与感觉相比,知觉反映的是客观事物的整体属性,是多种感觉协同活动的结果。知觉还受到各种心理特点如兴趣、需要、动机、情绪和态度等因素的影响,使人的知觉具有一定的倾向性。

(二) 知觉与感觉的关系

知觉以感觉为基础,但又不同于感觉,两者既相互区别又相互联系。

1. 感觉和知觉的联系

第一,感、知觉都是人脑对当前直接作用于感觉器官的客观事物的反映。客观事物是感觉和知觉产生的条件,没有客观事物作用于人脑,感觉和知觉是不可能产生的。感觉和知觉反映的都是客观事物的表面特征,形成的是对客观事物的感性认识。

第二,感觉是知觉的基础,知觉是感觉的深入和发展。感觉是知觉过程的重要组成部分,是知觉的前提和基础,人对客观事物的个别属性的反映越丰富、越精确,由此形成的知觉就越完整、越正确,两者联系越紧密。

第三,知觉是对感觉信息的整合。知觉的整合并不是各种感觉的简单相加,知识经验等因素对知觉的产生具有较大影响。

2. 感觉和知觉的区别

感觉和知觉是两种不同的心理现象,它们的区别主要表现在以下五个方面。

一是反映的客观事物的属性不同。感觉反映的是客观事物的个别属性,知觉反映的则是客观事物的整体属性。

二是生理机制不同。感觉是单个分析器活动的结果,知觉是多种分析器协同活动的结果。

三是反映的层次不同。感觉是介于心理和生理之间的活动,是以生理作用为基础的最简单的心理过程,只能认识事物的个别属性(低层次);知觉是纯心理活动,加入了个体主观因素,可以认识事物的整体和意义(高层次)。

四是经验的参与程度不同。感觉是人脑对客观事物的个别属性的反映,在此过程中,不需要或很少需要人的知识经验的参与,因此,相同的刺激会引起相似的感觉。知觉是在感觉的基础上产生的,需要人的知识经验等主观因素的参与,不同的人对同一刺激可能产生不同的知觉。

五是从严格意义上讲,感觉是天生的反应,是个体共有的普遍现象,而知觉却是后天学习的结果,具有很大的个别差异。

二、知觉的特性

(一) 知觉的选择性

我们周围的事物是多种多样的,在一定时间里,我们总是以少数事物作为知觉的对象，以便产生清晰的知觉，这就叫知觉的选择性。在知觉过程中，被知觉的事物好像从其他事物中突出出来，成为知觉的"对象"，而其他事物则退到后面去，成为"背景"。

图 3-4

花瓶与侧脸的双关图

知觉中的对象和背景的关系不是固定不变的，它常依据一定的主观条件相互转换。如图3-4所示，如果以白色为背景，则知觉到的是两个人的侧面像，如果以黑色为背景，则会知觉为白色的花瓶。

在大多数情况下，从知觉的背景中分出对象来并不困难，但是在某些情况下，要迅速地知觉出对象却不是一件容易的事。把对象从背景中区分出来一般取决于以下条件：

1. 对象与背景的差别

对象与背景之间的差别越大，从背景中区分出对象就越容易。反之，差别越小，区分就越困难。

2. 对象各部分的组合

对象本身各部分的关系组合也是我们把对象从背景中区分出来的重要条件。接近组合和相似组合的对象都有利于知觉的选择。接近组合，包括空间接近和时间接近的对象组合。相似组合主要是指形态、大小、颜色和强度等物理性质相似的对象的组合。

3. 对象的运动

在相对静止的背景上运动的刺激物，或在混乱运动的背景上朝向同一方向运动的刺激物都容易被区分出来而成为知觉的对象。例如，风平浪静的时候，在水中游动的鱼，我们会很容易发现它；又如观看大型舞蹈表演时，我们总是把那些向着同方向表演的演员看作一组，把他们从混乱而迷人的背景中区分出来。

区分出知觉对象的因素除上述客观条件外，还有知觉者的主观因素，如态度、兴趣、爱好、情绪以及有无确定的任务等，这些因素都会影响着对象与背景的区分。

（二）知觉的整体性

在过去经验的基础上，人具有把多种属性构成的事物知觉为一个统一整体的能力，这种特性叫做知觉的整体性。

知觉具有整体性的特点，尽管知觉的对象是复合刺激物，各部分具有不同的特征，人们依然将其作为一个统一的整体来知觉，决不分割为孤立的部分，有时甚至比它们的实际结构更加完整。如图3-5所示，人们倾向于将缺损的轮廓加以补充，使知觉成为一个完整的封闭图形。

知觉的整体性还表现在对于知觉过的对象，以后只要有对象的个别属性作用于我们的感官，我们就会对该事物产生完整的映像。例如，对曾经知觉过的一块大理石，只要看一眼，就能感到它是光亮的、坚硬的、冰冷的。尽管我们此时并没有触摸它，温度和硬度的刺激也没有作用于我们的皮肤，但是坚硬、冰冷的属性却已被包含在整体映像中了，因为对大理石的知觉是由多种分析器官实现的，多种分析器的兴奋

图 3-5 主观轮廓

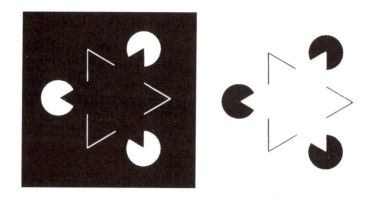

之间早已建立起了暂时神经联系,以后尽管只有视觉刺激发生作用,同样能引起整个暂时神经联系的再现。

知觉整体性依赖着两个基本条件:一是知觉对象本身的特点。例如,当知觉对象在空间、时间上接近时,容易知觉为一个整体;当对象的颜色、大小和形状等物理属性相似时,有组合成一个整体的倾向;当对象具有连续、对称、闭合等特点时,有较大组合的趋势,容易知觉为一个整体。这也称为知觉的组织原则。除此之外,知觉对象的强度也影响着整体的知觉,特别是知觉对象中那些主要的、关键的强成分常常掩蔽着不重要的弱成分,因此知觉某对象时,只要事物属性中关键或强的部分突出,就可形成整体知觉。

图 3-6 部分对整体的依赖

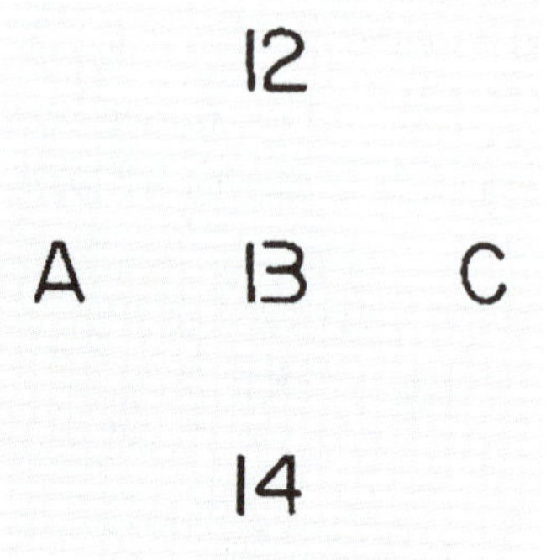

二是知觉的整体性还依赖于知觉者本身的主观状态。其中最主要的是知识与经验。当知觉的对象提供的信息不充足时,知觉者是以过去的知识经验来补充当前的知觉活动,使其形成具有一定结构的整体形象。因此,知识经验越丰富,越容易形成完整的知觉映像,使知觉更准确,更有效。(如图3-6所示)。

(三) 知觉的理解性

在知觉当前事物的时候,人总是在以往知识经验的参与下,以词为工具,对当前知觉的对象进行加工,并以概念的形式标志出来,知觉的这种特性称为知觉的理解性。

知觉的理解性是以知识经验为基础的,是人把对当前事物的直接感知纳入到已有的知识经验系统中去,从而把该事物看成某种熟悉的类别或确定的对象的过程。例如,当我们知觉某一事物时,我们总在想"这是什么""它叫什么",而说出它的名称也就意味着把它归到我们熟悉的一类事物中去了。因此知觉是一种主动寻求解释的过程,它与记忆和思维密切联系着。同样的一棵树,在画家和木匠的眼里,其价值是不一样的,就是两者知识经验的不同造成的。

知觉理解性的基本特征是用语词把事物标志出来。语词对人的知觉具有指导作用。特别是对于一些较复杂的难以辨认的事物，它可以帮助加快理解，减少知觉对象的不确定性。

（四）知觉的恒常性

在知觉过程中，当知觉的条件在一定的范围发生变化时，对知觉对象的映像仍然保持相对稳定不变，这叫知觉的恒常性。

知觉的恒常性普遍存在于各种知觉中，尤以视知觉的恒常性最为突出。例如，我们和所熟悉的人距离较远时，虽然他在我们的视网膜上的成像小了些，但我们绝不会把他知觉为另一个人；又如，无论是在强光照耀下，还是在暗光阴影处，我们总是把煤看成是黑色的，把雪看成是白色的。实际上，在强光下，煤所反射的光量要远大于暗光下雪所反射的光量，但人们绝不会黑白颠倒。这说明人的知觉不完全随客体的物理光学原理规律的变化而变化，而保持其相对的恒常性。

当然，并非在任何条件下知觉都能保持恒常性，影响知觉恒常性的主客观条件有下列几点：首先，知觉的对象通常是熟悉的，或是在熟悉的环境中被知觉的，有周围熟悉的事物作参照物。其次，被知觉的对象变化范围应适当，如果被知觉的对象距离太远，则大小及形状恒常性就会被破坏，如果色光太强，颜色恒常性也会消失。最后，知识经验也是保持恒常性的基本条件。比如，幼儿由于经验不足，知觉往往随环境变化而变化，一般把近物看得大些，把远物看得小些，不能达到守恒。

知觉的恒常性在认识活动和现实生活中有重要意义。它有利于人们精确地适应环境，在变化多端的条件下，形成事物稳定的知觉映像，正确地认识和了解事物的本来面貌。

三、知觉的信息加工过程

人的知觉过程是在过去已有经验的基础上对新信息进行辨认的过程，即信息加工的过程。知觉对信息的这种加工过程既可以是自下而上的，也可以是自上而下的。

1. 自下而上的加工

从外界环境所获得的感觉信息，经过大脑中已有经验的加工产生辨认和识别的过程，这就是自下而上的加工（bottom up processing）。经过自下而上的加工，外界刺激的物理特征被转化为比较抽象的心理表象。由于它是开始于外界刺激的数据而产生的加工，故也叫数据驱动加工（data driven processing）。如一个小孩见到一个黑皮肤的人，然后经过已有经验的加工，知觉到这是一个非洲人。

2. 自上而下的加工

有时个体可以运用已有的有关经验帮助知觉识别，这个已有经验包括知识文化背景、愿望和动机等。这种加工称为自上而下的加工（top down processing）。如对类似的新事物的辨认（包括再认），由于记忆中已有概念的影响，而对新信息进行了理解，这种自上而下的加工也叫概念驱动加工（concept driven processing）。如一个人想买一本新画册，走进一家书店，里面布满了书架，在出售各种新书，经过知觉辨认，这个人找到了这本新画册。

我们在知觉过程中既运用自下而上的加工,也运用自上而下的加工。

四、知觉的种类

根据不同的标准,可以对知觉进行不同的分类。根据知觉活动中占主导地位的感受器的不同,可将知觉分为视知觉、听知觉、嗅知觉、味知觉等。根据知觉对象的不同,可将知觉分为物体知觉(对物知觉)和社会知觉(对人知觉)。知觉还有一种特殊的形式就是错觉。

(一)物体知觉

物体知觉就是对物的知觉,对自然界中机械、物理、化学、生物等种种现象的知觉。任何事物都具有空间、时间和运动的特性,因而物体知觉又分为空间知觉、时间知觉和运动知觉。

1. 空间知觉

空间知觉(space perception)是人脑对客观事物空间特性的反映。包括形状知觉、大小知觉、深度与距离知觉、方位知觉等。空间知觉是一种较复杂的知觉,需要人的视觉、听觉、运动觉等各种分析器的联合活动来实现。空间知觉在人们的生活、学习中具有重要的作用。

2. 时间知觉

时间知觉(time perception)是人脑对客观现象的延续性、顺序性和周期性的反映。时间知觉既与活动内容、情绪、动机、态度有关,也与刺激的物理性质和情境有关。如同样一段时间,活动内容丰富的时候会觉得时间过得快,活动内容贫乏的时候会觉得时间过得慢。此外,由于年龄、生活经验和职业训练的不同,人与人之间在时间知觉方面存在着明显的差异。

3. 运动知觉

运动知觉(motion perception)是指物体在空间的位移特性在人脑中的反映。世界上万事万物都处在运动当中,因而,运动和静止是相对而言的。物体运动速度太慢或太快都不能使人产生运动知觉,人没有专门感知物体运动的器官,对物体运动的知觉是通过多种感官的协同活动实现的。当人观察运动的物体的时候,如果眼睛和头部不动,物体在视网膜的映像的连续移动,就可以使人们产生运动知觉。如果用眼睛和头部追随运动的物体,这时视像虽然保持基本不动,眼睛和头部的动觉信息也足以使人产生运动知觉。如果人们观察的是固定不动的物体,即使转动眼睛和头部,也不会产生运动知觉,因为眼睛和颈部的动觉抵消了视网膜上视像的位移。

(二)社会知觉

社会知觉就是对人的知觉,对由人的社会实践所构成的社会现象的知觉,具体包括对他人的知觉、自我知觉和人际知觉等。

1. 对他人的知觉

对他人的知觉指对他人的需要、动机、情感、观点、信念、性格等内部心理状态的知觉。

这种知觉主要是通过一个人外在的风度仪表、言谈举止、表情姿态等特征,来认识这个人内在的心理特点与品质,即"听其言,观其行,而知其人"。要对一个人形成正确、全面的认识,往往需要花费较长的一段时间。

2. 自我知觉

自我知觉即个体通过对自己的行为的观察而形成的对自己的思想、情感、能力、性格、道德水平等的认知。自我知觉的主体既是观察者,又是被观察者,自己观察自己,比较方便,但也容易当局者迷,"不识庐山真面目,只缘身在此山中。""人贵有自知之明",正确的认识和评价自己绝非易事。

3. 人际知觉

人际知觉是指对人与人之间的相互关系、彼此作用的知觉。这种知觉主要是在人际交往中发生的,以各种交际行为为知觉对象。人际知觉主要包括两个方面:一是对自己和别人相互关系和作用的知觉,二是对他人相互关系和作用的知觉。在人际知觉中,容易受到人的情感因素的制约,表现为亲则近之,疏则远之。

专栏 3-4

社会知觉的偏差

在对他人知觉时,常常会产生一些心理偏差,这些心理偏差就被称为社会知觉中的偏差,或者叫社会知觉的效应。常见的社会知觉偏差主要有以下几种。

(1)第一印象

第一印象是指与陌生人初次相见对对方产生的印象。第一印象鲜明、深刻且牢固,会形成一种固定的看法,影响甚至决定着今后的交往关系,在社会知觉中起重要作用。如对某人的第一印象良好,人们就愿意接近他,容易信任他,对他的言行能给予较多的理解,反之,第一印象恶劣,人们就不愿接近他,对他的言行不予理解,在社会知觉中造成"先入为主"的偏差。影响第一印象形成的主要因素,一方面是对方的外部特征的直接影响,另一方面是有关对方的间接信息的间接影响。第一印象只能作为对人的知觉的起点,而不能作为终点。这是因为第一印象不可能全面反映一个人的根本面貌,难免有主观性。只有历史地、全面地、发展地看待一个人,才能形成正确的对人的知觉。

(2)晕轮效应

晕轮效应是指对人的某些品质、特征形成的清晰鲜明的印象掩盖了其余品质、特征的知觉。这是以偏概全,"一俊遮百丑""一坏百坏"的主观倾向,即当一个人对另一个人的主要品质、特征形成良好或不好印象后,就会影响他对这个人其他方面的看法。好像一个人的头一旦被照亮了,就觉得全身都光亮了一样。

(3)刻板印象

刻板印象是指对社会上的各类人群所持有的固定的看法,或是对人概括、泛化的看法。刻板印象能潜藏于人的意识之中。比如,人们普遍认为山东人身材魁梧、正直豪爽、能吃苦耐劳；江浙人聪明伶俐、能随机应变。这是一种刻板印象，一旦形成了刻板印象，个体在对人认知时就会不自觉地、简单地把某个人归入某一群体中去，带来认知上的偏差。所以我们要善于从每个人的具体行为表现中去认识人，不能光凭刻板印象去认识、评价具体的个人。

（4）近因效应

近因效应是指在时间上最近获得的有关熟人的信息给人留下的深刻印象和强烈影响。在与熟人多次交往中，近因效应起很大的作用。熟人行为上表现出来的某种新异性会影响或改变第一印象的影响。我们认识一个人，既要看他过去的行为，更要看他现在的表现。近因效应与第一印象产生的条件是不同的。如果两个相互矛盾的信息先后进入人们的意识之中，如果人们认为前一个信息是真实的，后一个信息是虚假的，这是第一印象；如果人们对较近的或最近的信息印象较深，这就是近因效应。

造成社会知觉发生偏差的这些主观倾向，其发生都有一定的客观原因。只要认真对待，是可以加以克服和利用的。在人际交往中，人们可以合理利用它们发生的原理进行相互间的了解，改善人际关系。如可以有意识地整饰自己，给人留下良好的第一印象。

——韩永昌.心理学[M].上海：华东师范大学出版社，2009：55—56.

（三）错觉

错觉（illusion）是对事物的一种不正确的知觉。错觉不同于幻觉，幻觉是指没有相应的客观刺激时所出现的知觉体验。而错觉是在特定条件下对客观事物必然产生的失真的、歪曲的知觉。只要产生错觉的条件具备，错觉就难以避免，任何人都可能产生同样的错觉。幻觉与错觉的不同之处在于前者没有客观刺激存在，错觉则是对客观刺激的不正确反映。错觉是可以认识和利用的，生活和学习中可以利用错觉为自身服务，而幻觉没有任何利用价值。

错觉的种类很多，最常见的是视错觉，在视错觉中研究最多的是几何图形错觉。常见的几何图形错觉有线段长短错觉、方向错觉、线条弯曲错觉、大小错觉等。

1. 线段长短错觉

两条长度相等的线段，假如一条线段两端加上向外的箭头，另一条线段两端加上向内的箭头，则前者要显得比后者长得多，这被称为缪勒—莱耶尔错觉（如图3-7a所示）。两条等长的直线，一条垂直于另一条的中点，那么垂直线看上去比水平线要长一些，这被称为垂直—水平错觉，也叫菲克错觉（如图3-7b所示）。

2. 方向错觉

如图3-8（a）所示，由于背后倾斜线的影响，看起来竖线似乎向相反方向转动了，这也被称为策尔纳错觉；如图3-8（b）中画的是同心圆，看起来却是螺旋形了，这也被称为弗雷泽错觉。

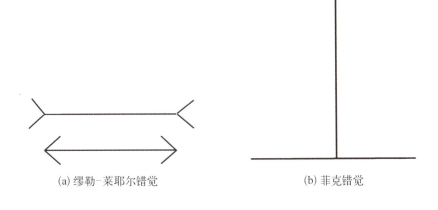

(a) 缪勒-莱耶尔错觉　　　　　　(b) 菲克错觉

图 3-7

(a) 策尔纳错觉　　　　　　(b) 弗雷泽错觉

图 3-8

3. 线条弯曲错觉

如图 3-9（a）所示，两条平行线看起来中间部分凸了起来，这也称为黑林错觉；图 3-9（b）中两条平行线看起来中间部分凹了下去，这被称为冯特错觉。

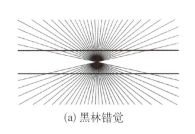 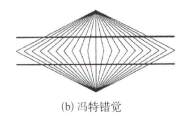

(a) 黑林错觉　　　　　　(b) 冯特错觉

图 3-9

4. 大小错觉

如图 3-10 所示，被大圆和小圆围在中间的两个圆面积大小相等，但看起来，左边被小圆围在中间的圆要大于右边被大圆围在中间的圆，这就是大小错觉，也叫艾宾浩斯错觉。

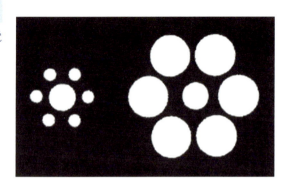

图 3-10
艾宾浩斯错觉

除了几何图形错觉外,还有形重错觉、方位错觉、时间错觉、运动错觉等。如一斤棉花与一斤铁,两者的物理重量是相等的,但是人们却觉得铁比棉花要重得多,这是形重错觉;飞行经验不足的驾驶员在海上飞行时,由于远处水天一色,找不到地标,失去了环境中的视觉线索,容易产生"倒飞错觉",可能引起严重的飞行事故,这是一种方位错觉。

研究错觉有重要的意义,揭示错觉产生的原因和规律,一方面有助于消除错觉对人类实践活动的不利影响,如在飞行员训练中增加有关情境的训练,从而消除错觉,避免飞行事故的发生;另一方面也可以更好地利用错觉为人类服务,如在生活中利用错觉原理,根据自身情况,恰如其分地打扮自己等。

第三节
感知觉规律在教育教学中的应用

一、了解直观教学的手段

"从生动的直观到抽象的思维"是人类认识发展的基本规律,学生的认识虽有其特殊性,但也不能离开这条基本的规律。俄国教育学家乌申斯基认为:"儿童一般是依靠形状、色彩、声音和触角来思考的,因此,直观教学对儿童是必须的,教学不应建筑在抽象的概念和词汇上,而应建筑在儿童能直观感受到的形象之上。"

小学、初中学生的抽象逻辑思维虽日益占据主导地位,但基本上还属于经验型,加之他们年龄尚小,积累的感性经验相对不足,因此,宜采取直观教学手段为学生提供丰富的感性材料,帮助他们顺利地理解和领会抽象的知识,为他们理论型逻辑思维的发展打下良好的基础。

教学中的直观形式主要有实物直观、模像直观和言语直观三种。实物直观是指通过观察实物标本、演示性实验、教学参观等方式,使学生对所学知识有一个真实、生动的印象,能帮助学生确切地理解教材,记忆深刻,但它的缺点是,事物的本质属性易被表面的非本质属性所掩盖,事物的内部情况不易观察,运动状态难以控制。模像直观是指通过图片、图表、模型、仪器、幻灯等方式模拟实物的形象而提供感性经验,模像直观可以摆脱实物直观的局限,根据教学目的的需要,可以把事物由近变远,由远而近,也可对事物进行扩大或缩小,突出重点,有助于学生理解抽象的内容。而且操作演示方便灵活,不易受时间与空间的限制,在教学中的作用是十分重要的。言语直观是指通过语言(书面和口头)的生动具体的描述、鲜明形象的比喻、合乎情理的夸张等形式,提供感性认识,加深学生对知识的理解。言语直观虽不如前两种生动、形象、逼真,但它可摆脱时空、设备与条件的限制,具有灵活、经济、方便的特点,是教师常用的一种教学方式,即使在实物、模象直观教学中,同样需要言语直观的配合。

教师在教学中可结合使用三种直观教学手段,提高教学效果。但在使用直观教学手段时,要注意适度,符合科学性,并根据教学的要求慎重选用。作为教师应确切地知道,教学中的直观只是一种手段而不是目的。在有限的教学时间内,教学形式变化频繁,过多使用直观材料,看上去热热闹闹,效果不一定好,反而会分散学生的注意力,降低他们的智力活动水平,使学生只是停留在肤浅地感知教材的水平上。在学生充分感知直观材料的基础上,教师应引导学生进行积极的思维活动,及时地将认识的材料进行总结归类,上升到一般的理论,这是感知过程的最后目标。只有这样,学生掌握的知识才是系统的、牢固的。

二、根据感知规律组织教学,提高教学质量

感知觉有一定的规律,作为教师来说,了解感知的规律,明确学生在什么条件下听得更清楚,看得更真切,反映得更明晰,并将此运用于教学,将会使学生不仅乐于学,而且善于学。

(一)适当的刺激强度,有利于引起清晰的感知

心理学实验证明,感觉器官对一定强度范围内的适宜刺激会表现出良好的感受能力。刺激过强或过弱都属于不适宜刺激,不能使学生获得清晰的感知。因此,教师在教学中应注意言语的运用,语调柔和亲切、声音适中,辅以一定的手势语言和表情,将更有利于学生的感知;板书时字迹要清晰,字不要过大或过小,画图时线条粗细要适中,以保证全体学生都能看明白。应该指出的一点是,这里的刺激强度是指相对刺激强度,教师在一个喧闹的教室里,即使声嘶力竭也不会比在一个安静的环境中娓娓细语有效果,因此,教学环境要力求安静。

(二)利用感觉器官的适应性,提高感知效果

刺激物持续作用于某一感受器将使其感受性提高或降低。根据这条规律,教师在讲课时语音语调应富于变化,以防单调的声音刺激导致学生听觉感受性的降低;授课方式要灵活多样,这样不仅能提高学生的学习兴趣,也能提高其感受性;体育教师上游泳课时,要让学生在下水前先用水浇湿全身,这样下水时皮肤才能适应水的温度;校舍的设计要注意采光面积不能过小,否则会导致学生在进入教室后要用较长时间适应暗光,造成视力的下降。此外,一门课程不宜频繁更换任课老师,因为学生对每一位新教师都会有一个适应过程。

(三)利用不同感觉的相互作用,提高感知效果

人的各种感觉之间不是孤立存在的,而是相互作用、相互影响。在教学中教师要适当运用这条规律。如教室的设计既要保证充分的采光面积,又要注意不要让阳光直射教室,以防强烈的光刺激降低视觉的敏锐度;上课或自习时,教室内要绝对的安静,以提高视觉的感受性;学生在独自阅读时可适度播放一些舒缓轻柔的乐曲(音量要小),以提高视觉感受性,增强阅读的效果;在上音乐欣赏课时,应避免强烈闪动的灯光等。

(四)利用对象和背景的对比与差别,突出感知对象

在性质或强度上对比的刺激物同时或相继地作用于感觉器官时,往往能使人们对它们的差异感知变得特别清晰。对象与背景的差别越大,对象越容易被选择出来进行感知。因此,教师在讲课时要注意语言的轻重缓急,对重点、难点部分,声音要宏亮,速度要放慢,或者采用突然停止讲话的方式以引起学生的注意;板书时要注意格式规范、字迹端正、排列整齐,必要时可用不同色彩的粉笔书写,以突出重点;对于容易混淆的知识内容,如字、词、公式、原理,要一一对比,讲清两者的异同,提高学生的分辨能力,获得鲜明的印象;在制作挂图、模型时,教具的不同部分,可用对比颜色(红绿、黑白、黄蓝等),特别是重要而不显眼的部分,通过颜色对比来提高感知效果;演示直观教具时应注意背景的选择,深色教具应选浅色为背景,浅色对象应选深色为背景。一位教师在做水的热胀冷缩实验时,把烧瓶中的水染成红色,背景衬上一张白纸,实验效果更好。

(五)采用化静为动的方式,提高感知效果

在相对静止的背景上,活动的事物易被感知。根据这条规律,教师在教学中应尽量多采用活动教具、活动卡片、活动画面、活动模型及电影、电视、录像、幻灯片、录音、广播等现代化的视听工具。如一位生物教师在讲"茎的输导作用"时,通过幻灯片教学让学生清晰地观察到茎韧皮部中的筛管自上而下输导叶光合作用制造的有机物,茎木质部中的筛管自下而上输导根吸收作用吸收的水和溶于水的无机盐的现象,比看挂图的效果更为生动形象。对于一些简图,教师可边讲边画,在这个过程中,学生不仅看到已经完成的图形,而且看到这个图形是如何组成的,起到帮助学生组织知觉信息的作用。把静止的信息转变为动态的信息,这十分有利于学习者的感知。正如教一个人如何做馅饼,最有效的方法是一步一步地做给他看,而不是给他看一个现成的馅饼或仅仅是口头描述。

(六)利用组合原理,增强感知效果

一般说来,距离上接近、形态上相似、具有连续、闭合等特征的事物,易于组成一个整体而被选择出来,成为知觉的对象。根据这条规律,教师应力求把教学过程中视听等方面的刺激物在时间、空间上组成系统,使学生易于形成整体的知觉,提高感知的效果。这样,教师在讲课时语言顿挫要适当,便于学生一句句地去感知;在讲课内容上要做到条理清晰,层次分明,加上必要的归纳,使所讲内容因"接近"而便于学生理解;板书设计条块合理,行距稍大于字距,书写优美流畅,使学生感到自然连续而提高视觉效果;讲课中范围明确,重点突出,就会产生"闭合"效果而便于学生系统地掌握知识;制作挂图或幻灯片

时，应注意事物之间的距离要恰当，在对象的背景上不要附加类似的颜色、线条或图形，以免产生不恰当的组合而形成错觉。

（七）使多种感官参与感知活动，提高感知效果

多种感官参与感知过程，可以从不同方面对事物的属性特点进行把握，能使感知更完整，更精确。因此，教师在教学过程中应尽可能让学生有更多的机会使用自己的多种感官。不仅让学生留心听，还要用心看，用手触摸，用鼻子闻，用头脑思考。在使用直观教具时，能让学生摆弄的，尽量让他们摆弄，能让他们制作的，尽量让他们自己制作。这样，在多种感官的参与下，使学生获得对事物的精确和全面的认识。

（八）运用语言提示，增强感知效果

语言提示能组织感知，有助于学生对感知对象的选择和理解，提高知觉效率。特别是当对象外部标志不明显而难于知觉时，语言提示更可以突出感知对象，帮助学生加以区分。语言提示还可以通过言语来唤起学生头脑中已有的经验，补充当前感知对象的欠缺，获得完整的知觉。根据这条规律，要求教师注意运用恰当的语言提示，引导学生感知教材。实践证明，教师一句关键性的提示，往往会使学生对整篇文章的立意、谋篇布局产生深刻的理解。教师应善于运用问题设计来引导学生的感知方向，提高学生的理解力。在使用直观材料时，由于直观教具制作上的限制，教师必须配合正确、生动的讲解和说明，使直观教具真正发挥其作用。对于不易觉察或难以辨别的感知对象，教师更应及时通过语言唤起学生头脑中已有的经验，去精确地感知该对象。

（九）充分了解学生原有的知识水平

在教学中，应当从学生已有的知识基础出发，在复习前面相关内容的基础上引进新的内容。只有充分了解学生原有的知识水平，才能科学地确定教学的起点，也只有适合学生实际水平的教学内容，才能真正引起学生的兴趣，促使他们集中注意，快速正确地理解内容。这是由知觉的理解性所决定的。从知觉的理解性出发，还应当考虑学生的生活经验，从学生的生活经验中选择适合教学需要的实例。如果发现学生缺乏必要的知识经验，教师应创造条件利用直观教学手段来补充学生的知识经验，帮助学生理解有关的理论知识。平时应要求学生多看、多听、多接触外界事物，通过参观、访问、参加社会实践活动等途径丰富学生的生活经验，以提高感知事物的能力。

三、学生观察力的培养

观察（observation）是一种有目的、有计划、贯穿着积极活动的知觉。它有三个基本特点：一是主动性。我们要观察什么，不是由于某个事物吸引人，也不是仅仅由于对它感兴趣，而是由目的任务决定的。因此，观察是一种主动的知觉，它与注意是紧紧联系在一起的。二是理解性。观察的目的是认识事物及其发展变化的规律。因而在观察时，我们总在运用已有的知识经验去对事物进行分析与综合、抽象与概括。观察的过程实际上就是一边知觉一边思考的过程。所以，观察也称为"思维的知觉"。三是持久性。观察不是

一次性的瞬时知觉,而是系统长久的知觉,必须长时间认真、仔细、全面系统地去进行。因此,在观察过程中,必须有非常稳定的注意来组织知觉。观察对学生的智力发展有重要意义。观察力是智力的重要组成部分。观察不仅能使学生从客观世界中汲取知识,而且在观察过程中,通过运用知识,还能使学生的知识经验活跃起来,启迪其思维。

观察力是观察的能力。它是经过后天系统训练,逐渐形成起来的一种带有个性特点的能力。求知欲、认知兴趣和动机是观察力形成的主要基础,知识与经验是观察力发展的重要条件。具有敏锐、深刻观察力的人,对事物看得全面,"见微知著",能迅速抓住事物的重要特征和本质。培养学生观察力应掌握以下几点:

(一)明确观察的目的、任务,培养观察的兴趣

观察的效果取决于观察的目的、任务的明确程度。20世纪中叶,40名心理学家聚集在西德某城市召开会议,会议主席曾设计了一个有趣的实验:在会议进行到一半时,突然冲进来两个人,在会场上搏斗了2秒钟。当这两人离去后,主席向与会者提议写下目睹记录,包括打斗场面,两人的外貌特征、穿着打扮等。结果错误率惊人,只有一个报告的错误率低于20%[①]。可见,没有明确的观察目的、任务,观察结果就会不精确。观察的目的性是观察力最重要的品质。观察没有明确的目的,不仅观察不会有成效,观察力得不到锻炼,还会养成东张西望、心不在焉、熟视无睹、懒散马虎的不良习惯。因此,不管进行何种观察,采用何种形式,都要有明确的观察目的。具体来说,观察什么,达到什么要求,具体的观察步骤、程序,采用何种方式以及具体方法等都要考虑周密,而且越具体越好,制定出观察计划。凡是长期、系统的观察,观察计划要用书面的形式详细规定下来;即使是短期、零星的观察,也要在头脑中有全盘的考虑。观察的目的性还意味着,观察时要勤于记录,记录应力求系统全面、详尽具体,正确清楚。它不仅是掌握第一手资料的可靠手段,也是确保观察精确性的宝贵方法。如果是长期观察,记录应持之以恒,坚持到底。否则,观察将功亏一篑。

除了明确观察的具体目的、任务外,还必须激发观察的兴趣。观察的兴趣是培养观察力的内部动力。有了观察的兴趣,人们就会孜孜不倦地勤于观察,使自己的观察力不断得以提高。培养观察的兴趣,关键要经常参与观察的实践活动,如观察周围熟悉的人、事、物,开展参观、访问、郊游等活动。观察实践活动不仅使一个人的观察力得到锻炼、提高,也可以从中获得丰富的知识,发现别人难以发现的问题,产生一种求知的满足感和欢快的情感体验,观察就会由被动转为主动,从而进一步激发起对观察的浓厚兴趣。

(二)掌握观察的方法

掌握观察的方法,学会观察很重要。在这方面应注意做好以下各项工作:

1. 在观察之前做好必要的知识准备

良好的观察是知识获得的前提,知识又是提高观察力的重要因素。一个知识渊博、经验丰富的人,在错综复杂的大千世界中,自然会容易观察到许多有意义的东西。比如古代的一块陶瓷片,考古学家们会从上面看出许多有价值的东西,而外行人则什么也看不出

---

① 杨善堂等.心理学[M].北京:人民教育出版社,2005:70.

来。因此,在观察前,教师要引导学生复习或预习有关的知识,让学生阅读和观察与对象有关的教科书、理论性文章、研究报告、经验介绍或图片、资料等,做到有备而来。

2. 观察要有计划、有步骤地进行

观察应具有一定的系统性,因此,在观察之前要制定好观察的步骤、顺序,先看什么,后看什么,是从整体到部分,还是从部分到整体,是从远到近,还是从近到远,都要预先设计好,保证观察的顺利进行,防止在观察过程中遇到意外情况而偏离了预定的目的、任务。

3. 观察时要善辨多思

良好的观察品质之一是善于发现细小的但却很有价值的事实,从司空见惯的现象中发现其内在的规律性联系。因此,观察必须伴随着积极的思维活动。如通过比较和分类,找出事物的异同,以便把握事物的最本质的特征;通过分析和综合,把握事物的整体和部分,以便区分出最本质的特点。善于思考,这是观察活动有所成效的关键所在。巴甫洛夫就是从狗吃食物而分泌唾液这一熟悉的现象中发现了大脑活动的秘密。在进行观察时,要善于提出问题,积极开动脑筋,并注意搜寻细节,不轻易放过任何例外的情况。

4. 要做好观察总结

观察告一段落后,要进行总结。这也是一个很重要的方面。往往有这种情况,一个人虽然观察得精细、条理,但不能将观察的结果完整而有层次地整理和表达出来,这也会削弱观察的效果。通过总结,可以检查观察的目的、任务是否完成,借此调整自己的行动计划,指导下一阶段的工作。总结可以是书面的,也可以是口头的。书面的除文字外,还可附上照片、图样。

(三)在实际训练中有针对性地培养自己良好的观察品质

在实际观察活动中,每个人的观察品质的差异会显露出来。如有的人在观察时只凭自己的兴趣,抓不住事物的要点;有的走马观花,观察肤浅;有的草率急躁,观察欠持久等,这些都不利于发展自己的观察力。我们在进行实际观察活动时,应及时纠正自己不良的观察习惯,逐步培养起良好的观察品质。

(四)在进行实际观察时还应注意的问题

1. 消除错觉干扰,纠正视觉错误

错觉现象的存在说明眼见不一定都为实,在观察时应警惕错觉的存在,注意排除错觉对事物真实性的干扰。在观察中要善于开动脑筋进行思考、辨析,不要看见什么就是什么。只要保持警觉,时时注意,总能够把错觉同客观事实区别开来。

2. 排除背景干扰,突出观察对象

观察对象总要在一定的背景中存在。对象和背景的差别大时,对象容易被区分,差别小时,则不易区分。例如,士兵在作战时常穿一身迷彩服,这是因为迷彩服与士兵作战时所处的自然界环境的颜色相似,从而缩小了背景与对象的差别,达到混淆敌人视线的目的。自然界的某些动物,有时也通过改变自身颜色来进行防卫。因此,要观察某个事物,必须首先把这个事物从众多背景事物中寻找出来,就是说,要训练自己善于排除背景干扰的能力,使研究对象突出出来。这就要做到:首先,从不同的角度进行观察,寻找突破口。

正面观察不出,就从反面观察;左边观察不出,就从右边观察。其次,抓住事物的显著特征。蛇皮尽管和树皮相仿,但活动的蛇却容易辨认出来。最后,设法扩大对象与背景在色彩、声调、形状等方面的差距。

3. 注意事物的发展变化,从不同的角度观察问题

苏东坡在《题西林壁》中吟道:"横看成岭侧成峰,远近高低各不同。"说明由于人和事物的相对位置的变化,被观察事物的某些属性也发生了变化。横看、侧看、远看、近看,庐山分别呈现出了不同的面貌。因此,要获得事物的全貌,就要变换看问题的角度,对事物进行全方位的观察。一方面,只从一个角度去观察,一点论看问题,无异于盲人摸象。以部分代替整体,就得不到正确的结论。另一方面,事物本身也在发生变化,斗转星移,变化万千。"不识庐山真面目,只缘身在此山中。"在观察客观事物时,要处理好观察计划和客观事物变化的关系。既要有明确具体的观察计划,又要有事物发展变化的心理准备。在执行计划时,不要太刻板,一成不变,而要时刻注意现场情况的千变万化,让计划适应已经变化了的客观事物。

4. 留心日常事物,积极开动脑筋

1962年的一天,美国麻省理工学院的谢皮罗教授在放浴缸水的时候,发现水旋涡是左旋的,这引起了他的注意和思考。后来他用实验的手段来研究这个问题,很快得出了水旋涡左旋与地球自转有关的结论。从洗澡水里发现的自然规律,还有阿基米德发现的浮力定律。像洗澡水这类日常生活事物,人们已司空见惯,熟视无睹,但有的人注意观察了,便会有所发现。这些伟大的科学家之所以能从容易被人忽视的小事中看到蕴藏着的普遍原理,是他们事事留心、思考的缘故。留心身边的事物,一方面要观察,一方面要思考,而后一点更为重要。观察事物时要多提几个为什么,提问、设疑是打开一切科学大门的钥匙。

本章小结

感觉是人脑对当前直接作用于感官的客观事物的个别属性的反映。知觉是人脑对当前直接作用于感官的客观事物的整体反映。知觉是在感觉的基础上产生的,但又不是个别感觉成分的简单相加。感觉与知觉既有联系也有区别。人的感觉器官对适宜刺激的感觉能力叫感受性。感受性用感觉阈限值来度量。感觉阈限分绝对阈限和差别阈限两种。感受性与感觉阈限成反比关系。各种感觉的发展、变化规律主要有:感觉的相互作用规律和感觉在实践中的发展规律。知觉的基本特性有整体性、选择性、理解性和恒常性四种。观察是一种有目的、有计划、贯穿着积极思维活动的知觉。观察力是智力的重要组成部分。在实践中要采取措施有针对性地培养和完善自己的观察力。运用感知觉的规律可以有效地提高教学的效果。

关键术语

感觉 感受性 感觉阈限 知觉 观察

讨论与应用

1. 阅读下面的材料，请结合本章所学知识，探讨关于盲人是依靠什么线索来避开障碍物的？

人们都知道盲人能觉察出障碍物的存在而无需碰到它。一个盲人走近墙壁时，在撞到墙壁之前就停下来了，这时人们常听到盲人报告说，他感觉到面前有一堵墙，他还可能告诉人们，这种感觉是建立在一种触觉的基础上的，即他的脸受到了某种震动的作用。为此，人们把盲人的这种对障碍物的感觉称为"面部视觉"。问题是，盲人真的是靠"面部"来避开障碍物的吗？

1944年，美国康奈尔大学的达伦巴史（K. M. Dallenbach）及其同事对盲人的"面部视觉"开展了一系列的实验验证工作。实验人员用毛呢面罩和帽子盖住盲人被试的头部，露出盲人被试的耳朵，往前走的盲人被试仍能在碰到墙壁前停住。然后，研究人员除去盲人的面罩和帽子，只把盲人的耳朵用毛呢包起来，在这种实验条件下，盲人被试一个一个地撞上了墙壁。

2. 阅读下面的材料，请结合本章所学知识进行分析：杭平为什么会出现这样的情况呢？

1998年5月20日晚，内蒙古乌海市巴彦乌素煤矿发生洪水冲灌的矿难，本来安全撤离的矿工杭平因主动下井通知同伴而遭洪水围困。他靠吃一头骡子的肉和喝井下的污水，在黑暗、饥饿、寒冷、恐惧中顽强支撑了34天，奇迹般地被救援并成为唯一的幸存者。上海吉尼斯总部授予他1998年度"中国被困矿井下生存世界最长者"称呼。获救后的杭平在很长一段时间内变得感觉迟钝，时常出现幻觉，难以和人正常交往。而且，杭平在家休养的一年中，常感到"头晕""记忆力下降""身体发软"。

3. 请分析教师这一行为的目的是什么？符合什么规律？

教师在板书生字时，常把形近字的相同部分与相异部分分别用白色和红色的粉笔写出来。

4. 请分析以下现象的原因。

A. 闭着眼睛倾听更清晰；B. 尖锐的声音会使人起鸡皮疙瘩并产生冷觉；C. 黄色调产生温暖的感觉，绿色产生清凉的感觉。

5. 请用本章学过的知识进行分析，为什么会出现这种现象呢？

苏联社会心理学家包达列夫做了以下实验：他向两组大学生出示了同一个人的照片，照片上的人的突出特点是下颌外翘，两眼内凹。在出示照片前对第一组被试说此人是罪犯，而对第二组被试说此人是一位科学家，然后让两组被试用文字描绘照片的相貌，并进行评价。第一组的评价是：深陷的双眼表明他内心的仇恨，突出的下巴表明其死不悔改。第二组的评价是：深陷的双眼表明其思想的深刻性，突出的下巴表明其克服困难的坚强意志等。

6. 试着思考，这是为什么呢？

当我们欣赏中国水墨画时，依然会把水墨画的荷花和荷叶知觉为水红色和墨绿色，黑白电视和黑白电影依然可以让我们感受到五彩缤纷的世界。

本章讨论与应用答题思路与要点
（扫描二维码）

本章复习思考题
（扫描二维码）

本章进一步阅读书目
（扫描二维码）

04 第四章 记忆

JIYI

　　亲爱的同学,记忆是与我们生活、学习密切相关的心理现象。很难想象,如果我们都失去了对过去经验的记忆,这个世界会变成什么样子。在生活中,为什么同样的知识,有的人过目不忘,有些人却复习很多遍都记不住呢?为什么我们在偶遇多年未见的老同学时,明明他的名字就在嘴边,却经常叫不出来?问问你身边的同学有没有相关经历。带着这些问题开始本章的学习吧!

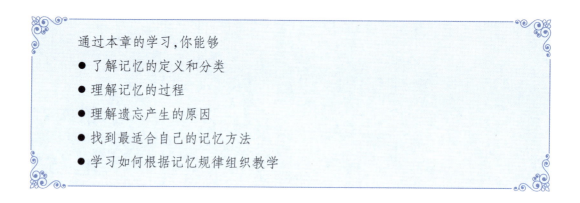

【本章结构】

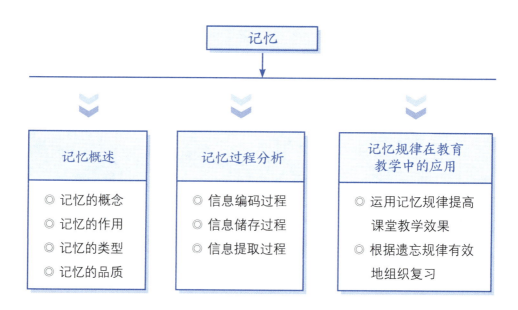

从1885年艾宾浩斯等人对记忆进行正式研究开始,人类对记忆的实验探索已经有一百多年的历史了。这一百多年来,心理学究竟研究了记忆的哪些内容?他们的研究又带给我们哪些启示呢?让我们一起走进记忆研究的世界。本章我们将学习有关记忆的内容,了解记忆的过程,学习如何提高自己的记忆能力。

第一节
记忆概述

一、记忆的概念

记忆（memory）是过去的经验在人脑中反映的心理过程。

所谓过去的经验，包括过去曾感知过的事物、思考过的问题、做过的事情以及体验过的情感。这些事物都会在头脑中留下一定的痕迹，随着时间的推移，这些痕迹有些会被强化，有些会趋于减弱、消退。在一定条件的诱发下，那些仍然保持在人的头脑中的痕迹会重新被激活、再反映。这些经历过的事物的痕迹的形成、保持及激活都属于记忆。例如："小时候你玩过哪些游戏？"，当看到这个问题的时候，你在脑海中浮现的就是过去的游戏场景。时间点非现在也非未来，而是指向过去。游戏的场景是你以前经历的事情，是过去的经验，这种现象反映的就是记忆。

二、记忆的作用

（一）记忆是人的心理活动和行为发挥作用的基础

记忆作为一种基本的心理过程，和其他心理活动密切联系着。它是信息存储的仓库和智力活动的基础，人类的大部分活动都需要记忆的参与。离开记忆，人从简单的行为到复杂的思维学习都无法进行。人要发展语言和思维，就必须保存词和概念；人要形成良好的行为习惯和人格特质，必须以记忆信息为支撑。可见没有记忆，个体就什么也学不会，也就没有心理的发展；没有记忆，就没有人类经验的积累，也就不会有现代文明，它联结着人类的过去和现在。

（二）记忆是学习的重要条件

俄国著名的生理学家谢切诺夫认为，"人的一切智慧的根源都在记忆"，记忆是"整个心理生活的基本条件"。对学生而言，要掌握人类几千年来积累下来的科学文化知识，把个体认识提高到当代水平，必须掌握记忆规律，掌握记忆的策略和方法，才能更好地提高记忆效果。

（三）掌握记忆规律对将来提高教学效率具有重大意义

从未来职业适宜性的角度看，掌握记忆规律有助于师范生从教后有针对性地提高教学效果。如果以后教会学生运用记忆方法和策略进行学习，既可以取得良好的教学效果，又能使学生受益终生。许多优秀教师的成功教学经验已经证明，掌握记忆规律、利用记忆规律进行教学,是取得教学效果的重要保证。

三、记忆的类型

（一）按记忆内容划分的记忆

1. 形象记忆（imaginal memory）

指以感知过的事物形象为内容的记忆。这些具体形象是来自五大外部感觉,既可以来自视觉,也可以来自听觉、嗅觉、触觉或者味觉。如人们对看过的优美山水、听过的乐曲的记忆就是形象记忆。这类记忆的显著特点是保存事物的感性特征,具有典型的直观性。

2. 语词—逻辑记忆（logic memory）

指以思想、概念或命题等形式为内容的记忆。如对数学定理、公式、哲学命题等内容的记忆。这类记忆是以抽象逻辑思维为基础的,具有概括性、理解性和逻辑性等特点。对于学生的学习来说,这类记忆是至关重要的,它既是学生学习新知识的基础,同时又影响着学生的抽象逻辑思维能力的发展。

3. 情绪记忆（emotional memory）

指以过去体验过的情绪或情感为内容的记忆。例如,我们对接到高校录取通知书、获得奖学金时的愉快心情的记忆。我们在认识事物或与人交往的过程中,总会带有一定的情绪色彩或情感内容,这些情绪或情感也作为记忆的内容而被存贮进大脑,成为我们的心理内容的一部分。情绪记忆往往是一次形成而经久不忘的,对人的行为具有较大的影响作用。例如,我们经常说"一朝被蛇咬,十年怕井绳",这就体现了对情绪——"怕"的记忆。情绪记忆的映象有时比其他形式的记忆映象更持久,即使人们对引起某种情绪体验的事实早已忘记,但情绪体验仍然保持着。

4. 运动记忆（motor memory）

指以人们过去的操作性行为为内容的记忆。凡是人们头脑里所保持的做过的动作及动作模式,都属于动作记忆。例如,我们上体育课时打乒乓球、练武术的套路,学习弹钢琴的过程,以及写字等都属于动作记忆。这类记忆对于人们动作的连贯性、精确性等具有重要意义,是动作技能形成的基础。

以上四种记忆形式既有区别,又紧密联系在一起。例如动作记忆中具有鲜明的形象性;逻辑记忆也经常伴随着情绪记忆。

（二）按记忆的保持时间划分的记忆

1. 瞬时记忆（immediate memory）

瞬时记忆又称感觉记忆（sensory memory）或感觉登记（sensory register）,是当客观刺激停止作用后,感觉信息在一个极短的时间内保存下来的记忆,是记忆系统的开始阶段。

瞬时记忆的特点：第一,时间极短。图像记忆的保持时间一般在1秒左右,声像记忆虽超过1秒,但不长于4秒。视觉后像属于瞬时记忆,若不加以注意,这种短暂的信息很快就会消失,若得以加工,就转入短时记忆。第二,容量较大。一般来说,凡是进入感觉通道的信息几乎都能被登记。第三,形象鲜明。感觉记忆储存的信息是未经任何处理,完全依据客观刺激所具有的物理特征进行编码,并按感知的先后顺序被登记,所以具有鲜明的形象性。

瞬时记忆的编码方式主要是图像记忆和声像记忆。图像记忆又称为视觉登记或图像储存,是指当作用于眼睛的图像刺激消失,视觉图像在视觉通道内被登记并保留瞬间的记忆。图像记忆是瞬时记忆的典型代表。声像记忆又称为听觉登记,指听觉系统对刺激信息的瞬间保持。

2. 短时记忆(short-term memory)

短时记忆是指对信息的保持时间大约在1分钟以内的记忆。短时记忆是信息从感觉记忆到长时记忆的过渡阶段。处在工作状态中的短时记忆,或者在完成当前任务时起作用的短时记忆,就是工作记忆。

短时记忆的特点:第一,时间很短。信息的保持在没有复述的情况下一般只有5—20秒,最长不超过1分钟。第二,容量有限。米勒(Miller)发表了《神奇的数字7±2:我们信息加工能力的局限》一文,明确提出了短时记忆的容量为7±2个组块,即5—9个组块,平均值为7。后来很多研究通过数字、单词、字母、无意义音节等各种实验材料得到的结果都和米勒一致。但短时记忆容量的值常常会因实验材料的不同而出现较大波动。为解释这一现象,米勒提出了"组块"的概念。所谓"组块"是指若干个小单位联合成大单位的信息加工过程。也可以说"组块"是指人们熟悉的记忆单位,可以是一个数字、一个字母,也可以是一串数字,一个词组或甚至是一个句子。第三,操作性强。处于短时记忆中的信息,可以进行操作和加工,正是在这个意义上,短时记忆又称作工作记忆。第四,易受干扰。短时记忆中的信息如果受到外来事物的干扰,就很容易产生遗忘。

图4-1 米勒

米勒(George A. Miller, 1920—2012),普林斯顿大学心理学教授。1960年他出版了与加兰特(Eugene Galanter)、普里布拉姆(Karl H. Pribram)合著的《计划和行为的结构》,概述了他们的认知心理学的概念。他最著名的文章是《神奇的数字7±2:我们信息加工能力的局限》,1956年发表于《心理学评论》。

短时记忆的编码方式有听觉编码和视觉编码两种,主要是听觉编码。在短时记忆的存储中,复述是短时记忆信息存储的有效方法。

3. 长时记忆(long-term memory)

长时记忆又称永久性记忆,是信息经过充分加工,在头脑中长久保持的记忆,也指记忆时间超过一分钟的记忆。

长时记忆有两个特点：第一是容量无限。长时记忆像一个巨大的图书馆，它储存了一个人对世界的认识，包括了以往感知过的各种事实、表象和知识。第二是信息保持时间长久。长时记忆中信息保持的时间可以用小时、日、月、年等单位来计算，甚至可以保持终生。

长时记忆中的信息以意义编码为主。意义编码有两种形式：表象编码和语义编码，它们又被称为信息的双重编码。表象编码主要加工处理非言语的对象和事件的知觉信息。语义编码是按言语发生的顺序以系统方式来表征信息的，包括言语听觉和言语运动两方面的信息。语义编码是长时记忆最主要的编码方式。

另外，图尔文也对长时记忆进行了研究，他将长时记忆分为两类，分别是情景记忆和语义记忆。情景记忆是指人们根据时空关系对某个事件的记忆，也指有关生活经验的记忆。语义记忆是指人们对一般知识和规律的记忆，与特殊的时间和地点无关，又称为语词逻辑记忆。我们对于公式、定理和规则的记忆都属于此类。

（三）按信息加工与存储的内容不同划分的记忆

1. 程序性记忆（procedural memory）

程序性记忆是指回忆如何做事情的记忆，包括对知觉技能、认知技能和运动技能的记忆。这类记忆往往需要多次练习才能逐渐获得，在利用这类记忆时通常不需要意识的参与。例如我们学习骑自行车、弹钢琴、写字、刷牙、系鞋带等都是通过练习而获得的程序性记忆。

2. 陈述性记忆（declarative memory）

陈述性记忆需要意识的参与，如我们在课堂上学习的各种课本知识和日常的生活常识都属于这类记忆。例如在学习游泳之前，我们可能读过有关的一些书籍，记住了某些动作要领，这种记忆就是陈述性记忆；以后我们经过不断练习，把知识变成了运动技能，真正学会了在水中游泳，这时的记忆就是程序性记忆。

（四）按记忆是否被意识到划分的记忆

1. 外显记忆（explicit memory）

外显记忆是指有意识提取信息的记忆，它是通过有意识的直接测验表现出来的。外显记忆强调的是信息加工和提取过程的有意识性，这一过程需要注意资源的参与。例如，在我们的头脑里保留着许多以前学过的唐诗宋词、乘法口诀或者如何骑自行车的记忆，对这些信息我们都能意识到，知道自己头脑中确有这些内容，而且是可以再认或回忆出来的。

2. 内隐记忆（implicit memory）

内隐记忆是指我们没有意识到，但确实存在着的过去的经验或记忆，它可以通过对记忆的无意识的间接测验表现出来。内隐记忆强调信息提取过程中的无意识性。例如，要求能熟练地打字的人立刻正确地说出键盘上字母的位置，许多人往往做不到，但在具体操作中，却不影响他们的打字速度，尤其是可以盲打，这说明他们有字母位置的内隐记忆。内隐记忆现象早在1854年就在遗忘症病人身上被发现了，这些病人不记得自己曾经拥有某方面的学习经历，但在他们完成相关任务的操作上却表现出了这些记忆。

专栏 4-1

内 隐 记 忆

沃林顿和韦斯克兰茨（Warrington & Weiskrantz, 1970）曾设计了一个经典实验，被试包括4名遗忘症患者（其中3人酒精中毒，1人颞叶受伤）和16名正常人。实验者先给所有参加者看一些词语，然后安排了两种测验：一种是直接回忆所学的词语；另一种是进行残词补全，即在字母组合（如__ab__）中补进字母，使之成为完整的词（如cable）。结果发现，遗忘症患者的回忆成绩远比正常人差，但在残词补全测验中，他们的成绩与正常人不相上下。遗忘症患者所具有的这种记忆，就是我们所说的内隐记忆，即在不需要人们有意识回忆的情况下，个体的经验自动地对当前任务产生影响而表现出来的记忆。这与我们平时所说的有意识记忆是不同的。也可以这样说，内隐记忆的内容无法被有意回忆，但可以在需要时被使用。正常人从语词认知、技能学习到社会认知诸方面，都存在内隐记忆现象。

20世纪80—90年代，心理学中关于"内隐"的研究很热门，如内隐记忆、内隐学习等。脑的活动除了有可以知晓、有意识的信息加工方式外，还可能有未被知晓、潜意识的但确实存在的信息加工方式。前者由于是可知的，常被称作信息的"外显加工"方式；后者由于是不知不觉的，常被称作信息的"内隐加工"方式。尽管目前科学家对人脑内隐加工的认识还不是很深入，但研究者普遍认为，人有相当大的一部分信息加工过程属于内隐加工方式，它无时无刻不在发挥作用，却又无法被人察觉或有意提取出来。自20世纪80年代开始，国内外许多学者对内隐记忆做了大量研究，将内隐记忆视为在不需要对特定的过去经验进行有意识或外显回忆的测验中表现出来的对先前获得信息的无意识提取（Graf & Schacter, 1985）。

——黄希庭，郑涌.心理学导论[M].北京：人民教育出版社，2015：367.

四、记忆的品质

为促使记忆高度发展，培养记忆力应以记忆的基本品质为目标。良好的记忆表现为在保证记忆高度精确的前提下，既要识记敏捷，又要保持长久，更要善于根据当前要求准确及时地把所需事物提取出来解决问题，满足要求。因此，记忆的良好品质可以归纳为以下四个方面：

（一）识记的敏捷性

识记的敏捷性是指记忆在速度上的品质。对于同一种材料，有些人能很快记住，有些人则需要很长时间。记忆的这种品质具有非常明显的个体差异。如《三国演义》中的张松，只把曹操新写的《孟德新书》看一遍后，就能一字不漏地背出来，而有的人虽然长久而刻苦地学习，识记效果也不理想。识记的敏捷性必须与其他品质结合起来才具有意义。

（二）保持的持久性

保持的持久性是指记忆在时间持续上具有的品质。人与人之间在保持的持久性方面具有显著的差异。如有的人识记过的事物能在头脑中保存很久，甚至终生不忘；有的人则所谓"记性好，忘性大"，识记过的事物保持不了多久。

（三）记忆的精确性

记忆的精确性是指所记住的事物精确无误的品质。这是记忆品质中最核心、最关键的品质。没有记忆的精确性，甚至精确性不高，记忆的其余品质都将失去应有的意义和实际价值。人与人之间在这方面表现的差异也非常突出。有的人记忆十分精确，而有的人记忆总是似是而非、错漏严重。

（四）记忆的准备性

记忆的准备性是指善于根据当前任务的要求把需要的信息从记忆中准确迅速地提取出来。个体之间差异较大，如有的人记住的信息多，但是在需要时不能准确迅速地提取出来；而有的人则能把解答当前任务需要的信息准确迅速地提取出来，表现为"对答如流""出口成章"。马克思在这方面的品质最为突出。法拉格在《回忆马克思》中提到，"无论何时，无论任何问题，都可以向马克思提出来，都能够得到你所期望的最详尽的回答……他的头脑就像停在军港里升火待发的一艘军舰，准备一接到通知，就开向思想的海洋"。记忆的准备性是使知识运用于实际的重要品质，它主要取决于记忆的组织是否到了系统熟记的程度，以及是否善于运用追忆的方法去寻找线索。

记忆的各种品质在不同学生身上有不同的结合，教师应该帮助学生认识自己在记忆上的特点，有目的地培养良好的记忆品质。

第二节
记忆过程分析

一、信息编码过程

无论什么类型的记忆，其基本过程均是由识记、保持、回忆或再认三个环节组成。从信息加工的角度看，其基本过程就是信息的编码、储存和提取。编码是信息的最初加工，对应信息的识记环节。储存是指被编码材料所获得的储存过程，对应信息的保持环节。提取是指被储存信息在随后某一时间的重现，对应信息的回忆或再认环节。简言之，编码获取信息,储存将它保存到需要的时候,而提取就是在需要的时候把它取出来。

(一)识记的类型

所谓编码(coding)就是人脑对外界输入的信息进行加工、归类并纳入记忆系统的过程,从而使这些信息成为适合记忆的形式。在人类的记忆系统中,编码有着不同的层次或水平,而且是以不同的形式存在着的。如视觉的信息编码、听觉的信息编码以及语义的信息编码等。采用哪种编码形式,取决于刺激的性质和主体的个人特点。此外,编码还包括对外界信息进行反复的感知、思考、体验和操作。新的信息必须与人的已有的知识结构形成联系,并汇入旧的知识结构中,才能被获得和巩固。但是,在某些情况下,当事物与人们的需要、兴趣、情感密切联系时,尽管只有一次经历,人们也能牢固地记住它。而这一识别、记住某种事物并在头脑中留下映像的过程,就是识记(memorization)。

1. 无意识记和有意识记

依据主体有无明确的识记意图和目的,是否付出意志的努力,可以将识记分为无意识记和有意识记。

无意识记是指没有预定目的、不需要意志努力而进行的识记。人偶然感知过的事物,阅读过的文献,在一定情况下体验过的情绪,当时没有刻意记忆它,但是有不少内容被记住了,事后可以回忆起来,或当其再度出现时可以认识它,这就是无意识记。人在生活中的很多信息都是通过无意识记储存在大脑中的,"潜移默化""耳濡目染"或"近朱者赤,近墨者黑"都可以理解为无意识记的结果。无意识记不需要意志努力,因此在识记过程中就不会很累,这恰是它的优势。教学中教师可以结合课程内容增加学生感兴趣的案例、视听资料,帮助学生利用无意识记学习,提高教学效果。但是由于无意识记没有目的,因此它很容易以个人兴趣为转移,难以保证识记内容的完整性。

有意识记是指有预定目的、经过一定意志努力并运用一定方法的识记。有意识记由于具有明确的目的性,因此能够更好地保证识记信息的完整性。在教育和生活中有意识记是更重要的,对于需要学习的知识、技能,都必须进行有意识记。

在一般情况下,有意识记的效果要明显优于无意识记。在实际教学中,教师应根据实际情况将二者有机结合起来,提高学生的识记效果。

2. 机械识记和意义识记

依据识记材料的性质和学习者对材料是否理解,可以将识记划分为机械识记和意义识记。

机械识记是指学习者在不理解材料意义的情况下,依据材料的外部联系,采取简单重复的方法进行识记。例如,对无意义的数字、人名、地名、电话号码、历史年代等的识记,大多采用机械识记。这种识记方法的缺点是花费时间多,消耗的能量大,效率相对较低,而且容易遗忘。机械识记最大的优点是对识记材料保持的准确性高。对于单词、语法、年代、人物等精确知识的识记,机械识记仍是必不可少的方法之一。

意义识记是指学习者依据材料的内在联系,通过理解进行的识记。例如,在分析、综合的基础上掌握某些概念,换句话说,就是在掌握材料内在联系的基础上达到识记的目的。例如,我们在读一篇文章的时候,可以分析它是说明文还是记叙文,它说明了什么客观事物和规律,它有哪些论点和依据,它的各个论点和依据之间有什么逻辑关系,以及这篇文章和过去学习过的材料、有关的知识、经验有何关系等。学生在学习的过程中除了分析学习内容的内在联系，还可以用自己的语言针对识记材料做学习提纲，这样也是利用意义识记，有利于知识的记忆和保持。意义识记最大的优点是记忆速度快，保持时间长久，易于提取，但不足的是记忆的精确性有所欠缺。

无论是在全面性和深刻性上，还是在长久性上，以理解为基础的意义识记比机械识记效果都好。因为只有理解了的材料才能在头脑中长期保持，才能在以后运用它们时很快地被提取出来。这是因为理解了的识记内容与过去巩固的知识经验建立了内在的联系。相反，不理解的内容即使暂时记住了，很快也会遗忘。艾宾浩斯曾对机械识记和意义识记的效果进行了对比研究，他识记12个无意义音节，需要16.5次才能成诵；识记36个无意义音节，需要55次才能成诵；而识记6节诗，其中有480个音节，只要7.75次就能成诵。该实验结果说明，意义识记在识记速度上优于机械识记。有的研究还证明，意义识记在记忆的全面性、牢固性上均优于机械识记。所以在教学过程中，教师应引导学生理解教学内容，使意义识记与机械识记结合起来，以达到最佳识记效果。

（二）影响识记的因素

在实际生活中，人们会发现那些与个体的兴趣、需要、活动的目的和任务相适合的、能激起情绪活动的事物，常常容易记住。也就是说，识记效果受到了很多因素的影响，总结起来，可以归纳为以下四个主要的方面。

1. 识记的目的和任务

一般说来，识记的目的和任务越明确具体，识记效果越好。识记材料如果能被直接操作或成为活动对象，识记效果会更好。针对识记的目的，有人做过一个实验，让被试计算印在颜色纸上的不同颜色的字母中的O。事后问被试实验用纸的颜色、除O外还有些什么字母、这些字母是什么颜色等，受试者回答错误的非常多。这证明没有明确的记忆目的，就不易产生清晰的记忆。在另一个关于识记任务的实验中，实验者给成人被试呈现一系列图形，让一组被试识记图片呈现的顺序，另一组被试只识记图形。实验结果表明，第一组有80%的被试、第二组只有43%的被试能正确记起图形的顺序。以儿童为被试的研究也得到相似的结果。成人经过12天后，第一组正确回忆的百分数仍和实验后一样高；儿童经过6天之后，曾有识记顺序任务的被试正确回忆的百分数显著降低，同没有识记顺序任务的被试相等。这个实验结果证明：识记目的和任务对成人和儿童的识记效果都有积极的影响，而对成人的影响更持久。

因为有了明确的识记目的和任务，人们就会把全部的识记活动集中在所要识记的对象上，而且会采取各种各样的方式和方法去实现它，所以识记的目的越明确，识记的效果越好。实践证明，长久的记忆任务比短暂的记忆任务的巩固性要好得多。依据这一规律，教师在教学实践中，不仅应当使学生知道教学的目的，以及每节课的重点和难点，知道哪些知识是学习的要点，不同知识点达到什么要求，记到什么程度。否则，学生会平均用力去识记知识，影响学习效果。

2. 识记材料的性质和数量

识记总是以一定的材料为对象，识记材料的性质、数量和其他属性自然会影响识记的效果。一般而言，直观、形象的材料比抽象的材料更易于识记，有意义的材料比无意义的材料易于识记，数量小的材料比数量大的材料易于识记。性质相同而难易不等的材料记忆的效果不同，容易的材料易于识记。难易不同的材料在识记进程中快慢也常有不同，识记容易的材料一般开始时进展较快，后来逐步缓慢下来；识记困难的材料，一般是开始时识记缓慢，后来逐步加快。

根据这一规律，教师在教学中应当注意为学生安排适当的识记材料数量，在一定时间内要求识记材料的数量不宜过多。如果过分加大数量，会降低识记效果，也影响学生的积极性。对于抽象材料，教师应尽可能采用具体直观形象的教学方式帮助学生采用形象记忆；对于难度较大的材料，教师可以结合以往的知识点，帮助学生搭建前后知识之间的联结，通过理解降低难度，帮助记忆。根据记忆材料的性质，采用不同的教学方式和记忆方式。

3. 不同感觉通道的影响

通过不同的感觉通道获取的信息，也就是不同的感官获得的刺激，记忆的效果也会不同。有实验研究也证实了多种感官的协同识记比单种感官的识记效果好。在实验中，让第一组被试只看某一识记材料，第二组只听同一内容，第三组既看又听。结果发现，视觉识记组可记住内容的70%，听觉识记组记住60%，视、听结合组可记住80.3%。可见，多种感官在识记活动中同时发挥作用，识记效果更佳。南宋朱熹有"读书三到法"，即心到、眼到、口到，也说明了多感官参与学习，效果会更好。

因此，在学习的过程中尽可能地让学生多感官参与学习，像生物、物理、化学等学科，能动手操作的知识，就通过实验，让手、眼、耳全部参与。不能操作的知识，例如语文、外语等学科，可以通过眼看、耳听、口说、手写，这样的记忆效果会大大优于单一感官的识记效果。

4. 识记方法

对于同一知识，采用不同的识记方法，识记效果也会不同。例如，在学习英语可数名词变复数的时候，"ch、sh"后都加"es"，采用机械识记的方法遗忘较快，而有同学说："ch、sh"在汉语拼音中的读法是"吃屎"，"吃屎"太特别了，要加"es"。这位同学采用谐音的方式记忆，记得会较快并且时间比较久。较快识记的材料不同，适用的方法也有差异，对不同个体而言，识记方法的恰当与否直接影响学习的效果。另外，编写识记提纲和不编写识记提纲也会影响记忆效果，有实验研究表明，识记同段文章，9天后检查，不编写识记提纲组遗忘43.2%，编写提纲组只遗忘24.8%。

良好的识记方法，就像是一个巨大的图书馆有了自己的信息检索系统，新信息可以按系统编入网络中，提取就十分方便。因此，教师在教学活动中应根据学生的年龄、个性差异以及学习科目和记忆材料的不同，指导学生学会运用正确的识记方法，例如分类记忆法、画思维导图、谐音记忆法、简缩歌诀记忆法等，以增强识记效果。

二、信息储存过程

（一）保持

保持是在头脑中对识记过的事物进行巩固的过程，保持是一个动态过程。识记的内容被存储后,并不是一成不变地保持原样,已有的知识经验会对这些内容进行加工、编码、再存储,使识记的内容随着时间的推移,不断地发生变化。

记忆内容的变化有质变和量变两种形式。保持内容质的变化,对不同的人而言,改变形式是不一样的,主要是指由于主体已有的知识经验以及对材料的认识、加工方式不同,人们存储的经验会发生不同形式的变化。卡密克尔(Carmickael)的一个实验研究(部分实验图形如图4-2所示)证实了质变大致有以下三种情况:第一,内容简略、概括,不重要的细节逐渐趋于消失;第二,内容变得更加完整、合理和有意义;第三,内容变得更加具体,或者更为夸张和突出。保持的量变有两个方面:记忆恢复和保持内容减少。一般来说,随着时间的延长,保持的内容会越来越少。但也有例外的情形,巴拉德(Ballard)在伦敦小学以12岁学生做实验,让他们用15分钟记一首诗,学习后第二天、第三天测得的保持量比学习后立即测得的保持量要高,这是记忆的恢复现象。这种现象在儿童中比成人中普遍,学习较难的材料比学习容易的材料更易出现,学习得不够熟练比学习得纯熟更易发生。

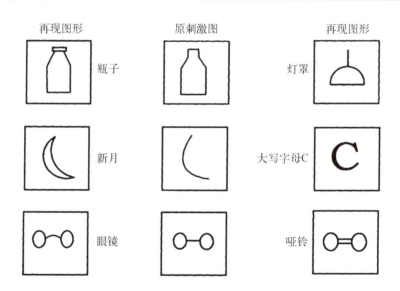

图 4-2 卡密克尔实验部分图形

(二)遗忘

1. 遗忘的概念

记忆保持的最大变化是遗忘(forgetting)。遗忘是指识记过的材料不能保持或者提取时有困难,或者回忆或再认有错误的现象。按照信息加工的观点,遗忘过程在记忆的不同阶段都存在。

遗忘基本上是一种正常的心理现象,是人心理健康和正常生活所必需的,因为感知过的事物没有全部记忆的必要,或者识记材料的重要性具有时效性。在学生的学习过程中也不是一切都需要记忆的,记忆的内容应具有选择性,正像清代郑板桥说的"当忘者不容不忘,不当忘者不容忘耳"。

2. 遗忘的种类

根据遗忘的时间,可分为暂时性遗忘(假性遗忘)与永久性遗忘(真性遗忘)。

暂时性遗忘指已经转入长时记忆的内容暂时不能被提取,但在适宜的条件下还可能恢复。暂时性遗忘经常是由于记忆线索的中断或者情绪过于激动或者紧张导致的。例如,假期里遇见多年不见的老同桌,明明知道对方的名字,但就是想不起来,等对方走了后,自己突然想起来了。这种现象称为"舌尖现象"(tip of tongue),属于暂时性遗忘。

永久性遗忘是指永久不能再认或回忆的遗忘。这种遗忘一旦发生便不能恢复。发生在瞬时记忆与短时记忆阶段的记忆材料未经注意而消失产生的遗忘都属于永久性遗忘。另外,长时记忆中的很多信息也会产生永久性遗忘。例如,从小学至今学过的知识中,很多知识再次被提起的时候,很多人都觉得自己没有学过。

3. 遗忘的进程

遗忘虽是一种复杂的心理现象,但其发生发展也是有一定规律的。德国心理学家艾宾浩斯(Hermann Ebbinghaus)最早对遗忘的进程进行了实验研究。

艾宾浩斯在实验中采用自己创编的无意义音节字表作为记忆材料,采用重学法(又称节省法)作为统计处理方式。自己既充当主试又充当被试,通过机械重复的记忆方法对字表进行系列学习,当识记到一次成诵的程度时便停止。然后间隔一段时间(7种不同的时距)后再测验自己还能记住多少。当有些音节不能恢复时,再重学这些音节,达到和第一次识记后相同的

图 4-3 赫尔曼·艾宾浩斯

赫尔曼·艾宾浩斯(Hermann Ebbinghaus,1850—1909),德国心理学家。1875—1878年游学于英国、法国,受费希纳的影响,开始用实验方法研究记忆。1890年,艾宾浩斯和他人共同创办了《心理学和感觉生理学杂志》。他在1885年出版了《关于记忆》一书。书中记载了以自己作为被试进行的记忆实验,提出了著名的"遗忘曲线",也被称为"艾宾浩斯曲线"。

恰能背诵的标准,以重学比初学节省诵读时间的百分比数作为保持量的指标。实验结果如表4-1所示,将实验结果绘制成曲线图,这就是著名的艾宾浩斯遗忘曲线(the curve of forgetting)(如图4-4所示)。

该曲线表明了遗忘的规律:遗忘的进程是不均衡的,在识记之后最初一段时间里遗忘量比较大,以后逐渐减小。即遗忘的速度是先快后慢,呈负加速。继艾宾浩斯之后,许多人重复了他的实验,所得的结果和艾宾浩斯的结论大体相同。艾宾浩斯的遗忘规律告诉我们时间影响遗忘,根据遗忘规律我们应该及时复习,才能取得较好的记忆效果。

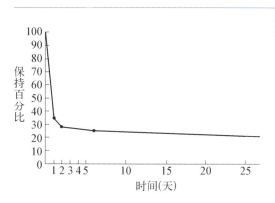

图 4-4 艾宾浩斯遗忘曲线

表 4-1 遗忘的进程

次序	时距（小时）	保持的百分数	遗忘的百分数
1	0.33	58.2	41.8
2	1	44.2	55.8
3	8.8	35.8	64.2
4	24	33.7	66.3
5	48	27.8	72.2
6	144	25.4	74.6
7	744	21.1	78.9

4. 影响遗忘的因素

遗忘的进程不但受时间的影响，还受到其他因素的影响，主要有以下几个方面：

（1）学习材料的数量和性质

需要记忆的材料越多，记忆就越困难，相反如果记忆材料越少，就越容易记忆。有意义的材料比无意义的材料遗忘得慢；形象、直观的材料比抽象的材料遗忘得慢；篇幅较长的、难度较大的材料遗忘得快。

（2）识记材料的系列位置

在回忆系列材料时，材料的顺序对记忆效果有重要影响。有实验研究发现，最后呈现的材料最先回忆起来，其次是最先呈现的那些材料，而最后回忆起来的是中间部分。这种在回忆系列材料时发生的现象叫系列位置效应（serial position effect）。简言之，在一段记忆材料中，位置处于前后两头的材料更容易记住，中间的容易遗忘。因此，在记忆的时候运用分散记忆，减小中间的部分，可以减少遗忘。

（3）识记的方法

同一材料采用不同的学习方法会影响记忆效果，一般，不同材料有较为适合的不同记忆方法。因此，学习者最好针对不同材料选择不同的记忆方法，以防止遗忘，例如，能理解性的材料最好采用以理解为基础的意义识记。

（4）识记者的态度

识记者对识记材料的需要、兴趣、情绪、动机以及重要性的认识等，都影响了遗忘的速度。凡是能引起主体兴趣，符合主体需要、动机，能激起主体强烈情绪的，一般不易遗忘；反之，则遗忘得快。学习者情绪差、动机弱、目的不明确都不利于记忆。在个体的工作、学习、生活上具有重要意义的材料遗忘得慢。例如，我们的银行卡密码对我们而言是很重要的信息，我们就会记得牢一些。

（5）学习程度

一般认为，对材料的识记没有一次能达到无误背诵的标准，称为低度学习；如果达到恰能成诵之后还继续学习一段时间，称为过度学习（overlearning）。实验证明，过度量超过50%时，记忆效果最好。

5. 遗忘的原因

心理学家对遗忘的原因有不同的看法，归纳起来有下述五种：

（1）衰退说

衰退说（decay theory）又称为记忆痕迹消退说，它认为遗忘是记忆痕迹得不到强化而逐渐衰弱，以致最后消退的结果。从巴甫洛夫的理论来看，记忆痕迹是人在认知活动和动作活动时大脑皮层上有关部位所形成的暂时神经联系，联系形成后在神经组织中会留下一定的痕迹，痕迹的保持就是记忆。记忆痕迹消退说很容易被人们接受，因为一些物理或者化学的痕迹有随时间衰退甚至消失的现象。但衰退说目前还没有得到精确有力的实验证明。

（2）干扰说

干扰说（interference theory）认为，遗忘是由于在学习和回忆之间受到其他刺激的干扰所致。一旦干扰被排除，记忆就能恢复，而记忆痕迹不会消退。干扰说可用前摄抑制和倒摄抑制来说明。

前摄抑制（proactive inhibition）是先前学习的材料对后来学习的材料的回忆或再认产生的干扰。这种现象为安德伍德（Underwood）的实验所证实。实验要求两组被试学习字表，第一组被试在学习前进行了大量的类似学习和练习，第二组被试没有进行这种练习。实验结果表明，第一组只记住了学习内容的25%，而第二组记住了70%。

倒摄抑制（retroactive inhibition）是后来学习的材料对先前学习的材料的回忆或再认产生的干扰。这种现象得到很多实验的证实，例如詹金斯（Jenkins）和达伦巴赫（Dallenbach）在实验中要求被试识记10个无意义音节，达到一次能背诵的程度。然后一部分被试即行入睡，另一部分则照常进行日常工作。结果发现，照常工作对回忆所学的材料起了干扰作用，其回忆效果低于学习后即行入睡组的效果。倒摄抑制受前后两种学习材料的类似程度、难度、时间安排以及识记的巩固程度等条件的影响。

另外，前面提到的系列位置效应，其产生的原因与这两种抑制的作用有关。由于材料的中间部分同时受到了前摄抑制和后摄抑制的影响，因而回忆时较困难，而首尾的材料由于只受到了一种抑制的影响，因而回忆的效果较好。

（3）压抑说

压抑说又称为动机性遗忘说，它认为遗忘是由于情绪或动机的压抑作用引起的，如果压抑被解除，记忆就能恢复。这种现象首先是由弗洛伊德在临床实践中发现的。他认为，有些经验之所以不能回忆，是因为在回忆的时候，个体会产生痛苦、忧愁，于是拒绝他们进入意识，将其储存在无意识中。只有当情绪联想减弱时，这种被遗忘的材料才能回忆起来。在生活中，由于情绪紧张导致遗忘的情景也很常见。例如考试时候由于情绪过分紧张，导致平时较熟的内容怎么也想不起来。

（4）提取失败说

遗忘之所以发生，不是因为存储在长时记忆中的信息消失了，而是因为我们在提取信息的时候没有找到适当的提取线索（retrieval cues）。一旦有了正确的线索，经过搜寻，所需要的信息就能提取出来，这就是遗忘的提取失败理论。例如，生活中有这样的经验：你认识某个同学，但是当有人问你是否认识的时候，你没有印象了。后来身边的人告诉你这个同学所在的班级、以往的趣闻等,有了这些线索后你就记起来了。这种遗忘就是没有找到适当的线索所导致的。

(5)同化说(认知结构说)

奥苏贝尔认为,遗忘实际上是知识的组织与认知结构简化的过程,即用高级的概念与规律代替低级的观念,使低级观念发生遗忘,从而提炼和简化了认识并减轻了记忆负担,这是一种积极的遗忘。用于解释有意义学习的保持与遗忘,他认为在真正有意义的学习中,前后相继的学习不是相互干扰而是相互促进的,因为有意义学习总以原有的学习为基础,后者的学习是对前面学习的加深和扩充。

专栏 4-2

记 忆 扭 曲

人们往往会扭曲自己的记忆。例如,仅仅是嘴上说说你身上发生了什么事情就可以让你倾向于认为它真的发生了,不管它事实上发生与否(Zaragoza,1998)。根据沙克特(Schacter,2001)的观点,这些记忆扭曲(memory distortion)可以通过七种独特的方式出现,好比"记忆的七宗罪"。

① 短暂。记忆消退得很快。比如,尽管大部分人知道辛普森在谋杀妻子的犯罪指控中被宣判无罪,但他们并不记得自己是从何处得知他被宣判无罪的。他们曾经说得出来,但是后来再也想不起来了。

② 心不在焉。人们有时在刷过牙之后又会去刷牙,或者进房间去找东西时,结果却忘了要找什么东西。

③ 阻滞。人们知道,有些事情应该记得,却回忆不起来。比如,遇见某个自己认识的人,却想不起名字,或者在努力回想一个单词的同义词时,虽然知道有一个很明显的同义词,但就是不能回忆起来。

④ 错误归因。人们经常记不住是在哪儿听见他们听说过的事情,或者在哪儿读到他们阅读过的东西。有时,人们会认为他们看见了自己并没有见过的东西,或者听见了他们并没有听到的事情。例如,目击者的证词有时不完全是真实的,因为我们会把自己所想的事情而不是我们事实上所看见的,认为是我们看见的事情。

⑤ 暗示。人们很容易受到暗示的影响,因此,如果有人暗示说他们见过某事,那么他们可能会认为自己记得曾见过它。比如,在荷兰,当人们被问及是否看见过一架飞机撞上一栋公寓大楼的电视片时,许多人回答见过,但实际上根本没有这样的影片。

⑥ 偏见。人们经常在回忆中带有偏见。例如,目前正经历着生活中巨大悲痛的人们很可能会回忆过去的痛苦,不管他们是否真的经历过这些痛苦。那些没有处在这类痛苦中的人们回忆过去的痛苦经历的可能性较小,这也几乎无关他们真实的过去经历。

⑦ 固执。人们有时候把某些事情当作非常重要的事情记住了,但从更广的角度看,这些事情并不那么重要。比如,有人有许多次成功,但只有一次重大的失败,或许他对这唯一一次的失败比这许多次成功记忆得更牢固。

——黄希庭,郑涌.心理学导论[M].北京:人民教育出版社,2015:384—385.

三、信息提取过程

(一)再认

再认(recognition)是过去经历的事物重新出现时,能够被识别和确认的心理过程。

在再认过程中,不同的人对不同的材料的再认速度是不一样的,这和影响再认的因素有关。影响再认的因素有以下几点:

1. 原有经验的巩固程度

如果过去的经验很清晰、准确地被保持,当再次出现时,一般能迅速、准确地予以确认。当再认出现困难时,人们常常要寻找再认的线索,通过线索达到对事物的再认。线索是再认的支点,如对久别重逢的朋友的再认一般要以身体的某些特征作为再认的线索。如果过去经验已经发生了泛化现象,就容易发生再认错误。

2. 原有事物与重新出现时的相似程度

相似程度会影响再认的速度和准确度,不同材料相似程度的高低影响不同。相似程度越高,则有利于再认,否则容易发生误认及错误的再认。

3. 个性特征

个性特征不同,人的心理活动速度和行为反应的快慢也不同。心理学家曾通过实验证实,独立性强的人和依附性强的人的再认有明显的差异。

(二)回忆

回忆(recall)也称为再现,是在一定诱因的作用下,过去经历的事物在头脑中再次呈现的过程。如在回答教师的提问时,学生要把头脑中所保持的与该问题有关的知识提取出来,这种提取过程就是回忆。

根据有无目的性,可以把回忆分为有意回忆和无意回忆。有意回忆是在预定目的的作用下对过去经验的回忆。例如,学生在考试的时候,对考试内容进行回忆。无意回忆是没有明确回忆意图或目的,映象是按照联想原则自然而然地被提取或复现。无意回忆的内容往往不连贯、不系统。触景生情就属于无意回忆。

根据有无中介因素参与回忆过程,可把回忆分为直接回忆和间接回忆。直接回忆是由当前事物直接唤起的对旧经验的回忆。间接回忆是借助中介因素而进行的回忆,这种回忆需要一定的意志努力才能实现。

追忆是间接回忆的特殊形式,它是通过积极的思维活动和较大的意志努力而进行的回忆。学生在解难题时对有关知识的回忆往往就是追忆。回忆过程特别是追忆，常常以联想为基础。

联想是事物之间的联系或关系的反映，是头脑中暂时神经联系的复活。联想在整个记忆过程中都有重要的作用。联想具有以下几个规律：

接近律。它是指在时间或空间上接近的事物形成的联想。如春—夏—秋—冬的联想为时间上的接近；东—南—西—北为空间上的接近。

相似律。它是以事物之间某些相似或共同特征为基础形成的联想。如鸟—飞机；鱼—潜艇等联想。

对比律。它是指由事物之间相反关系形成的联想。如真理—谬误；难—易等联想。

因果律。它是指因事物之间因果关系形成的联想。如骄兵必败、勤能补拙等联想。

（三）再认和回忆的关系

再认和回忆同属于记忆过程中的同一环节，即信息提取过程。但再认比回忆简单和容易，能回忆的材料一般都能再认，而能再认的材料不一定能回忆。从个体心理发展来看，再认比回忆出现得早。孩子出生后半年内，便可再认，而回忆的发展却要晚一些。

专栏4-3

法律中的再认与回忆

在法庭对案件的审判中，许多情况下法官和陪审团都是依据目击证人的证词来进行判断的。大家普遍相信目击证人的证词是正确和可靠的。但是孟斯特伯格发现，对同一事件，不同的目击者会有不同的描述，由此他对案件中证人证词的可信度表示了忧虑。有关的研究证实了孟斯特伯格的担忧，研究发现，目击者对事件的回忆会因为提问方式的不同有很大的差异。例如，在一项研究中，让被试看一部关于一起撞车事故的影片，然后要求被试对事故中车辆的行驶速度作出判断。结果发现，当问题是"车辆在冲撞时的速度是多少"时，被试对车速的判断超过65公里/小时；而当问题是"车辆在接触时的速度是多少"时，被试对车速的判断只有50公里/小时；一周之后，主试要求被试回忆事故中车窗是否被撞碎了，而事实上影片中的车窗玻璃并没有被撞碎。结果是，以"冲撞"字眼被提问的被试中有33%的人回忆说车窗玻璃被撞碎了，而以"接触"字眼被提问的被试中，这一比例只有14%。显然，在提问时，不同的字眼改变了被试对目击事件的记忆。

——彭聃龄.普通心理学[M].北京：北京师范大学出版社,2001：227.

第三节
记忆规律在教育教学中的应用

一、运用记忆规律提高课堂教学效果

(一)让学生明确识记的目的和任务

有意识记是教学活动中最主要的识记种类,教师应根据不同的教学内容,提出明确的识记任务要求。在每堂课上课之初,教师就可以让学生明确本节课的教学任务以及重难点,有了明确的识记目的后,有利于学生记忆教学的内容。

(二)充分利用无意识记的规律组织教学

在教学中,教师的讲课必须要生动形象,难度适中,教学形式要新颖、多样化,使学生能凭无意识记记住更多的知识。教师在教学中使学生无意记住更多的内容,是一种更高级的教学艺术。

(三)使学生理解所识记的内容并把它系统化

只有被理解的、系统的知识,才能长久地保持在记忆中,并在需要时很快地提取出来。教学的主要任务就是通过教师的讲解,使学生利用思维去理解所学的内容,使之对其建立起多方面的联系。教师还应把讲授的内容系统化,如果能把要识记的内容归结为公式、定理或归纳为几个方面,写成提纲,择要而记,就能有更好的识记效果。

(四)充分利用生动、具体的形象和表象进行教学

在教学过程中,教师应尽量利用生动的形象和表象帮助学生记忆。特别是对小学低年级的学生,形象记忆对他们来说较容易,抽象记忆较困难。对于小学高年级和中学生而言,教师也尽可能将抽象内容通过实物、模型或者言语进行直观化,这样既便于理解,也有利于记忆。

(五)合理安排教学

在安排课程的时候,学校应尽可能地避免把性质相近的课程排在一起,这样能减少材料相似性引起的前摄抑制、倒摄抑制对记忆的干扰。同时,教师要保证学生的课间休息,不要拖堂。课间休息有利于学生巩固上一节课所学的内容,提高保持效果;同时,也有助于减少由于前后课中记忆材料的间隔时间过短引起的前摄抑制、倒摄抑制对记忆活动的影响。另外,教师还应控制每堂课的信息投入量。过多的信息投入不利于学生课上对学习内容的消化、吸收和记忆,过少的信息投入不利于学生获取更多的知识。

（六）使学生处于良好的情绪和注意状态

情绪的组织功能在记忆活动中得到了明显的体现。积极愉悦的情绪状态有助于提高学生学习的效率，促进认知活动的进行，学生的注意力也更为集中。相反，如果上课时学生觉得枯燥无聊，消极的情绪经常起阻碍的作用，学生的注意状态也较差。

（七）培养学生良好的记忆品质，提高其记忆能力

良好的记忆品质无疑可以提高记忆能力，同时提高学习的效率。不同的记忆品质可以有针对性地采用不同的措施来培养。例如，通过布置各种定时性记忆作业并进行课堂提问，培养学生记忆的敏捷性；通过要求他们对识记材料进行深入的理解，使材料在头脑中系统化，进行合理的复习，培养其记忆的持久性；通过要求他们进行认真的识记和复习，使材料形成精确的联系和养成经常检查自己记忆效果的习惯，培养记忆的准确性；通过使他们对所学知识条理化、系统化和掌握追忆的技能，提高其记忆的准备性。

（八）教给学生记忆的方法

科学的记忆方法能够增强记忆，防止遗忘。常用的记忆方法有很多，包括自己的预习、复习策略都可以成为记忆方法，良好的记忆方法可以使人受益终生。下面介绍几种具体的记忆方法。

1. 谐音记忆法

利用谐音来帮助记忆是一种很有效的方法，尤其是针对无法理解的数字、历史年代、单词等难以记忆的材料，利用谐音在它们之间找出人为的有意义的联系，这样更便于贮存和回忆。例如，记忆单词救护车"ambulance"，利用谐音"俺不能死了"，再想象一个情景：一个人躺在救护车里想"俺不能死了"，这个单词记起来就容易多了。

2. 位置记忆法

位置记忆法也称为地点法，是通过与自己熟悉的某种地点序列相联系来记忆一系列名字或客体的方法。例如，我们经常记忆班级里的同学就是运用位置记忆法，谁坐在第一排，谁坐在第二排。

3. 简缩歌诀法

把记忆材料编成口诀或者押韵的语句来提高记忆效果的方法，叫做歌诀记忆法。这种方法把记忆材料分成组块来记忆，可以缩小记忆材料的数量，加大信息含量，便于提取。而且编口诀还增强了内容的趣味性，记忆内容有韵律、朗朗上口，容易记。例如，大家熟悉的二十四节气歌：春雨惊春清谷天，夏满芒夏暑相连，秋处露秋寒霜降，冬雪雪冬小大寒。

二、根据遗忘规律有效地组织复习

克服遗忘最好的方法是加强复习。要使学生获得巩固的知识，不能没有复习，复习效果的好坏并不机械地取决于复习的次数，而是取决于复习的正确组织。在教学过程中，为了有效地组织复习，必须注意以下几点：

（一）复习时机要得当

1. 及时复习

遗忘的规律是先快后慢，因此，复习必须及时，要在遗忘尚未大规模开始前进行。及时复习可以阻止通常在学习后立即发生的急速遗忘。所以，教师教授新知识后要及时地进行课堂练习，进行复习性提问、布置家庭作业等，让学生所学的知识得到及时复习。

2. 合理分配复习时间

根据复习在时间上分配的不同，可将复习分为两种：集中复习和分散复习。集中复习是集中在一个时间内，对所要识记的内容连续、反复地进行复习。分散复习是把要记忆的内容分在几个相隔的时间内进行复习。研究表明，一般情况下，分散复习效果优于集中复习。所以，组织学生复习时，应尽量采用分散复习。分散复习时，间隔时间的长短应根据复习内容的性质、数量、识记已经达到的水平等因素而定。一般地说，分散复习的时间间隔应是先密后稀，每次复习的遍数应是先多后少。根据这一规律，在学校的教学中，应当把功课的复习合理地分配在整个学期中，而不应只集中在期末考试之前。

（二）复习材料的量与次数要适宜

1. 合理掌握复习的量

一次复习内容的数量不宜过多，因为学习内容较多时相应的中间部分内容变多，而系列位置效应告诉我们，内容的中间部分受到干扰较多，容易忘记。因此，为了达到较好的学习效果，也要加强对内容的中间部分的复习。同时，为了防止复习内容间的相互干扰，复习中应注意安排适当的休息；复习过程中，不同学科交叉复习，避免相似的内容产生相互干扰。

2. 提倡适当地过度学习

因为有研究发现，当学习程度达到150%时，记忆效果最好，所以当学习内容记住后，再增加50%的学习次数，从而达到记忆的最佳效果。例如，记一个单词，读背4遍能达到默写程度，那么再增加2遍学习。

（三）复习方法要合理

1. 复习方法多样化

进行多样化的复习不仅能让学生感到新颖，有利于调动学生的兴趣和积极性，也有利于思维的练习和智力的提高。为了促使学生巩固地掌握知识，有时候可全面地复习，按部就班地复习，这种复习可普遍地恢复过去形成的联系，也有利于发现那些识记不牢固的部分。而更重要的是灵活采用多样化的复习方式，教师可采用提问、做练习、调查、讨论、实验操作或课外小组科技活动等种种形式，使学生对学习的有关知识进行复习、巩固。在学习与日常生活中，人们通常使用的复习方法有"理解法""背诵法""循环记忆法""练习和实验操作法"等。还有编写复习提纲、绘制图表、制作索引书目、制作卡片、剪报等，使脑内储存与外部储存结合起来，都有助于记忆内容的系统化。

2. 运用多种感官参与复习

多种感官参与复习可以更好地提高记忆效果。因此，在复习时应尽量运用多种感官参与,眼看、耳听、口读、手写要相互配合,在头脑中构成它们之间的神经联系,形成记忆痕迹,以后遇到其中的一种刺激信息,就可以激活多种相关的记忆痕迹,提高记忆效果。有研究发现,人的学习83%通过视觉,11%通过听觉,3.5%通过嗅觉,1.5%通过触觉,1%通过味觉。

3. 尝试回忆与反复识记相结合

研究表明,反复阅读与试图回忆相结合,比单纯通过反复阅读来进行复习效果要好。反复阅读与尝试回忆相结合的方法,能使学习者及时了解到识记的成绩,从而提高学习的兴趣,激起进一步学习的动机。同时,在每次回忆后,学习者可以及时检查记忆效果,在重新阅读时就会有针对性地集中精力攻克难点,纠正错误,不至于平均用力。

（四）掌握回忆的策略

1. 善用回忆技巧

回忆既是检验识记与保持效果的指标,也是识记与保持的目的。因此,提高回忆效果是很重要的。为了提高学生的回忆效率,教会学生善于运用回忆的技能和技巧,例如：运用联想进行回忆,运用推理进行回忆等。

2. 排除回忆过程中的干扰

培养学生的意志力,排除回忆过程中的干扰。干扰可能来自旧经验对心理状态的影响,也可能来自情绪的过分紧张,遇到这种情况,最好的办法是教育学生用自己的意志力克服紧张情绪,转移注意,暂时中断回忆。

专栏4-4

记忆研究怎样帮你准备考试

学生们在读了有关记忆研究的内容之后,询问最多的问题是："我怎样能马上用上这些？这项研究怎样帮助我准备下一次考试？"让我们来看看从研究结论中可以产生哪些建议。

① 编码特异性。就像你回想起的那样,编码特异性原则表明提取的背景应该匹配编码的背景。在学校的环境里,"背景"通常是指"其他信息的背景"。如果你总是在相同的背景下学习材料,你可能会发现在一个不同的背景下提取它很困难,所以,如果一位教授以一种稍微不寻常的方式来谈论一个话题,你可能会完全困惑。作为补救的办法,即使在学习的时候你也应该变换背景,重新组织你的笔记的顺序,问自己一些混在一起的不同课程的问题,构造你自己的新异组合。但是,如果你在参加一次考试时遇到障碍的话,试着产生尽可能多的提取线索来帮助恢复最初的背景："让我们想一想,我们是在学习短时记忆的哪一讲中听到这个内容的……"

② 系列位置。你从系列位置曲线得知,在非常广泛的情景下,呈现在"中间"的信息记忆最差。事实上,大学生对关于一些内容的中间部分测验题目比关于开始和

结尾部分的测验题目遗忘得更多。在听课的时候，你应该提醒自己要特别注意中间那段时间。学习的时候，你应该投入更多的时间和努力在要学习的材料上，以确保每次以相同的顺序学习这些材料。你可能也注意到了你现在读的这一章大约在本书的中间。如果你要参加覆盖所有课程内容的一次期末考试的话，必须特别仔细地复习这一章。

③ 精细复述和记忆术。有时当你学习以准备考试的时候，你会感觉像在设法获得"无组织的信息"。例如，你可能被要求记住大脑不同部分的功能。这种情况，你需要设法自己提供结构，设法以创造性的方式使用概念形成视觉表象或构成句子或故事。精细复述使你可以利用已经知道的东西使新材料更容易记忆。

④ 元记忆。关于元记忆的研究认为，人们通常对自己知道什么和不知道什么有很好的直觉。如果你处在一个有时间限制的考试情景下，就应该让直觉来指导你这样分配时间。例如，你可以快速地把所有测验题目读一遍，看看哪些题目给你最强烈的知道感。如果你正在参加一个考试，在这个考试中你会因为给错答案而被扣分，你应该特别注意你的元记忆直觉，这样就可以避免回答那些你感觉很可能错的问题。

——理查德·格里格（Richard J. Gerrig），菲利普·津巴多（Philip G. Zimbardo）.心理学与生活[M].王垒,王甦,等,译.北京：人民邮电出版社,2003：212.

本章小结

通过本章的学习，我们了解了记忆的定义、分类和品质，理解了记忆的过程包括识记、保持、再认或回忆三个环节；知道了遗忘的分类、遗忘的规律、遗忘的原因以及影响因素。在记忆基本知识学习的基础上，我们还学习了如何利用记忆规律组织教学，如何防止遗忘。

关键术语

记忆　短时记忆　遗忘　前摄抑制　倒摄抑制　过度学习

讨论与应用

1. 你能用本章学习过的知识来解释为什么打油诗能帮助我们更好地背下圆周率吗？

相传民国时期，在一所山间私塾中，一位先生要学生背诵圆周率，他要求学生必须准确背诵小数点后的22位数，即3.1415926535897932384626。临近中午，学生们依然没背下来，先生很生气，说："中午不许回家吃饭，继续背，什么时候背下来，什么时候回家。"教书先生是一个爱喝酒的人，自己上山找朋友喝酒去了。

待在教室里的孩子自然很生气，但依然没办法背下圆周率。忽然，一个机灵的学生编了一首打油诗，结果把圆周率后的 22 位数准确地背下来了。他把打油诗教给全体同学，待老师喝酒回来，学生们个个背得滚瓜烂熟。打油诗是这样写的："山巅一寺一壶酒，尔溜苦煞吾，把酒吃，酒杀尔，杀不死，溜而溜。"

2. 下列材料中，甲班保持量高的原因是什么？除此之外，你还知道哪些方法能提高记忆效果？

甲乙两班同学学习一段材料，甲班同学学习后不久就复习，乙班同学不复习，一周后，甲班同学的平均保持量为 83%，乙班同学的平均保持量为 25%。

3. 下列实验说明了我们的记忆在保持的过程中会发生变化，你知道会有哪些变化吗？

美国著名认知心理学家伊丽莎白·洛夫特斯做了一个实验：若抢劫者手里带的不是武器，有 49% 的受试者能够正确指认罪犯；但如果抢劫者携带武器，仅有 33% 的被试能够正确指认罪犯。一方面，人们对不协调和伤害性的物体关注更多，因此记得的其他细节相对减弱；另一方面，目击者在看见武器后会产生极大的恐惧感和压力，许多人误以为此种情况会强化记忆，事实上是强化了恐惧感。也许目击者会说："就是他干的，我永远也无法忘记这张脸……"但是，特定的场景在大脑中不断重演，错误的细节也随之一起出现，由此导致记忆发生扭曲。

第五章 想 象

XIANGXIANG

  亲爱的同学,你的脑海中是不是经常出现各种形象呢?那你有没有发现这样一个问题:在你脑海中出现的很多形象,有些是现实中存在的,有些是现实中不存在的,那么那些在现实中不存在的形象是怎么出现在你的脑海中的呢?希望通过接下来的学习,能帮助你解答以上的疑问。

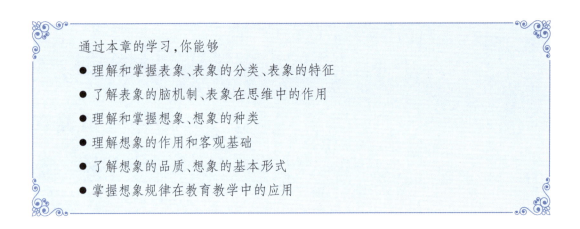

通过本章的学习,你能够
- 理解和掌握表象、表象的分类、表象的特征
- 了解表象的脑机制、表象在思维中的作用
- 理解和掌握想象、想象的种类
- 理解想象的作用和客观基础
- 了解想象的品质、想象的基本形式
- 掌握想象规律在教育教学中的应用

【本章结构】

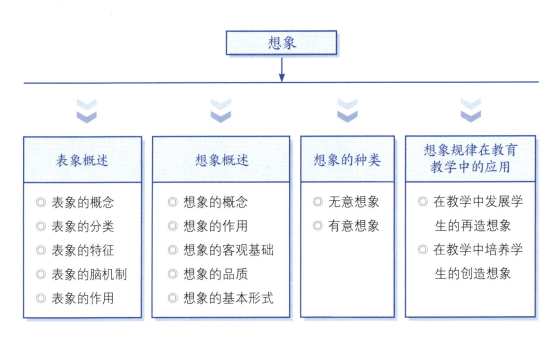

本章主要回答"什么是表象和想象"的问题,它有助于你更加专业地了解表象和想象的概念和内涵。我们从表象的概述开始,介绍表象的特征及不同种类,然后介绍想象的概念、种类,阐述想象的作用以及人脑进行想象的客观基础,最后分析想象规律在教育教学中的应用。

第一节

表象概述

一、表象的概念

表象（image）是指人脑对感知过的事物的形象的反映，是人脑以形象的形式对客观事物进行操作和加工的过程，是事物不在面前时对于事物的心理复现。

表象以感知觉所提供的材料为基础，没有对客观事物的感知，表象就无法形成。但是，表象不是感知觉的翻版，它是感知觉痕迹经信息加工后再作用的产物。

二、表象的分类

从表象产生的主要感觉通道来划分，表象可分为视觉表象、听觉表象、运动表象等。根据表象创造程度的不同，表象可分为记忆表象和想象表象。

（一）视觉表象、听觉表象、运动表象

1. 视觉表象（visual image）

人脑中的感知过的具有视觉特征（颜色、形状、大小等）的形象。视觉表象比较鲜明，是经常出现的表象形式。

2. 听觉表象（auditory image）

人脑中的感知过的具有听觉特征（音调、响度、音色和旋律等）的形象。在听觉表象中，言语听觉表象和音乐听觉表象最为鲜明和突出。

3. 运动表象（motional image）

在运动感知的基础上，在大脑中重现的动作形象或运动情景。动觉表象可以是视觉性的，也可以是动觉性的。

（二）记忆表象和想象表象

1. 记忆表象（memory image）

过去感知过的事物形象在人脑中的重现，保留了客观事物的主要形象特点。

2. 想象表象（imaginative image）

人脑在已有表象的基础上，通过加工改造与整合而形成的新形象。

专栏 5-1

"从我能记忆的时候起一直到现在，我经常是一个贫于视觉表象的人，即使是意

味很深的诗句也不能在我心目中引起图象。在睡意朦胧之际也没有产生过催眠式的视觉。当我回想什么时,我的记忆也不能提供事物的鲜明视象。经过意志的努力,我能对昨天下午发生的事情产生一种非常不鲜明的表象……但这种表象很不扎实,也绝对不能独立自在。它们和可见的实物的关系,就像荷马诗篇中的鬼魂和血肉之人的关系一样,它们在阴影下与人们会晤。只有当我发高烧时,我的表象才独立活动。"

——克雷奇(Krech)等.心理学纲要(上册)[M].周先庚,等,译.北京:文化教育出版社,1980:211.

三、表象的特征

(一)直观性

表象以生动具体的形象在人脑中出现,具有直观形象的特征。但是,它不同于感知觉的直接性特征。表象是人脑对感知过的事物的形象的反映,它所反映的是客观事物的大体轮廓和主要特征,不如感知觉那么鲜明、完整和稳定,具有模糊性。

(二)概括性

表象反映的是客观事物的形象,不是某个具体事物或事物的某个特征,而是相同事物或同类事物在不同条件下表现出来的共同特征,是一种归类了的事物形象。

(三)可操作性

由于表象是知觉的类似物,因此人们可以在头脑中对表象进行操作,这种操作就像人们通过外部动作控制和操作客观事物一样。

专栏 5-2

心理旋转实验

1971年,美国斯坦福大学的心理学家谢帕德(R. Shepard)和梅茨勒(Metzler)等做了一系列实验。他们以不同倾斜角度的正形象和反形象字母"R"为刺激物(如图5-1所示),观察被试确定它是正形象还是反形象需要的反应时间,以此说明被试对不同刺激的心理加工过程。实验结果表明(如图5-2所示),心理旋转具有连续性,对客体的心理旋转与物理旋转具有类似性,大多数被试要在头脑中想像地将两个物体调转到同一方向才能进行比较;而且意象在头脑中旋转的角度越大,作出判断的反应时越长,这就是著名的心理旋转实验。

——林崇德等.心理学大辞典[M].上海:上海教育出版社,2003:1406.

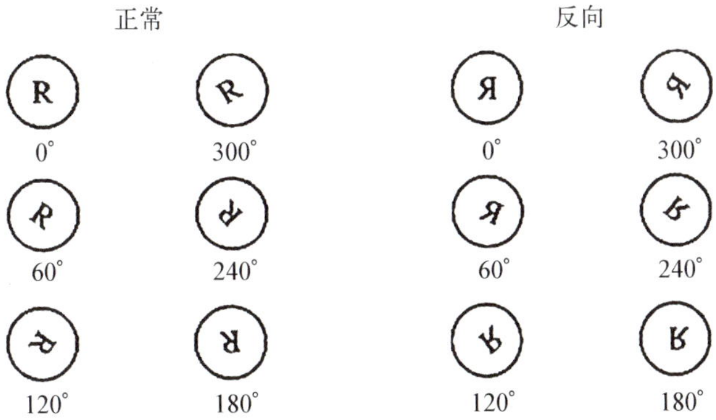

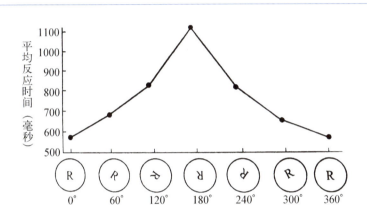

图 5-1 心理旋转实验刺激物

图 5-2 心理旋转实验结果

四、表象的脑机制

表象的脑机制是认知神经科学的重要研究领域。目前研究的主要问题是表象和知觉是否具有类似的脑机制。科斯林（Kosslyn）等人认为，视觉表象和视知觉是功能上的等价物，两者之间具有共同的神经机制；而另外一些研究者则认为，视觉表象和视知觉之间的神经机制并非完全相同。

早在20世纪70年代，毕思阿克（Bisiach）等人研究了两名颅顶受损的病人，这两名病人患有单侧性空间忽视症，即他们只能看到一侧的物体，而看不到另一侧的物体。结果发现，病人在视知觉中存在的问题，在表象活动中也会表现出来。

科斯林等人（Kosslyn）用正电子发射型计算机断层显像（Positron Emission Computed Tomography，简称PET）技术研究了表象的脑机制。实验采用了知觉任务和表象任务，发现由表象任务激活的脑区比由知觉任务激活的脑区更多。

加尼斯等人（Ganis）采用功能磁共振成像技术进一步研究了表象和知觉加工的脑机制。实验中，被试接受两种实验条件：一种是首先听到一个单词，然后形成单词所代表物体的表象；另一种是首先听到一个单词，然后马上看相应物体的图片，最后回答与图片相关的问题。结果发现，视觉表象和视知觉激活的脑区具有很大程度的重叠，其中额叶和顶叶重叠的程度较高，颞叶和枕叶的重叠程度较小。视知觉激活的脑区包含了视觉表象激活的脑区。研究结果表明,视觉表象和视知觉具有类似的脑机制。

然而结果并非如此简单,近年来有关脑损伤病人的研究发现,视觉表象和视知觉可能存在不同的脑机制。例如,在莫罗等人(Moro)的研究中,一个病人损伤的部位位于左半球的颞中回和颞下回,另外一个病人损伤的部位位于左半球枕—颞联合区和顶上小叶等区域。研究结果表明,病人在视知觉完全正常的情况下,视觉表象存在着较大的缺陷;视觉表象的缺陷可以发生在初级视觉皮层完好的情况下;左半球的颞叶在视觉表象的形成方面起着非常重要的作用。

综上所述,表象和知觉是否具有相似的脑机制,依然是有待进一步研究的问题。

五、表象的作用

(一)表象为概念的形成提供了感性基础

表象是认知过程的一个重要环节,它既有直观性,又有概括性。从直观性来看,它接近于知觉;从概括性来看,它接近于思维。表象离开了具体的事物,摆脱了感知觉的局限性,因而为概念的形成奠定了感性的基础。例如,对"动物"这个概念,孩子们常常用猫、狗、鸡、鸭等具体形象来说明。有了表象作支持,儿童更容易形成抽象的概念。

(二)表象促进问题的解决

表象在问题解决中的作用,早为人们所认识。例如,小学低年级学生在做算术题时,要有表象的参与;中学生在做几何题时,要依赖表象的支持;工程师在审阅建筑设计图纸时,倾向于在头脑中利用建筑物的形象来帮助思维。

在进行推理时,表象也有重要的作用。休腾洛切尔(Huttenlocher)等人给被试两个命题,如"汤姆比迪克高些""哈里比汤姆高些",要求被试说出谁最高、谁最矮,这时被试头脑中可能出现不同高度的圆柱体,并用它们代表汤姆、迪克和哈里。根据对表象的比较,被试直接说出了答案。

第二节

想象概述

一、想象的概念

想象(imagination)是人脑对已有表象进行加工改造、重新组合形成新形象的心理过程。

想象最突出的特征是在已有表象的基础上产生有关事物的新形象。这些新形象不同于亲身感知过的、简单再现于头脑中的记忆表象，它可以是个体从未亲身经历过、现实中尚未存在或者根本不可能存在的事物的形象。如我们没有机会亲自看到秦朝阿房宫的景象，但当我们读完杜牧的《阿房宫赋》之后，头脑中就会浮现出规模宏大、气势雄伟、建筑风格奇特的阿房宫的形象；还有机械设计师绘制的新机器的图纸，建筑师设计的新型建筑的图纸，文学作品中千姿百态的人物形象等，都是大脑对原有表象加工改造的产物。

想象是建立在已有表象的基础上，但不是已有表象的简单相加、胡乱凑合，而是经过一个合理的加工改造，重新组合的过程。

乍一看来，想象的形象新颖、离奇，很难在现实中找到其具体的"蓝本"，具有超现实性。其实想象同其他心理一样，不是凭空产生的。就构成新形象的材料来说，想象源于客观现实。如吴承恩笔下的猪八戒的形象是对头脑中已有的"肥胖的人体""猪头""钉耙"等储备的表象进行加工改造的结果。因此，想象也是对客观现实的反映，它是在感知材料的基础上形成的，没有相应的感性材料就不能产生想象。

二、想象的作用

（一）想象是人类劳动的必要因素

想象是人特有的一种心理活动，它是在劳动过程中发生和发展的。劳动要求人们预见行动的结果，因而人们在劳动之前，就要在头脑中形成"做什么"和"怎么做"的表象。想象造成劳动产品的心理模型，指导劳动过程的方向，这是人类劳动的主要特征之一。所以，马克思说："最蹩脚的建筑师从一开始就比最灵巧的蜜蜂高明的地方，是他在用蜂蜡建筑蜂房以前，已经在自己的头脑中把它建成了。劳动过程结束时得到的结果，在这个过程开始时就已经在劳动者的表象中存在着，即已经观念地存在着。"[①]

（二）想象使人的认识领域得到无限开拓与延伸

人脑能够通过感知揭示直接作用于感觉器官的事物的属性和意义。但是，在社会实践中，由于时间、空间及主客观条件的制约，我们常常遇到一些无法直接认识的东西。如宇宙间的星球、原始人类生活的情景等，这些空间上遥远的东西和时间上久远的事物，我们要直接感知很困难，甚至是不可能的。在这种情况下，可以借助想象的机制，弥补人类认识活动的时空局限和不足，超越个体狭隘经验的范围，对客观世界产生更充分、更全面、更深刻的认识。例如，《红楼梦》中的王熙凤的形象是无法直接感知的，但当人们读到"一双丹凤三角眼，两弯柳叶吊梢眉，粉面含春威不露，丹唇未启笑先闻"的文字描写时，人们通过已有的"丹凤""柳叶""粉面"等表象的作用，就能在头脑中想象出王熙凤的形象。

---

① 中共中央马克思恩格斯列宁斯大林著作编译局.马克思恩格斯选集：第二、三卷[M].北京：人民出版社，1972：202.

（三）想象具有预见作用

人类活动同动物本能活动的根本区别就在于活动的目的性、预见性和计划性，也就是说人能实现对客观现实的超前反映。人类的任何实践活动，无论是制造简单的工具，或者是进行艺术创作、科学发明，在活动之前，人们总是先在大脑中形成未来活动过程和活动结果的想象，并利用这些想象指导调节活动过程，实现预定的目的和计划。科学家的发明创造，工程师的工程设计，都是想象预见功能的体现。因此爱因斯坦曾说："想象力比知识更重要。"

（四）想象具有替代作用

现实生活中，由于各种因素的制约，人们的某些需要和活动不可能满足或全面实现时，就可以通过想象来代替，从心理上得到一定的补偿和满足。例如，在中国古典戏曲表演艺术中，许多布景和实物是通过演员形象化的动作唤起观众的想象，而获得良好效果的。戏曲中的骑马、过河、摆渡、开门、关门等都是通过想象来理解的。又如在游戏中，儿童借助想象满足其模仿成人的愿望，增长了知识和才干。若没有想象的参与，游戏就无法进行。可见，想象在儿童游戏中同样有着非常重要的作用。

三、想象的客观基础

我们在学习感知和记忆的概念时都曾强调过，感知和记忆都是反映客观现实的，其源泉和内容都来源于客观现实，通过想象形成的新形象有些是离奇古怪、荒诞不经的，如孙悟空、猪八戒、美人鱼等，这些形象在现实生活中是不存在的，这是不是说想象是脱离客观现实的呢？当然不是。任何一种心理现象都是来源于客观现实的。生活中没有孙悟空、猪八戒，但生活中有猴子、有猪、有人，将这些事物进行粘合，就创造出了生活中不存在的事物的新形象。因此，归根结底，想象依旧是建立在客观现实的基础上。此外，想象的具体内容还要受到一定社会历史条件的制约，带有一定的时代性。如孙悟空虽神通广大，手中的金箍棒可大可小，变化无穷，但毕竟是一根棒，而非机关枪、手枪等现代化武器，铁臂阿童木、超人都反映了不同时代科技发展的水平。想象具有时代性，不管想象出来的形象是多么奇特、荒诞不经，它们都是立足于客观现实的。

四、想象的品质

（一）想象的主动性

想象的主动性是指想象的积极性与目的明确性程度如何。想象的主动性良好的人，在一切活动中都积极主动地展开想象，看到现实中不满意、不合理、不科学的东西，便产生一种强烈的创造想象的欲望和动机，以积极的态度进行必要的知识积累和丰富的表象储备，能紧紧围绕所确定的主题和目的去积极思维，有计划、有步骤地展开自己的想象，并保持一定的方向，因而能比较顺利地取得成果。想象主动性差的人，对周围的事物缺乏敏感,抱残守缺,难以展开想象。即使展开了想象,也缺乏知识的准备,头脑中没有想象目的的稳固的表象,在想象过程中,常常东想西想,脱离主题,想象如同出笼的小鸟,漫天飞翔,新形象虽形形色色,但杂乱无章,不能实现创造的目的。

(二) 想象的丰富性

想象的丰富性是指想象内容的广阔性和充实性程度。想象丰富的人,能根据想象主题的要求,在广泛的领域和范围内展开多角度、多侧面、全方位的想象,从而产生出大量的新形象。如曹雪芹在《红楼梦》中成功地塑造了大观园里众多形态各异的人物群像,以及荣、宁两府奢侈豪华的生活情景,这些均反映出作者超人的想象丰富性。想象贫乏的人,其想象总是局限在狭小的范围内,内容也空泛、肤浅、平淡无奇。

(三) 想象的深刻性

想象的深刻性是指新形象反映事物本质的正确性和深透性程度。想象深刻的人,通过想象所产生的新形象是理性概括的,具有典型性的,因而能够反映客观事物的本质。文学家、艺术家塑造的一些典型人物的艺术形象,往往都十分深刻地反映了社会生活的某些本质方面,它给予人们的教益不亚于理论性的教科书。例如,曹植创作的"煮豆燃豆萁,豆在釜中泣;本是同根生,相煎何太急"痛斥曹丕对他的迫害,寓意深刻,感人肺腑。又如,有的漫画仅寥寥几笔,形象也不复杂,却寓意极深,这都是想象深刻性的表现。想象深刻性差的人,即使创造了新形象,也往往是感性的概括,缺乏典型性,没有代表性,不能由个别反映一般,由现象反映本质。

(四) 想象的新颖性

想象的新颖性是指想象的新异性和独特性程度。想象的新颖性程度强的人,想象所依据的表象是多种多样的,且又对其进行了复杂的改造,所产生的新形象与原型差别甚大,是前所未有、独特奇异的新形象。例如,一个中学生在作文中写道:"未来汽车都会装有一个'心情调色盒',它可以根据车主的心情而改变汽车的颜色。如果车主的心情很低落,汽车就会变成鲜艳的红色;如果车主刚下班,很疲劳,汽车就会变成清新、舒畅的绿色,使车主感觉自己仿佛置身于美丽的大草原上。如果你要到任何一个地方,只要说清楚详细地点,汽车就会自动向目标开去,并且是水陆空三用的。车上的雷达可以探测出路线上的障碍物,以免发生碰撞。"对于一个中学生来说,这种别开生面、独具匠心的想象,就表现了较好的新颖性品质。想象新颖性程度差的人,其想象囿于表象,因循守旧,"依葫芦画瓢",缺乏新意。

(五) 想象的清晰性

想象的清晰性是指新形象的鲜明性和生动性程度。想象清晰性程度良好的人,想象某一事物时,犹如在头脑里"看见了""听到了""闻到了"一样,活灵活现、惟妙惟肖。屠格涅夫写《父与子》时,仿佛自己就是巴扎洛夫,每天给他记日记;罗曼·罗兰为《约翰·克里斯朵夫》的主人公的命运担忧,以致每写一章都要白一些头发;福楼拜在《包法利夫人》的创作中,整日沉浸于所描写的情景中,当写到包法利夫人最后服毒自杀时,竟感到自己嘴里有砒霜的味道。这皆体现了作者想象的清晰性。想象清晰性程度差的人,头脑里出现的新形象常常是暗淡的、模糊的、片断的和不稳定的。

（六）想象的现实性

想象的现实性是指想象与现实的相关性程度。想象的现实性良好的人，能把自己的想象植根于现实之中，尽管可能超越现实，然而却是符合现实的要求和现实的发展方向的，且具有一定的社会价值，经过充分发挥能动作用，想象可以变为现实。想象现实性差的人，无视现实，想入非非，脱离实际，想象只是一些漂亮的肥皂泡，转瞬即逝。

五、想象的基本形式

想象过程是对形象的分析综合过程，它主要有下面几种形式。

（一）粘合

粘合是指把客观事物中从未结合过的属性、特征在头脑中结合在一起而形成新的形象。通过这种粘合活动，人们创造了许多童话和神话中的形象，如孙悟空、猪八戒、美人鱼等。这种创造都是将客观事物的某些特征分析出来，然后按照人们的要求，将这些特点重新配置，综合起来，构成了人们所渴望的形象，以满足人们的某种需要。

（二）夸张

夸张又称为强调，是指通过改变客观事物的正常特点，或者突出某些特点而略去另一些特点进而形成新的形象。如千手观音、九头鸟等形象，都是运用夸张而形成的想象，而漫画则是运用强调手段，着重突出事物的主要特征或者着重显示事物的某些方面。

（三）典型化

典型化是根据某类事物的共同特征创造新形象的过程，如在艺术构思中的各种装饰图案画中的花瓣、树叶等形象，就是来自各种植物的共同特征。布匹、瓷碗、小兜、暖水瓶等上面的图案，也是来自自然界的典型代表物。文学作品中人物形象的创造也是如此，作家往往是综合人物的典型特征之后创造人物形象的。

（四）拟人化

拟人化是把人类的特点、特性加在外界事物上，使之人格化的过程。例如童话故事中的小猫、小狗都会说话，自然界中刮风、下雨、闪电、打雷等现象也用"风婆""龙王""电母""雷公"等形象出现，这都是运用拟人化的方式创造出来的。

（五）联想

联想是由一个事物想到另一个事物的过程，它也可以创造新的形象。联想的活动方向服从于创作时占优势的情绪、思想和意图。某人在某种情绪状态下，由看到修理钟表联想到修理时间，进而联想到修理年代，这是一种异乎寻常的联想，它打破了日常联想的习惯，因而引发了新的形象。

第三节
想象的种类

根据想象时有无预定目的，可把想象分为无意想象和有意想象两种，再根据想象的新颖性、创造性的不同，把有意想象分为再造想象、创造想象、幻想三种。

一、无意想象

无意想象（involuntary imagination）也称不随意想象，它是人们在意识减弱时不由自主产生的一种想象。它没有特定的目的，只是在外部刺激的作用下自然而然进行的想象。例如，当我们抬头仰望天空中变幻莫测的浮云时，脑中就产生起伏的山峦、柔软的棉花、活动的羊群、嘶鸣的奔马等形象；当我们看到北方冬季玻璃上的冰花时，就会觉得它像梅花，像树叶等，这些都是无意想象的表现形式。梦是在睡眠状态下产生的一种正常的心理现象，是无意想象的极端形式。人在睡眠时，整个大脑皮层处于一种弥漫性的抑制状态，但仍有少部分神经细胞兴奋活跃，由于意识控制力的减弱，这些记载着往日经验的细胞便不随意地、不规则地结合在一起，形成了一个个离奇古怪、荒诞绝伦的梦境。不过"日有所思，夜有所梦"，无论梦境多么离奇，它仍然来源于客观现实，是对个体生活一种典型的无意想象。当人以全副精力投入到创造性活动中时，梦可能给人以启示，促进发明创造活动的顺利进行。

专栏 5-3

梦境究竟是什么

在生活中的每一个平常的夜晚，你都会进入到另外一个世界，这就是梦境。在过去，梦境是哲学家、通灵者和心理分析师才去研究的领域，而现在梦境已经成为了科学工作者们一个极其重要的研究领域。然而，梦境的实质究竟是什么，学者们还存在着争论。

精神分析学派的代表人物弗洛伊德和荣格（如图 5-3 所示）认为梦是潜意识过程的显现，是通向潜意识的最可靠的路径。或者说，梦是被压抑的潜意识冲动和愿望以改变的形式出现在意识中，这些冲动和愿望主要是人的性本能和攻击本能的反映。

霍布森从生理学的观点出发，认为梦的本质是我们对脑的随机神经活动的主观体验，这种神经活动完全没有逻辑联系，也不存在任何内在的含义。

——理查德·格里格（Richard J. Gerrig），菲利普·津巴多（Philip G. Zimbardo）. 心理学与生活[M]. 王垒，王甦，等，译. 北京：人民邮电出版社，2003：146—148.

图 5-3 荣格

荣格（Carl Gustav Jung, 1875—1961），瑞士心理学家。曾任国际心理分析学会会长、国际心理治疗协会主席等，他创立了荣格心理学学院，创立了人格分析心理学理论，提出"情结"的概念，把人格分为内倾和外倾两种，主张把人格分为意识、个人无意识和集体无意识三层。主要著作有《心理分析理论》《心理类型》《人类及其象征》等。

二、有意想象

有意想象（voluntary imagination）也称随意想象，是指有预定目的，在意识的控制下，自觉进行的想象。科学家提出的各种假设，文学艺术家在头脑中构思的人物形象，都是有意想象的结果。按新颖性、独立性和创造性程度的不同，有意想象又可以分为再造想象、创造想象、幻想。

（一）再造想象

再造想象（reproductive imagination）是根据言语的描述或图样的示意在头脑中产生有关事物新形象的心理过程。如我们看鲁迅先生的《孔乙己》时，头脑中出现穿长衫、站着喝酒的人物形象；机械制造工人根据图纸想象出机器的主要结构；人们看到祖国地形图，头脑中产生我国山川、湖泊、河流、公路、铁路、高原、平原的形象等，都属于再造想象。

再造想象产生的新形象是相对的，对于想象者来说是新的，而实际上是已经存在的事物形象。但是，再造想象仍然有一定的创造性。由于每个人的知识、经验、个性特征等主观因素的不同，再造想象的内容和创造水平必然有一定的差异。

再造想象对人类的各种实践活动，尤其是学习活动具有重要的意义。通过再造想象，可以帮助人们摆脱狭小的生活圈子，生动形象地认识自己没有感知过的或不可能直接感知的事物，扩大认识范围，充实主观世界。在教学过程中，教师通过生动形象的语言表述或图表、模型的演示，可以使学生通过再造想象在头脑中形成与概念相应的形象，从而深刻地理解教材，牢固地掌握知识。

形成正确的再造想象有赖于两个条件：一是正确理解语词的描述和图样、符号标志的意义。不懂外语的人，无法在头脑中形成外语作品中描绘的人物、场景的形象。在教学中，教师一方面要正确地运用语言，形象生动地描述事物或现象，另一方面还要有意识地进行各种符号的教学，促使学生把符号与相应形象结合起来；二是丰富的表象储备。有关表象储备越丰富，再造想象就越准确和充实。如果缺乏相应的表象储备，我们就不能进行顺利的再造想象。不论我们如何向一个先天性盲人描述朝霞的美丽，他也是无法想象的，因为他的头脑中没有颜色的表象，没有形状的表象。因此，教师要有计划地组织学生参观、访问、调查、进行实验操作等，并创造条件，尽可能地使用现代化教学手段，以丰富学生的表象。

再造想象的能力在我们的生活中是一种很重要的能力,它是我们理解和掌握知识所必不可少的。因为知识多半是间接经验,主要是以语言文字为载体来传授的,我们要达到真正的理解,就必须在头脑中形成与这些间接经验相应的事物的形象,否则,便不能真正的掌握。再造想象也是实现人与人之间的正常交流的重要条件。依靠再造想象,我们能够领会他人所说的话的含义,能够设身处地地想到他人的处境,人与人之间就可实现正常的交流、沟通和理解。

(二)创造想象

创造想象(creative imagination)是根据一定的目的、任务,在头脑中独立地创造出前所未有的新形象的心理过程。飞机设计师在头脑中构成一架新型飞机的形象;作家在头脑中构成新的典型人物形象等都属于创造想象。这些形象不是根据别人的描述,而是想象者根据生活提供的素材,在头脑中通过创造性地综合而形成的具有重大社会价值的新形象。

创造想象具有独立性、首创性、新颖性的特点,是人类创造性活动不可缺少的心理成分。无论是科学的发明,还是文艺创作,都必须首先在头脑中形成活动的最终或中间产品的模型,即进行创造想象,可见,创造想象是创造性活动的必要环节。没有创造想象,创造性活动就难以顺利进行。创造想象是一种比再造想象更复杂的智力活动,它的产生有赖于社会实践的需要、创造者强烈的创造欲望、丰富的表象储备、高水平的表象改造能力以及积极的思维活动等主、客观条件。

第一,要有急切的创造欲望和动机,这是激发创造想象的内部动力和首要条件。我们生活在一个急剧发展变化的社会当中,社会本身不断向人们提出创新的要求,这些要求一旦被人们所接受,将会极大地激发起个人的创造欲望和动机。

第二,广博的知识和丰富的表象储备是创造想象的前提和基础。创造想象不是一个凭空进行的过程,它也需要依赖我们头脑中储存的事物的表象和知识来进行。倘若没有丰富的知识和表象储备,曹雪芹是不可能创作出《红楼梦》这部鸿篇巨著的。爱因斯坦能够在物理学上取得伟大成就,与他从小广泛涉猎多种科学领域的经历是分不开的。

第三,积极的思维活动是创造想象的关键。创造想象不是一个凭主观愿望而胡思乱想的过程,而是在思维的参与和调节下有序地展开的。不善于积极的思考,不善于认识事物的本质和规律性联系,就不会有任何的创造想象。

第四,原型启发是创造想象的起点。我们进行发明创造时,任何一个新形象都不

专栏 5-4

缪斯必须是有形的,你在接下来的十年甚至二十年的时光中,必须坚持每天写一千字,试着让你的缪斯开始显形。学习足够多的文法,学习构建一个故事,让这个过程变成潜意识里的一部分,才不会遏制或者扭曲缪斯。好好生活,观察你的生活,养成良好的阅读习惯,探索你所阅读的内容,用来养育你最原始的缪斯。时时刻刻练习你的写作,反复训练、模仿,便能够打造出一个留住缪斯的洁净光明的空间。你需

> 要让她、他或者它，随便你怎么称呼，有空间去释放。训练过程中，你已经能放松自己，在灵感来临时，它便会自然地进入这个空间。
> ——雷·布雷德伯里（Ray Bradbury）.写作的禅机[M].巨超，译.南昌：江西人民出版社，2019：42.

是凭空捏造出来的，总要受到类似事物或模型的启发，我们就把这些类似事物或模型称为原型。原型对人们的创造发明有着重要的启发作用。如木工用的锯据说就是鲁班受锯齿草的启发而发明的。

（三）幻想

幻想（fantasy）是与个人的生活愿望相联系并指向未来的想象。

幻想是创造想象的准备阶段和特殊形式。它不同于再造想象，因为它比再造想象的创造性强。它也不同于一般的创造想象，区别在于：一方面，幻想与个人愿望相联系，幻想的事物是个人所追求、向往和憧憬的东西，而一般的创造想象不一定是创造者所赞美、向往的形象；另一方面，幻想不与当前的创造性活动直接相联系，不一定产生创造成果，仅是指向未来创造活动的前奏和准备，而一般的创造想象与创造性活动紧密相关。

根据幻想的社会价值和有无实现的可能性，可把幻想分为积极的幻想和消极的幻想。积极的幻想是根据事物的发展规律，并具有一定的社会价值和实现可能的幻想，一般称为理想。它是人前进的灯塔，能使人展望到未来美好的前景，激发人的信心和斗志，鼓舞人顽强地克服困难。而消极的幻想违背客观事物发展规律，且毫无实现的可能，一般称为空想。它是一种无益的幻想，常使人脱离现实，想入非非，以无益的想象代替实际行动，害怕艰苦的劳动和逃避困难。因此，在教学过程中，应重视青少年的理想教育，使他们从小树立远大崇高的理想。

第四节

想象规律在教育教学中的应用

一、在教学中发展学生的再造想象

再造想象在学生的学习过程中具有重要作用。

首先,学生可以借助教师在教学过程中的言语、教具、模型等,引起再造想象,形成与掌握自己不曾感知过或无法亲自感知的事物的形象。教师可以通过正确的语言描述和图像展示等,帮助学生利用再造想象去认识事物,了解宇宙、预见未来以及展现将来的生活场景等。

其次,再造想象是学生理解和掌握客观事物规律与内在联系必不可少的心理条件。掌握知识,获得经验,必须要有积极的再造想象。

最后,再造想象是思想教育的重要形式之一。用生动的语言对英雄人物、劳动模范、科学家等进行描述,可以在学生脑海中形成鲜明的榜样形象,从而加强思想品德教育的效果。

在教学中发展学生的再造想象,首先,扩大学生脑海中的表象储备。学生的记忆表象储备越多,展开再造想象的内容就越丰富。其次,帮助学生理解语言、模型等描述性关键词与实物标志的含义,以引起学生的再造想象。最后,唤起学生对教材内容的再造想象,由此加深对所学知识的理解和巩固。

二、在教学中培养学生的创造想象

创造想象是学生在目前和将来从事创造性活动的重要心理条件。在教学活动中,教师要通过课堂教学有意识地培养学生的创造性想象能力。

(一)丰富学生的表象储备

创造想象的程度与水平主要是由表象的数量与质量决定的。教师在教育教学活动过程中要创设条件,采取多种手段和运用不同方法来丰富学生的表象储备,改进表象的质量,以提高学生的创造性想象能力。要引导学生学会观察,获得感性经验,不断丰富学生的表象。表象是想象的基础,表象贫乏,想象也会枯竭。正确使用直观教具、引导学生深入地观察和分析事物,就能不断丰富学生的表象以发展其想象力。例如,在观察与实地考察的基础上,逐渐形成地形、地貌的鲜明而生动的表象,这正是学生形成"胸怀祖国,放眼世界"丰富想象力的基础。

(二)扩大学生的知识经验

想象并不是凭空产生的,它是人脑对客观现实的主观反映,除了需要有丰富的表象储备作为基础,还需要大量的知识与经验。人的知识经验越丰富,越广博,想象力就越丰富。为此,教师要鼓励学生在努力学习各科知识,打下坚实的理论知识基础的同时,广泛涉猎课外有益书籍,获得多学科、多领域的知识,并要积极参加各种课外活动。引导学生积极参加科技、文艺、体育活动等,不断丰富学生的生活经验,都能为发展想象力创造良好的条件。

(三)进行想象力训练

教师要结合各学科的教学活动,有目的地训练学生的想象力。例如:在上语文课时,可以让学生带着感情朗读课文,鼓励他们通过想象,体会作品中主人公的思想和感情,想象作品中叙述的事情发生的缘由以及可能的发展趋势;指导学生阅读健康有益的课外书籍,书籍是培养学生创造性想象的最好材料,通过书中的文字描述,能够发展学生的再造性想象,同时也能发展和激发学生的创造性想象;在音乐课上,歌词与乐曲也是激发学生情感和创造性想象的重要方式;开展绘画、手工雕刻、科技小制作以及文艺演出等活动,亦是培养和提高学生想象力的有效途径。引导学生积极思考，打开想象力的大门。想象和思维是紧密联系的。在教学和实践活动中，引导学生多问几个"为什么"，大胆探索，发展好奇心和广泛的兴趣与爱好，可以逐步打开想象力的大门，并发展学生的创造想象的能力。

（四）引导学生积极幻想

理想是符合事物发展规律、能够实现的幻想。积极的幻想对学生的学习生活具有直接推动作用。教师要把学生的幻想与学生的实际生活有机结合起来，既要培养学生具有远大的崇高理想，把自己的学习与祖国的现代化建设相结合，也要培养他们的科学幻想，鼓励学生从小具有向科学进军的志气和勇气，激励他们去发明创造。培养学生大胆幻想和善于幻想的能力，也具有重要意义。敢想是敢做的起点，幻想是创造活动的必要条件。对于学生的幻想，不要讽刺讥笑，应珍视、鼓励、引导，帮助他们把幻想转变成理想，把幻想同创造想象结合起来。

本章小结

表象是指人脑对感知过的事物的形象的反映；根据不同标准，可以将表象分为不同种类；表象有直观性、概括性、可操作性三个特征。表象能为概念的形成提供感性基础，能促进问题的解决；想象具有主动性、丰富性、深刻性、新颖性、清晰性和现实性的品质；想象有粘合、夸张、典型化、拟人化和联想五种形式；想象是人脑对已有表象进行加工改造、重新组合形成新形象的心理过程；想象是人类劳动的必要因素，可以使人的认识领域得到无限开拓与延伸，还有预见和替代的作用；想象是立足于客观现实的；想象根据不同标准，可以分为不同种类；再造想象在学生的学习过程中具有重要作用，在教学中培养学生的创造想象要做到丰富学生的表象储备、扩大学生的知识经验、进行想象力训练和引导学生积极幻想；在教学和实践活动中培养学生的想象力。

关键术语

表象　想象　无意想象　有意想象　幻想

讨论与应用

1. 阅读以下材料，分析其中所表现的想象的种类是什么？

材料一：苯在1825年就被发现了，此后几十年间，人们一直不知道它的结构。因为实在难以想像6个碳原子和6个氢原子怎么能够完全对称地排列、形成稳定的分子。1864年冬的某一天，德国化学家凯库勒坐在壁炉前打了个瞌睡，原子和分子们开始在幻觉中跳舞，一条碳原子链像蛇一样咬住自己的尾巴，在他眼前旋转。凯库勒明白了苯分子是一个环——一个六角形的圈圈。

材料二：在一口不深的井里，住着一条鱼和一只青蛙。它们俩是好朋友，都想出去看看。青蛙在外面周游一番回来了，它告诉鱼："外面有许多新奇有趣的东西。比如说牛吧，它的身体很大，头上长着两只弯弯的犄角，以吃青草为生，身上有着黑白相间的斑块，肚子下面长着四只粗壮的腿……"鱼听着听着,这时,在它的脑海里,出现了"鱼牛"的形象。

材料三:夏日的一天,许多小孩子在荷花塘边玩,一个孩子摘了一张荷叶,倒过来顶在脑袋上。鲁班看见了,觉得挺好玩,就问他:"你头上顶着荷叶干什么呀?"小孩子说:"太阳像个大火轮,顶着荷叶,就不怕晒了。"鲁班抓过一片荷叶来,仔细瞧了又瞧,朝头上一罩,又轻巧,又凉快。鲁班赶紧跑回家去,找了一根竹子,劈成许多细细的条,照着荷叶的样子,扎了个架子;又找了一块羊皮,把它剪得圆圆的,蒙在竹架子上。鲁班把刚做成的东西递给妻子,说:"你以后出门去带着它,就不怕雨淋太阳晒了。"鲁班的妻子瞧了瞧说:"不错不错,不过,雨停了,太阳下山了,还拿着这么个东西,可不方便了。要是能把它收起来,那才好呢。"鲁班就跟妻子一起动手,把这东西改成可以活动的:用的时候就撑开,不用的时候就收拢。这就是咱们今天的伞。

2. 请根据以下资料提供的线索,阅读《写作的禅机》并分析作者发展其创造想象的条件有哪些?

雷·布雷德伯里(Ray Bradbury,1920—2012),美国科幻小说家、散文家、剧作家、编剧、诗人,是二十世纪最伟大的作家之一。其代表作中的《华氏451》被美国国会图书馆选入"二十世纪最有影响力的一百本小说",并由法国著名导演弗朗索瓦·特吕弗拍成同名电影。《写作的禅机》是布雷德伯里所著的教你如何从头开始写作的书,也被美国《作家》杂志选入"十大最佳写作指导书"。该书共收录了12篇作品。它告诉读者,灵感从来不是人的天赋,可以通过后天养成;它还告诉读者如何养育灵感,如何用好的养育让灵感源源不绝……该书坦露的关于灵感和写作的秘密,对每一个写作者都非常实用。

第六章 思维

SIWEI

　　亲爱的同学,思维在生活中经常被我们提到,它是一种高级的认知过程。前面我们学习的感知觉只能反映客观事物的外部特征及其外在的相互联系,而要深入到客观事物内部,认识客观事物的本质属性及其内在的规律性联系,则要调动我们的高级认知过程——思维。那么,思维是什么呢?它有哪些种类,它的过程和形式又有哪些呢?请翻开本章,在阅读学习中寻找它们的答案吧。

通过本章的学习,你能够
- 理解思维的概念、特征、种类、品质
- 了解思维的一般过程和思维的形式
- 理解问题解决的过程、策略以及影响因素
- 了解思维规律在教育教学中的应用

【本章结构】

本章主要回答"有关思维的问题"。对思维的基本概念、种类、基本过程和思维的形式以及问题解决和创造性思维等进行了分析,最后探讨了怎样将思维规律运用到教学中去。

第一节

思维概述

一、思维的概念和特征

(一)思维的概念

思维(thinking)是人脑对客观现实间接和概括的反映。也可以说思维是人以已有的知识经验为中介,对客观事物的本质属性和规律性联系的间接和概括的反映。如我们通过对各种鸟的观察认识,对"鸟"的本质特征进行抽象、归纳,"鸟"的共同特征是"有羽毛""卵生""脊椎动物",从而得出鸟的概念,这就是思维的表现。

虽然思维与前一章讲的感知觉一样,都是人脑对客观事物的反映,但思维与感知觉又有根本的区别。从反映的内容来看,感知觉反映的是事物的个别的属性、表面的现象及事物之间的外部联系;而思维反映的是客观事物的共同的、本质的属性和事物的内部规律性及其必然联系。从反映的形式来看,感知觉属于感性认识,是对客观事物外部特征的直接反映;而思维属于理性认识,是对客观事物内在的必然联系的反映。思维和感知觉也有联系:感知觉是认识的低级阶段,是思维的源泉和基础;而思维是认识的高级阶段,是感知觉的进一步深化,在人的认识过程中处于核心地位。

通过感知觉,我们认识到事物的表面特征和表面联系;通过思维,我们获得对事物的本身特征与内在联系的认识。由感知觉到思维,实现了认识由感性到理性的飞跃,从而使我们对世界的认识达到一个更高的层次。

(二)思维的特征

思维具有概括性和间接性两个基本特征。

1. 概括性

思维的概括性是指思维能够把同类事物的共同的、本质的属性抽取出来加以概括,反映事物间的规律性联系。思维的概括性包括两层含义:第一,思维所反映的对象总是一类事物共同的本质特征和它们之间的规律性联系。如我们认识到水分子是由两个氢原子和一个氧原子构成的,它不仅指江河湖海里的水,也指我们饮用的水。这就是说,思维把握的是一类事物的共同特征,而不限于个别事物的个别特征。第二,人通过思维能从部分事物相互联系的事实中找到普遍的或必然的联系,并将其推广到同类现象中去。如借助思维,人可以认识温度的升降与金属胀缩的关系。这种概括促进人对客观事物的内在关系与规律的认识,有助于人们对现实环境的控制与改造。

2. 间接性

思维的间接性是指思维总是以一定事物为媒介来反映那些不能直接作用于感官的事

物。思维的间接性主要体现在三个方面：首先，思维可通过事物认识事物。如人们不能直接感知猿人的生活情景，但是考古学家通过化石可以思考古老的过去，复现出猿人的形象和当时的生活情景。其次，思维可通过事物的外部特征认识其内部变化及内在联系。如医生根据体温、血液、脉搏的变化与病人自诉等，就能诊断直接观察不到的病人内部器官的状态。最后，思维可通过语言和词反映有关事实，预测事物发展变化的进程等。正是由于思维的间接性，人们才可能超越时空的限制，认识那些没有感知或不可能直接感知的事物属性，揭露事物的本质、规律，从而了解过去，认识现在，预见未来。

思维的间接性和概括性是相互联系、相互促进的，人们通过抽象、概括，反映事物的本质属性及内在的规律性联系，然后再依靠思维活动获得的概念、法则、理论，通过推理判断，进行间接反映，从而使人的认识更加深刻。

二、思维的种类

（一）直观动作思维、具体形象思维和抽象逻辑思维

这种分类主要是根据思维的发展水平和思维的凭借物来进行划分的。

1. 直观动作思维

直观动作思维又称动作思维（action thinking），思维的凭借物依赖于实际的动作，动作停止，思维就无法继续。例如，摩托车出了问题，人们必须通过检查摩托车的相应部件，才能确定是车胎没气了，还是没油了。只有找出故障进行修理，才能排除故障。这种通过实际操作解决直观具体问题的思维活动，就是直观动作思维。3岁前的婴儿只能在动作中思考，他们的思维基本上属于直观动作思维。婴儿只有摆弄玩具才能玩耍，动作停止，他们的思维也就停止了。成人有时也要运用表象和动作进行思维，但这种直观动作思维的水平要比幼儿的直观动作思维高。

2. 具体形象思维

具体形象思维（concrete image thinking）是指人们利用头脑中的具体形象（表象）来解决问题。在幼儿期和小学低年级，儿童思维的主要形式是具体形象思维。例如，幼儿园大班的孩子在解答"3+5=？"时候，往往借助于具体的实物或者图片，比如手指、木棒或者图片中的小鸡等形象。艺术家、作家、导演、设计师等更多地运用形象思维。

3. 抽象逻辑思维

当人们面对理论性质的任务，并要运用概念、判断、推理等形式来解决问题时，这种思维称为抽象逻辑思维（abstract logic thinking）。例如，学生学习各种科学知识，科学工作者从事科学研究都要运用这种思维。幼儿在六岁左右出现抽象逻辑思维的萌芽，之后不断发展。

（二）经验思维和理论思维

1. 经验思维

人们凭借日常生活经验进行的思维活动叫做经验思维（empirical thinking）。例如，学前儿童根据他们的经验，认为"动物园里的都是动物""鸟是会飞的动物"，这些都属于

经验思维。由于知识经验的不足,这种思维易产生片面性,甚至得出错误或曲解的结论。

2. 理论思维

理论思维(theoretical thinking)是根据科学的概念和论断,判断某事物,解决某个问题。例如,我们说"心理是客观现实在人脑中的主观映象",就是理论思维的结果。这种思维活动往往能抓住事物的本质,使问题得到正确的解决。

(三)直觉思维和分析思维

1. 直觉思维

直觉思维(intuitive thinking)是人们在面临新的问题、事物和现象时,能迅速理解并作出判断的思维活动。这是一种直接的领悟性的思维活动,也是长期知识积累的结果。例如,科学家对某些偶然出现的现象,提出猜想或假说就属于直觉思维。直觉思维具有快速性、跳跃性、非逻辑性等特点。

2. 分析思维

分析思维也就是逻辑思维(logical thinking),它遵循严密的逻辑规律,逐步推导,最后得出合乎逻辑的正确答案或做出合理的结论。我们在解数学题的时候,较多采用的是分析思维。

(四)辐合思维和发散思维

1. 辐合思维

辐合思维(convergent thinking)又称为聚合思维,是指人们根据已知的信息,利用熟悉的规则解决问题。也就是从给予的信息中,产生合乎逻辑的结论,它是一种有方向、有范围、有条理的思维方式,往往有唯一的标准答案。例如,小明比小红高,小红比小亮高,问谁最高?回答这种问题时,运用的往往是辐合思维。

2. 发散思维

发散思维(divergent thinking)又称为辐射思维,是指人们沿着不同的方向思考,重新组织当前的信息和记忆系统中存储的信息,产生大量、独特的新思想。例如,如何保护城市的生态环境?回答这样问题的人们可以从不同的方向思考,想出诸如增加植被、减少环境污染、教育市民爱护环境等措施。这种思维方式在解决问题时,可以产生多种答案、结论或假说。但究竟哪种答案最好,则需要经过检验。

(五)常规思维与创造性思维

1. 常规思维

常规思维是指人们运用已获得的知识经验,按现成的方案和程序直接解决问题。如学生运用老师教的例题模仿解答类似条件的题目。这种思维的创造性水平低,对原有的知识不需要进行明显的改组,也没有创造出新的思维成果,因而称之为常规思维或再造性思维(reproductive thinking)。

2. 创造性思维

创造性思维(productive thinking)是指重新组织已有的知识经验,提出新的方案或程序,并创造出具有社会价值的、新颖的思维成果的思维活动。如伽利略的"自由落体定律"和达尔文的"生物进化学说"等划时代的理论,都是创造性思维的体现。创造性思维是人类思维的高级形式。许多心理学家认为,创造性思维是多种思维的综合表现。它既是发散思维与辐合思维的结合,也是直觉思维与分析思维的结合,它包括理论思维,又离不开创造想象等。

创造性思维的主要成分是发散思维,因此一般认为发散思维的特点也是创造性思维的特点。创造性思维具有三个特征:流畅性、变通性、独特性。

(1)流畅性

流畅性是指心理活动畅通无阻,灵敏迅速,能根据目的任务的要求,在短时间内联想到大量的事物。在限定的时间内说出的观念数量越多,越流畅。流畅性是发散思维最低层次的一个特征,它体现的往往是思维的数量。自由回忆是测量流畅性最常用的方法,如用汉字组词,要求用最后一个字组成下一个新词。如,从"幸福"这个词开始,可以自由回忆为:福气—气候—候鸟—鸟类—类别—别离—离开—开车—车窗……

(2)变通性

变通性是指思考问题时能随机应变,举一反三,触类旁通,不易受思维定势的影响,能产生超常的构想,提出不同凡响的新观点。这是发散思维较高层次的一个特性。如说出砖块的用途,如果只想到它在建筑方面的功能,不善于变通,所获得的答案的数量必然有限。相反,说出砖块除了可以盖屋修墙外,还可以用作自卫的武器,用来打狗、打坏人,可用作敲打的工具,往墙上钉钉子。这样一来,思维在不同的方向、范围内发散,变通性就大了。

(3)独特性

独特性是指能从前所未有的角度、观点去认识事物,提出超出一般人的某些独特的思想和见解。这是发散思维的最高层次的特性,它常常突破常规和经验的束缚,提出独到见解。比如,说圆形的东西有老鼠洞、小水珠;砖块可用作颜料等。人们往往用"亏你想得出来"来评价某个人的思维的独特性。

专栏6-1

创造力

"创新是一个民族的灵魂,是一个国家兴旺发达的动力。自20世纪50年代吉尔福德和托兰斯等人开始对创造力(creativity)进行心理学研究以来,这方面的研究工作越来越丰富。这些研究不仅触及个体因素,如创造性人格、创造性思维过程、创造性思维的测量和阶段等问题,也已逐渐扩展到创造性思维的脑科学基础、创造潜能的开发以及创造性思维的训练等文化和社会因素更为深入的问题。

美国心理学家加德纳(Gardner,1993)曾调查分析20世纪有着杰出创造的重要人物,其中包括弗洛伊德(心理学家)、爱因斯坦(物理学家)、毕加索(画家)、葛兰姆(舞蹈家)、艾略特(诗人)、甘地(思想家)等,发现有以下几点相似之处:① 有反传统倾向,对众所信守的传统规范存疑,因而在个人作为上不墨守成规,总想有所改进而臻于更新更好的境界;②对自己关心的问题肯深入钻研,在展现出超人的杰出成就之前,对相关问题研究所付出的心力至少连续了10年甚至20年;③在年轻时多半受到前人思想的启发及师长的指导与鼓励,因而立志上进,历经无数挫折失败,而终告成功;④个人生活感情层面较少,多半时间用于潜心研究,甚少享受安适的家庭生活。

  国内的研究中,童秀英和沃建中(2002)的研究发现,我国高中生创造性思维水平发展比较平缓,其中创造性思维最重要的品质即独特性在高一和高二之间发展较为平稳,但高三比高二有显著提高。谢光辉和张庆林(1995)曾对32名中国大学生实用科技发明大奖赛获奖者的人格特征进行研究,发现了低乐群性、高敏感性、高独立性和高自律性的特征。最近,李金珍等(2004)以9—16岁的中小学生为研究对象,采用实用创造力测验任务,探查了儿童创造力的发展特点。结果发现,儿童的创造力随年龄发展逐渐提高,但创造力新颖性、流畅性和变通性三个维度的发展并不均衡,流畅性和变通性在9—11岁比其他年龄阶段发展得更快。另外,家庭环境对于儿童的创造力有直接影响,也有间接影响,其中间接影响是通过影响创造性态度而得以实现的。胡卫平等(2004)将中学生科学创造力测验施测于英国6所中学的1190名青少年及中国2所中学的1087名青少年,对中英青少年科学创造力的发展进行了比较研究。结果发现:①青少年的科学创造力存在显著的年龄差异。随着年龄的增大,青少年的科学创造力呈持续上升趋势,但在14岁时下降;11—13岁、14—16岁是青少年的科学创造力迅速发展的关键时期。②青少年的科学创造力存在性别差异。英国女生的科学创造力比男生强,差异显著;中国男生的科学创造力比女生强,差异不显著。③中英青少年的科学创造力存在显著的差异。在创造性的问题解决能力方面,中国青少年明显高于英国青少年,但中国青少年在其他方面的科学创造力及总成绩则明显低于英国青少年。④中国青少年的科学创造力存在显著的学校类型差异。重点中学学生的科学创造力显著高于普通中学学生的科学创造力。

  在研究儿童的创造力发展时,有许多心理学家试图将创造性活动纳入认知活动的范畴,把创造性活动看成是智力活动的一个维度。但是,又有越来越多的研究者认识到活动主体的个性因素在创造性活动中起着关键的作用。例如,斯滕伯格(Sternberg,1988)认为,个性中兴趣和动机是人们从事创造性活动的重要驱力,可以驱使个体集中精力于所从事的作业。施建农(1995)认为,个体对创造性作业的态度对个体的智力导入量起到了一种开关作用。一个人的创造性态度越高,越容易投入更多的智力和精力,从而表现出更高的创造性。关于创造力的研究,还有人提出:普通人的创造力与天才的创造力是一个连续的整体,任何具有正常认知能力的人都有可能在某个领域有所创造,或者说常人都具有一定的创造力;所有的个体工作中都包含着某种程度的创造力;虽然在每个领域中都存在着创造性的个体差异,但这种差异不是一成不变的,而是可以通过一定途径使人的创造力得到培养和提高的。

  ——黄希庭,郑涌.心理学导论[M].北京:人民教育出版社,2015:442—443.

三、思维与语言的关系

语言是人类通过高度结构化的声音组合、书写、手势等构成的符号系统。语言既是个人内部思考的工具又是社会交际最重要的工具。

（一）语言与思维的联系

从思维的形式上来看，语言是个体思维活动的工具。语言既是标记（记录）思维活动成果的工具，又是人们互相交流思想的工具。思维的主要特点是概括性，其基本单位是概念。而语言的主要特点也是概括性，其基本单位是词。概念以词为工具而概括地反映客观事物。如，学生在课堂上听讲，是在教师讲课的语言刺激下进行思考。但是语言不是思维的唯一工具，思维也可以借助动作、表象等来进行。

从思维的内容和结果来看，思维是语言的内容，语言是思维的载体。思维借助于语言、词语来实现，语言也要依靠思维的内容和结果来充实和发展，二者密切联系在一起。

从思维的个体发展历史来看，思维与语言不是同步发展的，但是人的高级思维是伴随着语言的产生而逐渐产生、发展和提高的。个体发展过程中，当两岁左右的儿童掌握了语言后，抽象思维才逐渐增多并逐渐成为思维的主要形式。

（二）语言与思维的区别

语言和思维虽然有密切的联系，但是二者有着根本的区别。

从本质属性上来看，语言是人们交际的工具，而思维是人脑对客观事物间接概括的反映。语言是一种符号系统，是思维的物质外壳或思想的直接体现。

从与客观事物的关系来看，思维与外部世界是反映与被反映的关系，语言与外部世界则是标志与被标志的关系。

从规律性的适用范围来看，语言规律有民族性，思维规律则有全人类性。不同民族适用不同的语言，各有其语法规则，相互之间差异很大。而思维的规律性，不管在哪个民族，都是一样的。思维的发展顺序都是先有动作思维，然后出现形象思维，最后出现抽象逻辑思维。

专栏 6-2

语言获得的关键期

关键期（eritical period）是从生物学上确定的一段时间，指一个有机体做好最佳准备以习得某种特殊反应的时间。人类的语言习得有一些关键期。不到1岁的婴儿能辨别任何语言的音素，但在1岁末即已丧失了这种能力。出生后头几个月是磨炼母语音素的关键期。习得第二种语言的发音系统有一个关键期。与成年期习得第二种语言的发音相比较，幼儿期习得的第二种语言在几年之后所讲话语较少带某种口音，在喧闹情境中听这种语言较容易理解（Lenneberg, 1967；Snow, 1987）。

学习句法也有一个关键期,其重要证据是某些不幸儿童的遭遇。他们被禁止学习任何语言直到十几岁时。有个名叫珍妮的女孩,被人发现时已经14岁了。她从出生后20个月起就被绑在椅子上,一直没有人对她说话,也基本上没有社会交往。她的瞎了双眼的母亲匆忙给她喂食。她如果发出声音就要受到惩罚。她不会说话,被发现以后就由语言学家和心理学家们教她语言,但从未习得熟悉的句法。珍妮虽然学会了词并把一些词结合成简单句,却不能把简单句构成灵活的句子。这是因为她错过了学习句法的关键期(Curtiss,1977)。

对一种语言句法结构的理解也似乎有一个关键期。最有力的证据是对成人使用ASL(美国手势语)的研究。在已经使用ASL有30年或更久时间的成年人中,研究者可以清楚地区分出哪些人是在4岁前习得ASL的,哪些人是在4—6岁之间习得ASL的,哪些人是在12岁后习得ASL的。尽管经过了30年的使用,那些在儿童期以后习得ASL者对ASL中有区分性的句法结构的理解还是显得相对肤浅些(Meier,1991; Newport,1990)。

人类的婴儿有专司语言功能的特殊结构,对语言有特殊的敏感性,但如果出生后就与世隔绝,没有听到过说话,没有习得语言的机会,其专司语言功能的特殊结构便发挥不了作用。见诸报端的被人类救回的狼孩、猪孩、狗孩不会说话,只会像狼、狗、猪一样吼叫。他们回到人类社会后虽能学会一些词汇,但不能习得语言。这也表明语言习得有一个关键期。我们要抓住这个关键期,使儿童获得很好的语言能力。

——黄希庭,郑涌.心理学导论[M].北京:人民教育出版社,2015:463—465.

四、思维的品质

人的思维品质存在明显的个别差异,一般说来,良好的思维品质结构有以下特点。

(一)广阔性

广阔性指思路广泛,善于把握事物各方面的联系和关系,善于全面地思考和分析问题。古今中外的大思想家、科学家都具有明显的思维广阔性的品质。与此相反是思维的狭隘性。思维狭隘的人往往片面看问题,只凭有限的知识经验去思考,抓住一点不及其余,容易一叶障目,只见树木,不见森林。

(二)深刻性

深刻性指善于深入地钻研和思考问题,善于区分本质与非本质的特征,能抓住事物的主要矛盾,正确认识与揭示事物的本质规律。具有思维深刻性的大思想家、科学家都能在普遍的、简单的、已经为人所熟悉的现象中发现重大问题,并从中揭示出最重要的规律。与思维的深刻性相反的是思维的肤浅性。思维肤浅的人,在思维过程中往往被事物的表面现象所迷惑,看不到问题的本质,时常对重大问题熟视无睹,轻易放过,满足于一知半解,缺乏洞察力和预见力。

(三) 独立性

思维的独立性指善于独立地发现问题、思考问题、解决问题,不依赖、不盲从、不武断。具有独立性的人,不依赖于现成的答案,善于独立思考,独立发现问题、分析问题,并善于运用新方法、新途径去解决问题。与思维独立性相反的是思维的依赖性。具有依赖性的人遇事不能独立思考,表现为缺乏主见,易受暗示,过分崇拜权威,盲目迷信,人云亦云,常常放弃自己的观点。

(四) 批判性

批判性指一个人能否依据客观标准进行思维并解决问题的品质。具有思维批判性的人,有明确的是非观念,表现为既能正确地评价他人的思维成果,又富有自我批判性;即能坚持正确的东西,又能随时放弃自己曾坚持的错误观点。与思维批判性相反的品质是思维的随意性。思维具有随意性的人考虑问题时往往主观自负,随心所欲地得出结论,评判事物不能坚持客观标准,缺乏自我批判性,易受个人情绪左右,或者遇事随波逐流。

(五) 灵活性

灵活性指思考和解决问题时,思路灵活,不固执己见,善于发散思维,解决问题,足智多谋,随机应变。与灵活性相反的品质是思维的固执性。具有固执性的人表现为固执、刻板,思想僵化、墨守成规。

(六) 敏捷性

敏捷性指思路清晰,解决问题迅速,又能当机立断,不优柔寡断,不轻率从事。郭沫若形容周恩来思考问题"似雷电行空,如水银漫地"就是指这种特点。与思维敏捷性相反的品质是思维的迟钝。这种品质表现为思路堵塞、优柔寡断,在新的情况面前束手无策,一筹莫展。

(七) 逻辑性

思维的逻辑性是指考虑和解决问题时思路鲜明,条理清楚,严格遵循逻辑规律。具体来说,便是提出问题明确,不模棱两可;推理严谨,层次分明;论证充分,有的放矢,有说服力;结论证据确凿。思维的逻辑性反映了一个人思维条理性方面的特点。缺乏思维逻辑性的人,思路混乱且跳跃性大;论点缺乏证据,推理易出现逻辑错误;陈述无顺序性,常出现语无伦次的现象。

第二节
思维的一般过程和形式

一、思维的一般过程

思维是一个非常复杂的心理活动过程。它表现为对作用于人脑的客观事物进行分析、综合、比较、归类、抽象、概括、具体化、系统化等过程,这就是思维过程,也称为思维操作(thinking operation)。其中,分析与综合是思维的基本过程,它贯穿于人的整个思维活动之中,其他过程都是通过分析、综合来实现的,或者说是分析、综合过程的主要环节。

(一)分析与综合

分析是在头脑中把事物的整体分解为部分、方面或个别特征的思维过程。如我们把电脑分解为显示器、机箱、鼠标、键盘等,逐一进行了解;把动物分解为头、尾、足、躯体;把一篇文章分成字、词、句子、段落分别进行讲解等,均属于分析。

综合是在头脑中把事物的各个部分、方面、各种特征结合起来进行考虑的思维过程。如把若干节体操动作组合为一整套广播操来研究其价值;把机器的各种零配件结合成一个整体来考虑其性能;把一个学生的思想品德、智力水平、学业成绩、健康状况等方面联系起来,加以评价,做出结论等,就是综合。

分析与综合有不同的水平,首先,较简单的是动作思维中的分析综合。这是结合具体的操作,在分析具体物体时,把物体的零部件取下来,或者再把它们安装成整体,以考察其功能的思维过程;其次是形象思维中的分析综合。这种分析综合是在头脑中对事物的表象进行分析或联合的思维过程。最后,较复杂的是抽象思维中的分析综合。它是对词语所标志的事物的分析综合,是利用公式定理和原则,在头脑中把某种抽象的知识划分出来或加以联合的思维过程。

(二)比较与归类

比较是在头脑中把各种事物或现象加以对比,确定它们的异同的思维过程。比较的基础是客观事物间的差异性和同一性。正因为事物或现象之间存在着性质上的异同、数量上的多少、形式上的美丑、质量上的好坏等,我们才有可能在思维活动中进行比较。比较可以在同一事物或现象之间进行,也可以在不同类但具有某种关系或联系的事物或现象之间进行。

归类是在人脑中根据客观事物或现象的共同点和差异点,把它归入类别中去的思维过程。归类是在比较的基础上,将具有共同点的事物划为一类,再根据更小的差异将他们划分为同一类中的不同属性或特征,以揭示事物一定的从属关系和等级体系的思维活动。

比较是思维的重要过程,也是重要的思维方法,在人们的认识活动中有着极其重要的作用。有比较才有鉴别，只有通过比较才能找到事物间的共同点和差异点，才能进一步进行归类。教学活动中，教师应尽量运用变式教学，使学生能更多地利用比较的方法，正确理解知识，辨析概念，合理归类，突破教学上的难点。

（三）抽象与概括

抽象是在头脑中把同类事物或现象的共同的、本质的特征抽取出来，并舍弃其个别的、非本质特征的思维过程。如我们从粉笔、毛笔、钢笔、圆珠笔、中性笔等对象中，在头脑中抽出它们"能写字"的共同本质特征，舍弃它们不同大小、形状、构造、颜色等方面的非本质特征，就是思维的抽象过程。

概括是在头脑中把抽象出来的事物的共同的、本质的特征综合起来，并推广到同类事物中去的思维过程。如通过抽象得出结论："有生命的物质叫生物"，并把这个结论推广到植物、动物和微生物等一类事物中去的思维过程就是概括。

抽象、概括同分析、综合及比较紧密联系着。抽象主要是在分析、比较的基础上进行的；概括主要是在抽象、综合的基础上进行的，没有抽象和综合就不可能进行概括。

概括有两个层次：初级经验的概括与高级科学的概括。前者是在感知觉、表象水平上对事物的外部特征的概括，如幼儿把穿白大褂的人都当作医生；后者是对事物内部的、本质特征进行的概括，如一切定理、定义、概念等都是高级概括的产物。概括是一种特殊形式的综合，是概念形成的重要基础。

（四）具体化与系统化

具体化是人脑把经过抽象、概括而获得的概念、原理、理论应用到某一具体对象上去的思维过程，也就是用一般原理去解决实际问题，用理论指导实际活动的过程。具体化在人的思维过程中有着重要的作用。它能把抽象的理性认识同具体的感性认识结合起来，是启发思考与发展认识的重要环节。通过具体化的思维过程，可以更好地理解一般的原理和规律，也可以使已经总结出来的原理得到检验，并不断扩大、深化和发展。

系统化是在头脑中根据事物的一般特征和本质特征，按不同的顺序与层次组成一定系统的思维过程，如心理学研究的对象是心理现象，心理现象分为心理过程和个性心理、心理状态三部分，心理过程分为认知、情绪情感和意志三部分。这就是我们在头脑中对心理学内容系统化的过程。

系统化是在比较和分类的基础上实现的，也是思维过程中不可缺少的环节。系统化的知识便于在大脑皮层上形成广泛的神经联系，因此系统化在学习过程中有着非常重要的意义。

二、思维的形式

（一）概念

1. 概念的含义

概念（concept）是人脑对客观事物共同的本质特性的反映。在抽象与概括的基础上，人脑中便形成各种不同的概念，概念是判断的基础，用判断进行推理，形成科学原理法则，因而人能正确认识和改造现实。概念是思维最基本的单位。

概念包括内涵和外延两部分。内涵指概念所反映事物全部的共同本质的属性；外延指具有这些共同本质特性的全体对象。概念的内涵和外延是反比关系，内涵越大，外延越小；内涵越小，外延越大。

概念是用词语来标志的。概念和词语是紧密联系而又相互区别的。二者的联系表现在词语是概念的物质外壳，概念给词语一定的意义和内容。但是，概念是心理现象，词语是概念的物质标志，二者不能混淆。

2. 概念的种类

（1）具体概念和抽象概念

根据概念所反映的客观事物属性的抽象与概括程度，可把概念分成具体概念和抽象概念。

具体概念（concrete concept）是指人脑根据客观事物的外部特征形成的概念。例如：在幼儿面前呈现香蕉、苹果、皮球、口琴等物，要求他们分类。如果幼儿将苹果与皮球归为一类，香蕉与口琴归为另一类，说明他们主要是根据物体的外在形状，如圆、方等来分类的，由此形成的概念主要是具体概念。

抽象概念（abstract concept）是指人脑根据客观事物本质属性以及内在联系形成的概念。例如，幼儿能够将香蕉与苹果归为一类，将口琴与皮球归为另一类，说明他们是按照面前事物的本质属性及内在联系进行分类的，由此形成的概念则是抽象概念。

（2）合取概念、析取概念和关系概念

根据概念所反映的客观事物属性的数量及其相互关系，可把概念分成合取概念、析取概念和关系概念。

合取概念（conjunctive concept）是根据一类事物中单个或多个相同属性或特性而形成的概念，这些属性或特征在概念中必须同时存在。例如，"毛笔"这个概念就有两个属性——"用毛制作"和"写字工具"，这两个属性同时存在，才形成"毛笔"这个合取概念，如果只有其中一个属性那就不是毛笔了，比如只有"用毛制作"，那可能是刷子等其他物品。

析取概念（disjunctive concept）是指概念所包含的客观事物可同时具备两个要求的属性，也可以只涉及其中之一。例如，"好学生"这个概念，既可以是学习好的，也可以是品质好的，还可以是品学兼优的。

关系概念是指根据客观事物之间的关系而形成的概念。例如，高低、上下、左右、大小、前后等，都是根据客观事物之间的相对关系或内在联系构成的概念。

（3）前科学概念和科学概念

根据概念形成的途径，可把概念分为前科学概念和科学概念。

前科学概念（prescientific concept）又称日常概念，是个体在日常生活中通过人际交往的经验积累而形成的概念。前科学概念受个人生活范围和知识经验的限制，往往不能把握客观事物的本质属性，概念的内涵常常包含事物的非本质属性，存在片面性，甚至可能是错误的。例如，小学生往往认为"蛾子不属于动物"或者"蘑菇不属于植物"。

科学概念（scientific concept）指在科学研究中，经过假设和检验后逐渐形成的、反映客观事物本质属性及内在联系的概念。一般而言，那些可以用语言进行阐述与解释的科学概念，是在有计划、有目的的教学过程中获得的。例如，学习数学、物理学、生物学、心理学、教育学和社会学等学科的定义、定律、原理等。随着社会科学技术的发展，人类对客观事物认识的深化，科学概念的内涵和外延也在不断地完善与丰富。

3. 概念的形成

概念形成（concept formation）是指个体通过反复接触大量同一类事物，从而获得此类事物或现象的共同特征或共同属性，并通过肯定（正例）或否定（反例）的例子加以证实的过程。

概念形成一般经历三个阶段：抽象化—类化—辨别。抽象化是通过了解事物的属性或特征，对具体事物的各种特征与属性进行抽象。类化是在抽取共同属性或者特征后，根据事物特征或者属性的相似性或共同性，将类似的属性或特征加以归类。辨别是概念形成的最后一步，是对客观事物进行分辨。辨别渗透于概念形成的全过程，从抽取事物的属性或特征，到对这些属性或特征进行归类，最后到对客观事物的属性或特征之间的差异进行认识，都存在辨别。

（二）判断

判断（judgment）是肯定或否定事物具有某种属性的思维形式，是思维的基本形式之一。判断以概念为基础。例如"企鹅是鸟"，就是判断的思维形式。一切判断都是借助于语言、词汇并用句子形式来实现的。

判断可分为：直接判断与间接判断。直接判断多以感知形式出现，可用言语，也可用动作表达。例如，问幼儿飞机和汽车哪个跑得快？幼儿会说汽车，因为他亲眼看到的是汽车，这是直接判断。间接判断是借助推理来实现的思维判断形式，是事物之间的条件、空间、时间、因果等关系的反映。

（三）推理

推理（reasoning）是一种间接判断。它反映判断和判断之间的联系。是由一个或几个相互联系的已知判断推出合乎逻辑的新判断的思维形式。

推理的种类可分归纳推理和演绎推理两种。归纳推理是从特殊事例到一般的推理过程。例如"水加热变成气体""煤油加适度热变成气体""酒加热变成气体"等，故推理"液体加热变成气体"。演绎推理是从一般到特殊具体的推理过程。例如，"所有金属能传热"是大前提（一般），"铜是金属"是小前提（特殊具体），结论为"铜能传热"。

专栏 6-3

推理中常见的错误

人们在推理过程中并不总是按照逻辑规则的，现实生活中，人们的推理经常受到一些因素的影响。

1. 典型特征的作用

典型特征是指一个或一类事物有代表性的特征。例如，有位陌生人告诉你，有一个人很矮,很瘦,喜欢吟诗。然后他要你猜一猜这个人是某大学的古典文学教授还是一位卡车司机。你会如何回答?很多人的答案会是教授。但是这个结论几乎肯定是错误的,因为在全人口中,卡车司机的比例比教授大得多,何况还限定了是某大学的古典文学教授。人们之所以忽略基础率(即教授在全人口中的比率)而出现这样的错误,是因为人们受到上述描述的典型特征的影响。人们倾向于认为教授喜欢吟诗,而卡车司机不会。这就是典型特征的影响。

2. 信息可及性

人的推理容易受到记忆中的信息的易提取程度,即信息可及性的影响。容易想起来的事情也是比较容易当作经常发生的事情。例如,乘坐飞机的危险大还是乘坐汽车的危险大?很多人回答是飞机,这是因为只要有飞机失事,全世界的媒体都会报道,使人产生很深的印象。汽车虽然危险,但由于报道很少,印象不深,反而觉得不怎么危险了。

3. 具体化

具体化是指把一个抽象的概念看做或当做具体的存在。例如,一个学生得不到学士学位,就抱怨说:"这个大学不想给我学位证!",好像大学可以像一个个体一样行为,事实上,大学什么都不能做。

4. 诉诸权威或名誉

诉诸权威或名誉这是一个常见的逻辑错误。广告商经常使用人们的这种推理错误来误导消费者。比如用明星来包装产品,即使这些明星根本就不具备实质性的专业知识。最阴险和最有攻击性的就是利用权威学者的影响力,例如用一个诺贝尔奖获得者来宣布一个和他的研究毫无关联的结论。

——邵志芳.思维心理学[M].上海:华东师范大学出版社,2007:104—110.

第三节

问题解决

一、问题解决的内涵

(一)问题及其种类

问题(problem)就是个体不能用已有的知识经验直接加以处理并因此而感到疑难的情境。

问题的形式有很多。按照问题的结构可以分为：结构良好的问题和结构不良的问题。结构良好的问题（well-defined problem）也称为有结构的问题，是指已知条件和要达到的目标都非常明确，个体按一定的思维方式即可获得答案的问题。结构不良的问题（ill-defined problem）也称无结构的问题，是指已知条件与要达到的目标都比较含糊，问题情境不明确，各种影响因素不确定，也不容易找出解答线索。

任何问题都有三个基本成分：一是初始状态，是指对已知的问题情境和条件的描述；二是目标状态，是指具有构成问题结论或结果的描述，或者具有问题所要求的答案；三是存在的限制或障碍，即对该问题正确解决的方法不直接显现，需要通过间接思考才能达到。

（二）问题解决

问题解决（problem solving）是指为了从问题的初始状态到达目标状态而采取一系列具有目标指向性的认知操作的过程。

问题解决具有以下特征：

1. 目的性

问题解决具有明确的目的性，它总是要达到某个特定的目标状态。例如，做梦由于缺乏明确的目标，所以不是问题解决。

2. 序列性

问题解决包含一系列的心理活动，即认知操作，如分析、联想、比较、推论等。而且这些心理操作是存在一定序列的，一旦序列出错，问题就无法解决。

3. 认知性

问题解决活动必须由认知操作来进行，即通过内在的心理加工实现的问题解决，是在有特定目标但没有达到目标的手段的情境中，运用特定领域的知识和认知策略实现目标的一种思维活动。例如，证明几何题就是一个典型的问题解决过程。几何题中的已知条件和求证结果构成了问题解决的情境，而要证明结果，必须应用已知的条件进行一系列的认知操作。操作成功，问题就得以解决。

二、问题解决的过程

问题解决的过程一般可分为发现问题、理解问题、提出假设和检验假设四个阶段。其中，提出假设是问题解决的关键阶段。

（一）发现问题

发现问题就是认识到矛盾的存在并产生解决矛盾的需要和动机。从完整的问题解决过程来看，发现问题是其首要环节。爱因斯坦曾经指出，提出一个问题往往比解决一个问题更重要。因为解决问题也许仅仅是一个数字上或实验上的技能问题而已，而提出新问题，是从新的角度看问题，需要创新性的想象力，而且标志着科学的真正进步。

（二）理解问题

理解问题也称为明确问题，就是从笼统、混乱、不确定的问题中，找出问题的主要矛盾和关键因素,把握问题的实质,使问题的症结明朗化,从而确定解决问题的方向。能否迅速明确问题,依赖于两个因素,一是全面系统地掌握感性材料,二是已有知识经验的多寡。知识经验越丰富,越容易从一系列纷繁复杂的问题中区分出主要问题。

(三)提出假设

明确问题后,解决问题的关键就是根据问题的性质,运用已有的知识和经验,找到解决问题的可能途径和方案,选择恰当的问题解决操作步骤。提出假设是问题解决的关键阶段。假设是科学研究的"前哨"和"侦察兵",是解决问题的必由之路,科学理论正是在假设的基础上,通过不断地实践而发展和完善的。

(四)检验假设

问题阶段的最后步骤是检验假设。假设是对问题解决方案的探索和设想,假设是否正确,需要借助一定的手段来检验。检验假设就是通过一定的方法来确定假设是否合乎实际、是否符合科学原理。检验假设分为直接检验和间接检验,间接检验的结果是否正确,最终还要由直接检验来证明。

三、问题解决的思维策略

布鲁纳(Bruner)在研究人工概念时最先提出思维策略的概念,他发现人们在解决概念形成问题时自觉与不自觉地在运用着某种思维策略。纽厄尔和西蒙认为,在问题解决过程中,有如下两类通用的问题解决策略:算法式策略和启发式策略。

图 6-1 布鲁纳

布鲁纳(Jerome Seymour Bruner,1915—2016),美国教育心理学家、认知心理学家。对认知过程进行过大量研究,在词语学习、概念形成和思维方面有诸多著述,对认知心理理论的系统化和科学化作出了巨大贡献,是认知心理学的先驱,是致力于将心理学原理实践于教育的典型代表,也被誉为杜威之后对美国教育影响最大的人。主要著作包括《教育的文化》《意义行为》《论认知:左手随笔》《教育过程》等。

(一)算法式策略

算法式策略(algorithm strategy)是指在解决问题时的一套规则,它能够指明在问题空间中的解题步骤,以及搜索所有可能算式或途径,直到选择到有效方法解决问题。简言之,算法式策略就是把解决问题的方法一一尝试,最终找到解决问题的答案。算法式策略的特点是,只要一个问题有解题规则,那么只要按照其规则进行操作,问题总能得到解决。

例如，皮箱上的密码锁，如果有一天忘记密码，可以按照一定规则，循环拨号，一一尝试，最终总能找到密码。

但运用算法式策略解决问题时也会碰到困难。其一是不能肯定所有问题都有自己的解题规则，有些问题也许没有规则，有些则尚未发现其规则；其二是有些问题按规则一步步求解，工作量实在太大，以至在事实上无法运用此类策略求解。

（二）启发式策略

启发式策略（heuristic method）是凭借经验来解决问题的策略。这里有所谓解题的经验规则，它不能保证问题一定能得到解决，但却常常能有效地解决问题。王甦认为，"现在一个极有影响的看法认为，人类解决问题，特别是解决复杂问题，主要是应用启发式策略。"启发式策略也有多种。这里仅介绍应用范围最广的几种。

1. 手段—目的分析策略

手段—目的分析策略（mean-end analysis）的基本思想是从认识问题解决的目标和现有状态之间的差距着眼，通过设立若干子目标，通过实现一系列的子目标最终达到总目标。纽厄尔和西蒙曾以"河内塔"问题来说明这种解决问题策略的具体应用过程。有A、B、C三根立柱，在A柱上套有直径由小到大排列的圆盘（如图6-3所示）。要求将A柱上的三个圆盘全部移动到C柱上。移动的过程中，可以借助B柱，但是必须遵守两个规则：每次只能移动一个圆盘，二是无论何时大盘不能压住小盘。

图 6-2　西蒙

西蒙（Herbert A. Simon, 1916—2001），又名司马贺，美国著名经济学家、社会学家、心理学家、计算机科学家，认知心理学的奠基者。曾获国家科学奖，1953年当选美国国家科学院院士，1978年获诺贝尔经济学奖。

对这个问题的解决至少需要经过以下步骤：将1盘从A柱上移动到C柱，将2盘从A柱移动到B柱，将1盘从C柱移动到B柱，将3盘从A柱移动到C柱，将1盘从B柱移动到A柱，将2盘从B柱移动到C柱，将1盘从A柱移动到C柱。这样最终解答了问题。在解答问题的过程中，可以分解为三个子目标，先后顺序分别是3盘移动到C柱，2盘移动到C柱，1盘移动到C柱。这种策略体现的就是手段—目的分析策略。

2. 爬山法

爬山法（hill climbing method）是类似于手段—目的分析法的一种解题策略。它是采用一

图 6-3

河内塔问题示意图

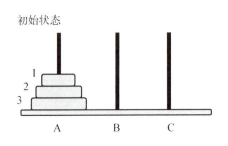
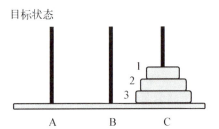

定的方法逐步降低初始状态和目标状态的差距,以达到问题解决的一种方法。爬山法犹如一个人登山,为了爬到山顶,需要从山脚一步一步登上山峰。爬山法和手段—目的分析法的不同在于,后者包括这样一种情况,即有时人们为了达到目的,不得不暂时扩大目标状态与初始状态的差异,以有利于达到最终目的。

3. 反推法

反推法(inverse method)又称为逆推法或者逆向搜索(backward search),该策略的基本思想是,从目标状态出发向初始状态反推,直至达到初始状态为止,然后再由初始状态沿反推路线步步正向求解。

这一策略与手段—目的策略正好相反,不是由初始状态朝目标状态推进而是由目标状态向初始状态反推。例如,在一个两人参加的数字游戏中,有10个珠子,每次每人只能拿1、2或3个珠子,双方轮流拿,谁拿到最后一个珠子就算输了。如果从初始状态考虑选择每一步究竟拿几个珠子,则很难取胜,而从目标状态反推,问题便易解了。目标状态是把最后一个珠子留给对方,由于每次都有三种可能选择,所以倒过来留给自己的那个状态应该是2、3或4个珠子。为此必须要造成对方处于5个珠子的状态,而要做到这点,就又必须使自己处于6、7或8个珠子的状态。于是,自己取胜的第一步是必须使对方面临9个珠子的状态,也就是轮到自己先拿,就拿1个珠子。若对方先拿,则在对方拿后,自己拿的珠子数被这样的一个阶段目标状态决定:使对方面临5个珠子的状态(如图6-4所示)。

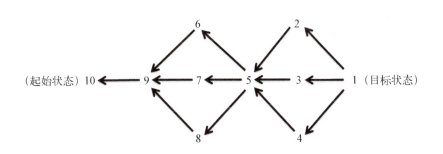

图 6-4

数字游戏反推示意图

四、影响问题解决的心理因素

影响问题解决的因素有很多,但已有的心理研究发现,以下几种心理因素具有一定的典型性。

(一)情绪状态

个体在怎样的情绪状态(emotional state)下进行问题解决的思维活动,对活动的效果有直接的影响。这也是情绪的调节功能在问题解决情境中的具体表现。美国著名心理学家西蒙也指出:"由于在活动着的人身上,行为动机和情绪对认知行为的过程有重要影响,所以思维和问题解决的一般理论应该结合这些影响。"一般说,高度紧张和焦虑会抑制思维活动,阻碍问题解决,而愉快和兴趣状态则为问题解决的思维活动提供良好的情绪背景。

(二) 动机强度

动机 (motive) 虽不直接调节人的思维活动,但会影响个体思维活动的积极性。然而,研究表明,动机强度并不总是与问题解决的思维活动效率成正相关。太低的动机强度自然不能调动个体问题解决的积极性,不利于充分活跃个体思维活动,但过高的动机强度也会造成很大的心理压力,反而抑制思维活动,降低解题成效。因此,适中的动机强度最有利于问题的解决。并且这一动机强度的适中点还会随问题解决的难度而变化。一般说,越是复杂的问题,其动机强度的适中点越是偏低一些。

(三) 定势作用

定势 (set) 也称为思维定势,是由先前活动所形成的并影响后继活动趋势的一种心理准备状态。它在思维活动中表现为一种易于使用习惯的方式解决问题的倾向。我们生活中常玩脑筋急转弯,而这个"弯"往往就是我们的一种思维定势。定势在问题解决中的作用有积极与消极之分。在解答常规问题时,定势往往起积极作用,而在解答创造性问题时,定势往往起阻碍作用。

卢钦斯 (Luchins) 的量杯实验是说明定势消极作用的一个典型。该实验要求被试计算如何用不等容量的杯子量出一定数量的水 (如表6-1所示)。实验组从例题之后逐解所有8道题,而控制组则在例题之后只做第6、7、8题。结果实验组的81%的被试受例题1—5题所形成的定势影响,套用B-A-2C的算法求解第6、7、8题,使算法重复,而控制组则由于未受此定势的影响,100%被试都采用非常简捷的方法求解第6、7、8道题。克服定势消极作用的办法是具体情况具体分析,一旦发现自己采用习惯使用的方式解决问题发生困难时,不要执意固守,而应退出旧思路,寻求新方法。

表 6-1 卢钦斯的定势实验

题序	三个杯的容量(夸脱)			要求量出的水的容量(夸脱)
	A	B	C	
1	21	127	3	100
2	14	163	20	99
3	18	43	10	5
4	9	42	6	21
5	20	59	4	31
6	23	49	3	20
7	15	39	3	18
8	28	59	3	25

（四）功能固着

功能固着（functional fixation）是指个体在解决问题时往往只看到某种事物的通常功能，而看不到其他方面可能有的功能。这是人们长期以来在日常生活中所形成的对某种事物的功能或用途的固定看法。例如，一般认为不锈钢杯子是用来盛开水的，白衬衫是用来穿着的，而不易想到，在必要时可以把不锈钢杯子当蜡烛台，把衬衫当画布。但在问题解决中，有时正是由于克服了这种功能固着才找到新的求解思路。邓克（Duncker）的实验证实了功能固着对解决问题的消极影响。他让两组被试使用同样5种工具来解决5个问题。实验组被试在解决问题前先对工具的习惯用法进行练习，以增强功能固着的影响；控制组则无此练习，直接解决问题。结果实验组成绩远低于控制组，功能固着的消极影响十分显著（如表6-2所示）。

表 6-2 邓克的功能固着实验

组别	工具	练习	解决问题	参加人数	成绩 %
实验组	钻子	钻洞	支撑绳索	14	71
	箱子	盛物	做垫脚台	7	43
	钳子	打开铁丝结	支撑木板	9	44
	秤锤	称重量	做钉锤用	12	15
	回形针	夹纸	做挂钩用	7	57
控制组	同		同	10	100
	实验组	无	实验组	7	100
				15	100
				12	100
				7	86

（五）迁移影响

迁移（transfer）是指已获得的知识经验对解决新问题所产生的影响。迁移有正迁移和负迁移之分。正迁移是已获得的知识经验对解决新问题有促进作用，负迁移是已获得的知识经验对解决新问题有阻碍或干扰的影响。例如，学会骑自行车反而影响学骑三轮车，属负迁移。根据美国心理学家贾德（Judd）的理论，只有当一个人对其知识经验进行概括，掌握其要义，才易于将知识经验迁移到新问题解决的情境中去。美国心理学家布鲁纳则更进一步强调，迁移的关键在于领悟事物之间的关系，基本概念或原理掌握得越深透，则越能实现正迁移。

（六）原型启发

原型启发是指在其他事物或现象中获得的信息对解决当前问题的启发。而能给人获得解决问题启发的事物叫做原型（prototype）。作为原型的事物或现象是多种多样的，存在于自然界、人类社会和日常生活之中。阿基米德从身体浸入浴缸将水溢出的现象获得启发,解决了皇冠含金量的鉴别问题;上海铁道医院医生从汽车方向盘的外形中获得启发,解决了人造瞳孔角膜的透气问题;科学家则从动物的形态、动作和某些机体结构中获得启发,解决了大量生活、生产和军事上的问题,并形成仿生科学。原型启发关键是要做生活中的有心人,不断积累丰富的知识,并善于发现有关事物或现象与当前所要解决问题之间的某种内在联系,以从中获得有益的启迪。

(七)酝酿效应

当一个人长期致力于某一问题的解决而又百思不得其解的时候,如果暂时停止他对这个问题的思考,去做别的事情,几个小时、几天或几周之后,他可能会忽然想到解决的办法,这就是酝酿效应(incubation effect)。日常生活中,对一个问题我们有时候会不知道从何入手,这时思维就进入了酝酿阶段,当我们茅塞顿开的时候,突然会有类似阿基米德的惊叹,这时酝酿效应就绽放出了思维之花,问题就会得到顺利解答。宋代诗人陆游的"山重水复疑无路,柳暗花明又一村"就是这一心理的写照。

(八)问题的特征

问题本身的特征影响问题解决,例如问题是抽象还是具体、问题的表征方式等。一般而言,问题越抽象、问题呈现时的空间组织(即知觉方式)与原有经验越不符,会阻碍问题的解答;相反,如果问题呈现的知觉方式与人们已有的知识经验越接近,问题就越容易解决。例如,已知圆的半径为 2 cm,求圆的外切正方形面积(如图6-5所示)。显而易见,图B呈现的问题情境要比图A容易。

图 6-5 问题特征对问题解决的影响

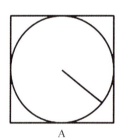
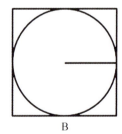

A　　　　　　　B

(九)个体的智能与个性

个体的智能水平高低以及气质、性格等个性差异也影响解决问题的效率。理想远大、意志坚强、情绪稳定、谦虚勤奋、富有创造精神等优良个性品质,都会提高解决问题的效率。反之缺乏理想、意志薄弱、情绪不稳定、骄傲懒惰、墨守成规等消极的个性品质都将有碍于问题的解决。

专栏6-4

问题解决中的直觉

先看两个问题。

问题一：一种突发急性传染病可导致600人死亡。医生有两种选择：若使用A药，可救活200人；若使用B药，有1/3的机会是600人全被救活，2/3的机会是600人全部死亡。医生应选择哪种药？

问题二：有600人生命垂危。医生必须作出选择：若使用A药，400人会死亡，若使用B药，有1/3的机会是无一人死亡，2/3的机会是600人全部死亡。医生应选择哪种药？

大多数人在问题一中选择A药，在问题二中选择B药。这很奇怪，这两个问题其实是一样的，但为什么会出现不同的选择呢？唯一的不同之处在于问题表述的角度，问题一是讲有多少人能活，问题二则是讲有多少人会死。然而，甚至那些意识到先后答案有矛盾的人们也很难作出一致的选择。

可见，人们在判断与决策时经常依赖于直觉而不是逻辑。直觉（intuition）是一种不依赖清晰推理的、快速的、冲动性的思维方式。它可以很快得出答案，但也可能导致错误，有时甚至是十分严重的错误。心理学家卡尼曼和特韦尔斯基（Kahneman & Tersky, 1972, 1982）花了大量时间研究人在面对不确定问题时如何进行决策、如何进行预测，结果发现，人在判断时带有下列普遍性的严重缺陷。

① 代表性启发错误。人们在进行判断时常会因为直觉而落入陷阱。例如，下面有两种可能发生的情况，请你判断，哪种情况更有可能发生？一种情况是，格拉芙将输掉第一局，但最终会赢得比赛的胜利；另一种情况是，格拉芙将输掉第一局。卡尼曼和特韦尔斯基发现，大多数人选择第一种可能性。但是，这种凭直觉作出的回答忽视了一个重要的事实，那就是概率结果。例如，我们抛一枚硬币，图案面朝上的概率是50%；抛两枚硬币时，它们都是图案面朝上的概率只有25%。因此，真正发生第二种情况的可能性比第一种要小。卡尼曼和特韦尔斯基相信，人们选择"格拉芙将输掉第一局，但最终会赢得比赛的胜利"是基于一种叫做代表性启发（representativeness heuristic）的直觉错误。也就是说，当一种选择看上去更能代表我们已知的东西时，我们就会赋予这种选择更多的权重。因此，人们会把有关一位职业网球手应有行为的心理模型与格拉芙的信息进行比较，而第一种情况中的信息似乎与这种心理模型更为接近，所以，尽管第一种情况离事实更远，但看上去显得更可能发生。

② 忽略基础比率错误。凭直觉判断容易犯的第二种错误是忽略基础比率（base rate）或事件发生的潜在可能性。在一个实验中，研究者告诉被试，将向他们介绍100个人的情况，其中有70名律师和30名工程师。然后，在那100个人中随便抽出一个人，让被试猜这个人是律师还是工程师。所有被试都回答，此人70%可能是律师，30%可能是工程师。接下来，研究者给被试一段如下描述："迪克是一位30岁

的男士,已婚但没有孩子。他有很高的成就动机,能力很强,在他工作的那个领域将会十分成功。他的同事们都很喜欢他。此人的职业是什么?"注意,这个描述并未给出任何关于迪克职业的新信息,律师或工程师的比率仍是70%对30%。然而,此时大多数被试的答案却成了50%对50%,直觉上,似乎他是工程师或律师的可能性是相等的。这种猜测中完全忽视了潜在的基础比率。有时候,对潜在比率的忽视可能是一件好事。例如,目前的美国的离婚率约50%,如果对此念念不忘,还有多少人愿意结婚呢?此外,对于许多高风险的工作,人们宁愿忽视事故发生的基础比率,认为自己将是特例,否则有多少人会去从事高风险的工作呢?但有时候,对潜在比率的忽视也可能是一件坏事。例如,那些吸烟、酒后开车或不系安全带的人之所以为所欲为,就是因为他们不去考虑吸烟致病的潜在可能性或相当高的交通事故发生率。

③ 问题建构方式引起的直觉错误。卡尼曼和特韦尔斯基的研究结论表明,导致直觉错误的最普遍的原因是问题表述的建构方式(framing)或问题的组织方式对判断的影响。正如我们在选择用药的例子所看到的那样,一个问题的表述方式稍有不同,就可使人们给出不同的答案。一般来说,看问题越全面,就越有可能作出最合理的决策。但现实的情况是,许多问题并没有一个明显的正确答案,而人们常会片面地看待这些问题。例如,在选择职业时,明智的做法是综合考虑收入、工作条件、工作满意度、所需技能、未来前途等因素,但在现实中,人们在进行决策时往往只是考虑某一个方面,比如,"我喜欢写作,所以我要当记者","我想挣钱,当律师挣得多","我在照相方面有天分,我要当摄影师"。如此片面和狭隘地建构问题,必然增大出现决策错误的可能性。

以上讨论了在不确定情况下的一些直觉错误。目前,有关直觉决策的研究结果被广泛应用于医学、商业、军事、投资、金融和国际关系等领域,即训练人们在作决策时要三思而后行,以减少失误。但另一方面,诺贝尔经济学奖获得者、著名心理学家西蒙提出人的"有限理性"的观点,认为人们的认识是有限的,因此往往会以更简单、更节省脑力的"满意原则"取代"最佳原则"。这很有道理,平常我们的种种判断与决策往往是有时间限制的,很多时候容不得我们反复斟酌,只能追求让自己满意就行了。无论如何,请记住,简洁清晰的思维才是解决问题的捷径。

——黄希庭,郑涌.心理学导论[M].北京:人民教育出版社,2015:433—435.

第四节
思维规律在教育教学中的应用

一、科学概念的掌握

概念的掌握是在个体发展过程中借助词语来实现的,是对人类已有概念的有组织的学习过程。概念掌握虽不像概念形成那样曲折漫长,但也是分阶段的复杂的学习过程。拿儿童对于数的概念的掌握来说,就经历了不同阶段:数的实际意义认识阶段;数的顺序、大小的理解阶段;数的分解组合能力阶段;数的概念展开阶段等。其他概念掌握也如此,都要经历从具体到抽象,从模糊到精确,从感性到理性,从简单到复杂的发展趋势。

概念是学生进行判断与推理的基础。可以通过平日生活来获取日常概念,但是日常概念往往可能不科学。获得科学概念的主要途径就是学校学习。学生在专门的教学形式下,通过教师的引导掌握概念的内涵和外延而形成科学概念。根据概念形成的规律,教师在教学中应注意做到以下几点。

(一)以感性材料作为概念掌握的基础

教学不能仅限于对概念内涵作抽象地讲解,还应当向学生提供足够的与概念本质属性有关的感性材料。知识越直观、越具体,学生理解起来就越容易,依据内容的不同可以采用事物直观、模像直观和言语直观三种形式。如果学生还没有相关的知识经验,就应让学生观察实物、标本、模型进行实验、参观等;如果学生已经具备了这些经验,就应通过生动的语言唤起学生头脑中相应的表象。不论采用何种方式,所提供的材料都必须具有鲜明的代表性、典型性,以充分体现事物的本质特征。

(二)充分利用过去的知识经验

在日常交往和个人积累经验的过程中形成的日常概念,一般都没有经过严密的思维加工,并且受个人经验的限制,往往不能准确地反映事物的本质属性,常有错误和曲解。当日常概念与科学概念的内涵基本一致时,对概念的掌握起积极影响,反之则起消极作用。我们也可以在教学中发挥它的积极作用。例如,日常的"邻居"概念有助于对"邻角""相邻数"的理解;对于数学中"元角分"的应用,也可以借助场景引起学生以前的购物经验,这样便于学生理解题意。

(三)突出重要特征,充分利用"变式"

所谓变式(variation)是指在组织学习感性材料时,从不同角度、方面和方式变换事物非本质的属性,以便揭示其本质属性的过程。运用变式对帮助学生消除日常概念的消极影响,突出事物的本质特征,防止扩大或缩小概念的内涵或外延有重要意义。变式不充分或不正确,往往会产生内涵混淆,外延扩大或缩小的概念错误。如大多数鸟都会飞,但会飞不是鸟的本质属性,鸟的本质属性是有羽毛。学生把会飞的蝙蝠、蜻蜓、蝴蝶等动物都当作鸟类,把鸡、鸭、鹅排斥在鸟类之外,就属于这类错误。当然,变式不应是无休止的,而应选择适当的、典型的方式进行。

(四)正确运用语言表述,明确概念的本质特征

事物的本质属性被揭示出来以后,就要用下定义的方法,用简明、精确的语言把它固定下来,它起着组织、整理和巩固思维成果的作用。及时并正确下定义,有助于概念的掌握,概念的内涵往往是通过下定义的方式来固定的。正确地下定义是掌握概念的重要标志,一要语言简练、准确,不该是循环、否定、比喻性的;二要从学生的实际水平出发下定义。

(五)在实践中运用概念使概念具体化

概念的运用既是学习概念的目的,也是检验概念掌握的标志。教学实践也证明,概念用于实际后,学生对概念更加熟悉,并加深理解,大大提高了掌握概念的自觉性和积极性。因此,教师要重视学生概念的实际运用。学生实际运用的方式有:用概念解释事物、用概念解决实际问题等。

(六)形成正确的概念体系

正确的概念体系既能帮助学生快速理解概念,也能帮助学生区分概念之间的区别和联系。学生在形成了正确的概念体系后,也就真正掌握了概念的本质,既有利于对新概念的理解,也有利于旧知识的巩固和充实。

应当明确,学生掌握概念并非有固定模式,它既可由感性开始,从具体到抽象;也可由理性开始,从抽象到具体。但是,无论是从感性开始,还是从理性开始,无论是从抽象开始,还是从具体开始,都必须遵循感性和理性、具体和抽象相结合的原则。

二、问题解决能力的培养

在学校情境中,大多问题解决都是通过解决各科中的具体问题来体现的,这就意味着培养学生问题解决的能力要结合具体的学科知识。具体可以从以下几个方面入手。

(一)帮助学生调节解决问题的动机水平

在问题解决过程中,学生的动机是制约思维活动和解题效率的一个不可忽视的心理因素。耶克斯—多德森定律显示,动机强度偏低和过高都不利于问题解决。学生在学习过程中易暴露的问题是:在平时作业时,容易出现动机强度偏低,从而造成思维积极性不足;在测验或考试时,容易出现动机强度过高,从而导致思维功能削弱。因此,首先让学生明白动机水平对自己问题解决的影响,进而学会调控自己的动机水平,平时抓紧,考试放松,从而让自己取得最佳的解题效果。

（二）调控问题解决时的情绪状态

在解题过程中，学生的情绪也是影响思维活动和解题效率的一个不可忽视的心理因素。在情绪方面，诸如悲伤、愤怒、忧郁等负面情绪都不利于学生解题，而在测验或考试解题时，最主要的干扰则来自于焦虑、紧张的情绪状态。适度的紧张有时可以提高问题解决的效率，但是过度的紧张只会压抑思维。因此，教师可以教学生通过深呼吸和冥想等方式来调节自己的情绪，让自己处于平和、愉悦的心境之中，以取得最佳的解题效果。

（三）帮助学生正确表征问题

在学科教学中，学生在解题时首先是理解题意，在头脑中形成良好的问题表征方式。在头脑中构建的表征方式越具体、直观、形象，越有助于问题解答。另外如前面图6-5所示，已知圆的半径为2 cm，求圆的外切正方形的面积。表征方式越贴近已有的知识经验，问题解答起来就越容易。

（四）帮助学生养成对问题进行分类的习惯

当学生准确理解语意之后，就应进而判断问题类型，以便将当前问题纳入自己头脑中已形成的问题类型之中。这就需要学生在平时对解题类型进行归纳，以便在头脑中形成相应的认知结构，为正确解题创造必要条件。另外，面对问题要善于去伪存真，把握问题实质，找到它在头脑中某类型问题的原型。

（五）利用迁移的积极影响，克服某些定势的消极作用

当学生把题目纳入一定的类型之后，就可以利用已有的解题知识、经验使问题的解决既便利又快捷，这其实是在利用正迁移的积极影响。但同时又应防止可能出现的某些定势的消极作用。有时同一类型题中也有些不同的变异，完全套用已有的解法则又会失之偏差，有时会钻进死胡同而不能退出。因此，解题时不仅要正确判断题目类型，而且一旦发现问题，要及时分析、审视，善于变通，换角度求解。

（六）教授与训练问题解决的方法和策略

当有些问题不能简单归入某一类型，或运用已有知识一时不能求解时，应积极运用一些解决问题的策略。例如，手段—目的策略、反推策略等。但这些策略只是解决问题的一般策略，结合各学科的具体实际，教师还应多给予更具体的解题策略的指导，使学生真正掌握学习的方法。这样才能做到既促进学科学习中的问题解决，又促进学生思维能力的发展。

（七）解题后鼓励学生反思

学生解题时一旦求解结束便如释重负，往往忽视解题后的反思。而对解题的反思是发展学生元认知思维、理顺解题思路和积累解题技巧的重要环节。教师可以指导学生对解题的过程、解题途径、解题方法的多样性及对题目的归类进行思考，以便提高思维的深刻性和系统性。

三、创造性思维的培养

较强的思维能力和创造能力不是与生俱来的,而是后天培养教育的结果。教师不仅要传授知识,而且要教会学生掌握知识所必需的思维和创造的策略和方法,培养他们良好的思维品质,发展创造思维能力,使他们学会学习,学会创造。

(一)创设宽松接纳的教学环境,调动学生创造的积极性

教师应给学生创立一个能支持标新立异或容纳偏离常规者的环境,让学生感受到心理安全或者心理自由,给学生创设较为宽松的学习的心理环境。这样才能真正调动学生的内在积极性和主动性。在教学中,教师可以设置开放性问题,激发学生创造的欲望。对于老师提出的开放性问题,不管学生的回答正确与否,都应对学生积极参与和爱动脑筋的品质进行表扬,消除学生对答错问题的恐惧。对于学生提出的各种问题,不应忽视或者讥讽,而应接纳并赞许其有求知欲和好奇心。如果对学生的意见有所批评,应解释理由。

(二)运用启发式、发现式等教学方法培养学生独立思考与探究的能力

在教学的过程中,如果采用"满堂灌""死记硬背"的方式,那学生可能只是记住了内容,虽然考试成绩不会太差,但是能力不高。而如果能依据教学内容灵活采用发现式、启发式等教学方式,让学生自己动手动脑,经过自己的思考或与同学的交流来得出自己的结论,学生不仅体验了科学探究与学习的乐趣,获取了成就感,而且也学会了独立思考与探究。

(三)优化知识结构,提高语言表达能力

语言是思维的工具。学生掌握了语言这个工具,就能自如地表达自己的想法,思维也会更加条理清晰。所以提高言语能力是提高思维能力的重要条件。而言语的内容来源于知识的学习,知识是提高创造能力的基础。因而,优化学生的知识结构与提高学生的言语表达能力,都能促进学生创造性思维的发展。

(四)采用头脑风暴等方法进行创造性思维训练

头脑风暴也称为脑激励法,其核心思想是把产生的想法和评价想法区分开。基本做法是,教师先提出问题,然后鼓励学生寻找尽可能多的答案,不必考虑答案的正确性,教师也不评论,一直到所有可能的答案都提出来了为止。延迟对答案做评论既可以鼓励学生多提答案,也能防止他们怕说错受批评而不敢说。头脑风暴可以训练学生的发散思维,培养思维的灵活性、变通性等良好的思维品质。

(五)培养创造型人格

创造性思维的发展不仅与智力因素有关,同时也与非智力因素,特别是人格特征关系密切。研究发现具有创造性的人格具有以下特点:浓厚的认知兴趣,旺盛的求知欲和强烈的好奇心;敏锐的观察力,富于想象,具有捕捉机遇的能力;较强烈的进取心和较高的抱负水平,自信心强,且能有效地进行自我激励;较强的独立性,从众行为少,有开拓创新精神,不受传统观念束缚等。

本章小结

思维是指人以已有的知识经验为媒介,对客观事物的本质属性和规律性联系的概括的、间接的反映;思维具有概括性和间接性两个基本特征。思维过程包括分析与综合、比较、抽象与概括、具体化与系统化;思维有概念、判断和推理三个形式;问题解决有两类问题解决策略:算法策略和启发式策略,其中启发式策略包括手段—目的分析策略、选择性搜索策略和反推法;影响问题解决的因素有情绪状态、动机强度、定势作用、功能固着、迁移影响、原型启发、酝酿效应、问题特征和个体的智能水平与个性特征;要在教学中运用构成良好的问题空间的教学策略、有效填补认知空隙的教学策略和解题后再反思的教学策略;促进学生思维的深刻性、灵活性、批判性、敏捷性品质的培养。

关键术语

思维　直观动作思维　具体形象思维　抽象逻辑思维　创造性思维　分析　综合　概念　问题解决

讨论与应用

1. 阅读下面的案例,回答问题。案例中该同学测验的是幼儿心理发展的哪个方面?老师为什么说他可能弄错了,请你给他指出来。

有一名实习生在幼儿园进行了一次简单的"幼儿××水平测验",他设计了两个题目:Ⅰ"设 A>B,B>C,请小朋友说说 A 和 C 哪一个大";Ⅱ"小王同学比小李同学高,小李同学比小张同学高,请问小王和小张两位同学谁高"。他选用"随机取样"方式在大班选用了题目Ⅰ,在中班选用了题目Ⅱ,可出乎意料,他发现中班幼儿的思维发展水平高于大班。他满意地把这个新发现告诉老师,老师说他可能弄错了……

2. 阅读下列两个案例,用你学过的知识,解释案例中两名幼儿的思维特点以及对教育的启示。

案例一:茵茵已经上了中班,她知道把两个苹果和三个苹果加起来,就有5个苹果。但是当你问她2加3等于几?她直摇头。

案例二:3岁的佳佳上小班了,玩橡皮泥时,他往往没有计划性。橡皮泥搓成团就说像包子,搓成长条就说是油条,长条橡皮泥卷起来就说是麻花。

3. 阅读下面的材料,说明实验中哪个因素影响了问题的解决,以及实验结果对教学工作有何启示?根据学过的内容,指出问题解决还受到哪些因素的影响?

研究者设计了一个"两绳问题"的实验,在一个房间的天花板上悬挂两根相距较远的绳子。被试无法同时抓住,这个房间里有一把椅子,一盒火柴,一把螺丝刀和一把钳子。要求被试把两根绳子系住。问题解决的方法是:把钳子作为重物系在一根绳子上,从而把两根绳子系起来。结果发现只有39%的被试能在10分钟内解决这个问题，大多数被试认为钳子只有剪断铁丝的功能，没有意识到还可以当做重物解决问题。

本章讨论与应用答题思路与要点
（扫描二维码）

本章复习思考题
（扫描二维码）

本章进一步阅读书目
（扫描二维码）

本章测量量表
（扫描二维码）

第七章
注 意
ZHUYI

　　亲爱的同学，你在课堂上是否经常听到老师说"集中注意认真听"呢？这是每个老师经常会在课堂上强调的话语，可见"注意"对于课堂学习效果有很大的影响。那怎么才能在课堂上做到集中注意听老师讲课呢？通过本章内容的学习，希望能帮助你对"注意"有更深的认识。

通过本章的学习,你能够
- 掌握注意的概念与特点
- 了解注意的功能、分类与品质
- 明确注意产生和维持的条件
- 掌握注意的规律
- 学会运用注意的规律进行教学

【本章结构】

本章主要回答"注意是什么"的问题。它有助于你更加专业地了解与注意这个心理活动有关的主要原理,包括注意的概念、注意的种类、注意的品质以及注意的规律。不仅如此,通过学习还能帮助你在教学中运用注意规律的途径与方式,以提高学生的注意力品质。

第一节 注意概述

注意（attention）是一切心理过程的开端。它在人的心理活动中起组织和调节作用，因而又是心理过程顺利而有效进行的保证。没有注意，就不会有人的认知，也就不会有人的情感和意志。注意是什么？注意有什么特点？注意有哪些功能？注意可以如何分类？学习本章，我们首先需要弄懂这些问题。

一、注意的概念与特点

（一）注意的概念

注意是大家很熟悉的一种心理现象，在生活中随处可见。例如，学生上课时专心地听老师讲课，聚精会神地思考老师提出的问题，认真完成老师布置的作业，在这些活动中，学生并不是什么都看、都听、都记，而是把意识指向和集中于与学习有关的内容上，这就是注意。在心理学上，注意就是指心理活动对一定对象的指向和集中。

（二）注意的特点

注意有两个特点：指向性和集中性。

1. 注意的指向性

注意的指向性是指在某一瞬间，人们的心理活动或意识选择了一定的对象，而离开了其余对象。在千变万化的世界中，每时每刻都会有大量的刺激作用于我们的感官，但我们并不是把所有的刺激都作为我们的反映对象，而是有选择性的。我们只去选择那些对机体来说是重要的、有意义的刺激来进行反映，而对那些不重要的事物就不去注意或注意得很模糊，以此保证意识的准确性和完整性，以及在哪个方向上进行活动。意识的指向不同，人们从外界接受的信息也不同。

2. 注意的集中性

注意的集中性是指意识不仅指向于某一客观事物，而且全神贯注于这个客观事物，深入到客观事物内部中，使心理活动表现出一定的强度和紧张度。注意集中时心理活动会离开一切无关的事物，并且抑制多余的活动，这样就保证了意识的清晰、完善和深刻。然而这时对于那些没有受到注意的事物，就意识不到了。例如，当一个人全神贯注地读书时，他听不见周围环境中的噪声喧闹，所谓"视而不见，听而不闻"，就是注意对事物高度集中的结果。

注意的指向和集中是同一注意状态的两个方面，两者是不可分割的。指向是集中的基础，同时又必须通过集中表现出来。例如，学生上课听讲，他的心理活动不是指向教室里的一切事物，而是有选择地指向教师的讲课内容，并对其做较长时间的保持，并且离开一切与听课无关的事物，这样才能对老师的讲课留下清晰、深刻的印象。

注意是心理活动的重要组成部分，但注意本身不是一种独立的心理过程，不能直接实现对客观事物属性和特征的反应，它没有自己特定的反应对象。当我们在说"注意"的时候，总是表达了"注意看""注意听""注意想"的含义。当一个人在注意着什么的时候，也就在感知着什么，或记忆着什么，或思考着什么。这就是说，注意是不能独立存在的，它总要伴随着其他心理过程同时出现。同时，注意虽没有自己特定的反应对象，不能直接反应客观事物，但它却是一切心理活动的开端和基础，是一切心理活动的共同特征，它维持和保证着各种心理活动的有效进行。注意看，才能看清楚；注意听，才能听明白。相反，如果没有注意的参与，人的意识水平就会下降，就会视而不见，听而不闻，学习和工作就很难取得成效。因此，注意是保证心理活动能够顺利进行的必要条件。注意虽不是一个独立的心理过程，但作为一种独特的心理现象，有其自身的结构和运行机制，按照系统论的观点，人的注意是一种动态的、变化的过程。只要人有意识，人的意识就会连绵不断，一种注意结束了，另一种注意会同时开始，人的注意就像江河那样连绵不断、永不停歇。

二、注意的功能

注意是整个心理活动的引导者和组织者，它使心理活动处于积极状态并获得必要的驱动力。注意有三种主要功能。

（一）选择功能

周围环境每时每刻都给人们提供了大量的刺激，带来了丰富的信息。但是，并不是所有的刺激对人们都是重要的，人们也不是对所有信息都感兴趣（人们在注意周围事物时是有选择性的）。注意使人的心理活动有选择地指向那些对主体来说是重要的、有意义的信息来进行反映，并排除无关刺激的干扰。人脑的这种选择重要刺激、排除无关刺激的干扰的能力就是注意的选择功能。注意的选择功能表现为心理活动对一定对象的指向与集中，因而是注意的基本功能，注意的其他功能都是在它的前提下发挥作用的。

（二）保持功能

注意能够使人的心理活动维持在被选择的事物上，并对其进行深入的加工，直到行为完成、目的实现为止。例如，围棋选手在对弈时，为了战胜对手，可以全神贯注注意棋盘几小时；外科医生为了抢救病人可连续数小时站在手术台前，集中注意做手术。当心理活动发生以后，注意能使活动对象维持在意识状态中，得到清晰、准确的反应，注意的保持功能确保了人的意识活动的顺利进行。

（三）调节和监督功能

注意可以协调、控制和监督心理活动的正常机能，使人的心理活动沿着一定的方向和目标进行，并且还能提高人们的意识觉醒水平，使心理活动根据当前的需要做出适当的分配和及时的转移，以适应千变万化的环境。如汽车司机随时注意交通情况，根据变化及时改变行车的速度和方向,以确保行车安全。注意的调节和监督功能保证人能更好地适应周围环境的变化,更好地认识和改造世界。

三、注意的分类

根据注意有无预定目的和意志努力的程度不同,可把注意分为无意注意、有意注意和有意后注意三种。

(一)无意注意

无意注意又称不随意注意(involuntary attention),是一种没有预定目的并且不需要意志努力的注意。例如,大家正在上课,突然从门外闯进来一个人,这时,大家会不约而同地把视线投向这个人,不由自主地对他发生了注意。在这种情况下,我们对要注意的事物没有任何心理准备,注意的引起和维持,既不依靠明确的目的任务也不依靠意志的努力,而主要取决于刺激物本身的性质。从这个意义上说,无意注意是一种消极被动的注意,是注意的初级形式。同时,因无意注意不需要意志努力,因而它不易使个体产生疲劳,这是它的优点。

(二)有意注意

有意注意也叫随意注意(voluntary attention),是指有预定目的、需要付出意志努力的注意。例如,当我们阅读一篇科研论文时,由于认识到学习这篇论文的重要性,便自觉地将注意集中于文章的内容上;当学生在学习中遇到困难或环境中出现干扰因素时,须通过意志的努力,使注意力维持在要学习的东西上,这都是有意注意的过程。有意注意是在目的的支配下有意识地、主动积极地发生的一种注意,是人类所特有的一种注意的高级发展形式。但由于有意注意需付出一定的意志努力,因而易使主体产生疲劳。

(三)有意后注意

有意后注意(postvoluntary attention)是在有意注意的基础上产生的有预定目的、不需要意志努力的注意。有意后注意是注意的一种特殊形式。它同时具有无意注意和有意注意的某些特征。一方面,它类似于有意注意,具有自觉的目的、任务;另一方面,它又类似于无意注意,不需要付出意志努力。如个体在从事某一活动时,开始时很枯燥,对它没有兴趣,需要意志努力才能完成,但随着活动的逐步开展及知识经验的积累与丰富,个体逐渐对活动本身产生了浓厚的兴趣,这时不再需要意志努力就能维持自己的注意力了,有意注意转化为有意后注意。

值得注意的是,有意注意和无意注意虽然有区别,但是在人的生活中,二者往往是不能截然分开的。因为任何一种工作都需要这两种注意的参加。倘若单凭无意注意去从事某种工作,那么工作不仅会显得杂乱无章,缺乏计划性和目的性,而且也难以持久。同时,任何工作总会有困难或干扰,总会有单调乏味的过程,因此需要有意注意的参加,工作才能完成。然而单凭有意注意从事工作,需要进行紧张的努力,付出巨大的能量,时间久了,会使人感到疲劳,所以必须有无意注意参加,工作才能持久。在人的每项活动中,往往既需要无意注意也需要有意注意。

第二节 注意的规律

掌握注意的规律是在教学中应用注意规律,取得好的教学效果的前提。注意的外部表现,注意发生的相关理论,产生无意注意、有意注意和有意后注意的条件等都是重要的规律。

一、注意的外部表现

人的注意发生时,常常伴随着特定的心理变化和外部表现。注意最显著的外部表现有:

(一)机体的适应性运动

人在注意时,有关的感觉器官会做朝向运动,如注意看时,视线集中在某物体上,举目凝视;注意听时,把耳朵转向声源,侧耳倾听;注意思考问题时,常常眼睛呆视,双眉紧皱,凝神沉思。这些举目凝视、侧耳倾听、凝神沉思都是注意的适应性动作。

(二)无关运动的停止

当人的注意高度集中时,有关的肌肉会处于紧张状态而使无关的动作停止下来。如学生集中注意力看黑板时,手与脚的下意识的小动作会停止下来,只有眼睛做着有规律的扫描运动。

(三)内脏器官的适应性变化

人的注意高度集中时,血液循环和呼吸系统都会发生相应的变化,一般规律是:肢体血管收缩,四肢血流量减少,头部血管舒张,大脑血流量增多。饭后不宜立即进行学习的道理即在于此。同时,呼吸变得轻微而缓慢,吸气时间变得急促短暂,呼气时间相对延长,当注意达到高峰时,甚至会出现屏息现象。此外,当紧张注意时,还会出现心跳加快,牙关紧闭,握紧拳头等现象。

注意的外部表现可作为研究注意的客观指标。一般来说,注意的外部表现和注意的真实情况是一致的,根据注意的外部表现,可以了解人的内心活动。但在特定条件下,人可以通过假象来掩盖注意的真实情况,可能会出现所谓貌似注意实际不注意,或者貌似不注意实际注意的现象。如学生在课堂上用眼睛盯住老师一动不动,表面上一幅认真听讲的样子,而实际上,他的注意力可能完全不在教师讲课的内容上,而是指向与教学无关的其他事情。因此,在判断一个人是否注意时,还必须进行多方面的观察和了解。

二、注意发生的相关理论

（一）过滤器理论

1958年，英国心理学家布罗德本特（Broadbent）根据双耳分听的一系列实验结果，提出了解释注意的选择作用的一种理论——过滤器理论（filter theory）（如图7-1所示）。布罗德本特认为：神经系统在加工信息的容量方面是有限度的，不可能对所有的感觉刺激进行加工。当信息通过各种感觉通道进入神经系统时，要经过一个过滤机制。只有一部分信息可以通过这个机制，并接受进一步的加工；而其他信息就被阻断在它的外面而完全丧失了。布罗德本特把这种过滤机制比喻为一个狭长的瓶口，当人们往瓶内灌水时，一部分水通过瓶颈进入瓶内，而另一部分由于瓶口狭小、通道容量有限而留在瓶外了。这种理论也叫瓶颈理论或单通道理论。

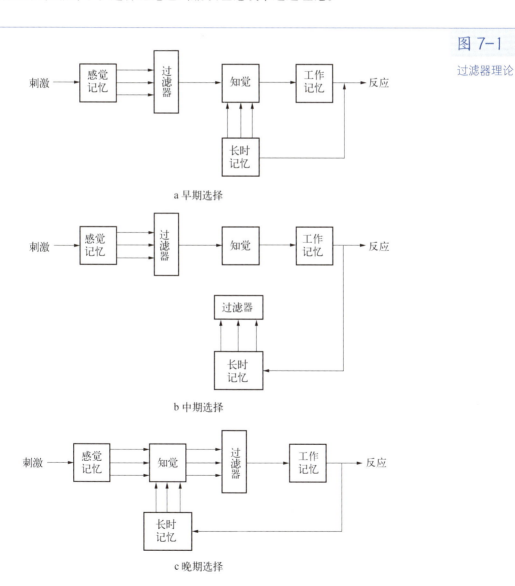

图 7-1 过滤器理论

（二）衰减理论

特瑞斯曼（Treisman）提出了衰减理论（attenuation theory）（如图7-2所示）。衰减理论主张，当信息通过过滤装置时，不被注意或非追随的信息只是在强度上减弱了，而不是完全消失。特瑞斯曼指出，不同刺激的激活阈限是不同的。有些刺激对人有重要意义，如自己的名字、火警信号等，容易激活。当它们出现在非追随耳的通道时，容易被人们所接受。

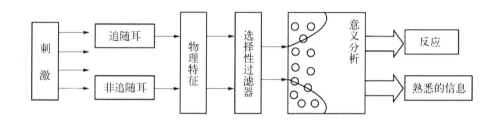

图 7-2　衰减理论

（三）容量分配理论

"容量分配模型"由心理学家卡里曼（Kahneman）提出。容量分配理论（capacity allocation theory）试图把注意看成是一组对刺激进行归类和识别的认知资源或认知能力。这些认知资源是有限的。当刺激越复杂或加工任务越复杂时，占用的认知资源就越多。当认知资源完全被占用时，新的刺激将得不到加工。[1] 例如，当人驾驶车辆行驶在无人的高速公路上，可以一边开车，一边和车内的人说话。他之所以能够边开车边聊天，是因为这些活动所要求的注意容量没有超出他所能提供的容量。若在行人拥挤的街道上开车，大量的视觉和听觉刺激占用了他的注意容量，他也就不能再与同伴聊天了。

专栏 7-1　注意的生理机制

注意的生理机制是很复杂的，是大脑皮层中枢与皮层下中枢协同活动的结果。

注意首先与大脑皮层下脑干网状结构（由延脑、脑桥、中脑组成）的活动有密切关系。脑干网状结构的功能是调节和控制心理活动的激活水平，当外界刺激作用于人的感受器时，外界信息通过一条通道直接到达大脑皮层——特殊传入通路；它还通过另一条通路即经过网状结构后弥散到大脑皮层——非特殊传入通路，使大脑皮层处于激活状态。只有处于激活状态，大脑区域感受到的信息才是最清晰、最精确的。

---

[1] 彭聃龄.普通心理学[M].北京：北京师范大学出版社，2012：227—233.

实验表明,将动物的脑干网状结构切断后,动物就会陷入沉睡状态。临床上脑干损伤的病人,主要症状是长期处于睡眠状态或梦样状态。

另外,高级的有意注意还与大脑额叶的功能有密切的联系。

随着应用事件相关电位(ERP)技术、脑磁图(MEG)技术、正电子发射断层扫描(PET)等新技术用于神经心理学研究,发现认知活动在大脑皮层都有相应的功能区或功能单元定位,如视觉定位在枕叶部位;听觉定位在颞叶区。结果表明,当注意指向一定的认知活动时,可以改变相应的大脑功能区或神经功能单元的激活水平,从而对当前的认知活动产生影响。

——张朝,李天思,孙宏伟.心理学导论[M].北京:清华大学出版社,2008:220.

三、注意产生和维持的条件

(一)无意注意产生的原因

无意注意的产生有主客观两方面的因素:一是刺激物本身的特点,二是人的主观状态。

1. 刺激物本身的特点

(1)刺激物的强度

环境中出现的强烈刺激,如一声巨响、一道强光、一阵浓烈的气味、一次猛烈的碰撞,都可引起人的无意注意。一般来说,刺激的强度越大,越易引起人的注意。同时,对无意注意来说,起决定作用的往往不是刺激物的绝对强度,而是刺激物的相对强度,即刺激物强度与周围物体强度的对比。比如,当夜深人静时,一些微弱的声音如钟表的滴答声、冰箱的嗡嗡声会引起我们的注意,而这些声音在嘈杂的白天就不会引起我们的注意。

(2)刺激的变化和运动

在静止的背景上,运动、变化的刺激物容易引起人们的无意注意。如街道边闪动的霓虹灯、夜空中划过的流星,极易吸引人们的视线;教师在讲课时突然的停顿,也会马上引起思想开小差的学生的注意。

(3)刺激的对比

刺激物与周围环境在大小、形状、颜色和持续时间方面形成明显的对比差异时,易引起人们的注意。如"万绿丛中一点红""鹤立鸡群"等,特别显眼,就是对比的作用。

(4)刺激的新颖性

新颖、奇特的东西易成为人们注意的对象,而刻板、千篇一律的寻常刺激就不易引起人们的注意。经常来往的大街上突然竖起了一个巨型的新广告牌,引得路人纷纷注目;常见面的同事或同学突然穿了一件漂亮的衣服,不免会多看她(他)两眼。

2. 人的主观状态

(1)需要和兴趣

凡能满足人的需要、引起人的兴趣的事物,都容易吸引人们的注意。如一张报纸上有各种信息报道,球迷容易注意有关球赛的消息,找工作的人则特别注意招聘广告。

(2)情绪与期待

情绪在很大程度上影响着无意注意。一个人在心情舒畅时对平时不太在意的事物也会产生注意;而在心绪不佳时,即使是对平时感兴趣的事物也会视而不见、听而不闻。凡是人们期待着的事物,都容易引起注意。例如,中国古代章回体小说常用"欲知后事如何,且听下回分解"作为每一回的结尾,使读者形成一种期待心理,吸引读者一回回地读下去。

(3)知识经验

在一个人的知识经验的范畴内,并能在原有的基础上增加新知识的事物,易引起人们的无意注意。一个没学过高等数学的人,很难对杂志上刊登的高等数学方面的论文产生兴趣,这是因为他缺乏必要的知识经验。一个人所具有的知识经验的水平,直接影响着他对注意对象的选择。一般来说,具备一定基础并具有进一步探索的欲望是产生无意注意的最佳知识结构。

(4)身心状态

人的身心状态对无意注意也有重大影响。当一个人身患疾病、身心疲惫时,很难对事物产生注意;而当一个人身体健康、精力旺盛时,最容易对新鲜事物产生注意并且保持长久。实验证明,工作时出现的差错数量在工作日快结束时会增加,多是由于疲劳状态使注意难以集中造成的。

(二)维持有意注意的条件

1. 对活动目的的确定与理解

我们知道,有意注意是一种有预谋的注意,目的越明确越具体,对目的理解得越深刻、越清楚,完成任务的愿望越强烈,有意注意越容易引起与维持。否则,目的不明确,对活动目的的理解很肤浅,完成活动的愿望不强烈,态度消极,就极易被无关事物所吸引,在活动中漫无目的,有意注意就难以维持。

2. 稳定的间接兴趣

兴趣是人们进行活动的一种动力,当人们对某一事物发生兴趣时,就会推动人们去注意、认识该事物。兴趣有两种,一种是直接兴趣,一种是间接兴趣。直接兴趣是指个体对活动的过程或活动本身感兴趣;间接兴趣则是指个体对活动结果感兴趣。如果说,无意注意依赖于人的直接兴趣,那么,有意注意则主要依赖于人的间接兴趣。如学习外语时需要背诵大量的单词,易使人感到枯燥乏味,但由于认识到学习外语的重要性和作用,通过掌握外语来更好地吸取外国先进的科学技术,于是支持他把学习过程坚持下去。间接兴趣越深厚,个体对活动对象产生的有意注意就越稳定。

3. 意志努力

有意注意也叫意志的注意,个体的意志力对有意注意的维持起着重要的作用,尤其是在个体对注意对象缺乏兴趣,又有内外干扰的情况下,个体意志坚强与否直接影响有意注意的维持;相反,意志薄弱,害怕困难的人,不可能有良好的有意注意。

4. 活动的合理组织

在目的、任务明确的前提下,是否善于组织活动,也是引起和维持有意注意的重要条件。研究表明,形式单一的活动易使人产生厌倦和疲劳感,从而导致注意的分散;反之,灵活多样的活动有利于提高大脑的兴奋性,从而增加注意的稳定性。同时,在生活中养成良好的学习和工作习惯,起居饮食有规律,这样,在规定的时间内,就能迅速地集中起自己的注意力。相反,一个没有良好生活习惯的人,整天处于忙乱状态,他在必要时就难以组织起自己的注意。此外,把智力活动与某些外部操作结合起来,也有利于注意的维持。如在看书时适当做点笔记,可以帮助人们更好地集中注意。

(三)产生有意后注意的条件

1. 与人们对活动目的的认识有关

当认识到活动目的的重要性并能长期坚持不懈地从事这一活动时,有意注意才有可能发展为有意后注意。

2. 与活动的熟练程度和知识经验有关

一个人在开始从事某种活动或学习一门课程时,会因不熟练而产生困难,需要一定的意志努力才能坚持活动。以后当通过努力,对从事的活动熟悉并有较丰富的知识时,便会产生兴趣,因而就不需要那么大的意志努力来维持注意,这时有意注意便转化为有意后注意。

四、注意的品质

(一)注意的范围

注意的范围也叫注意的广度(attention span),是指一个人在同一时间内能清楚地把握对象的数量。在同一时间内,人能清楚地看到或听到的东西,其数量是有限的。注意的范围可通过测量来确定。如用速示器测量视知觉的注意范围,结果表明在不超过1/10秒的时间内,成人从速示器中所能把握的对象是4—6个彼此不相联系的外文字母,8—9个黑色圆点或3—4个几何图形。

影响注意范围的因素有很多:首先是对象的特点。如果被注意的对象具有实际的意义,容易被理解;排列集中有规则,能构成相互联系的整体,则注意的范围较大,反之,范围缩小。1859年,汉密尔顿(Hamilton)做了一个实验,他在地上撒了一把石子,发现人们很不容易同时看到六个以上的石子。如果把石子两个、三个或五个组成一堆,人们能同时看到的堆数和单个的数目几乎一样多,因为人们会把一堆看作一个单位。其次是活动的目的、任务的明确程度和个人的知识经验。任务简洁,目标明确,个体关注的范围较大;任务复杂,需要更多地去注意细节或目标模糊时,关注的范围较小。个人的知识经验越丰富,整体知觉能力较强,则有助于扩大注意的范围;经验贫乏,则使注意的范围缩小。

> 专栏 7-2
>
> 有学者对体育运动与儿童注意广度的关系进行实验研究,实验对象为小学五年级在校生。随机整班抽取五年级的五个班的学生为被试,其中的四个班作为实验组,另外

的一个班作为控制组,每个组均包括男女生被试在内。其中两个实验班进行足球学习,两个实验班进行乒乓球学习,小强度、中强度各一班。实验共进行12周,每周3次,每次30分钟(不包括准备活动与结束阶段),实验内容以足球、乒乓球各项目的基本技术教学为主,并采用适当的比赛形式开展各项目的教学活动。实验采用前、后测,前测在教学实验开始前一周进行,后测在锻炼12周后的一周进行,前、后测均在星期三下午进行团体施测,以保证施测的前后一致性和不同组别的一致性。实验组的教学由两名教学经验丰富的教师担任,相同项目的教学由同一个老师进行,并保持教学内容相同。控制组的活动安排以自习或阅览图书为主。实验结果表明:①足球锻炼对少儿的注意广度有显著影响,且中等强度的锻炼效果好于小强度的锻炼效果。②乒乓球锻炼对少儿的注意广度的影响不明显。③强度因素对注意广度的影响不明显,但不同强度的乒乓球与足球锻炼,其效果有一定的差异。④性别因素对注意的广度无显著性影响。

——吴广宏.足球与乒乓球锻炼对小学生的注意广度影响的实验研究[J].北京体育大学学报,2005(12):1726—1727.

(二)注意的稳定性

注意的稳定性(stability of attention)是指注意长时间地保持在某一对象上。这是注意在时间上的特征。注意的稳定性是人们完成实践活动的保证。学生没有稳定的注意,就难以领会知识,获得系统的经验;工人没有稳定的注意,就不能安全有效地进行生产操作,难以按质按量地完成生产任务。注意的稳定性不等于注意的静止不动,人的注意是有起伏现象的。如图7-3所示,可以明显的观察到注意的起伏(attention fluctuation)。注视该图,你会发现两个方形的相对位置不是固定不变的,并且几个立方体的位置也不是固定不变的。短时间的注意起伏不会影响活动的完成。注意的稳定性是指虽然所接触的对象和行动本身可以变化,但是活动的总目标始终不变。

注意的稳定性与人的主观状态和对象的特点有关。活动态度积极,责任心强,良好的学习与工作习惯,较强的抗干扰能力,情绪稳定,身心健康,可使人的注意力稳定

图 7-3

注意的起伏

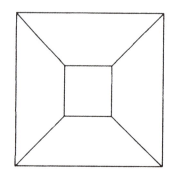
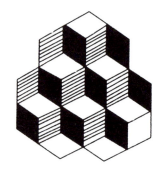

持久。注意对象的特点也会影响注意的稳定性。如果活动的对象是单调的、静止的，注意就难以稳定；如果注意的对象是复杂的、变化的、活动的，注意就容易稳定。

与注意的稳定性相反的品质是注意的分散（或称分心）。注意的分散就是注意离开了当前应指向和集中的对象，而指向了无关的对象。分心是注意的一种障碍和缺陷。有些学生上课时总是东张西望、左顾右盼，这是他们学习后进的一个重要原因。教师应及时了解学生的这种缺陷，帮助他们养成良好的注意习惯。

> **专栏 7-3**
>
> 注意力缺损多动症，或 ADHD，描述的是那些表现出持续的、与年龄不相符的、并不足以导致破坏其主要生活活动的注意力分散、多动和冲动的儿童。
>
> ADHD 这一术语可能是新的，但表现出过分多动和行为失控的儿童却历来都有。在 1845 年，德国神经病学家海黎胥·霍夫曼在他写的一本儿童故事书里对多动进行了描述，这是已知的有关多动症的最早记录之一。他用幽默的诗句描述了"坐立不安的菲力"就餐的场景：怎么坐都不爽，左晃晃，右摇摇，前扭扭，后挪挪，椅子眼见要翻倒；菲力高声叫，拉住桌布魂儿慌，稀里哗啦一声响，杯盘刀叉落满堂。
>
> 1994 年，一篇关于 ADHD 的名为《驱力过度的生活》的文章引起了瞩目，其间对男孩达斯提·恩的行为进行了描述：
>
> 达斯提下楼吃早餐，50 磅重的身体上的每一块肌肉都在疯狂地跳动。达斯提先从橱柜里拖出一盒麦片，紧接着开始用手抓麦片，用脚踢盒子，房间里顿时到处都是麦片碎屑。在他终于搞坏了清理麦片碎屑的簸箕之后，他开始转向下一个目标，把卫生间里的三卷手纸拖了出来，然后弄得满屋子都是。
>
> 尽管菲力和达斯提相隔 150 多年，但两个孩子用餐时的行为都是 ADHD 典型的基本症状。两个男孩的注意力都难以集中——不能集中在目标行为上，多动——动个不停，冲动——行事毫不考虑。
>
> ——埃里克·J·马什（Eric J. Mash），戴维·A·沃尔夫（David A. Wolfe）. 异常儿童心理［M］. 徐哲宁，苏雪云，译. 上海：上海人民出版社，2009：134.

（三）注意的分配

注意的分配（distribution of attention）是指在同一时间内把注意指向两种或几种不同的对象与活动上。如教师一边讲课，一边观察学生的反应；学生一边听课，一边记笔记；司机一边双手操纵方向盘，一边注意路面情况。所谓"眼观六路、耳听八方"，就是注意的分配现象。注意的分配是完成复杂工作任务的重要条件。但是，同时把注意分配到几种活动上也不是轻易就能做到的。一手画方、一手画圆，可能哪个图形也画不好；初学钢琴或骑自行车，很容易顾此失彼。

因此，注意的分配是有条件的。首先，在同时进行的几种活动中，只有一种是不熟悉的，需要集中注意力去做，而其他活动所需要完成的动作比较熟练或者已经达到自动化的程度，只需稍加留意或者使之处于注意的边缘即可。其次，同时进行的几种活动之间的关系也很重要。如果同时进行的几种活动的性质和内容有密切的联系，或者通过训练把各项活动的动作组合成为一个整体的操作系统，那么注意的分配就可以顺利进行。现实生活处处要求人们能够将注意很好地分配。注意分配的能力是在实践中锻炼出来的，我们应该努力培养和锻炼自己注意分配的能力。

> **专栏 7-4**
>
> 使左手画方，右手画圆，令一时俱成，虽执规矩之心，迴剟劂，而不能者。由心不两用，则手不并运也。
>
> ——刘昼.《刘子新论·专学》

（四）注意的转移

注意的转移（shifting of attention）是指根据新任务的要求，主动及时地把注意从一个对象转移到另一个对象上，或在同一活动中从一种操作转向另一种操作。注意的转移是注意的动力特征。注意的转移与注意的分散不同。前者是根据任务的需要主动地、有目的地把注意从一个对象转到另一个对象；后者是在需要稳定注意的时候受无关刺激的干扰离开了当前应当注意的对象。

在人类的正常生活和工作中，随着活动的变化、任务的更新，需要人们的注意能及时迅速地转移，以保证新任务的完成。注意的转移有一个过程。我们常说"万事开头难"，指的就是注意还没有完全从别的活动转移到新的活动上来。注意转移的快慢和难易程度常依赖于前一活动的性质、前后活动的关系以及人们对前一活动的态度。如果前一活动中注意的紧张度高，前后活动关系较小，或人们依然沉浸在前一活动中，注意的转移就很困难。此外，注意的转移还与人们的神经类型和已有的习惯有关。神经类型灵活的人比非灵活型的人注意转移要迅速且容易些；已养成良好注意转移习惯的人比没有养成这种习惯的人更能迅速实现注意的转移。

第三节

注意规律在教育教学中的应用

我们已经掌握了许多注意的规律，在教学实践中该如何运用呢？本节主要内容包括如何运用教学规律组织教学和如何培养学生的注意品质。

一、运用注意规律组织教学

(一) 根据注意的外部表现了解学生的听课情况

人在注意时,有关的感觉器官会做朝向运动,如举目凝视、侧耳倾听等,这样可得到最清晰的印象。当人的注意高度集中时,有关的肌肉会处于紧张状态而使无关的动作停止下来。如学生集中注意力看黑板时,手与脚的下意识的小动作会停止下来,只有眼睛做着有规律的扫描运动。人的注意高度集中时,血液循环和呼吸系统都会发生相应的变化,一般规律是:肢体血管收缩,四肢血流量减少,头部血管舒张,大脑血流量增多。同时,呼吸变得轻微而缓慢,吸气时间变得急促短暂,呼气时间相对延长,当注意达到高峰时,甚至会出现屏息现象。此外,当紧张注意时,还会出现心跳加快,牙关紧闭,握紧拳头等现象。

根据注意的这些外部表现,我们就可以判断一个人是否集中注意力了,这对从事教育工作和其他行业的人有着重要的意义。不过,注意的外部表现和注意的内心状态也有不一致的情况。上课时有的学生看似注意听讲,实则已想入非非或已注意其他事物。此外,由于人可以控制自己的表情,内心十分注意而表面上却可以装出一副心不在焉的样子,使外部表现与内部状态不一致,此时需要人们仔细分辨。

(二) 运用无意注意规律组织教学

无意注意主要是受客观外界的刺激而不由自主地发生的一种注意形式,它对教学活动可产生两种截然不同的作用。一种是消极作用,由于教学活动以外的偶发事物分散了学生的注意,干扰正常的教学活动;另一种是积极作用,通过对某些刺激物特点的有意识地控制来吸引学生的注意,提高教学效果。运用无意注意的规律进行教学的目的,是使无意注意发挥积极作用,避免消极作用,使学生轻松愉快地进行学习。

1. 创造良好的教学环境

良好的教学环境是避免无意注意产生消极影响的重要因素。校园作为学生活动和娱乐的重要场所,要保持安静、整洁、优美、清新,避免噪音和有害空气的污染。在校园适宜的地方,可书写名人学者的格言警句,以陶冶学生美好的心灵,为学生在课堂上稳定集中地学习营造一种良好的氛围。教室的布置要朴素、简洁,富有教育意义,不要有不必要的张贴和过多的装饰。教室内空气要流通,光线要充足。教师的衣着要朴素大方,言语表情勿矫揉造作。学生要养成铃响即进教室的良好习惯,不迟到,不早退,不随意进出教室,以防影响他人注意的稳定和集中。

2. 注意教学内容的组织

凡能够满足需要、符合兴趣的刺激物易成为无意注意的对象,因此,教师在组织教学内容时,应充分考虑学生已有的知识经验,选材时难易要适当。教材过难,会脱离学生已有的知识经验;教材过易,所讲的内容学生早已熟悉,这两者都将造成学生注意力的分散。研究表明,能吸引学生兴趣并使之保持稳定注意的,既不是他们完全不了解,也不是他们完全熟悉的教材,而是与他们已有的知识相联系的内容。这样,在教学时,教师应在学生已有知识的基础上,把教学内容安排得丰富些,要时刻向学生介绍一些与本学科有关的最新研究成果。

3. 教学方法要多样化

单调、呆板的教学方法会使学生觉得索然无味，失去学习的兴趣。生动灵活的教学方法则有助于调动学生的学习兴趣，维持学生的注意。教师上课时除采用传统的讲授法这一教学方法外，还应穿插运用其他教学方式，如讨论、角色扮演、课堂小实验等方式，活跃课堂气氛，提高学生通过动手、动脑发现知识并获得知识的能力，避免教师"一言堂"使学生感到厌倦的局面。此外，教师还可以配合教学内容使用录音、录像、投影、幻灯、多媒体、网络等电化教学设备及模型、模象等直观教具，进一步丰富教学形式。但在使用直观教具时，应注意不要让其成为分散学生注意力的源头。正确的做法应是先对教具进行适当的掩饰，待需要时再呈现给学生。

4. 注意观察学生的反应

教师上课时应随时注意观察学生注意力集中的情况，一旦发现学生走神、分心、做小动作等，就应当设法及时予以制止，如采用目光凝视、摇头示意、提问或干脆突然停止讲课等方式，把学生的注意力重新拉回到课堂上来，尽可能不要当场训斥学生，以免干扰集体的注意力，打断其他同学的思路。

（三）运用有意注意的规律进行教学

从本质意义上来说，学生的学习更多的是一种自觉的、有目的的、以一定方式组织起来的活动。学生如果只凭兴趣去学习，学习活动势必难以持久，也不能获得系统条理的知识，而且学习过程中总会遇到干扰和障碍，这样，教师必须唤起和维持学生的有意注意。

1. 明确学习的目的和任务，激发学生学习的自觉性

明确的目的和任务是唤起和维持学生有意注意的重要条件。只有目的、任务明确了，学生的注意力才能做到有的放矢，抓住重点、难点，去看、去听、去记、去想，学习才有成效。否则，看书乱看、听课乱听、眉毛胡子一把抓，就难以取得令人满意的效果。一般地，教师在开始讲授一门新课时，应首先说明学习这门课的总的目的、任务和意义，在每一节课开始时，也应向学生说明本节课的主要任务和所需解决的问题，在讲到重点、难点时预先向学生提示一下，这些做法都有助于学生根据目的、任务来积极地组织自己的注意。

2. 培养稳定的间接兴趣

教师既要引导学生明确目前的学习目的和任务，同时要让他们明了长远的学习目标和意义，使他们能认识到学习的重要性和肩负的责任，把自己个人的学习与社会的需要及自己的前途联系起来，培养学生对学习后果的兴趣，即间接兴趣。在教学中，间接兴趣可以成为支持学生为既定目标而努力奋斗，产生克服困难的力量和保持高度有意注意的动力。

3. 培养学生克服困难和干扰的意志力

有意注意是"意志的注意"，因此，激发学生克服困难和干扰的意志力，也是维持学生有意注意的重要途径。教师可以通过各种教育教学活动，培养学生的意志力，如向学生讲述伟大人物锻炼意志力的故事，以树立榜样，激发学生的自制力。此外，教师还应对学生进行组织性和纪律性教育，建立正常的教学常规，并一贯严格要求学生，促使学生养成良

好的注意习惯,也可使意志薄弱的学生借助外界的力量集中注意。

4. 合理地组织课堂教学

教师在课堂上要严密、紧凑、合理地组织教学,精心设计教学环节,做到环环相扣,使每一教学环节都有充实的活动内容;面向全体学生安排与提出富有启发性的问题,让所有的学生都投入紧张的学习活动,使他们没有分散注意的机会,从而保证有意注意长时间地处于稳定状态。

(四)运用注意相互转换规律进行教学

在教学工作中,单纯依靠无意注意,会使教学活动缺乏目的性和计划性,学生容易对知识浅尝辄止,遇到困难容易半途而废。反之,过分强调有意注意,学生容易疲劳,容易丧失对学习本身的兴趣,造成注意的分散。因此,教师要善于运用注意相互交替与转换的规律组织教学,使教学活动成为学生心向往之并乐意为之的事情。针对一节课来说,教师首先应通过组织教学将学生的注意力由上一节课或课间活动的有趣对象引导到课堂教学中,讲明本节课的主要教学目标及应掌握的知识点,引起学生的有意注意。接着可巧妙设计问题,采用启发式教学,引发学生对新课题、新内容的兴趣,产生无意注意。随后,在讲到重点、难点时,要提醒学生特别注意,由无意注意转入有意注意。在紧张而努力的有意注意之后,通过教学方式的改变,如适当运用直观材料或趣味性的资料使之转入无意注意。下课之前,学生的注意容易涣散,此时教师应向学生提出要求,布置作业,将学生的注意力集中到应该完成的学习任务上来。总之,一节课就是这样各种注意形式相互交替和转换,从而使学生的注意有张有弛,始终保持稳定集中。当然,这种注意交替与转换,没有固定的模式,教师可根据教学的中心任务、教学的难度及学生注意力发展水平与表现巧于安排。

二、培养学生良好的注意品质

(一)增强注意的稳定性

注意稳定性不佳往往与意志力薄弱、情绪不稳定有关,因此注意稳定性的训练应从这两方面入手。具体的做法有以下几种。

1. 自我暗示法

在开始学习或工作时,先在心里对自己说:"集中注意力!不管其他的事,先把目前的事情做好。"工作学习一段时间后注意力容易分散,这时对自己说:"不要开小差,坚持一下把工作完成!"工作结束后,可对自己进行一下口头奖励,如说:"我真行!""我真棒!""下一次我可以做得更好!"

2. 循序渐进法

有的人已经养成了注意力易分散的不良习惯,为纠正此习惯,可采用循序渐进的方法。起初,先给自己找一些难度较小、时间较短、自己感兴趣的事情去做,然后使任务难度加大,时间加长,最后迫使自己去完成不感兴趣但必须去完成的工作或学习任务,使自己注意力稳定的时间逐步延长。

3. 干扰训练法

为磨练自己的意志力,可故意增加一些干扰,提高自己抗干扰的能力。干扰刺激可以是电台广播、电视节目、外界的嘈杂声等,训练时应遵循干扰刺激从小到大、训练时间从短到长、任务由易到难的原则。

4. 放松法

人在情绪波动时也易引起注意力的分散。这时,可首先采用一些放松的方法使自己平静下来,再进行工作或学习。如深呼吸法,先深深地吸一口气,再慢慢地呼出去,反复做几次,可帮助自己稳定心神。再如,肌肉放松法,先紧紧地握起拳头,然后慢慢地松开,也可使自己情绪稳定。

(二)注意广度的训练

训练注意广度的目的在于提高自身的整体知觉能力,具体做法如下:

给自己列一张数字表,表中的数字都是无规则的(如下所示),然后划去任意两个数之间的某个数,这些数字都可自己选定,如划去"1"和"8"之间的"6"字等。

```
1 5 3 4 9 6 3 8 2 5 4 7 9
3 0 3 7 1 5 4 2 6 9 8 7 4
4 2 7 3 0 1 5 6 4 9 2 3 8
```

划数字训练的评分方法是计算划对、划错和漏划三种数据。全部划对的数字的总和称为粗分,划错的加上二分之一漏划的称为失误,粗分减去失误称为净分。用公式计算即为:

净分=划对数−(划错数+1/2漏划数)
失误率=【(划错数+1/2漏划数)/划对数】×100%

通过比较多次训练间的净分和失误率,可以看出自己的注意广度是否得到扩大。

(三)注意分配的训练

提高注意分配的能力,关键在于训练自己熟练掌握与活动有关的技能,并使技能达到自动化或半自动化的程度。这是顺利实现注意分配的最基本的条件。比如拍球画圈练习:(1)老师给第一个学生一个篮球和一张A4白纸。(2)让学生在座位上坐着,用一只手拍球,同时要求学生用另外一只手在白纸上画圆圈。(3)每个学生都要如此进行训练。(4)每次训练2分钟,休息1分钟,共进行五个轮次。

(四)注意转移的训练

改善注意转移的品质可以通过提高主体的自我控制能力来实现。具体做法如下:
按以下规则出两道题:
第一题:写两个数,把一个数写在另一个数的上边。例如4和2,然后把它们加起来,把和的个位数写在右边的上方,像下面所示的那样,再把上面的那个数移到下面,继续这样做……

```
4 6 0 6 6 2 8 0
2 4 6 0 6 6 2 8
```

第二题：起始的两个数与上述相同，然后把两个数的和的个位数写在右边的下方，把下面的数移到上面，继续这样做……

```
4 2 6 8 4 2 6 8
2 6 8 4 2 6 8 4
```

稍加练习后，随便请个人来，让他每隔半分钟向自己发出命令："第一""第二""第一""第二"等，听了命令后，画一竖杠，立即改做另一题，尽可能准确而迅速地完成作业。检查后就会发现，错误主要发生在两题转换之间。通过多次练习，自我控制能力得到提高，做题的错误率会减少，转换的速度也会加快。

本章小结

注意是心理活动对一定事物的指向和集中。它是心理过程有效进行必不可少的心理前提。它是一种独特的心理现象，它具有选择、保持、调节和监督三种功能。注意的品质有注意的广度、注意的稳定性、注意的分配和注意的转移四种，它们是有效地完成工作和学习任务的重要保证。注意可划分为无意注意、有意注意、有意后注意三种，每种注意形式都有各自的规律。运用这些规律在教学中可以提高教学效率，在自我完善中可以提高个人的注意品质。

关键术语

注意　无意注意　有意注意　有意后注意　注意的稳定性　注意的分配　注意的转移

讨论与应用

1. 阅读以下材料，分析其中所体现的注意理论。

鸡尾酒会效应是指人的一种听力选择能力，因常见于鸡尾酒会上而得名。它是指在各种声音混杂的鸡尾酒会上，有音乐声、谈话声、酒杯餐具的碰撞声等，但我们都可以将注意力集中在欣赏的音乐或与别人的谈话上，而对周围的其他声音充耳不闻。但是如果这时有人说到我们的名字或提到我们感兴趣的事情，我们会立即有所反应。该效应揭示了人类听觉系统中令人惊奇的能力。鸡尾酒会效应能够让多数人将很多其他无关的声音关掉，只选择听自己关注的那一个声音。还有一个类似的情况是，人们能够从毫不关注的兴奋点中立即识别对自己来说重要的文字信息。

2. 试用心理学的有关理论加以分析。

在教学中有这样一种现象，有些老师非常重视兴趣对学生学习的影响，主张"要让学生在笑声中掌握知识"，每次上课学生都兴趣盎然，笑声满堂。但是笑过之后学生却头脑空空,每到考试便手足无措。

3. 请用心理学注意的有关知识分析一下原因。

为了把课上得生动形象,王老师带去了不少直观教具,有实物、图片,还有模型。进教室后,王教师就把这些教具放在桌子上,或挂在黑板上。他想今天的课效果一定很好,可是结果并非如此。

第八章
情绪、情感
QINGXU、QINGGAN

  亲爱的同学，是否有人问过你"今天感觉怎么样"，或者你曾经说过"我今天感觉不太开心"。这里的"感觉"与你前面已经学过的"感觉"含义是否相同？或者你是否注意到你身边有些人看上去总是兴高采烈，而有些人却常常愁眉不展，这是什么原因呢？请带着这些问题学习本章的内容吧。

通过本章的学习,你能够
- 了解情绪、情感的概念
- 理解情绪、情感的分类
- 掌握情绪、情感的规律
- 掌握调节情绪的方法
- 学会在教学中运用情绪、情感的规律

【本章结构】

本章主要是回答"什么是情绪""什么是情感"的问题。它有助于你更加科学地认识情绪、情感的概念和内涵;明确情绪、情感产生的生理机制;掌握情绪、情感的类型;理解情绪、情感的一般性规律;了解如何更有效地在教学中发挥情感因素的积极作用,以及如何提高自己的情感修养。

第一节
情绪、情感概述

一、情绪、情感的概念

情绪（emotion）、情感（affection）是人对客观事物产生的一种态度体验。情绪、情感是人对客观现实的反映，但它不是反映事物本身，而是反映了人对该事物的态度。情绪和情感总是由客观事物引起，离开了具体的客观事物，人不可能产生情绪和情感，世界上没有无缘无故的爱与恨，就是这个道理。客观现实是情绪、情感产生的源泉，人的情绪、情感是对客观现实的反映，但是，这种反映与感觉、知觉、思维不同，感觉和知觉是以映像的形式反映客观事物的本身，思维是以概念的方式反映客观事物，而情绪、情感则是以体验的方式来反映客观事物。例如，看到一位同学谈吐文雅，行为端庄，我们会产生好感。这种好感的产生尽管来自该同学本身，但好感所反映的却是我们对该同学的表现态度，是对该表现的一种体验或感受。

专栏 8-1

> 莱昂纳多5岁了而且非常可爱，他还能做许多5岁孩子们能做的事情：玩拼图、搭积木，以及和成年人一起玩猜谜游戏。但是与其他5岁的孩子不同，莱昂纳多从来没有为他的能力感到自豪，也未曾对他妈妈生气，或者厌倦他的功课。那是因为莱昂纳多处在一个无法感受任何情绪的状态中。他从来不会感到高兴或者伤心、快乐或者失望、害羞、嫉妒、恼怒、兴奋、感激或者悔恨。他从来没有笑或者哭过。他的妈妈花了好多年教他做出各种情绪的面部表情，例如惊奇和伤心，以及怎样觉察他人的表情。莱昂纳多知道当有人对他说友好的话时，他应该微笑，而且他应该时不时抬起眉毛来表达对别人说的话感兴趣。但是他妈妈敏锐地发现：莱昂纳多只是做出妈妈教他的表情，因为莱昂纳多是一台机器。
> ——丹尼尔·夏克特（Daniel Schacter），等.心理学[M].傅小兰，等，译.上海：华东师范大学出版社，2016：313.

二、情绪、情感的关系

情绪和情感是两个既有区别又有联系的概念。其区别在于：

（一）从需要的角度看

情绪是和有机体的生物需要相联系的体验形式，如喜、怒、哀、乐等；情感是同人的高级的社会性需要相联系的一种较复杂而又稳定的体验形式,如与人交往相关的友谊感、与遵守行为准则规范相关的道德感、与精神文化需要相关的美感与理智感等。

(二) 从发生的角度看

情绪发生较早,为人类和动物所共有,而情感发生得较晚,是人类所特有的,是个体发展到一定阶段才产生的。新生儿只有悲伤、不满、高兴等情绪表现,通过一定的社会实践才逐渐产生形成如友爱、归属感、自豪感、责任感、道德感等情感体验。

(三) 从表现形式看

情绪一般发生得迅速、强烈而短暂,有强烈的生理的变化,有明显的外部表现,并具有情境性(由具体情境而产生,随情境的变化、消失而变化、消失)、冲动性(爆发力强,力度大)、动摇性(变化快,不稳定)。而情感是经过多次情感体验概括化的结果,不受情境的影响,并能控制情绪,具有较大的稳定性;情感由于只与对事物的深刻性认识相联系,因而深沉,具有深刻性;情感更多地表达内心体验,很少产生冲动,具有内隐性。

情绪和情感虽然有各自的特点,但又是相互联系、相互依存的。情感是在情绪的基础上形成的,反过来,情感对情绪又产生巨大的影响,它们是人感情活动过程的两个不同侧面,二者在人的生活中水乳交融,很难加以严格的区分。从某种意义上说,情绪是情感的外部表现,情感是情绪的本质内容。

三、情绪、情感的分类

(一) 情绪的分类

1. 情绪的基本形式
(1) 快乐

快乐是指盼望的目标达到或需要得到满足之后,解除紧张时的情绪体验。如亲人相聚时的"高兴",学习获得好成绩时的"愉快",工作取得成就的"满意"等,都是快乐的情绪。但是有一些情绪,如怜悯、奇怪、惊奇等,既不是明显的快乐,也不是明显的不快乐。

快乐的程度取决于愿望的满足程度。一般说来,可以分为满意、愉快、欢乐、狂喜等。引起快乐情绪的原因很多,如亲朋好友的聚会、美好理想的实现、宁静明亮的学习环境等都可以引起快乐的情绪。如果愿望或理想的实现具有意外性或突然性,则更会加强快乐的程度。

(2) 悲哀

悲哀是与所热爱的对象的失去和所盼望的东西的幻灭相联系的情绪体验。引起悲哀的原因比较多,如亲人去世,升学考试失意,自己所珍爱的物品丢失等,都会引起悲哀的情绪体验。

悲哀的程度取决于失去对象的价值。此外,主体的意识倾向和个性特征对人的悲哀程度也有重要的影响。根据悲哀的程度不同,可分为遗憾、失望、难过、悲伤、极度悲痛等不同的等级。悲哀有时伴随哭泣,使紧张释放,缓解心理压力。在比较强的悲哀中,常常伴发失眠、焦虑、冷漠等心理反应。

（3）愤怒

愤怒是由于外界干扰使愿望实现受到压抑，目的实现受到阻碍，从而逐渐积累紧张而产生的情绪体验。引起愤怒的原因有很多，如恶意的伤害、不公平的对待等都能引起愤怒的情绪。愤怒的产生取决于人对达到目的的障碍的意识程度，只有个体清楚地意识到某种障碍时，愤怒才会产生。

愤怒的程度取决于干扰的程度、次数及挫折的大小。根据愤怒的程度，可把愤怒分为不满意、生气、愠怒、激愤、狂怒等。

（4）恐惧

恐惧是有机体企图摆脱、逃避某种情景而又苦于无能为力的情绪体验。引起恐惧的原因有很多，如黑暗、巨响、意外事故等。恐惧的程度取决于有机体处理紧急情况的能力。

在快乐、悲哀、愤怒、恐惧四种基本情绪中，快乐属于肯定的积极的情绪体验，它对有机体具有增力作用。而悲哀、愤怒、恐惧通常情况下属于消极的情绪体验，对人的学习、工作、健康具有消极的作用，因而应当把它们控制在适当的水平上。但在一定条件下，悲哀、愤怒、恐惧也可以起到积极的作用，如战士的愤怒有利于他们在战场上勇敢战斗；对可怕后果的恐惧有利于个体提高责任感与警惕性；悲哀可以使人"化悲痛为力量"，从而摆脱困境。

2. 情绪的基本状态

根据情绪发生的强度、持续时间的长短及外部表现的情况，可将情绪分成心境、激情、应激等。

（1）心境（mood）

心境是一种使人的心理活动都染上某种相应色彩的微弱而持久的情绪状态。其特点表现为：第一，和缓而微弱，似微波荡漾，有时人们甚至觉察不出它的发生；第二，持续时间较长，少则几天，长则数月；第三，它是一种非定向性的弥散性的情绪体验，在人的心理上形成了一种淡薄性的背景，使人的心理活动、行为举止都蒙上一层相应的色彩。例如，人在得意时感到精神爽快，事事顺眼，干什么都起劲。失意时，则整天愁眉不展，事事都感到枯燥乏味。

心境产生的原因是多种多样的。个人生活中的重大事件，诸如事业的成败、工作的逆顺、人际关系的亲疏、健康状况的优劣，甚至自然界的事物，如时令气候、环境景物等都可以成为某种心境形成的原因。除了由当时的情境而产生的暂时心境外，人还能形成各自独特的稳定心境。这种稳定的心境是依人的生活经验中占主导地位的情绪体验的性质为转移的。例如，有的人朝气蓬勃，在他的生活中愉快的心境便占主导地位；有的人失望忧愁，在他的生活中忧伤之情便占主导地位。对心境起决定性影响的是一个人的世界观。

心境有消极和积极之分。积极的心境，使人振奋愉快，能推动人的工作与学习，激发人的主动性与创造性；消极的心境则使人颓丧悲观，妨碍人的工作和学习，抑制人的积极性的发挥。人应充分发挥其主观能动性，正确地认识、评价自己的心境，消除消极心境的不良影响，培养坚强的意志，增强抗御外界不良刺激和干扰的能力，树立正确的理想和信念，有意识地掌握自己的心境，做心境的主人。

（2）激情（passion）

激情是一种强烈的、爆发式的、持续时间短暂的情绪体验，如欣喜若狂、暴跳如雷、悲恸、绝望等。激情有以下四个特点：第一，激情具有激动性和冲动性。激情一旦产生，人完全被情绪所驱使，言行缺乏理智，带有很大的冲动性和盲目性；第二，激情维持的时间比较短，冲动一过，激情也就弱化或消失了；第三，激情具有明确的指向性。激情通常由特定的对象所引起，如意外的成功会引起狂喜，理想破灭会引起绝望，黑暗、巨响会引起恐惧等；第四，激情具有明显的外部表现。在激情状态下，人的内脏器官、腺体和外部表现都会发生明显的变化，如暴怒时"面红耳赤"，绝望时"目瞪口呆"，狂喜时"手舞足蹈"等。

引起激情的原因是多方面的，对人有重大意义的事件（如巨大的成功、亲人的亡故）、对立意向的冲突、过度的抑郁和兴奋，都可能导致激情的产生。从生理上看，激情是外界的超强刺激使大脑皮层对皮下中枢的抑制减弱甚至解除，从而使皮下的情绪中枢强烈兴奋的结果。在激情状态下，人的认识范围缩小，理智下降，不能正确评价自身行为的意义及结果，控制自己的能力减弱，不能很好地约束自己，往往会做出令人吃惊的蠢事。但是，如果以激情是不可控制的或以激情爆发来原谅自己的错误，也是不正确的。人能够意识到自己的激情状态，也能够有意识地调节和控制。

激情具有双重作用。激情如果伴随着冷静的头脑和坚强的意志，它可以成为动员人的所有潜能积极投入行动的巨大动力。如许多诗人、艺术家常常是在激情状态下迸发出灵感，妙思横溢，完成不朽的杰作的；许多爱国志士也往往是在激情状态下做出轰轰烈烈、可歌可泣的英雄壮举。激情如果是不符合社会要求的、对机体有害的，就起消极作用。青少年犯罪中常见的就是激情犯罪。可见，激情的意义是由它的社会价值决定的。

（3）应激（stress）

应激是在出乎意料的紧急和危险的情况下所引起的高度紧张的情绪状态。当人遇到紧张危险情境又需迅速采取重大决策时，就可能导致应激状态的产生。在应激状态下，人可能有两种表现：一是目瞪口呆，手足失措，陷于一片混乱之中；二是急中生智，冷静沉着，动作准确有力，及时摆脱险境。

出乎意料的危险情景或面临重大压力的事件，如火灾、地震、突遭袭击、参加重大的比赛、考试等，都可能是应激状态出现的原因。

应激有积极的作用，也有消极的作用。一般的应激状态能使有机体具有特殊的防御排险机能，能使人精力旺盛，使思想特别清楚、精确，使人动作敏捷，推动人化险为夷，转危为安，及时摆脱困境。但紧张而又长期的应激会产生全身兴奋，注意和知觉范围狭小，言语不规则、不连贯，行为动作紊乱。在意外的情况下，人能不能迅速判断情况并做出决策，有赖于人的意志力是否果断、坚强，是否有类似情况的行为经验。另外，思想觉悟、事业心、责任感、献身精神等也是在应激状态下防止行为紊乱的重要因素。

人如果长期处于应激状态，会有害于身体健康，严重的还会危及生命。加拿大生理学家谢尔耶（Selye）于1974年曾提出：应激状态的延续能破坏一个人的生物学保护机制，使人降低抵抗力，易受疾病侵袭。他把应激反应分成三个阶段：第一阶段为惊觉阶段。表现为肾上腺分泌增加，心率上升，体温和肌肉弹性下降，血糖和胃酸度暂时性增加。在这种情况下，有可能出现临床休克。这是能量聚积阶段。第二阶段为阻抗阶段。表现为前阶段症状消失,身体动员许多保护系统参加应激,使身体代谢水平提高,肝脏释放糖分,使血糖增加。这个阶段如果延长(过度)则会使身体内的糖大量消耗,下丘脑、脑垂体和肾上腺系统过度活动,给内脏带来物理损伤,出现胃溃疡、胸腺退化等症状。这是能量的释放阶段。第三阶段为衰竭阶段。有机体体力耗竭,导致重病或死亡。这是能量衰竭阶段。

(二)情感的分类

根据社会性需要是否获得满足而产生的情感主要有道德感、理智感和美感。这是人类社会历史发展过程中形成的高级的社会情感。

1. 道德感

道德感(moral feeling)是人们运用一定的道德标准评价自身或他人的行为时所产生的一种情感体验。如敬佩、赞赏、憎恨、厌恶等。

人们在相互交往中掌握了社会上的道德标准,并将其转化为自己的社会需要。人们看到一定的言语行为和观察到一定的思想意图时,总是根据个人所掌握的道德标准加以评价,这时人所产生的情感体验即为道德感。如,当别人或自己的言论、行为、意图符合自己的道德标准时,便产生满意的、肯定的体验;否则,便产生消极的、否定的体验。可见,道德感是由人们所掌握的道德观念、道德标准决定的。

在不同的历史时代、不同的社会制度、不同的阶级中,道德标准是不同的。因此,道德感总是受社会生活条件的制约,受阶级的制约。如封建社会的男尊女卑、君君臣臣、父父子子的道德伦理纲常就不适应于今天的社会。在社会主义制度下,爱国主义情感、国际主义情感、集体主义情感、责任感、义务感等才是社会主义社会所提倡的道德感。

道德感虽然受社会生活条件的制约、受阶级的制约,但是就全人类来讲,是有共同的道德标准的。例如,对社会义务的承担,对自己国家的热爱,对老弱病残的扶助等,任何社会都是宣传和倡导的,而对吸毒、凶杀、叛国等任何社会也都是加以杜绝、禁止的。

2. 理智感

理智感(rational feeling)是人们认识和追求真理的需要是否得到满足而产生的一种情感。它在认识活动中表现为:对事物的好奇心与新异感;对认识活动初步成就的欣慰与高兴的体验;对矛盾事物的怀疑与惊讶感;对判断证据不足时的不安感;对问题解答的坚信感;对知识的热爱、真理的追求;对偏见、迷信、谬误的憎恨;对错失良机的惋惜;对取得巨大成就的欢喜与自豪等。

理智感同人的认识活动的成就的获得、需要的满足、对真理的追求及思维任务的解决相联系。人的认识活动越深刻,求知欲望越强烈,追求真理的情趣越浓厚,人的理智感就越深厚。理智感不仅产生于认识活动之中,而且也是推动人们探索、追求真理的强大动力。天文学家哥白尼在回顾自己所走的道路时说,他对天文的深思产生于"不可思议的情感的高涨和鼓舞"。

虽然理智感对全人类表现出更多的共性,但它仍受社会道德观念和人的世界观的影响,因而,人们对科学的热爱,对真理的追求,都反映了每个人鲜明的观点和立场。

3. 美感

美感(aesthetic feeling)是人对客观事物或对象的美的特征的情感体验。它是由具有一定审美观点的人对外界事物的美进行评价时所产生的一种肯定、满意、愉悦、爱慕的情感。

美感与道德感一样，是受社会生活条件所制约的。在不同的社会历史发展阶段，不同的社会制度下，不同的风俗习惯及不同的阶级中，人的审美标准是不同的，因此，对各种事物美的体验也是各不相同的。正如马克思所指出的那样："忧心忡忡的穷人甚至对最美丽的景色都无动于衷；贩卖矿物的商人只看到矿物的商业价值，而看不到矿物美的特性。"

虽然美感具有阶级性与民族性，受社会历史条件的制约，但仍存有全世界共同享有的美感。例如，美丽的自然景观能给大多数人带来美感。因此，美感的某些内容是存在共同性的，但是，这并不能否定美感的阶级性与社会性。

第二节
情绪、情感的规律

情绪、情感与认知过程既有联系又有区别，情绪、情感的产生依靠认知，情感与情绪也会影响认知；情绪、情感的外部表现是我们可以分辨情绪的直接而有效的办法。

一、情绪、情感与认知过程的关系

（一）情绪、情感与认知过程的联系

情绪、情感与认知过程是紧密联系的。认知过程是产生情绪、情感的前提和基础。有了对事物本身属性的认识，才能有主客体之间需求关系的反映，从而产生情绪与情感，没有对事物的认识就不能产生情绪和情感。没有某种感觉，就不可能有某方面的情调，所以聋者不觉噪音之讨厌，盲者不知丽色之可喜。当人听到并知道是节日的礼炮声或是激战的炮声时，便有不同的态度体验，这是与知觉相联系的情绪和情感。当人们回首欢乐的童年、学业和事业的成就、甜蜜的爱情、遭受的挫折、惊险的场面时，便会产生不同的态度体验，这是与记忆相联系的情绪和情感。在日常生活中，人对某些问题和事件，越想越高兴，越想越生气，越想越后怕，则是思维和想象的结果。

（二）情绪、情感与认知过程的区别

首先，认知过程反映了客观事物本身的属性，而情绪、情感过程则是反映主客体之间的需求关系。单纯对客观事物的认知不能产生情绪与情感，只有客体和主体之间的需求

关系的反映才产生情绪与情感。例如两个在考试中得20分的学生，都认识到20分意味着不及格，但两个学生的学习目的、学习动机不同，因而一个抱着无所谓的态度，另一个则深感羞愧。

其次，认知过程的随意性较强，人可以随意地感知、注意、记忆、想象和思考，也可以随意地停止这种认知活动。而情绪、情感过程只有通过认知作用才具有某些随意的性质。

> **专栏8-2**
>
> ### 沙赫特—辛格的激活归因情绪理论
>
> 沙赫特（S. Schachter）和辛格（J. E. Singer）提出的情绪归因论（attribution theory of emotion）认为，情绪既来自生理反应的反馈，也来自对导致这些反应情境的认知评价。因此，认知解释起两次作用：第一次是当人知觉到导致内脏反应的情境时，第二次是当人接受到这些反应的反馈时把它标记为一种特定的情绪。沙赫特认为，脑可能以几种方式解释同一生理反馈模式，给予不同的标记。生理唤醒本来是一种未分化的模式，正是认知过程才将它标记为一种特定的情绪。标记过程取决于归因，即对事件原因的鉴别。人们对同一生理唤醒可以作出不同的归因，产生不同的情绪，这取决于可能得到的有关情境的信息。
>
> ——黄希庭.心理学导论[M].北京：人民教育出版社，2007：492.

二、情绪、情感的外部表现

（一）情绪、情感与机体变化

情绪、情感是在大脑皮层的主导作用下，皮层和皮下中枢协同活动的结果。它们发生时除了产生独特的喜、怒、哀、乐等主观体验外，还伴随着一定的机体生理变化和外部表现。

1.机体的生理变化

伴随情绪、情感的产生，有机体内部会发生一系列的生理变化。这些变化主要表现在呼吸系统、循环系统、消化系统以及内外腺分泌的变化上。例如，人在紧张时，肾上腺活动增强，促进肾上腺分泌增多，引起血糖增加，同时呼吸加快，心率加速，血压升高，脑电出现高频率、低振幅的β波（频率为14—30次/秒，振幅为5—20 μV），皮肤电阻降低，唾液腺、消化腺和肠胃蠕动等活动减少。而人在高兴时，肾上腺活动正常，肾上腺分泌适当，呼吸适中，血管舒张，血压下降，皮肤电阻上升，唾液腺、消化腺和肠胃蠕动活动加强等。这种变化的差距是十分明显的。以呼吸系统为例，在不同的情绪状态下，呼吸的频率乃至于呼气和吸气的比例都会产生明显变化；在悲痛时，每分钟呼吸9次，高兴时17次，积极动脑筋时20次，愤怒时40次，恐惧时竟达64次。

由于情绪的这种独特的生理特性,因而情绪也就与一个人的健康发生密切关系。我国古代就有"喜伤心""怒伤肝""忧伤气""思伤脾""悲伤肺""恐伤肾""惊伤胆"之说,现代医学更是明确地提出了身心疾病的概念。

> **专栏 8-3**
>
> ## 测 谎 仪
>
> 　　当人说谎的时候,身体会不由自主地产生一些特殊的变化。而测谎仪就是利用这些变化,来发现人到底有没有说谎。人在说谎的时候,身体语言也会发生变化,例如:脸色发红,心跳突然加速,一直吞咽口水,不敢直视对方的眼睛等,总之跟平常的身体反应很不一样。测谎仪能把身体发生的变化一一记录下来,如一个人的呼吸、血压、脉搏、脑电波等。专家在询问了各种问题后,会将测谎仪所显示出来的不同的人体反应做比较。如果被测者对于每种问题的反应都一样,没有较大的起伏,那么这个人说的很可能是真话;相反,如果前后反应有许多差异,那么说谎话的可能性就很大了。
>
> ——大米原创,雨霁编绘.最热最热的76个科学知识[M].杭州:浙江少年儿童出版社,2012:20.

2. 情绪、情绪的外部表现

情绪、情感发生时,人的身体各部位的动作、姿态也会发生明显变化,这些行为反应被称为表情。表情是人际交往的一种形式,是表达思想、传递信息的重要手段,也是了解情绪、情感体验的客观指标。人类的表情主要有面部表情、身段表情与言语表情三种。

(1) 面部表情(facial expression)

人的面部表情最为丰富,它通过眼部肌肉、颜面肌肉和口部肌肉来表现人的各种情绪状态。眼睛是心灵的窗户,各种眼神可以表达人的各种不同的情绪和情感。例如,高兴时"眉开眼笑",悲伤时"两眼无光",气愤时"怒目而视",恐惧时"目瞪口呆"等。眼睛不仅能传情,而且可以交流思想,因为人们之间有些事情不能或不便言传,只能意会。因而观察他人的眼神,可以了解他人的内心愿望,推知人们对事物的态度。眉毛的变化也表现出不同的情绪状态,如展眉欢欣,蹙眉愁苦,扬眉得意,低眉慈悲,横眉冷对,竖眉愤怒等。口部肌肉同样是表现情绪的主要线索,例如嘴角上提为笑,下挂为气,憎恨时"咬牙切齿",恐惧时"张口结舌"。就连表情肌肉有所退化的鼻子和耳朵也能表示人不同的心态,如轻蔑时耸鼻,恐惧时屏息,愤怒时张鼻,羞愧时"面红耳赤"等。据心理学家埃克曼(Danl Ekman)的研究,人的面部表情是由七千多块肌肉控制的,这些肌肉的不同组合能使人同时表达两种情绪。所以,人的面部表情是丰富多彩的。

(2) 身段表情(bodily expression)

身段表情是通过四肢与躯体的变化来表现人的各种情绪状态。如从头部活动来看,点头表示同意,摇头表示反对,低头表示屈服,垂头表示丧气。从身体动作来看,高兴时"手舞足蹈",悔恨时"顿足捶胸",惧怕时"手足失措"。

（3）言语表情（verbal expression）

言语表情是通过音调、音速、音响的变化来表现人的各种情绪状态。如高兴时语调激昂,节奏轻快;悲哀时语调低沉,节奏缓慢,声音断续且高低差别很少;爱抚时语言温柔,和颜悦色;愤怒时语言生硬,态度凶狠。有时同一句话,由于语气和音调的不同,就可以表示不同的意思,如"怎么了？"既表示疑问,也可以表示生气、惊讶等不同的情绪。

> **专栏8-4**
>
> 达尔文（1872）在《人类和动物的表情》一书中指出,现代人类的表情和姿势是人类祖先表情动作的遗迹,即人类的情绪表达是从其他动物类似表达进化而来的。这些表情动作最初具有适应意义,以后就成为遗传的东西被保存下来。例如,婴儿用笑容和啼哭来表达他们舒适、满足、困倦、饥饿、疼痛的感受,从而保持其生存适应。达尔文曾随英国皇家海军环游世界,在南洋诸岛部落中,观察不同文化之下的不同种族的人,发现基本情绪的面部表情在各种族间是一致的。正因为表情具有其生物学根源,所以许多最基本的情绪,如喜、怒、哀、乐等原始表情是具有全人类性的。
>
> ——黄希庭.心理学导论[M].北京:人民教育出版社,2001:515.

三、情绪、情感的功能

情绪、情感具有驱动功能、调节功能、信号功能和感染功能。情绪、情感作为信号的功能比语言信号的功能还要强大,感染功能为人与人之间的情感交流提供了可能。

（一）驱动功能

情绪、情感的驱动功能是指情绪、情感对人的行为活动具有增力或减力的作用。它能够驱使个体进行某种活动,也能阻止或干扰活动的进行。例如,一个人在高涨的情绪下会全力以赴,克服种种困难,达到自己追求的目标;如果一个人情绪低落,则会畏缩不前,知难而退。从这种意义上讲,情绪和情感具有某种动机的作用。美国心理学家奥尔兹（James Olds）的动物心理实验也证明了这一点。他将生物电极埋入大白鼠丘脑内的快乐中枢,并让大白鼠学会压杠杆以获得生物电的刺激,引起快乐的冲动。于是,大白鼠会竭尽全力去压杠杆,追求快乐。大白鼠压杠杆的平均速度可达2000次/小时,最高峰可达100次/分钟,并且可以持续15—20个小时,直到精疲力尽,进入睡眠状态为止。美国心理学家利铂（Leeper）认为,"感情本身就是动机",而汤姆金斯（Tomkins）则进一步将情感视为第一性动机,提出生物内驱力只有经过情感体系放大才具有动机的作用的观点。可见,情绪、情感对个体行为的动机作用是明显的。

图8-1 詹姆斯·奥尔兹

詹姆斯·奥尔兹（James Olds，1922—1976），美国心理学家。奥尔兹最为著名的研究乃是他关于大脑"奖励中枢"的发现。过去一直认为，只有像视觉、听觉和语言这类功能才定位于脑内特定的部位，而像快乐和痛苦这类情感则各自以脑的整体活动为特征。其代表作为《电刺激老鼠的中隔区和其他部位所产生的阳性强化》。

（二）调节功能

情绪、情感的调节功能是指情绪和情感对个体的活动具有组织或瓦解的作用。这种作用一方面表现为情绪和情感产生时，会通过皮下中枢的活动引起身体各方面的变化，使人能够更好地适应所面临的情境。例如，面对突如其来的险情，恐惧感会使人产生"应激反应"，引起体内一系列生理机能的变化，使人更好地适应变化的环境。另一方面表现在情绪和情感对认识活动和智慧行为所引起的调节作用，影响着个人智能活动的效率。前苏联心理学家基赫尼洛夫（Kihnilov）就明确提出了思维活动受情绪调节的观点，认为"协调思维活动的各种本质因素正是同情绪相联系，保证了思维活动的重新调整、修正，避免刻板性和更替现存的定势"。实践也证实，心情愉快时思路格外灵敏，心情沮丧时，思路则变得迟钝、混乱。

（三）信号功能

情绪、情感的信号功能，首先表现为人与客观事物之间的关系产生了一种意外变化的信号。客观事物作用于人，特别是原有的主观状态不能适应这种客观事物刺激时，人的神经、化学机制就会被激活，并发生特殊信号，促使人改变活动方式，并采取新的应付措施。这时的人就会产生不同的内心体验，或愉快，或不愉快，或满意，或不满意等。其次，人的各种情绪、情感无不具有特定的表情、动作、神态及语调，构成了表达人的内心世界的信号系统。通过这种信息的传递，个体可让他人识别正在体验着的情绪状态，也可向他人传递自己的某种愿望、观点和思想，从而使自己对事物的认识和态度具有鲜明的外露特色，更容易为他人所感知、所接受。正因为如此，情绪、情感的信号功能在特殊的人际交往——教学中有着重要的作用，有时，它比语言信号的作用还要巨大。

（四）感染功能

情绪、情感的感染功能是指个体的情感对于他人的情感施予影响的效能。当情绪或情感在个体身上发生时，个体会产生相应的主观体验，还会通过外部的表情动作为他人所觉察、感受，并引起他人相应的情绪反应。西方心理学把这种现象称为移情或情感移入（empathy）。心理学研究表明，一个人的情感会影响他人的情感，而他人的情感还能反过来再影响个人原先的情感,人与人之间的情感发生相互作用,正是情绪、情感的感染功能所导致的必然结果。情绪、情感的这一功能为人与人之间的情感交流提供了可能性,使个体的情绪、情感社会化,同时也为通过情感影响、改变他人情感开辟了一条途径。

四、自我防御机制

当个体处于应激状态时,自然而然采用的应对方式有:压抑、否认、文饰、置换等。

(一)压抑

压抑(repression)是个体将意识不能接受的欲念、情感冲动和记忆放逐到潜意识中去,使之不能被意识所觉知,以避免产生焦虑、恐惧、愧疚的过程。比如,个体对过去痛苦经历的压抑。在压抑过程中,那些太具有威胁性或太痛苦的冲动或记忆内容被个体从意识中排除出去,压抑进了无意识层面。然而,被压抑的经验并未真正消失,只是处于潜意识状态,它会积极寻找宣泄的出口。

压抑与理智的克制不同,克制是一个人欲望、冲动或本能无法达到、满足或表现时,有意识地去控制、想办法延缓其满足需要,越是成熟、有修养的人越能使用克制来调节和管理自己的情绪;而压抑则是把自己原有的欲望、需求都摒除于意识之外,弄得自己无法自由行动,过分的压抑会导致神经症的出现。

(二)否认

否认(denial)是指无意识地歪曲现实或重新解释有关痛苦的事实,以减少内心的焦虑和痛苦。如痛苦或焦虑难以应付时,个体不去注意情境有威胁性的方面,或改变情境的含义,而是将情境感受为不那么危险或重要,以逃避现实,减轻内心的焦虑。与压抑不同,它是个体有选择地注意并重新对事件进行解释的过程。

(三)文饰

文饰也叫合理化作用(rationalization),指用一种自我能接受、超我能宽恕的理由来代替自己行为的真实动机或理由,用于为自己的失败或错误找辩护托词,而不承认自己理性所不能容忍的行为的真正动机、需要和欲望,以避免精神上的痛苦。文饰作用又可分为酸葡萄心理(因未达到预定的目标,就否认该目标具有价值和意义)和甜柠檬心理(因达到的现有目标与预定目标不符,无法实现预定目标,就提升现有目标的价值和意义)。它们都是以似是而非的理由来证明个体行为的正确性,以保持内心的安宁。比如:一些经常考试不及格的学生不认为考试不及格是一种失败,甚至干脆直接说考试及不及格对他没有任何影响或意义,他根本就不在乎考试结果。

(四)置换

置换(replacement)是指处于应激状态或行为和心理受挫的个体因对方的地位或权势等不能表现出侵犯行为,转而采取转移侵犯的方式,其目的在于满足自己的需求和冲动。比如,学生在学校被老师批评后,向身边的其他人发火。青少年的情绪波动较大,在应激状态中比较容易采取置换的应对方式,因自己受挫和不快而迁怒于人,甚至将怒气发泄到社会上,应当注意尽力克服。①

第三节
情绪、情感规律在教育教学中的应用

一、学生情绪的调节

(一)认识到情绪对身心健康的重要性

良好的情绪能促进身心健康,而情绪失调会破坏身心健康。例如,长期压抑悲伤和哭泣容易引起呼吸系统的疾病,抑制会引发癌症,不表达情绪会加速癌症的恶化,对愤怒的压抑与心血管疾病、高血压的发病率有着密切联系。因此,探讨情绪调节过程与健康的关系应该是研究情绪调节的一个重要方面。②

> **专栏8-5**
>
> **主观幸福感**
>
> 有研究小组调查了46个国家的8557名参与者。参与者要求回应某些陈述,以评估他们的生活满意程度,比如从"强烈反对"到"强烈赞同"的7点量表上回答"我的生活几乎接近了我的理想"。他们在最后一周还要用9点量表——从"一点儿也不"到"一直都是"——来表示他们感到积极情绪(如自豪、感恩和爱意)和消极情绪(如内疚、羞耻和嫉妒)的频率。结果发现这些测量数据中存在一致关系。即,参与者有着更多的积极情绪体验和更少的消极情绪体验时,他们报告的生活满意度更高。不过,积极情绪对生活满意度判断的影响约两倍于消极情绪。结果还发现某些跨文化差异。比如,人们为保证日常生存而必须付出的努力程度存在文化差异。在生存都成问题的文化里,生活满意度的判断较少取决于积极情绪体验。
>
> ——理查德·格里格(Richard J. Gerrig)、菲利普·津巴多(Philip G. Zimbardo).心理学与生活[M].王垒,王甦,等,译.北京:人民邮电出版社,2016:393.

---

① 李红.心理学基础[M].北京:高等教育出版社,2009:283—284.
② 彭聃龄.普通心理学[M].北京:北京师范大学出版社,2012:446.

（二）恰当地表露情绪

亚里士多德说过，任何人都可能发火，但要做到为正当的目的，以适宜的方式，对适当的对象，适时适度的发火，可不容易。能否恰当地表露自己的情绪，直接关系到你和他人的交往状况。在现实生活中，我们难免会受到委屈，也难免因意见分歧或者兴趣不同而产生人际矛盾与冲突，而在你表达自己的不满或者阐述自己看法时，控制好自己的情绪是十分重要的；否则，你不仅不能解决问题，反而会激怒对方，使得问题变得更加严重。因为情绪的外部表现——表情会即刻对接受者发生作用，所以你的热情或者冷淡、愤怒或者镇静会立刻影响到对方。有时交往的双方是可以对分歧进行交流和深入地探讨的，但由于你的动怒，使得双方不欢而散，结果反而加深了双方的隔阂，恶化了彼此的关系。在相反的情况下，即使对方因某种原因处于愤怒之中，而如果你能给予一个镇定的微笑，也会对平息对方的怒气起到很大作用。

当然，恰当地表露情绪并非是要我们做一个虚情假意的人，但作为一种交往的规则，我们应该明白，如果真实的情感可能伤害你所爱的人，那就需要掩盖起来，代之以虽然不够真实但却无害的表情。这种表情规则也正是我们的社会礼仪的组成部分，善于利用这些规则，可以产生积极的效果。

（三）善于理解他人

恰当地表露情绪，既是为了自己不至于显得鲁莽和缺乏修养，也是为了他人。当我们需要表达自己的某种体验时，应该考虑对方所能承受的限度，也就是不仅要考虑自己的感受，而且还应该从对方的角度去着想。这种能够设身处地地体验他人情绪的能力在心理学中被称为移情能力。具有良好移情能力的人，既能分享他人的情感，即所谓"快乐着你的快乐，悲伤着你的悲伤"，又能客观地理解、分析他人的情感。显然，能够分享和理解他人的情感可以最大限度地获得对方的好感，因为我们每个人都希望自己被人关心、被人理解。

心理学的研究表明，具有移情能力的个体更愿意为他人提供帮助，能产生更多的助人行为，因为他们能深切地感受别人的痛苦和不幸，能体验他们的需要和愿望。同时具有移情能力的人也是一个侵犯性动机很低的人，当一个人能够感受到自己的行为可能对他人造成伤害的时候，就能够抑制伤害他们的冲动，而几乎所有犯强奸、抢劫、盗窃、诈骗和伤害他人罪的人，都有一个共同特征，那就是没有移情能力。所以，在学校和家庭教育中，我们更应该重视对个体移情能力的培养。比如，在家里哥哥欺负了妹妹，父母应该说："你看看你让妹妹好伤心"，就比说"你怎么这么淘气"要好得多，因为前者就是让孩子去注意自己的不良行为给别人带来了痛苦。如果在教育中能够有意识地对儿童的移情能力加以引导和培养，那么他们长大以后就更能关心别人、帮助别人，同时也会大大减少对他人的侵犯行为。

（四）增强对生活的适应能力

不健康的情绪不会无缘无故地产生，通常是由一定原因造成的。但是，在同样的客观条件下，有的人不管生活怎样起伏变化，始终不改愉快乐观的精神面貌；有的则在生活的变动前,时喜时怒,时悲时愁,使情绪随之动荡。这除了与人的生活态度、胸怀度量有关外,还与有没有适应生活的能力有关。在生活中,有眼泪,有欢笑,有冷嘲热讽,也有热情与友谊,如果不能适应这些变化,情绪就会受到伤害。如果具备了良好的适应能力,就会做到不管环境、条件、生活、人际关系如何变化,都能坦然处之,理智对待。

适应能力,首先是指接受生活现实的能力。人往往容易接受那些令人高兴、满意的现实,而不易接受那些令人扫兴、失意的现实。但是,面对现实中不愉快的事情,靠闹情绪、发牢骚是不能解决的,因为现实毕竟是现实,它不会因人不接受就不复存在。要想改变这些不愉快的现实,最好的办法就是承认它、接受它,然后再想办法来对付它、解决它。其次,适应能力还包括正确地估价自己。不能正确地评价自己,也会给生活带来不适应。例如,对自己的能力估计过高,就容易使人产生挫折感与失败感,长此以往就会造成人格的变态发展。有的会萎靡不振,自暴自弃;有的会变得固执己见,怨天尤人;有的甚至变得凶狠暴躁,嫉妒怨恨,表现出强烈的冲动性。

(五) 培养幽默感

幽默是自觉地用表面的滑稽逗笑形式,以严肃的态度对待生活事物和整个世界,激发人类心理某种情感的一种智慧。具有幽默感的人善于从烦恼中解脱出来。在人际交往中,幽默有助于消除敌意,缓解摩擦,防止矛盾升级。例如,在某俱乐部举行的一次招待会上,服务员倒酒时,不慎将啤酒洒到一位宾客那光亮的秃头上。服务员吓得手足无措,全场人目瞪口呆。这位宾客却微笑着说:"老弟,你以为这种治疗方法会有效吗?"在场的人闻声大笑,这位宾客的话不仅打破了尴尬的局面,也给自己和服务员解了围。可见,幽默是一种好的适应工具,它可以使本来紧张的情绪变得轻松,使窘迫的场面在欢声笑语中消弭。

要成为具有幽默感的人,可以从以下几个方面入手:其一,要学会自嘲,在面对生活中的苦难和别人的挖苦时,可以通过自嘲来化解。例如,苏格拉底娶了一位漂亮的泼辣妇人,这位夫人动不动就对他无礼谩骂。别人问苏格拉底"为什么要娶这么个夫人"时,他回答说:"擅长马术的人总要挑烈马骑,骑惯了烈马,驾驭其他的马就不在话下。我如果能忍受得了这样的女人,恐怕天下就再也没有难于相处的人了。"通过自嘲化解生活中的无奈,也是人生智慧的体现;其二,要扩大知识面。幽默是一种智慧,必须建立在丰富知识的基础上,一个人拥有广博的知识,就能做到谈资丰富、妙语成言;其三,学会使用双关语言,所谓双关,也就是说出的话包含两层含义。其四,训练正话反说,或者反话正说。就是说出来的话所表达的意思与字面意思相反。

(六) 培养良好的性格特征

情绪、情感的健康与否还与人的性格有着密切的关系。性格坚强者,遇到失意与伤心之事能挺得住,性格软弱者,则容易被不良情绪所左右;性格豪爽者,不会因芝麻大小的事引起情绪上的波动,而心胸狭窄者,则常常喜欢斤斤计较,容易产生情绪上的波动。而且,许多不良的情绪往往可以从性格上找原因。如,容易忧愁的人,往往都具有好强、固执、不善于与人交往的性格特征;情绪上经常处于犹豫、疑虑的人,性格上往往表现为被动、拘谨、依赖性大,缺乏独立性与创造性;情绪上容易烦躁的人,则性格上过于敏感,且习惯将愤懑的情绪埋入心底。可见,要保持健康的情绪状态,必须优化自己的性格特征,克服性格方面的缺陷。如性格外向的人,要注意掌握自己心境的变化,多运用思维的力量来要求自己沉静、平稳,遇事冷静思考,克制冲动,防止情绪骤然爆发而破坏宁静的心境;性格内向的人,要学会暴露与排遣不良的情绪,遇到不愉快的事、想不通的问题不要郁积于心。当不良的情绪已经产生时就多从性格方面找找原因,如果因脾气暴躁引起情绪多变,就应该首先克服暴躁的情绪;如果是心胸狭窄引起的情绪不快,就应开阔心胸,放宽度量;如果是多愁善感引起的情绪上的波动,则着意培养开朗豁达的胸怀。

(七)学会消释与克服不良情绪

不良情绪一旦产生,就要及时地消释它,克服它。消释与克服不良情绪的方法很多,主要有:

1. 学会通过正常的途径来发泄和排遣不良情绪

不良情绪的发泄,其实质在于把危害身心健康的能量排遣出来,以减轻情绪的强度。否则,如果压抑太大,就会影响人正常的认识活动,甚至造成身心反应性疾病。但宣泄的方式要合理、适当,不能通过伤害别人来发泄自己的愤怒。宣泄的方式有很多,可以采取转移的方法,如劳动、跑步,当人精疲力竭时,气恼之情就会基本平静,郁积的怒气也就消失一大半;也可以采用倾诉的方法,比如向亲朋好友诉说自己内心的苦恼,或写信痛斥引起你情绪的烦恼者,然后再把信撕掉;甚至还可以大哭一场,痛哭之后,人的悲伤之情一般会减少许多。

2. 理智地消除不良的情绪

要想理智地消除不良的情绪,首先必须承认不良情绪的存在,不能对其持回避的态度;其次,在承认后分析产生这一情绪的原因,弄清楚为什么苦恼、忧愁与愤怒。这样,通过理智分析、正确认识客观事物,使不良的情绪消除;最后,如果的确有可恼、可怒、可忧的理由,就要寻找适当的方法与途径来解决。如果因考试焦虑不安,就应把精力集中到学习上,减少自己的忧愁;如果因人际关系没搞好而苦恼,就要认真分析原因,问题在自身,就要克服自身的毛病,问题在别人,可主动与别人交换意见,以消除误解,达到相互间的了解。

专栏 8-6

合理情绪治疗

合理情绪治疗(Rational-Emotive Therapy,简称RET)也称"理性情绪疗法",是帮助求助者解决因不合理信念产生的情绪困扰的一种心理治疗方法,是20世纪50年代由阿尔伯特·艾利斯(A. Ellis)(图8-2)在美国创立的。合理情绪治疗是认知心理治疗中的一种疗法,因它也采用行为疗法的一些方法,故被称为一种认知—行为疗法。其理论认为引起人们情绪困扰的并不是外界发生的事件,而是人们对事件的态度、看法、评价等认知内容,因此要改变情绪困扰不是致力于改变外界事件,而是应该改变认知,通过改变认知,进而改变情绪。他认为外界事件为A,人们的认知为B,情绪和行为反应为C,因此其核心理论又称ABC理论。例如:两个同事一起上街,碰到他们的总经理,但对方没有与他们打招呼,径直过去了。这两个同事中的一个认为:"他可能正在想别的事情,没有注意到我们。即使是看到我们而没理睬,也可能有什么特殊的原因。"而另一个却可能有不同的想法:"是不是上次顶撞了老总一句,他就故意不理我了,下一步可能就要故意找我的岔子了。"两种不同的想法就会导致两种不同的情绪和行为反应。前者可能觉得无所谓;而后者可能忧心忡忡,以至无法平静下来干好自己的工作。从这个简单的例子中可以看出,人的情绪及行为反应与人们对事物的想法、看法有直接的关系。在这些想法和看法背后,有着人们对一类事物的共同看法,这就是信念,前者在合理情绪疗法中称之为合理的信念,而后者则被称之为不合理的信念。合理的信念会引起人们对事物适当、适度的情绪和行为反应;而不合理的信念则相反,往往会导致不适当的情绪和行为反应。人们坚持某些不合理的信念,长期处于不良的情绪状态之中,最终将导致情绪障碍也就是C的产生。

——阿尔伯特·埃利斯.理性情绪[M].李巍,张丽,译.北京:机械工业出版社,2014:2.

图8-2 阿尔伯特·艾利斯

阿尔伯特·艾利斯(Albert Ellis, 1913—2007),美国临床心理学家,合理情绪行为疗法的创始人。最初他所用的名称为理性治疗(Rational Therapy,简称RT),1961年改为理性情绪疗法(Rational Emotive Therapy,简称RET),1993年又更改为"理性情绪行为疗法",他被美国媒体称为"心理学巨匠"。其代表作有《理性情绪》《理性生活指南》等。

3. 文学创作

文学创作也是排遣不良情绪的一种方法。在中国历史上,许多爱国的仁人志士,忧国家之忧、愁人民之愁,既报国无门又无人诉说,如鲠在喉,不吐不快。于是把"不快""愤怒"升华成惊天地、泣鬼神的文字。如屈原被逐,愁愤而作《离骚》;司马迁受辱,发愤著书,终成《史记》;辛弃疾壮志未酬而作《长短句》等,借此使高尚的情感得以表达,使伤害的心灵得以慰藉。至于李清照的"莫道不销魂,帘卷西风,人比黄花瘦",则更是通过对词的创作表达对丈夫的思念、宽慰寂寞难耐之心的一种排遣。当然,作者并不一定是有意识地采取创作的方式来消除忧愁,但在客观上却起到了这样的作用。

4.通过心理活动进行适当的自我调节

当不良情绪产生时,还可以采取心理调节的方法。心理调节的方法有很多,其中常见的有:

其一,自我鼓励法,即用生活中的哲理或某些明智的思想来安慰自己。要对自己说:犯错误不要紧,只要认识了能改正就好;实验失败遭到嘲讽,要对自己说:失败乃成功之母;改革遇到挫折,要对自己说:不经巨大的困难,不会有伟大的事业。在痛苦与打击面前,一个人只有有效地进行自我鼓励,才会感到有力量,才能在痛苦中振作起来,树立起生活的信念,驱除不良的情绪。

其二,语言暗示法。语言暗示法对人的心理乃至行为都有着奇妙的作用。当人被不良情绪所压抑时,通过语言的暗示作用可以调节与放松心理上的紧张状态,使不良的情绪得以缓解。如,要发怒时,你可以用语言暗示自己"不要发怒,发怒会把事情变坏的";陷于忧愁时,提醒自己"忧愁没有用,于事无益,还是想想办法好";当有较大的内心冲突和烦恼时,可以用"不要怕,定下心,会好的"等给自己以鼓励与安慰。只要是在松弛平静、排除杂念、专心致志的情况下进行这种言语的自我暗示,对情绪的好转会起到明显的作用。进行语言调节时应注意暗示语应根据自己的目的而定,并且制作上要简短、具体、直接肯定,默念时要在头脑中浮出相应的形象且在心中反复默念,以加强自我暗示的程度。

其三,请人疏导法。不良的情绪光靠自身调节是不够的,还需借助于别人的疏导。心理学家认为,人的心理处于压抑的时候,有节制地发泄,把苦闷倾吐出来是有益的。当一个人被不良情绪困扰时,找个知心人谈谈,听听好朋友的意见是大有好处的。俗语讲:"快乐有人分享,是更大的快乐,而痛苦有人分担,就可以减轻痛苦。"何况,当人的情绪压抑时,向朋友倾诉苦恼,从朋友处得到的不仅仅是安慰,还有开导和解决问题的具体方法。心理学家的研究还证实,向异性朋友倾诉苦恼会收到更好的效果。对男性而言,他的话容易被女性理解和体谅,女性温柔的性格和婉转的语言像一剂良药,可以解除男性精神上的紧张与不愉快;对女性来说,男性是她忠实的听众,她的言谈更容易得到男性的赞同,因而女性可将不便在同性面前表露的情感与内心世界在男性面前尽情表露,从而减轻心理的压力。可见,异性间的友谊有助于摆脱紧张、抑郁的情绪。

其四,环境调节法。环境对人的情绪、情感同样起着重要的作用。如,安谧、宁静的环境使人心情松弛、平静;杂乱、尖厉的噪音却使人急躁、焦虑。因此,改变环境,对不良的情绪调节会起到一定的作用。的确,当人被不良的情绪压抑时,出去走走,大自然的美景会使人胸怀旷达,身心愉悦。绿色的世界,蓬勃的生机,会令人心旷神怡,精神振奋,忘却烦恼,解除精神上的紧张与压抑。

其五,呼吸调节法。这种方法在如瑜伽等的训练中历来被重视,它在调节人的情绪方面也起着积极的作用。具体做法是:先闭上眼睛,努力使心情平静,然后深深吸气,吸时要慢,充分吸气后,几秒钟内停止呼吸,然后把气徐徐吐出,吐气时要比吸气时还慢。一边做深呼吸,一边在每次吐气时心中数着"一、二、三……"数到十再回头重数,连续几次后,身心就会松弛,情感得以缓解。这种方法很容易将注意力从情感冲动转到自身的呼吸上,将精神统一到呼与吸的行为上,从而达到控制冲动、平息激情、恢复理智、实现自制的目的。

二、情绪、情感规律在教学中的作用

学校教育是教师和学生共同参与的双边活动,也是特定情境中的人际交往活动。无论是处于教育主导地位的教师,还是处于教育主体地位的学生,都是有思想、有感情的个体。因此,教学活动中师生之间不仅有认知方面的信息传递,也有情感方面的信息交流。重视教学中的情感因素,发挥其积极作用,是教师在教学过程中不可忽视的一个重要方面。具体做法如下。

(一) 要在教学中确定情感目标

人们在分析教学过程时,总倾向于把注意力集中于教学中的认知系统,而往往忽视情感系统。事实上,教师、学生和教材既是构成教学中认知系统的三个基本要素,也是构成教学中丰富而复杂的情感现象的三个源点。教师的情感包括对教育和教学工作的情感、对所教学科及其有关知识内容的情感、对学生的情感、主导情绪状态和情绪表现(即表情运用状况)等。学生的情感包括对学校学习活动的情感、对所学课程及其有关知识内容的情感、对教师和其他同学的情感、主导情绪状态、课堂情绪气氛和情绪表现等。教材虽是物,但其内容直接或间接地反映了人类实践活动的情况,又是教育者按一定社会、阶级、时代的要求编写而成,在不同程度上体现了教育者的意志,因而其内容本身也不可避免地蕴含大量的情感因素。因此,当教师和学生围绕着教材内容展开教学活动时,不仅认知因素,情感因素也被激活了,形成情知信息交流的回路。在教学中对情知回路的有效调控,自然同时能产生认知和情感两方面的教学效果。因此,教学不仅要有认知目标,也要有情感目标。在教学中可确定如下情感目标:

① 让学生处于愉悦、饱满、振奋的情绪状态之中,为认知活动也为情感的陶冶创设良好的情绪背景。

② 让学生在接受认知信息的同时获得各种积极的情感陶冶。

③ 让学生对学习活动本身产生积极的情感体验,形成良好的学习心向——好学、乐学的人格特征。

(二) 在教学中通过认知调控情感

在认知与情感并存的教学活动中,教师不仅可以通过自身的情感调控学生的学习情感,也可以通过情知交互作用,从认知上调控学生的情感,这是一条以知促情的重要途径,其具体做法是:

1. 精心选择教学内容

布卢姆(Benjamin Bloom)在《教育过程》一书中明确指出:"学习的最好刺激乃是对所学材料的兴趣。"对于中学生来说,在教学活动中,真正能引起他们积极的情绪体验的,莫过于教学内容本身所具有的内在魅力。诚然,教学内容是根据学科教学大纲和教材选定的,但任课教师在这方面仍有一定的灵活性、主动性和创造性。苏联教育家巴班斯基认为:"学校经常碰到教学大纲和教科书存在缺点的现象。但我们认为,全部工作都取决于教师,一个知识渊博的、热爱自己工作的、生气勃勃的、精力充沛的教师一定会使任何教学大纲变活,并补正最差的教科书。"因此,教师可以,而且也应该根据学生的实际情况、学科发展的现状和社会政治文化生活的变化,对教学内容作适当调整、增补,以求精心选择。事实上,所选择的教学内容的好坏,会直接引起学生完全不同的情绪体验。南斯拉夫著名教学论专家弗·鲍良克(Vladimir Poljak)说过:"教师选择的教学内容可以是枯燥、单调的;可以不带个人的主观积极的情绪色彩,只是客观地提出一系列的事实与概念。当然,这将在学生那里产生不满足的情绪感受。相反,教师选择的教学内容若是高质量的,那么它们就能引起学生满足的感受,教学活动使他们激动、感兴趣、思想集中、开心、兴奋。"[①]

2. 巧妙组织教学内容

从教学内容的选择到教学内容的呈现,中间还有一个组织、加工的过程。通过这一过程,不仅将所选择的教学内容有机地组织起来,以体现内在的逻辑联系,而且更重要的是,还要显示这些教学内容内在的魅力。例如,我们应尽可能地将经典性的教学内容与当代社会、现代科技联系起来,使学生对教学内容产生明显的时代感;将某些看来相当枯燥而又必要的教学内容与生动的事例、有趣的知识联系起来,使学生对教学内容产生明显的趣味感;将某些看来似乎简单易懂的教学内容与学生未曾思考过的问题、未曾接触过的领域联系起来,使学生对教学内容产生明显的新奇感,从而激起学生学习的热情。

3. 择优采用教学形式

这里的教学形式是相对于教学内容而言的一个广义的概念,它包括教学的模式、策略、方法和手段等。在国内外教学中已出现各种各样的教学模式,仅美国师范教育专家乔依斯(Joyce)和韦尔(Weil)就从上百种教学模式中挑选出发现法、掌握学习法、非指导性教学法等25种模式,而与模式相配合的各种策略的运用就更多了。教学方法也层出不穷,至于教学手段,随着互联网技术以及录音、录像、投影、电影、幻灯片、多媒体等电化教学技术、设备的发展,也呈多样化趋势。这些都为教师教学形式的择优采用创造了有利条件。这里的关键是因"材"择法,根据不同的教学材料和教学对象的不同特点选择最佳教学形式,以满足学生在特定教学情景中的需要,产生相应的积极情绪体验。

(三)在教学中充分挖掘各方面的情感因素

在教学中通过充分挖掘情感因素,使学生处于良好的情感氛围之中,不仅有利于学生各种情感的陶冶和培养,而且也有利于促进和优化学生的认知活动。

1. 充分挖掘教材内容的情感因素

如前所述,教师、学生和教材是形成课堂教学中情感现象的三个源点。因此,对教材内容的情感性处理是以情生情、调控学生情感的一个重要方面。充分挖掘教材内容的情感因素,是指在教学内容向学生呈现的过程中,教师从情感角度着眼,对教学内容进行必要的加工处理,使之能充分发挥情感因素的积极作用。教材内容可粗分为两类:一类含有丰富的情感因素,以文科类教材内容为主;另一类本身缺乏情感因素,以理科教材内容为主。对于前者,教师要注意发掘教材内容中蕴含的情感因素,并善于以表情的方式表现出来;而对于后者,教师则要设法赋予教材内容以某种情感色彩。后者处理难度大,也更易为人们所忽视。然而,如果处理得当,在理科类教材中也能充分发挥情感因素的积极作用,陶冶学生的情操,实施寓乐于教。如陈景润的中学数学老师就曾用极为形象、生动、富

[①] 刘红华.满足学生求知的情感体验[J].文学教育(下),2009(8):153.

有情感的语言来激起学生探索数学奥秘的热情。

2. 注重教师情感的自我调控

作为教学中另一个重要的情感源点,教师情感的自我调控具有特别重要的意义。这是因为情感具有感染功能,教师的情感会在教学过程中随时随地影响学生的情感,起着极为重要的调控作用。在这方面教师要特别注意两种调控:一是教师情绪状态的调控。有不少教师没有意识到这一问题的重要性,对自己的情绪由着兴致、不加调控,有的还出于错误的认识,为体现教学的严肃性而故意绷着脸,表现出"冷静""沉着""严厉"的教态,这都会影响学生的情绪,产生消极效果。正确的做法是,教师在教学活动中要始终调控好自己的情绪,处于饱满、振奋、愉悦、热忱的状态,以感染学生的情绪、活跃教学气氛,为学生的认知活动创造最佳的情绪背景,特别是在教师由于种种原因导致自己在情绪不佳时走进教室,更要以教师的责任感和敬业心调控自己,不在学生面前表现出来。二是教师对所教学科的情感调控。以往教师考虑的是如何教好自己所教的学科,而往往没有意识到自己对所教学科的情感会潜移默化地影响学生对该学科学习的情感和态度。教师对教材冷漠的态度会影响学生的情绪,进而阻碍学生学习的积极性;而教师在教学中充分表达自己对所教学科的热爱,学生也会受到感染进而充满热爱知识的感情。因此,优秀的教师不只是传授知识、培养能力,而且还将自己对学科执着追求的精神、热爱的感受带给学生,以激起学生情感上的共鸣。

3. 加强师生之间的情感的交流

在教学活动中,师生之间不仅交流认知,也交流情感;不仅交流教学内容中的情感,也交流着师生人际间的情感。而师生人际间的情感也会通过迁移功能影响学生对教学活动、教学内容的情感和态度。我国古代教学名著《学记》中"亲其师,信其道"之说,便深刻揭示了这一道理。而师生情感交流的核心是爱心融入。这就要求教师从职业道德的高度认识师爱的意义,培养师爱情感,并掌握施爱的艺术。具体方法如下:

(1)施爱于细微之处

俗话说,"于细微之处见深情。"往往在师生交往的细微之处最能使学生感受到教师真诚而深厚的爱。对学生一道目光的友好接触,对其名字的一声亲切呼唤都会产生师爱的魅力。

(2)施爱于需要之时

根据情绪发生的心理机制,教师首先应考虑如何将自己的师爱之情化为满足学生某些合理而迫切的需要的行为,这样才能从根本上引发学生的积极情感反应,促进师生在教学中的情感交流。

(3)施爱于意料之外

根据情绪发生的心理机制,客观事物超出的预期越大,产生的情绪强度也越大。因此教师要使自己的行为真正引起学生情感上的振动,从而产生师生情感上的炽热的碰撞,那么教师就要设法在师生交往中使学生产生某些出乎意料的感觉。

(4)施爱于批评之中

师爱具有明显的教育性,这是一种严与慈相结合的爱。教师不仅要怀着一片爱心去鼓励、赞扬学生的点滴进步,也要怀着同样的爱心去批评、指正学生的缺点错误。由于批评易引起学生不悦、反感甚至恼怒的情绪,因此,在批评时仍能让学生感受到教师的拳拳之心、真挚之情是不容易的,这恰恰也是批评教育的艺术性之所在。

（5）施爱于学生之间

教师一方面把自己对学生的爱直接施予学生,另一方面也要通过学生集体将爱传递给学生。这不仅有利于直接促进学生间的情感交流,增强集体的凝聚力,而且也有利于学生更深切地感受到蕴含在学生间情感背后的师爱。

（6）施爱于教学之余

不仅在教学中,在教学之外也有大量的师生接触,教师不仅要关心学生的学习,也要关心学生的生活、心理需要等,注意课外的"感情投资"会获得教学中意想不到的效果。

本章小结

情绪、情感是客观事物是否符合人的主观需要而产生的态度体验,它在认识的基础上产生,又推动人的认识过程不断深入。情绪、情感发生时要伴随着机体的变化,并有驱动、调节、信号、感染的功能。它还从性质上、强度上、激动性上、紧张度上表现出一定的两极性。人的情绪有快乐、悲哀、愤怒、恐惧四种形式。人的情绪可分为心境、激情、应激,而人特有的高级的社会情感包括道德感、理智感、美感。

情绪、情感在人的学习中起着十分重要的作用,教师要重视教学中的情感因素,努力发挥其积极作用。

关键术语

情绪　情感　心境　防御机制　情绪调节

讨论与应用

1. 请运用情绪、情感原理分析文中人物的行为。

……范进三两步走进屋里来,见中间报帖已经升挂起来,上写道:"捷报贵府老爷范讳高中广东乡试第七名亚元。京报连登黄甲。"

范进不看便罢,看了一遍,又念一遍,自己把两手拍了一下,笑了一声,道:"噫！好了！我中了！"说着,往后一跤跌倒,牙关咬紧,不省人事。老太太慌了,慌将几口开水灌了过来。他爬将起来,又拍着手大笑道:"噫！好！我中了！"笑着,不由分说,就往门外飞跑,把报录人和邻居都吓了一跳。走出大门不多路,一脚踹在塘里,挣起来,头发都跌散了,两手黄泥,淋淋漓漓一身的水。众人拉他不住,拍着笑着,一直走到集上去了。众人大眼望小眼,一齐道:"原来新贵人欢喜疯了。"老太太哭道:"怎生这样苦命的事！中了一个甚么举人,就得了这个拙病！这一疯了,几时才得好？"娘子胡氏道:"早上好好出去,怎的就得了这样的病！却是如何是好？"（节选自［清］吴敬梓《范进中举》）

2. 阅读以下材料,用情绪、情感理论进行分析。

国外医学人员在对吓死者的尸体解剖后发现,死者的心肌细胞均受到了不同程度的破坏，心肌中央夹杂着许多玫瑰色的出血点，说明出血过多，损坏了心脏功能。而对120名从心室纤维颤动的死亡线上救治的病人进行追踪，发现其中1/5的病人在发作前遭受过极度惊恐等激烈的情绪波动，从生理上揭开了"吓死人"的奥秘。

美国的科研人员通过实验证明，人不仅可以被突然吓死，而且也可以被逐步恐吓致死，他们将死刑犯的双眼蒙住，用滴水代替滴血，同时不断地对死刑犯说："你的血液在不断地被抽出，现在你身上的血已被抽了1/5……1/4……1/3……"犯人惊恐万分，终因心理无法承受而死去。

3. 阅读以下材料，分析其中揭示的消除不良情绪的方法。

"己所不欲，勿施于人"出自《论语·颜渊》，意思是如果自己不希望被人此般对待，自己也不要那般待人。

"所以无论何事，你们愿意人怎样待你们，你们也要怎样待人"出自《圣经·马太福音》，意思是用你希望别人对待你的态度去对待别人。

本章讨论与应用答题思路及要点
（扫描二维码）

本章复习思考题
（扫描二维码）

本章进一步阅读书目
（扫描二维码）

本章测量量表
（扫描二维码）

09

第九章
意 志
YIZHI

亲爱的同学，还记得这些故事吗？明代医药学家李时珍三次府试落第后立志钻研医学，他一面刻苦攻读前人留下的经典医学著作，一面到全国各地进行医疗实践和调查访问，历时27年，在他61岁那年，写出了《本草纲目》的初稿；北宋政治家、史学家、文学家司马光花了19年的时间编写了《资治通鉴》；西汉史学家、散文家司马迁在狱中受宫刑后写下了传世之作《史记》等。那么，这些人是凭借什么取得如此巨大的成就呢？希望通过本章的学习，你能从中找到答案。

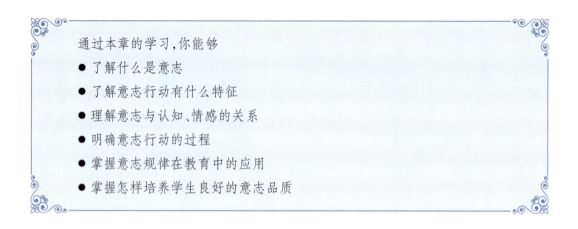

【本章结构】

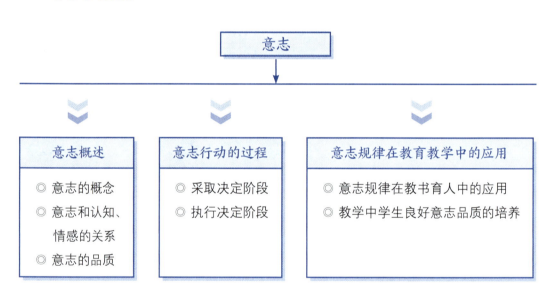

本章主要是回答"什么是意志""意志品质""意志行动的过程""意志规律在教育中如何应用"等方面的问题。学习本章有助于你把握意志行动的过程,明确意志规律在教书育人中的应用,并能够在今后的教学中加强对学生良好意志品质的培养,帮助学生形成良好的意志品质。

第一节
意志概述

一、意志的概念

意志(will)是人自觉地确定目的,并有意识地支配、调节自己的行动,克服困难以实现预定目的的心理过程。

意志是人常见的心理现象,也是人类所特有的心理现象,是意识能动性的集中表现。它具体表现为人的意志能够对自身的行为进行自觉的发动和控制两个方面。前者表现为推动人们去从事那些有利于目的实现的行为,后者表现为制止那些不利于目的实现的愿望和行为。比如,为了实现某一目的任务,人不得不去努力认识事物的规律,不得不放弃某些令他愉快却有碍目的实现的行为,控制自己的某些情绪而去完成那些使他感到吃力、费劲甚至要作出一定牺牲的行为。做一个决定,坚持一个目标,放弃另一个目标,都是意识能动性的表现。

> **专栏9-1**
>
> ### 意志与自由
>
> 人的意志是不是自由的?在这个问题上,哲学及心理学史上有过两种极端的见解。唯意志论者叔本华和尼采认为人的意志行为是不受任何东西约束的,可以绝对自由,为所欲为。所谓自由意志(free will)是指行为在任何情况下都是受个人意志控制的。行为主义者华生则否认人的意识,否认意志自由,认为人的行为完全是由外界刺激所决定的。前者是极端的唯心论,后者是极端的机械论,都是错误的。
>
> 辩证唯物主义认为,人的意志是自由的但又是不自由的。说它是自由的,因为在一定的条件下,人可以根据自己的意愿自主地选择目的,发动或制止某种行动,按某种方式、方法行事;说它是不自由的,因为人的一切愿望、一切行动都必须符合客观规律,否则,将一无所成。
>
> 从开始懂得使用火和石头工具的那一天起,人类就向自由迈进了第一步。随着对客观规律的认识越多,越能运用客观规律,人类的意志也就越自由。人类掌握了更多自然界的规律和社会发展的规律,才有可能获得更大的自由。意志的社会历史制约性主要表现在两个方面:一是人的意志的自由度是受社会历史条件制约的;二是人们对意志品质的评价是以具体的社会历史条件为转移的。
>
> 一个人掌握的自然科学和社会科学的知识越多,越善于运用客观规律,他对世界

> 的改造也就越主动、越自由。而这种能力的获得又有赖于人的主观努力,即需要勤奋地学习、勇敢地探索、不断地实践。
>
> ——黄希庭.心理学导论[M].北京:人民教育出版社,2007:497—498.

意志总是和行动联系在一起的。意志调节、支配行动,又通过行动表现出来。受意志支配的行动叫做意志行动(volitional movement)。意志与意志行动是两个既有区别又有联系的概念。首先,意志是一个在头脑内部进行的内隐的心理过程,而意志行动则是显露于外的;其次,意志调节支配意志行动,意志行动必须包含意志因素,没有意志就没有意志行动。最后,意志又必须通过意志行动表现出来,没有意志行动的意志不是意志,只能是一种空想。

人的意志行动有三个特征:

1. 自觉的目的性

这是意志行动的首要特征。人的意志首先是与行动的目的密切联系在一起的。无意识的本能活动和盲目的冲动行为或一些习惯动作都不含有或很少有意志的成分。人在认识客观现实并感到某种需要的时候,就会确立目的并依据它去自觉地组织自己的行动:计划行动,约束自己,抑制与达到目的不相适应的意图或行动,加强与达到目的相适应的行动,或通过变革客观现实来满足自己的需要。所以,意志总是与人的有目的的、有组织的行动密切相联系,意志是人所特有的。动物也有行动,但多是一些低级的适应性行动,是无意发生的偶然的动作。正如恩格斯所说:"一切动物的一切有计划的行动,都不能在自然界上打下它们意志的印记。这一点只有人才能做到。"① 意志行动反映意志水平的高低,它们随着目的水平而转移,目的越高尚,目的的社会意义越大,意志的水平也就越高。

2. 与克服困难相联系

这是意志行动最重要的特征。人们为了实现一定的目的,往往需要克服不同种类和程度的困难。意志总是通过困难才能表现出来,如果我们所做的某些活动,如吃饭、穿衣、走路等,可以毫不费力地完成,那不是意志行动,只有那些需要克服一定的困难,付出一定意志努力的行动,才能称为意志行动。如学生要获得优异成绩就得忍受学习的单调和寂寞的痛苦;教师要教好学生就要不断地进行辛苦的备课;运动员要获得冠军就得进行枯燥的日复一日、年复一年的训练等。因此,没有困难就不可能有人的意志,克服困难就成了意志行动的核心。

阻碍人们实现目的的困难有内部困难和外部困难两类。内部困难是指来自人自身的障碍。它包括心理和生理两种,心理上的困难如信念的动摇、情绪的冲动、能力的缺乏等,生理上的困难如健康状况不佳等。外部困难是指外部条件客观上造成的障碍,如恶劣的天气、人手不足、缺乏必要工作条件等。要克服这些困难,个体就必

---

① 恩格斯.自然辩证法[M].北京:人民出版社,1971:157—158.

须充分发挥自我意识和积极能动作用,对自己的活动和行为进行自觉地组织和调节。正因为如此,人们往往把克服困难的程度当作衡量人意志强弱的标准。克服困难的程度愈高,人的意志愈坚强,反之,人的意志愈薄弱。

3. 以随意动作为基础

人的行动是由动作组成的。动作有随意动作和不随意动作两种。不随意动作是指那些无预定目的的、也无需努力的、不由自主的动作。它是人在无意识或意识减弱的状态下做出的,如本能动作、习惯性动作或睡眠状态的动作。随意动作则是由意识调节控制的,在后天生活实践中学会了的、有目的的动作,如学生想学好功课,必须学会写字、阅读、操作、实验等。如果不具备这些学会了的随意动作,意志行动就无法实现。一系列的有意识动作连贯统一起来,就是人的意志行动。必要的随意动作愈熟练,人的意志就愈容易发挥。可见,意志行动必定是随意性的,随意动作是意志行动的基础。但是,并不是所有的具有自觉性或随意动作都带有意志努力的性质。例如,饥饿时想吃食物充饥,从家里的柜子里取出食物就行了。这种行动是有意识的、有目的的,但无需意志努力就能做到。只有当行动有困难时,如我们的战士在战斗中几天几夜喝不上水,有食物吃也会遇到相当大的困难——严重缺水,口干舌燥,难以下咽,这就需要做出巨大的意志努力。所以意志必然与困难相联系,没有困难的随意行动是无意志可言的。

专栏9-2

意志的生理机制

意志行动是通过一系列随意运动来实现的。控制机体运动的皮质主要在中央前回。运动区对一定部位肌肉的支配,具有精细的机能定位。大脑皮质运动区由许多呈纵向柱状排列的多细胞单元(运动柱)组成。运动区的细胞与皮质的其他部位有广泛的神经联系;来自皮肤、肌肉和关节的冲动以及来自额叶和颞叶等部位的信息,为运动区调节运动提供了所需的信息;"运动柱"内细胞之间的环路使不同层次的细胞广泛作用,最后离开皮质的锥体细胞和非锥体细胞,对输入信息和指令信息的总和发生反应。大脑皮质的随意运动是通过锥体系统和锥体外系统的协同活动完成的。其中锥体系统的机能是对敏捷灵活的活动进行精细调节,锥体外系统的机能则主要与调节肌肉紧张、肌群的协调性运动有关。

大脑额叶在意志行动中具有非常重要的意义。大脑额叶是形成意志行动的目的的器官,它随时将活动的结果与预先拟订的目的进行比较。鲁利亚等(Лурия,汪青等译,1983)的研究表明,额叶损伤的患者丧失了形成行动的愿望,不能独立地产生行动计划,行动的意识调节受到严重的破坏。患者不能借助语言所形成的动机而产生某种行动。例如,用言语指示要求额叶受伤的患者抬起手来,如果这时患者的手放在被子下面,他只是模仿地重复着"是,是抬起手……",但不会先从被子下面把手抽出来,然后再抬起来,不能对自己的动作进行调节。额叶严重损伤时,随意运动程序的

> 机制遭到破坏。这与运动区损伤时,运动的执行环节遭到破坏是不同的。
>
> 　　此外,网状结构在行为的意志调节中也有重要的意义。因为行为的意志调节必须以大脑皮质的优势兴奋中心为前提,要使大脑皮质建立优势兴奋中心,必须高于正常的动力供应。而网状结构则是皮质动力供应的特殊电池和操纵台。
>
> 　　总之,意志行动是大脑的许多复杂的神经过程相互作用的结果,其中中央前回运动区和额叶起着十分重要的作用。但是,由于意志活动的复杂性,其生理机制还远未探明。
>
> ——黄希庭.心理学导论[M].北京:人民教育出版社,2007:499—500.

二、意志和认知、情感的关系

首先,意志和认知过程有密切的联系。意志的产生是以认知为前提的。意志的一个特征是具有自觉的目的性。人的任何目的,都是在认知活动的基础上产生的。个人在确定目的、选择方法和步骤时,要考虑客观形势,分析主观条件,回顾过去的经验,设想将来的结果,拟定方案,编制计划,并对这一切进行反复的权衡和斟酌。所有这些都必须通过感知、记忆、思维、想象等认知活动才能实现。而意志对认知也有很大的影响。人的各种认知活动都可能遇到一定的困难,要克服这些困难就需要作出意志努力。

其次,意志和情感也有密切的联系。情感既可以成为意志行动的动力,也可以成为意志行动的阻力。当某种情感对人的活动起推动或支持作用时,它就会成为意志行动的动力。当某种情感对人的活动起阻碍或削弱作用时,这种情感就会成为意志行动的阻力。消极的情感对意志行动的干扰作用取决于一个人的意志品质:意志坚强者可以克服这些消极情感的干扰,把意志行动贯彻到底;意志薄弱者则可能被这些消极情感所压倒,使行动半途而废。意志也可以控制情感,使情感服从于理智。总之,在个人身上,认知、情感和意志总是密切联系在一起的。只是由于研究上的需要,我们才从不同的侧面对统一的心理活动进行分析而已。

最后,意志对人格的形成和发展具有十分重要的意义。孟子曰:"富贵不能淫,贫贱不能移,威武不能屈,此之谓大丈夫。"[1]法国生物学家巴斯德(L. Pasteur)曾说,立志、工作、成功是人类活动的三大要素。立志是事业的大门,工作是登堂入室的旅程,这旅程的尽头就有个成功在等待着。这些都说明,意志对健全人格的养成具有极为重要的作用。

三、意志的品质

意志品质是指一个人在实践过程中形成的比较稳定的意志特点,是人的性格的

---

[1] 孟轲.孟子·滕文公下[M].太原:山西古籍出版社,1999:93.

重要组成部分。评价意志品质的好坏,根本的一条是要看意志活动的社会价值;判断一个人的意志力强弱,则要看意志表现的程度。

良好的意志品质有如下四个方面。

(一) 自觉性

自觉性(independence)是指人对行动的目的及其社会意义有正确而深刻的理解,并能主动支配自己的行动使之符合于该目的。这种品质来自于人的正确的观点、信仰和世界观。具有自觉性品质的人,能认识到行动的社会意义,能够自觉、有效地控制和调节自己的行动,一心为实现预定目的而勇往直前。例如,一个想学好专业课的学生,不用父母和老师的督促,就可以自觉设定计划,并贯彻执行。

与自觉性相反的意志品质是受暗示性和独断性。受暗示性表现为盲从、没有主见,对自己的行动目的缺乏正确的认识,行动时缺乏信心;容易屈从别人的影响,为他人言行所左右,在行动中任意改变自己的行动目的,没有明确的行动方向。独断性是受暗示性的另一个极端,表现为盲目地、毫无理由地拒绝别人的意见和劝告,一意孤行,固执己见。因此,受暗示性和独断性是妨碍人们进行认识和实践活动的不良的意志品质。

(二) 果断性

果断性(decisiveness)是指人善于明辨是非、不失时机地采取行动,并实现目的的意志品质。具有果断性品质的人善于审时度势,能全面而又深刻的考虑行动的目的及其达到的方法,善于对问题情境做出正确的分析和判断,洞察问题的是非真伪。这种能力使他们在应对心理冲突时能当机立断,不踌躇,在采取行动时敢作敢为,在不需要立即行动或情况发生变化时,又能立即停止已做出的决定和行动。在复杂情境中所表现出来的高水平的果断性并不是每个人所固有的,果断性必须以正确的认识为前提,以大胆勇敢和深思熟虑为条件。果断性是意志坚强者的优良品质。

与果断性相反的意志品质是优柔寡断和草率武断。优柔寡断的主要特征是顾虑重重,"前怕狼,后怕虎"。在作出决定时总是犹豫不决,一直处于心理冲突状态,到了紧急关头,仓促作出决定后又反悔;执行决定时,常常对决定采取怀疑态度,表现出徘徊观望、踌躇不前。草率武断往往是缺乏思考而又轻举妄动的倾向。这种人不善于洞察事物的发展变化,自己缺乏经验,又不善于向他人学习。作出决定时往往凭一时冲动,草率从事。这种人的决断尽管是迅速的却是缺乏充分根据的,其结果必是失败多于成功。优柔寡断和草率武断都是缺乏克服困难的精神,不敢正视困难或总是逃避困难,是一种意志薄弱的表现。

(三) 坚韧性

坚韧性(hardiness)是指一个人在执行决定时,百折不挠地克服一切困难和障碍,去完成既定的目的的意志品质。具有坚韧性品质的人,能够长久地坚持自己行动的合理性,不为外界条件所迷惑。即使在失败时也不泄气,而是更加坚定、果断,百折不回,始终以饱满的精神,坚持不懈地去实现既定的行动计划,并能灵活地采取新措施,直到最终实现目的。所谓"富贵不能淫,贫贱不能移,威武不能屈"正是意志坚定的表现。

与坚韧性相反的意志品质是动摇性和执拗性。动摇性表现为缺乏坚强的毅力，遇到困难就怀疑预定的目的和所采取的方法，不能长期地控制自己的行动，容易放弃或改变自己的决定，不善于迫使自己去完成预定的计划，见异思迁，虎头蛇尾，有始无终。执拗性表现为对自己的行动缺乏正确的理性认识，我行我素，固执己见，不能根据已经变化的形势灵活地采取对策，也不能放弃那些明显不合理的决定。这种人最后只能在无情的现实面前碰壁，因为抛弃事物发展规律的人也终将被规律所抛弃。

专栏9-3　坚韧性也许是一种综合性的意志品质

坚韧性（hardiness）是卡巴莎（Kobasa, 1979; Kobasa & Maddi, 1981, 1982）用来解释为什么有些人可以顺利应对压力事件，而另一些人则不能而提出的一个概念。她认为坚韧性由三个相互关联的成分构成：承诺（commitment）指个体对于生活目的和意义的感知；控制（control）指相信命运掌握在个人手里，能通过自己的努力来改变生活；挑战（challenge）指个体认为变化是生活的常态、成长的动力。坚韧性人格的承诺、控制和挑战三种成分缺一不可。

在卡巴莎等人看来，坚韧性强的人好奇心强，总能在自己的经历中发现乐趣和意义（承诺），并且相信自己的观念和行为有一定的影响力（控制），还期盼着日常生活有所变化，认为变化是发展的重要动力（挑战）。这些信念和倾向对个体应对压力事件很有用。对于坚韧性强的人来说，变化所带来的压力不仅是很自然的，而且是有意义的甚至是乐事。他们会立刻做出相应的果断行动来了解新情况，将其纳入原定计划中，并从中吸取对将来有用的经验。通过这些方式，坚韧性强的人降低了对压力事件的压力感。相反，坚韧性差的人，总是感到自己和周围环境都没什么意思、没有意义，甚至很危险。他们面对难题感到无能为力，认为生活最好不发生任何改变。当遇到压力事件时，由于他们的人格无法提供或提供很少的缓冲作用，因此可能会损害其身心健康。又如面临失业，坚韧性强的人会采取行动积极寻找另一份工作（控制），还会到同行或主管那里调查自己为什么会被辞退（承诺），同时，还会想到这可能是重新计划职业发展的一个机会（挑战）。但面对同样一件事，坚韧性差的人就会手足无措（无力感），逃避问题（逃避），并感到事态无法逆转（威胁）。

虽然有一些研究支持坚韧性人格的存在，但对它到底由哪些成分构成却有争议。与三成分模型相矛盾的有下列一些研究。

坚韧性中的承诺和控制具有相关，但挑战与此二者关系不大（William, Wiebb & Smith, 1992; Costantini, Solano, DiNapoli &. Bosco, 1997）。

坚韧性的人应具有承受能力（持续承受生理和心理的痛苦的能力），力量（抵抗压力、应激和困难的能力），勇敢（勇气、大胆和冒险的特质）、控制能力（施加权力和影响力的能力）。坚韧性的内涵应当更丰实，三个成分不足以说明坚韧性（Gross & John, 1998）。

> 西方学者所发现的坚韧性与大五因素中神经质、外向性有关。但我国学者发现外向性中的活跃、合群、乐观，善良中的利他、诚信、重感情，以及处世态度中的自信、淡泊都与坚韧性有关（王登峰、崔红，2005；邹智敏、王登峰，2007）。
>
> 总之，坚韧性人格这个概念尚需用实证研究进一步加以澄清。从本章提及的意志品质来看，坚韧性也许是一种综合性的意志品质。
>
> ——黄希庭.心理学导论［M］.北京：人民教育出版社，2007：520—522.

（四）自制性

自制性（self-control ability）也叫自制力，是指善于控制和支配自己行动的心理品质，包括自觉、灵活地控制自己的情绪和动机，约束自己的行动和言语等。具有自制性意志品质的人，既善于抑制与自己预定目的相反的愿望、动机及不良情绪，又善于迫使自己去执行已采取的决定，使行动朝向预定的目的。自制性是坚强意志的重要标志。马卡连柯曾说："坚强的意志——这不但是想什么获得什么的那种本事，也是迫使自己在必要时放弃什么的那种本事……没有制动器就没有汽车，而没有克制就不可能有任何意志。"

与自制性相反的意志品质是任性和怯懦。任性表现为不顾社会的需要和影响，不能约束自己的行为，感情用事，任意而为。这种人在顺利的情况下倾向于为所欲为，忘乎所以，易为激情所控制；在不顺利的情况下，不能忍受困难和挫折，不能清醒地分析挫折的原因，容易一错再错。怯懦表现在行动时畏缩不前，惊慌失措，是受暗示性、优柔寡断等不良品质的必然结果。两者都是意志薄弱的表现。

第二节 意志行动的过程

意志是通过一系列的意志行动表现出来的。意志行动过程可以分为采取决定和执行决定两大阶段。

一、采取决定阶段

这是意志行动的开始阶段，也是准备阶段。它决定着意志行动的方向和行动的方法、步骤，是完成意志行动不可缺少的开端。人在行动之前，先要在头脑里考虑为什么要行动，怎样去行动，然后采取决定。这一阶段主要包括解决可能产生的种种动机斗争，明确目的，选择适当的方式与策略，制定具体的行动计划等一系列环节，最后作出决定作为本阶段的结果。它是具体意志行动之前的主观对客观的反映过程。

（一）动机斗争

人的意志行动是由一定的动机引起的，这是因为人的意志行动总是指向一定的目的，而一定的目的又是由一定的动机所引起的。动机是在需要的基础上形成的，是由需要转化而来的。人的需要多种多样，由需要而产生的动机也是复杂多样的。各种动机可能和平共处，也可能相互矛盾、冲突。这种动机之间的矛盾冲突，就称作动机斗争。动机斗争解决以后，个体才能确定行动目的，意志首先表现在动机斗争之中。

图9-1　库尔特·勒温

库尔特·勒温（Kurt Lewin，1890—1947），德裔美国心理学家，拓扑心理学的创始人，实验社会心理学的先驱，格式塔心理学的后期代表人，传播学的奠基人之一。其主要著作有《人格的动力理论》《拓扑心理学原理》等。

各种动机间的矛盾冲突是复杂多样的。德国著名心理学家勒温（Lewin）按照动机冲突的形式把它分为三类：

1. 双趋冲突（approach-approach conflict）

两种能满足需要的目标具有同等的吸引力，但只能选择其中之一时所产生的动机冲突，叫做双趋冲突。例如在特定的时间，既想完成家庭作业，又想参加同学的生日晚会等。"鱼与熊掌不可兼得"①时出现的冲突也属于这种类型。显而易见，当两种目标的吸引力比较接近或相同时，解决双趋冲突就非常困难；当两种目标的吸引差别较大时，解决冲突就比较容易。

2. 双避冲突（avoidance-avoidance conflict）

同时遇到两个需力图回避的威胁性目标，但只能回避其一时所产生的动机冲突，称为双避冲突。例如小孩生病了，既不想打针，也不想吃药，由此引起的动机冲突就是双避冲突。应该看到，双避冲突有时由于人们接受了其中一个目标而趋于解决。

3. 趋避冲突（approach-avoidance conflict）

同一目标既有吸引力，又有排斥力，人既希望接近，同时又不得不回避，从而引起的动机冲突叫做趋避冲突。例如，想参加竞赛，又害怕失败；既想学习成绩好，又害怕辛苦，在这些情况下的动机冲突属于趋避冲突。

以上是三种基本的冲突方式，但在实际生活中，有更复杂情境出现的可能性。即人们面对着两个或两个以上的目标，而每个目标又分别具有吸引和排斥两个方面的作用。人们不能简单地选择一个目标，而回避或拒绝另一个目标，必须进行多种选择，由此引起的动机冲突叫多重趋避冲突（double approach-avoidance conflict）。例如，当一个人看到某

---

① 孟轲.孟子·告子上[M].太原：山西古籍出版社，1999：176.

地以丰厚的物质待遇招聘职员时,就可能引起这种冲突。一方面,他想到在这个地方工作的许多好处,如工资高、住房条件也不错等,同时他又担心去一个新城市可能遇到的问题,如生活不习惯、语言不通、举目无亲等;另一方面他又想,留在原单位工作,虽然工资住房条件差些,但生活已稳定下来,亲朋好友都聚集在周围。这种对各种利弊得失的考虑,就会产生多重趋避冲突。解决这种冲突,需要人们对各方面的情况做深入地分析思考,因而花费时间较长。

动机冲突的另一种分类是从性质上分的,一般可分为原则性的和非原则性的两种。凡是涉及个人愿望与社会政治原则、道德规范相矛盾的动机冲突,属于原则性的动机冲突。如在公共场所看到损害公共设施的行为,这时是挺身而出还是事不关已高高挂起;周末既有同学聚会,又有集体的义务劳动,是选择同学聚会还是参加义务劳动的心理矛盾等,都是原则性动机冲突。解决这类动机冲突时,往往会伴随着激烈的内心斗争,引起巨大的精神紧张和不同程度的痛苦情绪。如何抉择往往能表现出个人的价值取向、意志水平及人性特点。因为动机冲突的过程,实质上就是对各种动机权衡轻重,评定其社会价值的过程。凡是不与社会政治原则、道德规范相矛盾而仅是个人兴趣爱好方面的动机冲突,属于非原则性动机冲突。例如周末去看电影还是去跳舞;课外活动是跑步还是踢球等都属于非原则性动机冲突。一般说来,这类冲突的内心斗争不那么激烈,持续时间也不长,无论怎样取舍都无可厚非。

(二)确定行动目的

通过动机斗争,解决了心理矛盾后,就进入了确定目的的过程。意志行动是一种有目的的活动,没有明确目的的行动就不能称其为意志行动。因此,在行动之前必须先确定所要达到的目的,这是意志行动的前提。

目的越深刻(即社会意义越大)、越具体,则由目的所引起的毅力就越大。目标越远大,它对行动的动力就越大。在远大的目标之下,应再确立一些近期的目标,否则,遥远的目标反而会使人懈怠。例如,做一个有教育情怀、专业基础扎实的教师,这是师范院校的学生学习的较长远的目的,而在学校的学习中提高自己的思想觉悟水平,学好各门课程,提高教育教学能力,锻炼好身体,这又是比前一目的更具体而较近的目的。为实现这个德、智、体全面发展的目的,又可以规定每一项更为具体、更近期的目的。可见,行动的目的是存在不同层次的。但是眼前的目的任务必须从属于更长远的宏伟目标,其间必须保持一致,才能取得成功。

(三)选择行动策略与方法

行动目的的确定以后,就必须考虑选择和拟定达到这个目的的策略与方法。因为没有正确的策略与方法不可能实现行动的目的。行动策略与方法的拟定,直接关系到行动的失败。

在通常情况下,达到同一目的的方法可能不止一种,因此必须根据意志行动的要求和主客观的条件进行权衡和选择。在拟定或选择某一种策略和方法之前,要了解、比较各种方法的优缺点以及采用后可能导致的后果等。然后,根据客观事物的发展规律、社会需要、道德规范以及自己的主观条件等去选择有效的策略和方法。

（四）制定行动计划

确立了行动的目的，选择了合适的策略和方法，下一步就要制定行动的具体计划，以保证行动时少出差错，少走弯路，顺利地实现行动目的。制定计划要全面了解情况，进行认真分析研究，考虑到各种可能性，抓住重点，突出矛盾，制定切实可行的行动计划。

总之，经过动机斗争，确定行动目的，选择行动策略与方法，制定行动计划，采取决定阶段就完成了。作出决策，标志着意志行动的准备阶段的结束，随即进入执行决定阶段。

二、执行决定阶段

执行决定阶段是意志行动的关键阶段，也是意志努力集中表现的阶段。通过深思熟虑做出有根据的决定，这只表明意志行动有了一个良好的开端。但要实现计划，达到最终目的，还需要艰苦的努力去付诸实施，这才是意志活动的中心环节。如果不付诸行动，准备阶段的一切也就失去了意义和价值，意志行动也就不复存在。所以执行决定，这是从"头脑中的行动"过渡到实际中的行动，这才是主观见诸客观的过程。在执行决定中，人必然会经受各种尖锐的矛盾、冲突的折磨，必然要克服更多更大的实际困难，经受实践中成功与失败的考验，因而它更能充分体现出人的意志。所以，执行决定才是意志行动的中心环节。

执行决定的过程是克服困难的过程。人在意志行动中，不可能是一帆风顺的，总会遇到这样或那样的困难和挫折。在执行决定阶段，这些困难会表现得更加明显与突出。困难有两种：一种是内部困难，即主观上的困难。如未被完全排除的消极动机，或者在行动过程中产生相反的动机、目的，干扰行动的进程；或者个人原有的懒惰、保守、动摇等消极品质和知识经验不足，身体情况欠佳等阻碍行动的进行。另一种是外部困难，即客观条件方面的障碍。如物质条件的不足，客观情况的改变，时间、空间上的不利，来自他人的干扰、讽刺和打击等，这些都能够对决定的执行起很大的阻碍作用。内部困难和外部困难是相互联系、相互影响的。

执行决定的过程必然有成功也会有失败。面对成败，我们需要运用意志来调节自己的心理反应。面对成功，精神振奋、信心百倍，同时又能清醒地认识到成功只是相对的，只是人生道路上的一个新的起点。面对失败，不颓废，百折不挠，顽强斗争，坚持到底；同时又能冷静分析失败原因，总结教训，以利再战，直至胜利。这就是高超意志水平的表现。

意志行动的两个阶段是紧密联系的，没有意志行动的准备阶段，行动就会失去方向；而缺少意志行动的执行阶段，再好的决定也失去了意义。在实际的意志行动中，这两个阶段常常是紧密联系和反复交织的。

第三节
意志规律在教育教学中的应用

一、意志规律在教书育人中的应用

在教书育人的过程中,教育者要高度重视青少年意志的锻炼和培养,充分运用意志的有关规律,以促进青少年的学习与成长。

(一)以知促意,激发学生的意志行动

知即认知,是人们对学习目标、意义和结果的认识、判断和评价。它是通过传授和实践活动形成的。它一经形成,就成为人们确定其对客观事物的态度与行为准则的内在原因。所以,认知是意志的基础和前提,是意志行动达到最终目标的根本保证。

在教学中,要让学生明确学习目标,以此激发学生的学习动机,并唤起积极行动去实现这一目标。行为目标越明确,就越能正确把握行动的方向,对行动的推动力量也就越大。因此,教师应多采用目标定向或目标导向的方法,引导学生的意志行动,促进其完成学习任务。同时,在学习过程中,教师要利用一切机会、采取多种方式积极引导学生认清学习的重要意义,并引导学生在学习中战胜自我,激发学生通过意志努力去获得学习上的成功。

(二)以情促意,增强学生的意志力量

情即情感,是人们对事物的爱憎、好恶的态度和内心体验,是认识与行动的纽带和桥梁。情感和意志有着密切的关系。情感可以说是一种动力系统,是个体意志形成的催化剂。因此,教学活动中,教师应充分运用这一规律,在提高学生认识的同时,必须引起学生情感上的共鸣,使他们在学习实践活动中体验愉快和满足,以增强学生克服困难的意志力量,使之达到完成学习任务的目的。

首先,教师要与学生建立起和谐、亲密的师生关系,将学生对教师的情感迁移到学习中去。"亲其师,则信其道",学生的向师性特点在教学活动中起着不可估量的作用。其次,在具体的教学活动中,教师在对学生进行评价时,要以正向的、鼓励性的评价为主,要尽量让学生看到自己的成绩和进步。这样才能使学生产生愉悦感,增强自信心,以促使他们敢于接受更高目标的挑战。否则,会令学生沮丧、失望,从而失去自信。因此,教师宜在教学中遵循"小步子"原则,即让学生达到的行为目标不可太高,让学生获得足够多的成功以及由此而带来的积极情感体验,从而增强学生的意志力量。

(三)以行促意,锻炼学生的意志品质

行即行为,是人们在认知、情感和意志的支配和调节下所采取的实际行动。行为是人

的品质的一个重要外部表现,是衡量一个人品质水平的根本标准,特别是意志品质水平。意志表现为实际行动中的一种坚持精神,是人们在履行义务和责任过程中克服内心障碍和外部困难的决心与毅力。

学校的日常教学活动是学生的主要活动内容。教师可以通过日常教学中具有一定困难程度的活动来磨练学生的意志,这样既有助于意志品质的培养,又促进学习任务的顺利完成,能获得一举两得的效果。因此,教师在教学活动中可以有意设置一些困难情境,让学生经受适度的挫折,使他们在战胜挫折的过程中磨砺意志。但在实际操作中要注意:一要把握时机。一般说,最好在学生的意志水平达到一定程度,对具体学习活动的意义、目的有一定认识,并在有相应的情感激励的条件下实施,才能取得好的效果,否则会产生负面影响;二要注意个别差异。如对心理承受能力较强而又骄傲自满的学生,可较多使用这类方法以锻炼其意志,反之则应慎用这类方法。

二、教学中学生良好意志品质的培养

良好的意志品质不是天生的,而是在后天的生活实践中通过学习而逐步形成和发展起来的,是有意识培养的结果。良好意志品质的培养主要从以下几个方面入手。

(一)加强科学的世界观、人生观教育,增强责任感

学生的一切意志行动都受一定的动机和目的调节、支配,加强正确的目的、动机教育,不断提高学生的动机水平,有利于培养学生坚强的意志品质。要使学生确立明确的目的,其核心就是要培养学生具备科学的世界观和人生观。因为只有树立了科学的世界观,学生才能正确地制定行动目的,并对一切个人的、团体的思想和行为做实事求是的正确评价,明辨是非、善恶和荣辱;只有树立了科学的世界观,学生才能具有高度的责任感,明确生活目的和追求崇高理想。一个具有高度责任感的人,会最大限度地与各种不利因素作斗争,会自觉克服懒惰、散漫等不良习惯,形成良好的坚定性和自制力。

因此,要教育学生把崇高的理想同眼前的学习、工作、生活结合起来,用理想来指导自己。只有这样,才能在学习和工作中有坚定的决心和高度的责任感,不被任何困难吓倒,有克服困难的勇气、毅力和动力,从而形成良好的意志品质。

(二)引导学生在实践活动中磨练意志,获得经验

意志是在克服困难的实践活动中逐渐发展起来的,如按时完成学习任务,遵守课堂纪律,执行委托的社会任务等,都可以锻炼学生的意志。教师除结合教学内容或通过主题班会等方式向学生讲述意志锻炼的意义、方法外,还应组织好学生的各种实践活动。

组织学生进行实践锻炼应注意抓好以下几个方面的工作:第一,行为训练要有目的性、计划性,从简到繁,逐步深入。第二,向学生提出的活动任务要有一定的难度,同时又是他力所能及的。例如,要求他们坚持独立完成各种作业,坚持参加科技小组的活动,坚持各种体育锻炼,坚持为集体做好事等。对青少年来说,这些要求都有一定的难度,但又是他们能够做到的,因而对于培养他们意志力的坚定性、自觉性很有好处。第三,根据学生意志品质上的差异,采取不同的锻炼措施。意志力的培养既包括整体水平的发展,也包

括个别意志品质的完善,在培养的过程中应该针对个体不同的意志发展状况,采取具体的有针对性的措施。例如,对于容易盲从、轻率行事的学生,教师应当多启发他们的自觉性,培养他们对社会集体的义务感和责任感;对于怯懦的学生,则应多鼓励他们克服困难,并对克服困难的方法和技术给予指导;对于依赖性强的学生,则应多鼓励他们独立完成任务,不要越俎代庖;对于自制力差的学生,则要让他们学会善于调节和控制情感的本领,要让学生逐步学会预料到挫折和失败带来的后果,使他们有足够的忍受挫折和失败的思想准备,从而减弱激情的反应,同时,鼓励他们的勇敢行为,克制冒险和蛮干的行为。

(三)发挥集体和榜样的教育作用

青年学生有强烈的集体观念。集体对个人意志品质的培养有着重要的作用。在良好的班级体里,同学们团结互助、关心集体、热爱集体、尊重集体,愿意完成集体委派的任务,并努力为集体争光。如果个人对他所属的集体具有归属感,他就会重视集体的意见,按照集体的要求行动,自觉约束自己的行为,关心其他成员,维护集体的荣誉,并在行动中表现出自己的才智、决断力和自制力,以获得集体的认同。而这种归属感和认同感又可以成为其进步发展的动力。

青年学生崇拜榜样,喜欢模仿榜样的行为。榜样的教育作用是无声的力量。教师除了用科学家、发明家、革命先烈以及文艺作品中的优秀人物来陶冶学生的意志外,还要善于从学生周围的生活中,从学生熟悉的人物中,特别是从他们同龄人中选取典型,为他们树立坚强意志的榜样。随着少年学生对榜样人物进行学习、模仿,其意志品质便会被内化为学生自己的良好意志品质。当然,教师自身的榜样作用也很重要,所以教师要以身作则,以自己良好的意志品质为学生树立榜样,这对培养学生良好的意志品质将起到不可估量的作用。

(四)教育学生加强意志的自我锻炼

外因通过内因而起作用。在培养学生良好的意志品质过程中,周围人的影响、榜样的力量、教师的要求等都必须转化为学生内在的自我需求,才能发挥作用。青年学生的自我意识已经有了一定的发展,他们具备了一定水平的自我教育能力,这就为学生意志的自我锻炼提供了前提条件。因此,教师应当正确引导学生制定自我锻炼的计划,掌握自我锻炼的方法,有始有终,持之以恒,加强意志的自我锻炼,并逐步养成自我评价、自我监督、自我控制的习惯,形成良好的意志品质。

"冰冻三尺,非一日之寒。"[①]坚强的意志是经过无数件小事的锻炼而逐步培养起来的,青年学生只有在小事上锻炼自己的意志,才可能在重大的事情上表现出坚强的意志来。有的学生误认为小事可以马虎,大事才能考验人的意志。事实告诉我们,小事都不能克制自己的人,做大事则难免会失败。正如高尔基所说:"哪怕是对自己一小点的克制,也会使人变得坚强起来。"教师要引导学生从小事做起,在平时的劳动、工作、学习和生活中,遇到各种困难都要尝试去克服,从而使学生的意志品质得到锻炼和发展。

---

① 王充.论衡·状留篇[M].长沙:岳麓书社,2015:250.

专栏 9-4

习得性无助

美国心理学家塞利格曼1967年在研究动物时提出了习得性无助。他用狗做了一项经典实验,起初把狗关在笼子里,只要蜂音器一响,就给以难受的电击,狗关在笼子里逃避不了电击。多次实验后,蜂音器一响,在给电击前,先把笼门打开,此时的狗不但不逃,而是不等电击出现就先倒地开始呻吟和颤抖。本来可以主动地逃避却绝望地等待痛苦的来临,这就是习得性无助。

1975年塞利格曼用人当受试者,结果使人也产生了习得性无助。实验是在大学生身上进行的,他们把学生分为三组:让第一组学生听一种噪音,这组学生无论如何也不能使噪音停止。第二组学生也听这种噪音,不过他们通过努力可以使噪音停止。第三组是对照组,不给受试者听噪音。当受试者在各自的条件下进行一段实验之后,即令受试者进行另外一种实验:实验装置是一只"手指穿梭箱",当受试者把手指放在穿梭箱的一侧时,就会听到一种强烈的噪音,放在另一侧时,就听不到这种噪音。实验结果表明:在原来的实验中,能通过努力使噪音停止的受试者,以及未听噪音的对照组受试者,即第二组和第三组受试者,他们在"穿梭箱"的实验中,学会了把手指移到箱子的另一边,使噪音停止;而第一组受试者,也就是说在原来的实验中无论怎样努力,也不能使噪音停止的受试者,他们的手指仍然停留在原处,听任刺耳的噪音响下去,却不把手指移到箱子的另一边。为了证明"习得性无助"对以后的学习有消极影响,塞利格曼又做了另外一项实验:他要求学生把下列字母排列成单词,比如 ISOEN,DERRO,可以排成 NOISE 和 ORDER,学生要想完成这一任务,必须掌握34251这种排列的规律。实验结果表明:原来实验中产生了无助感的受试者,很难完成这一任务。随后的很多实验也证明了这种习得性无助在人身上也会发生。

——李红.现代心理学[M].成都:四川教育出版社,2009:143—144.

本章小结

本章主要介绍了意志的含义、意志行动的特征、意志的品质,以及意志与认知、情感的关系,还对意志行动的过程进行了分析,了解了意志规律在教育中的运用,为培养学生良好的意志品质提供了一定的策略和方法,为师范生从事教育教学工作奠定了必要的基础。

关键术语

意志　意志品质　意志行动　动机冲突

讨论与应用

1. 请阅读以下案例,思考谈迁的故事反映了什么?谈谈为什么坚强的意志可以促使人获得成功。

中国古代的惊世之作《国榷》,就是明末清初史学家谈迁含辛茹苦,历经二十余个春秋，六易其稿，撰写400多万字，于五十多岁时完成的。但是天有不测风云，书稿意外失窃了。面对这个沉重的打击，谈迁并没有气馁，相反他强忍悲痛，克服各种困难，又经过四年的不懈努力，终于完成新稿。

2. 请结合本章所学谈谈你的看法。

如果规定自己在3个月内减肥25公斤，或者一天必须从事3个小时的体育锻炼，那么对这样一类无法实现的目标，最坚强的意志也无济于事。而且，失败的后果会将自己再试一次的愿望化为乌有。在许多情况下，将单一的大目标分解成许多小目标不失为一种好办法。打算戒酒的鲍勃在自己的房间里帖了一条标语——"每天不喝酒"。由于把戒酒的总目标分解成了一天天具体的行动，因此第二天又可以再次明确自己的决心。到了周末，鲍勃回顾自己七天来的一系列"胜利"时信心百倍，最终与酒"拜拜"了。

3. 请结合案例分析，如何培养学生坚强的意志力。

在美国，人们为了保护鹿，就杀掉了鹿的天敌——狼。于是鹿的数量剧增。鹿群们由于终日无忧无虑地饱食于林中，结果体态变得蠢笨，植物因为鹿群迅速繁殖和践踏而凋零，继而鹿由于缺少充分的食物及安逸少动所带来的捕捉而大批死亡。无奈，人们只有把狼再请进来，鹿群们又恢复了蓬勃生机。

本章讨论与应用答题
思路与要点
（扫描二维码）

本章复习思考题
（扫描二维码）

本章进一步阅读书目
（扫描二维码）

本章测量量表
（扫描二维码）

第十章
个性心理与行为动力
GEXINGXINLIYUXINGWEIDONGLI

　　俗话说:"人心不同,各如其面。"意思是说人的个性是千差万别、各不相同的。为什么说人的个性是不同的?人的个性包括哪些?亲爱的同学,请翻开本章,在随后的学习中一起探索个性的"奥秘"吧。

通过本章的学习,你能够
- 理解掌握个性的概念、结构和特点
- 了解什么是需要、动机和兴趣
- 了解需要、动机和兴趣的种类
- 理解和掌握马斯洛需要层次理论及其在教育中的应用
- 掌握学习动机与学习效果的关系
- 了解学习动机理论
- 掌握怎样激发和培养学习动机
- 理解兴趣的品质
- 理解兴趣的激发和培养

【本章结构】

```
                    个性心理与行为动力
        ┌──────────┬──────────┬──────────┐
        ▼          ▼          ▼          ▼
     个性概述      需要         动机        兴趣
    ◎ 个性的概念  ◎ 需要的概念  ◎ 动机概述   ◎ 兴趣的概念
    ◎ 个性的结构  ◎ 需要的种类  ◎ 学习动机概述 ◎ 兴趣的分类
    ◎ 个性的特征  ◎ 需要层次理  ◎ 学习动机理论 ◎ 兴趣的品质
                   论及其在教  ◎ 学习动机的培 ◎ 学习兴趣的培养
                   育中的应用    养和激发
```

本章主要是回答"个性""需要""动机"及"兴趣"等方面的问题。学习本章可以帮助你了解什么是个性、如何培养和激发学生的动机和兴趣。我们首先介绍个性的概念、结构及其特征,了解需要、动机和兴趣的内涵及其种类,然后探讨需要、动机理论及兴趣的品质,最后学习动机和兴趣的激发与培养,为将来从事教育教学工作奠定基础。

第一节 个性概述

一、个性的概念

个性（personality）是指个体在生活中形成的比较稳定的个性倾向性和个性心理特征的总和，它反映了一个人的独特的心理面貌。

个性也叫人格，源于古希腊文"persona"，是指演员在表演时为扮演角色所戴的面具。在古代，带这种面具可以表示剧中人物心理的某种典型性。饰演的角色不同，所戴面具也不同，这与我国京剧的脸谱有相似之处。如宋朝的清官包拯就是黑脸，黑脸一般代表刚正不阿，不媚权贵，他的黑额头上有一白月牙，则表示其清正廉洁。心理学沿用这一概念的含义，把一个人在人生舞台上所扮演的角色的种种心理活动风格称为个性。个性是个体生活经历在心理上的反映，它一方面体现了人比较稳定的需要、动机、兴趣、信念、价值观等个性倾向性方面的特点，另一方面也反映出人的能力、气质、性格等个性心理特征的差异，正因为有了个性，人的心理表现才千差万别，独具特色。

理解和把握个性的概念，要注意两个要点：

其一，个性的稳定性。个性一经形成就具有比较稳定的特点，不会轻易改变，不能把个体身上随时的变化都理解为个性。例如，某人从不助人，但某天却心血来潮帮助别人一次，就不能说他有助人为乐的个性，因为这不是他身上稳定的特点。

其二，个性是指一个人的心理品质的总和。个性概念中强调的总和，是各种心理特征在一个人身上独特的结合，而不是各种特征的机械相加，正是这种独特的结合，使每个人显示出自己的特色。

在当今强调展现个性的时代，青少年在学习和理解个性的概念时，要学会处理好展示自己的个性与尊重他人的个性的关系，这样才能使个性知识更好地为自身服务。第一，学会展现个性，但不可唯个性。每个人都有自己的个性，也应力求表现自己的个性，如果世界上的每一个人都缺乏个性，人的心理特点就会千篇一律，毫无特色和生机可言；但人也不应使自己的个性太强，甚至无法与人相处，个性太强的人，过于强调自己与他人的不同，和所有人都没有共同语言，就无法与人相处，无法处理好人际关系，因而在生活中也就易孤独，不利于自身的发展。第二，学会尊重他人的个性，即尊重他人独特的人格特点。所谓"国有国格，人有人格"，每一个人由于经历不同，都会形成各不相同的个性特点，这就要求人们在相处时要学会尊重他人的个性特点和习惯，不应强求别人和自己一样，更不能强求他人改变。这一点在青少年人际交往中尤其重要。

二、个性的结构

个性与人格一词虽有共同的词源，但二者在应用时代表的内涵却是不同的。来自西方心理学体系的人格一词，它的内涵较小，主要包含气质和性格的内容，不包括个性倾向性中的动机、需要、价值观等内容，也不包括能力。来自苏联心理学体系中的个性一词，涵盖了动机、需要等个性倾向性的内容，也包括了能力、气质、性格等个性心理特征的成分，内涵更大，它与心理过程共同构成了人的心理现象。从保证知识结构完整性的角度，本书更倾向于选用个性的概念。从心理结构上分析，个性是一个复杂的、多侧面的、多层次的系统，它由个性倾向性、个性心理特征和自我意识三个密切联系、不可分割的子系统构成。

（一）个性倾向性

个性倾向性（personality trend）也叫个性的动力系统，是指决定个体对待客观事物的态度与行为的内部动力系统。它决定着人对现实的态度，主要由需要、动机、兴趣、信念和世界观等成分组成。需要是个性倾向性的源泉和基础；动机是个性发展的内驱力；兴趣是个性发展最现实、最活跃、最能动的因素；理想、信念、世界观是个性心理的核心，是个性倾向性的集中表现，是人意识到的需要系统，它指导着人的行动，影响着人的整个心理面貌。

个性倾向性中的这些成分是相互联系、相互作用的。但其中总有一个成分占主导地位，占主导地位的倾向性成分对其他各个成分起支配作用，并影响其他心理活动。就人的整个心理现象而言，个性倾向性是人的一切心理活动和行为的最高调解者，也是个性的积极性的源泉。

（二）个性心理特征

个性心理特征（psychological characteristic of personality）是指个体身上经常表现出来的本质的、稳定的心理特征。它表明一个人的比较典型的心理活动和行为，它主要包括能力、气质、性格等。能力是保证活动成功的个性心理特征；性格标示着人对现实的态度和与之相应的行为方式的特征；气质标志着人在进行心理活动时，在神经过程的强度、速度、稳定性、灵活性等动态性质方面的独特结合的个体差异性。它们最直接地表现了人们之间的差异的具体内容，因而也叫个体的特征系统。

（三）自我意识

自我意识（self-consciousness）是人对自身以及对自己同客观世界的关系的意识。主要包括自我认识、自我体验和自我调节，它是个性结构中最重要的组成部分。人们正是通过对自我的认识和评估，来调节、控制自己的思想和言行，使之符合客观现实的条件，并使得个性的发展逐步趋于完善和成熟。因此，自我意识也称个性的自我调节系统。

专栏10-1

描绘积极的自我意向

不管我们是否意识到，在我们每个人的心灵深处都有一副关于"自己是什么样的人"的自画像，虽然它不够清晰，但是却详细描绘着你的一切方面。这就是心理学里所说的自我意象（self-image）。

心理学家曾经对一个中学篮球队进行过这样一个研究：他们把水平相似的队员分为三个小组，告诉第一个小组停止练习投篮一个月，第二个小组在一个月中每天下午在体育馆练习投篮一小时，第三组在一个月中每天在自己的想象中练习投篮一个小时。结果，第一组由于一个月没有练习，投篮平均水平由39%降到37%，第二组由于在体育馆中坚持了练习，平均水平由39%上升到41%；第三组在想象中练习的队员，平均水平由39%提高到42.5%。这真是很奇怪！在想象中练习投篮怎么能比在体育馆中练习投篮提高得快呢？很简单，因为在那些球员的想象中，所投出的球都是中的！通过想象，球员们为自己描绘出成功的自我意象，并最终在行动上获得了成功。

自我意象的作用正是在于它树立了你对自己的根本的看法和感受。正像投篮一样，一个人的自我意象是可以通过训练而改变的，我们可以让它变得美丽多彩。我们完全有权力，也有能力重新为自己描绘一幅美丽的自画像。既然这样，还等什么呢？开动脑筋，放开想象，描绘一个积极的自我吧。

——林崇德，申继亮.大学生心理健康读本[M].北京：教育科学出版社，2005：193.

三、个性的特征

（一）稳定性与可变性

个性的形成都经历了一个长期反复的过程。它是个体通过教育和参加社会实践，逐渐形成的一定的行为动机、理想、信念、价值观，在一定倾向性的指引下，使自己的心理面貌在不同的生活情境中都表现出一贯的品质，构成稳定的人格。个人身上会表现出许许多多的心理特点，但构成人格特征的是指那些经常出现的、比较稳定的特征。一个人在各种场合，如在家中、在学校、在团体中、在运动场上一贯表现出粗心大意，就说明他具有粗心的性格特点。

个性的稳定性是相对的。人的个性是在社会生活过程中形成的，并随着社会生活的改变而发展变化的。一个人随着年龄的增长、生活条件与实践活动的改变、教育的作用和自己的主观要求，在不同程度上是可以改变个性的。

（二）独特性和共同性

个性最突出的一个方面便是它的独特性，亦即个别性。个性的独特性是指人的心理倾向、个性心理特点和心理过程的独特结合。人们的兴趣、爱好极其多样，能力各异，在气质和性格的表现上也是各有特色，正如"人心不同，各如其面"。世界文学名著之所以千古流传、深入人心，主要原因之一就是作者成功塑造了典型的、个性独特鲜明的人物。《西游记》中的孙悟空、《水浒传》中的李逵、《红楼梦》中的林黛玉，个个角色鲜活，心理特点独特，给人留下深刻的印象。因此，人的个性表现是极端个别化的，每个人都是独特的，绝无仅有的。个性的独特性主要是由人自身的素质不同,人所处的社会生活环境及其所接受的教育影响的不同造成的。

个性的共同性是指人的个性具有共同的特征。由于人们的个性受共同的社会经济、政治和文化生活环境影响而形成,因此个性中包含有民族的心理特点,每个人都具有本民族的思想感情、文化传统和习俗。在阶级社会中,个性还包含有阶级和集团的心理特点,每个人都具有本阶级、本集团的需要和世界观。因此,就使得人的个性在体现个人独特的心理特征的同时,又体现出本阶级、本民族所具有的精神面貌。从这个意义上讲,人的个性是个别性与共同性的统一。

(三) 生物性与社会性

人是生物实体,也是社会实体。人具有生物属性,也具有社会属性。人格结构中的气质和智力就更多地体现着人的生物性,而兴趣、理想、信念等则主要是在社会的影响下形成的。

作为一个自然实体,人通过遗传所获得的先天素质,如身体的构造、形态、感官及神经系统的特性等是构成人格形成的物质基础,虽不能预定人格的发展方向,却影响着人格发展的进程和人格形成的难易。作为一个社会实体,人处在各种社会关系中,总是通过接受各种社会影响来协调自己的心理与行为,逐步形成了一个人的个性。没有人的社会生活条件,人就无法社会化。人的生物性因素和人的社会性因素,虽然对人的个性形成与发展共同起作用,但二者比较起来,生物性因素总属于次要地位。

第二节
需要

一、需要的概念

需要(need)是个体和社会的客观需求在人脑中的反映,是个人的心理活动与行为的基本动力,是个人活动积极性的源泉。

需要是有机体内部的一种不平衡状态。这种不平衡状态包括生理的和心理的不平衡。例如,血液中水分的缺乏,会产生喝水的需要;血糖成分下降,会产生饥饿求食的需要;失去亲人,会产生爱的需要;社会秩序不好,会产生安全的需要等。在需要得到满足后,这种不平衡状态暂时得到消除;当出现新的不平衡时,新的需要又会产生。

需要是由个体对某种客观事物的要求引起的。这种要求可能来自有机体的内部,也可能来自个体周围的环境。例如,人渴了需要喝水,这种需要是由机体内部的要求引起的;父母的"望子成龙"使孩子积极向上,孩子的这种需要是由外部要求引起的。当人们感受到这些要求,并引起个体某种内在的不平衡状态时,要求就转化为某种需要。需要总是指向能满足某种需要的客体或事件,即追求某种客体,并从客体中得到满足。没有客体、没有对象的需要,不指向任何事物的需要是不存在的。

需要是个体活动的基本动力,是个体行为动力的重要源泉。人的各种活动或行为,从饥则食、渴则饮,到从事物质资料的生产、文学艺术作品的创作、科学技术的发明与创造,都是在需要的推动下进行的。

二、需要的种类

人的需要是多种多样的,可以从不同的角度对其进行分类。

(一)自然性需要和社会性需要

根据需要的起源,可以把需要分为自然性需要和社会性需要。

自然性需要又称机体需要、生物性需要或生理性需要,是指与维持个体生存和种族延续相联系的需要,包括对饮食、休息、排泄、运动、繁衍后代等的需要。生理需要是人类最基本、最原始的需要,是人和动物共有的。但人的生理需要和动物的生理需要有本质的不同。动物直接从自然界摄取物质满足需要,而人则使用工具改变自然物品的形式,并创造新的物品满足需要。

社会性需要又称心理性需要,是指对维持社会生活所需求的事物的反映,是与人的社会生活相联系的需要,如对交往、劳动、奉献、成就等的需要。社会需要是后天习得的,是人所特有的高级需要。这种需要是从社会要求转化而来的,当个人认识到社会要求的必要性时,社会要求就转化为个人的社会需要。

(二)物质需要和精神需要

根据需要的对象,可以把需要分为物质需要和精神需要。

物质需要是指个体对物质对象的需要。这种需要既包括维持生命机体的低级需要(如食物、安全、性等),也包括人的高级的社会物质的需要(如豪宅、名车、高级家用电器等)。

精神需要是指个体精神文化方面的需要。这种需要在人的社会生活中具有重要意义。如认知、交往、道德、劳动、审美、成就等方面的需要。

上面所说的这些不同类型的需要不是截然分开的,在很大程度上它们相互依存。

专栏10-2

中小学生需要的研究

辽宁师范大学教育系杨丽珠教授等人于1998年研究了中小学生的需要,他们用三种形式的问卷测试了1080人(男女生各半,包括小学生、普通中学生和城市重点高中生)。该项研究表明,我国中小学生需要结构的发展是多维度、多层次的统一体。包括28种需要,分为7类,每类又有4个层次,见表10-1。

——杨丽珠.中小学生需要倾向性发展研究[J].辽宁师范大学学报,1989(02): 25.

表 10-1 中小学生需要结构模式

需要的种类	需要的层次
生理和物质生活需要	1. 水、空气、阳光、食物、睡觉等 2. 吃得好一些，穿得舒服一些 3. 家庭的现代化 4. 安静的学习环境
安全与保障需要	1. 身体健康、体魄健壮 2. 人身安全、不受欺负 3. 生活安定、和平幸福 4. 升入理想学校或有个好工作
交往和友谊需要	1. 父母和老师的爱 2. 同学之间团结友爱 3. 结交诚实、正直的朋友 4. 异性朋友的爱
尊重与自尊需要	1. 平等与公正 2. 信任与理解 3. 尊重与自信 4. 独立与自主
课外活动与精神生活需要	1. 玩小动物，做游戏 2. 课外读物 3. 文体活动 4. 艺术欣赏、文学评论
学习与成才需要	1. 新铅笔、新书包 2. 好老师、好课本、学好功课 3. 丰富知识，多方面能力，优秀品质 4. 革命理想，正确人生观
奉献与创造需要	1. 为他人做好事 2. 搞小科研，搞小发明 3. 关心国家大事，尽职尽责 4. 拼搏，干一番大事业

三、需要层次理论及其在教育中的应用

关于需要的结构，在心理学界存在不同的理论观点，其中马斯洛（A. H. Maslow）的需要层次理论（hierarchical theory of needs）（如图10-1所示）影响较大。下面重点介绍一下马斯洛的需要层次理论。

（一）马斯洛的需要层次理论

马斯洛认为人是一体化的整体，人类的基本需要是按优势出现的先后或力量的强弱排列成等级的，即所谓的需要层次。马斯洛提出人类有五种基本需要：生理需

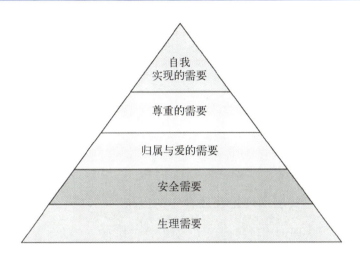

图 10-1

马斯洛的需要层次理论

要、安全需要、归属与爱的需要、尊重的需要、自我实现的需要,各层次需要的基本含义如下:

生理需要(physiological need)。人对空气、水、食物、睡眠、性的需要等。它们在人的所有需要中最重要,也是最有力量的。如果一个人的生理需要得不到满足,其他的需要均会被推到次要的地位。当人落水之后,在为得到空气而拼命挣扎时,就会体会到自尊和爱的需要是多么不重要了。

安全需要(safety need)。它表现为人们要求稳定、安全、受到保护、有秩序、能免除恐惧和焦虑等。例如,多数人希望得到一份较安定的职业,还有人愿意参加各种保险,这些都表现了他们的安全需要。婴幼儿由于无力应付环境中的不安全因素的威胁,他们的安全需要就显得尤为强烈。

归属与爱的需要(belongingness and love need)。个人要求与其他人建立感情的联系,如结交朋友、追求爱情,参加一个团体并在其中获得某种地位等,就是归属与爱的需要。在这里,马斯洛特别提到爱的需要,他认为爱是一种两个人之间健康的、亲热的关系,它包括了相互依赖。他指出,缺乏爱,会抑制人的成长以及潜力的发展。爱应该包括两方面,即给别人的爱和接受别人的爱。

尊重的需要(esteem need)。它包括自尊和他尊。自尊需要的满足会使人相信自己的力量和价值,使其在生活中变得更有能力,更富有创造性。相反,缺乏自尊会使人感到自卑,没有足够的信心去处理面临的问题。他尊是希望受到他人的认可和尊重。这看似与归属需要类似,但是这种渴望被赞美的需求还与对名声、权力、地位的渴望联系在一起。

自我实现的需要(self-actualization need)。就是促使自己的潜能得以发挥,追求实现自我理想的需要,希望自己越来越成为所期望的人物,完成与自己的能力相称的一切,即人的价值的完满实现。在人生道路上自我实现的形式是不一样的,带孩子的妇女或开卡车的妇女、一个在流水线上工作的男人或做炊事工作的男人,他们都有机会去完善自己的能力,满足自我实现的需要。

马斯洛认为,这五种需要都是人的最基本的需要。这些需要是天生的、与生俱来

的,它们构成了不同的等级或水平,并成为激励和指引个体行为的力量。他认为各层次需要之间有以下一些关系:

① 一般来说,这五种需要像阶梯一样,从低到高。一个层次的需要获得满足后,就会向高一层次的需要发展。我国古语所谓的"仓廪实而知礼仪,衣食足而知荣辱"说的就是这个道理。

② 这五种需要不是都能得到满足的,越是靠近顶部的成长型需要,满足的百分比越少。

③ 同一时期,个体可能同时存在多种需要,因为人的行为往往是受多种需要支配的。每一个时期总有一种需要占支配地位。

(二)马斯洛的需要层次理论在教育中的应用

马斯洛的需要层次理论比较接近现实,对教育工作有一定的参考价值。只有满足学生合理的、可以实现的最基本需要,他们才会努力学习。教师还应注意培养学生的高级需要,并创造条件,使学生的自尊心、集体感、荣誉感得到相应的满足,促使学生向自我实现的方向发展。

当然,我们在分析和应用该理论时,也要看到其局限性。首先,它只强调了个人的需要、个人的意识自由、个人的自我实现,而没有提到社会实践对个人需要的制约性以及人的需要的社会性。其次,它过于强调个人的内在价值,他的自我实现论并没有突破西方个人本位的意识形态的束缚。再次,马斯洛把人的需要统统说成是先天的,与生俱来的,这就模糊了人的生理需要与社会需要的差别,降低了后天生活环境和教育对人的需要的发生发展所起的作用。最后,马斯洛的需要层次理论还缺乏科学实验的依据和客观的测量指标,还有待于在社会实践中作进一步的检验。

第三节

动机

一、动机概述

(一)动机概念

动机(motivation)是指引起和维持个体行为,并将该行为导向某一目标,以满足个体某种需要的内部动力(动机是为实现一定目的而行动的原因)。动机一词,来源于拉丁文"movere",即推动(to move)的意思,是一个解释性的概念,用来说明个体为什么有这样或那样的行为。人从事任何活动都有一定的原因,这个原因就是人的行为动机,即人的一切有意识的行为,都是由动机引起的,并受动机的调节与支配。

(二)动机产生的条件

引起动机必须满足两个条件,即内在条件和外在条件。

1. 内在条件——内驱力

需要是个体进行活动的基本动力。人的各种活动,从觅食求生、学习交往,到创造发明、回馈社会等,都是在需要的推动下进行的。需要就是引起动机的内在条件,动机是在需要的基础上产生的,离开需要的动机是不存在的。但是,需要不一定都产生动机行为,只有当个体的需要达到足够的强度,推动人们去行动,并把活动引向某一目标时,需要才能变成实际行动的动机。这种驱使有机体产生行为的内部动力,就是内驱力(drive)。

需要是内驱力的基础,当机体缺乏某种东西而产生需要时,机体内环境的相对稳定便遭到破坏。例如,需要水分或需要食物时,机体内的细胞内外的水的渗透压或血液中的糖分遭到了一定水平的破坏,这种生理变化所产生的需要便对机体形成紧张的内驱力,从而导致求饮、求食行为,以恢复相对稳定。内驱力大致与需要成正相关。例如,饥饿的人比饱食的人具有较强的内驱力;而又饿又渴的人比只是饥饿的人具有更大的内驱力。

人的内驱力和需要一样有生理性内驱力和社会性内驱力两种。由生理需要而驱使机体产生一定行为的内部力量,称为原发性内驱力或生理性内驱力,如饥饿内驱力、口渴内驱力等;由责任感等后天形成的社会性需要所产生的内驱力,称为继发性内驱力或社会性内驱力。一般说来,社会性内驱力对原发性内驱力起调节作用。

2. 外在条件——诱因

人的动机行为不仅受到内部需要的"推动",也会受到外部刺激的"拉动"。例如,饥饿会促使有机体去寻找食物,但饱食者看见美味佳肴也会引起食欲,即使已吃饱也会再次进食。因此,外部刺激也是引起动机的一个原因。凡是能够引起机体动机行为的外在刺激,均被称为"诱因"(incentive)。它是引起动机的另一个重要因素。诱因又可分为正诱因和负诱因。凡是有机体因趋向或接受而获得满足的刺激物,称为正诱因;凡是个体逃离或躲避而获得满足的刺激物,称为负诱因。例如,如果一个人对食物很讲究,那么,色香味俱全的食物是正诱因,而残羹冷炙则是负诱因,但是当这个人极度饥饿又没有东西可食时,即使是残羹冷炙,在他眼里也是美味佳肴,这时残羹冷炙又成了正诱因。诱因可以是物质的东西,也可以是精神的东西。例如,教师对学生的肯定和赞扬,是一种激发学生学习的诱因。

当然,由需要转化为动机的两个条件并不是绝对的。当其中一项达到足够的强度时,另一条件即使不具备或不充分,也能引起人们的动机行为。所以,一般认为人的动机行为既可由需要引起,也可由外界事物引起,但往往是内在条件与外在条件交互影响的结果。

(三)动机功能

动机作为内在的动力,对人的行为有四种功能:

1. 激发功能

动机是个体能动性的一个主要方面,它具有发动行为的作用。人的各种行为都体现着他所需要的客观事物对其行为的激发作用。当面临的刺激与当前的动机有关时，个体的行为更容易被激发。例如，感到寒冷的人，有取暖的需要，附近的柴火、引火物等更能够引起他产生烤火的行为；饥饿的人会对与食物有关的刺激特别敏感，更容易激起其觅食的行为。动机力量的大小，是由动机的性质和强度决定的。一般认为，中等强度的动机有利于任务的完成。

2. 指向功能

动机不仅能激发行为，而且能将行为指向一定的目标或对象。动机不一样时，活动的方向和目标也不同。如在学习动机的支配下，人们可能去图书馆或教室；在休息动机的支配下，人们可能去电影院、公园或娱乐场所。

3. 维持和调节功能

动机具有维持功能，它表现为行为的坚持性。活动产生以后，动机维持着该活动始终朝着既定的目标进行，并调节着活动的强度和持续时间。如果活动达到了目标，动机促使有机体终止这种活动；如果活动尚未达到目标，动机将驱使有机体维持或加强这种活动，或转换活动方向以达到某种目标。动机的维持作用是由个体活动与他所预期的目标的一致程度来决定的。当活动指向个体所追求的目标时，这种活动就会在相应动机的维持下继续下去；相反，当活动背离了个体所追求的目标时，这种活动的积极性就会降低，或者完全停止下来。

人的行为动机在具体活动中的体现是很复杂的。相同的活动可能体现不同的动机；不同的活动也可能由相同或相似的动机所支配，并且人的一种活动还可以由多种动机所支配。例如，同样是勤奋努力学习的行为，有的学生是为了自己的人生追求而自发学习兴趣，有的是为了得到老师的表扬和家长的认同，有的是为了获得丰富的物质奖励。又如，一个成就动机很强的人，会在学习、生活、工作等各个领域勇于进取，不甘人后。

（四）动机分类

动机是多种多样的，可以从不同的角度和侧面对动机进行分类。

1. 从动机的起源看，可以分为生理性动机和社会性动机

生理性的动机又称原发性动机、原始性动机、生物性动机，是以机体的生理需要为基础的动机，包括饥饿、口渴、睡眠、性欲、排泄的动机等。

社会性动机又叫继发性动机、习得性动机、心理性动机，是以人们的社会性需要为基础的动机，包括成就动机、交往动机、威信动机等。由于社会性动机是后天习得的，所以在人与人之间有着很大的个别差异。

2. 从动机的动力来源看，可以分为内部动机和外部动机

这是所有动机划分中心理学家们公认的一种划分方法，此法对教育实践具有相当重要的应用价值。内部动机是指由个体内在需要引起的动机。动机的满足是在活动之内，不在活动之外。活动本身就能引起人的兴趣，是活动者追求的目的。例如，有的学生的学习动机是由学习者本人自行产生的，学习活动本身就是学习者所追求的目的，而不是为了老师和家长的赞扬和奖励。可见，内部动机中的成功感或兴趣比外部动机中的单纯为了金钱或物质利益既经济又更富有积极作用。

外部动机是指个体由外部诱因所引起的动机。例如，学生为了得到老师和家长的赞

扬而努力学习,或者为了得到物质奖励而学习。这些活动的推动力均来自活动外部的刺激,都是外部动机。外部动机可以转化为内部动机。教育实践证明,要提高学习积极性,必须使外部动机转化为内部动机,让学生从学习中产生学习兴趣,力求不断深入地探索事物的奥秘;同时强调内部动机的激发,也不应忽略外部动机的应用,对学生外部动机的激发可以使学生已形成的内部动机处于持续的激起状态。

3. 从动机的影响和持续作用的时间看,可分为近景的直接性动机和远景的间接性动机

近景的直接性动机是由对活动本身的直接兴趣所引起的,这类动机比较具体,与活动本身有较切近的关系,实际效能明显,但是这种动机持续时间短,影响范围小,不够稳定,容易受偶然因素的影响,易随情境的改变而改变。不过,在一定时期内,这种动机对具体的活动有着直接的推动作用。

远景的间接性动机一般是与活动的社会意义和个人前途相关联的,它多来自对活动的深刻意义的认识。这类动机一旦形成,就具有稳定性和持久性,不易为情境中的偶然因素所改变,持续作用的时间也较长。但是,一般来说,远景的间接性动机与当前进行的活动没有过多的直接联系,所以对当前活动的直接推动作用较小。

二、学习动机概述

(一)学习动机的概念

学习动机是推动学生进行学习活动的一种内部动力,是激发个体进行学习活动、维持已引起的学习活动,并使行为朝向一定的学习目标的一种内在过程或内部心理状态。它是在社会生活条件和教育的影响下逐渐形成的,不同的社会和教育对学生的学习有着不同的要求,所以反映在学生头脑中的学习动机也是不完全相同的。

(二)学习动机的分类

为了对学生的学习动机有所了解,首先要对其进行分类。学习动机的分类方法很多,这里只列举两种对教学实践有影响的分类。一种分类是把学习动机分为内部动机与外部动机,这在前面的动机分类里已有叙述,这里就不再赘述;另一种是把动机分为认知内驱力、自我提高内驱力和附属内驱力。这是美国心理学家奥苏贝尔的分类。

图 10-2 戴维·保罗·奥苏贝尔

戴维·保罗·奥苏贝尔(David Pawl Ausubel, 1918—2008),美国认知教育心理学家。先获宾夕法尼亚大学学士学位(1939)和哥伦比亚大学心理学硕士学位,后又获布兰迪斯大学医学博士(1943)和哥伦比亚大学心理学博士(1950)学位。1950—1974年任伊利诺伊大学教育研究所教授。1975年转任纽约州立大学研究生院与大学中心教授,1978年退休为名誉教授。后开办诊所,任精神病医生。曾获桑代克奖。主要著作有《自我发展与个性失调》《青少年发展的理论与问题》《儿童发展的理论与问题》《教育心理学:一种认知观》等。

奥苏贝尔指出："一般称之为学校情境中的成就动机，至少包括三方面的内驱力决定成分，即认知内驱力、自我提高内驱力和附属内驱力。"他认为，学生所有的指向学业的行为都可以从这三方面的内驱力加以解释。当然，随着儿童年龄的增长，这三种成分在个体身上的比重会有改变。

认知内驱力（cognitive drive），即一种要求了解和理解知识、掌握知识的需要，以及系统地阐述问题并解决问题的需要。这种内驱力，一般说来，多半是从好奇的倾向中派生出来的。但个体的这些好奇倾向，最初只是潜在的而非真实的动机，还没有特定的内容和方向。它要通过个体在实践中不断取得成功，才能真正表现出来，才能具有特定的方向。因此，学生对于某学科的认知内驱力感兴趣，远不是天生的，主要是获得的，也有赖于特定的学习经验。在有意义的学习中，认知内驱力可能是一种最重要和最稳定的动机了。这种动机指向学习任务本身，即为了获得知识，满足这种动机的奖励即知识的实际获得是由学习本身提供的，因而也被称为内部动机。

自我提高内驱力（ego-enhancement drive），是个体因自己的胜任能力或工作能力而赢得相应地位的需要。这种需要从儿童入学开始，日益显得重要，成为成就动机的主要组成部分。自我提高的内驱力与认知内驱力不一样，它并非直接指向学习任务本身。自我提高的内驱力把成就看作是赢得地位与自尊心的根源，它显然是一种外部动机。从另一个方面说，失败对丧失自尊是一种威胁，因而也能促使学生在学业上做出长期而艰苦的努力。

附属内驱力（affiliated drive），是一个人为了保持长者们（如家长、教师等）的赞许或认可而表现出来的把工作做好的一种需要。它具有这样三个条件：第一，学生与长者在感情上具有依附性。第二，学生从长者方面所博得的赞许或认可（如被长者视为可爱的、聪明的、有发展前途的人，而且受到种种优惠的待遇）中将获得一种派生的地位。所谓派生地位，不是由他本身的成就水平决定的，而是从他所自居和效法的某个人或某些人不断给予的赞许或认可中引申出来的。第三，享受到这种派生地位乐趣的人，会有意识地使自己的行为符合长者的标准和期望（包括对学业成就方面的标准和期望），借以获得并保持长者的赞许，这种赞许往往使一个人的地位更确定、更巩固。

（三）学习动机与学习效果的关系

1. 学习动机的水平影响学习效果

动机与学业成就密切相关。美国的尤古罗格卢（Uguroglu）等人分析了232项动机测量与学业成就之间的相关系数，发现其中98%是正相关。这意味着高的动机水平导致高的学业成就。[1]但是在现实生活中，我们也经常看到：有的学生学习动机很强，但成绩却不好，而有的学生学习动机不强，学习成绩却不错。这是由于动机与效果不是直接关系，而是间接关系。动机是以行为为中介来影响效果的。人的行为除了受动机的控制和调节外，还受其他主客观因素的影响。所以，为了提高学习成绩，激发正确的学习动机固然重要，但却不是唯一的充分条件，还应该尽可能改善制约学习活动的各种主客观条件，诸如改进学习方法，提高学习能力，加强辅导等。

---

[1] 韩永昌.心理学[M].上海：华东师范大学出版社，2009：197.

2. 学习动机的强度影响学习效果

动机有加强学习的作用。研究证明，成就动机强的学生比成就动机差的学生更能坚持学习，学习成绩也更好。美国洛厄尔的研究说明了这一点。洛厄尔选择两组成就动机强弱不同而其他条件相同的大学生作被试，比较他们的学习效果。实验任务是要求他们用一些打乱了的字母去构成普通的词（比如，打乱了的W、T、S和E去构成WEST）。将19名成就动机强的学生和21名成就动机弱的学生成绩作比较，图10-3中的结果表明：成就动机较强的被试在这项学习任务中能够取得不断的进步，而成就动机弱的学生则没有取得明显的进步。

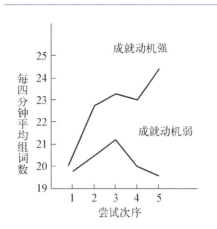

图10-3 成就动机强弱对学习的影响

学习成绩的好坏有激发和削弱学习动机的作用。学习成绩好，满足了原有的学习需要，可促进学习动机的加强；学习成就差，原有的学习需要得不到满足，受到惩罚，使学习动机进一步削弱。

但是，有时学习动机过强，学生处于紧张状态，反而会降低学习效率。如，在考试前做了充分准备，并认为一定能得高分的学生，可能在考试中发挥不出实力，甚至考不及格。这就是动机过强而降低了效率的事例。为了取得最好的学习成绩，学生的学习动机应维持在一个适当的水平上。一般说来，从事比较容易的学习活动，动机强度的最佳水平应当高一点；而从事比较困难的学习活动，动机强度最好低一点。这就是耶克斯—多德森定律（Yerkes-Dodson Law）①（如图10-4所示）。

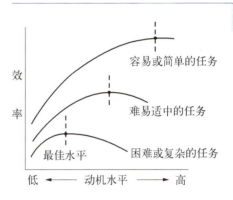

图10-4 耶克斯—多德森定律

实践发现，动机强度的最佳水平点还会因人而异，表现出个别差异。进行同样难度的学习活动，有的学生动机强度的最佳点可能要高一些，另一些学生动机强度的最佳点可能要低一些，这就需要教师的正确指导。

三、学习动机理论

人类的动机很复杂，心理学家对动机的解释也是多种多样的，因此需要我们学会在不同的情境中利用不同的动机理论来理解人们的行为。

---

① Kantowitz B H, Sorkin R D. Human Factors: Understanding People-System Relationships[M]. New York: John Wiley&Sons, 1983: 606.

（一）强化理论

学习动机的强化理论是由行为主义学习理论家提出来的，其早期代表人物是新行为主义心理学家斯金纳。他不仅用强化来解释操作学习的发生，而且也用强化来解释动机的引起。他认为人为了达到某种目的，一定要采取一定的行为作用于环境。当这种行为的后果有利于达到目的时，这种行为就会再次出现；当这种行为的后果不能达到目的时，这种行为就会消失或减弱。以这种观点看，人的行为动力就是强化，斯金纳所谓的强化就是增大行为发生的概率事件。按此理论，任何学习行为的获得就是应该增强报偿。因此，在学习活动中采取各种外部手段，如奖赏、赞扬、评分、等级、竞赛等都可以激发学生的学习动机。

强化理论也认为强化有外部强化和内部强化之分。外部强化是外部或他人给予行为者的强化；内部强化是自我强化，即行为者在活动中获得成功而增强的成就感和自信心。这两种强化都能增强学习者的学习动机。强化理论还认为，强化有正强化和负强化之分。正强化是指对行为者的奖励性刺激，以提高行为发生的概率；负强化是撤销那些令人厌恶的或惩罚性的刺激，以提高行为发生的概率。

斯金纳将强化理论用于人的学习上，发明了程序教学法和教学机。他强调学习应遵循小步子和及时反馈的原则。根据他的研究成果，他提出了行为强化的五条原则：① 经过强化的行为趋向于重复发生。例如，当学生的某行为获得教师的称赞后，该生此行为就增加了重复出现的可能性。② 应该根据强化对象的不同而采取不同的强化措施。学生的年龄、性别、个性以及家庭环境不同，强化的方式也应该不同。③ 小步子前进，分阶段设立目标，并对目标给予明确的确定和表述。④ 及时反馈。⑤ 正强化比负强化效果更好。

强化理论在教育工作中的运用很广泛，但它也有许多不足。这主要表现在强化理论过分强调引起行为的外部力量，而不关心个体内部发生的各种心理过程和相应的条件，忽视甚至否定了人的学习行为的自觉性和主动性。

（二）归因理论

在各种有影响的动机理论中，归因理论最为强调认知的观点，其指导原则和基本假设是：寻求理解是行为的基本动因。学生们试图去解释事件发生的原因，他们试图去为他们的成功或失败寻找能力、努力、态度、知识、运气、帮助、兴趣等方面的原因。当前对实践应用影响最大的是加利福尼亚大学的韦纳（B. Weiner）教授。

图 10-5 韦纳

韦纳（B. Weiner, 1935—　），美国著名的认知心理学家，发展了比较著名的归因理论。他曾发表了有关情绪和动机的许多文章和15本著作。自1965年以来，他一直任教于加利福尼亚大学。主要研究方向有因果性归因、情绪、心情的影响、亲社会行为等。他的主要贡献有归因理论、动机心理学、情绪心理学。主要著作有《动机和情绪的归因理论》等。

韦纳认为：能力、努力、任务难度和运气是人们在解释成功或失败时知觉到的四种主要原因，并将这四种主要原因分成控制点、稳定性、可控性三个维度。根据控制点维度，可将原因分成内部的和外部的；根据稳定性维度，可将原因分成稳定的和不稳定的；根据可控性维度，又可将原因分成可控的和不可控的。这一关系可用表10-2表示。

表 10-2 成功与失败的归因[1]

控制点	稳定性程度	
	稳　定	不　稳　定
内　部	能力 "我很聪明"成功 "我很笨"失败	努力 "我下了功夫"成功 "我实际上没下功夫"失败
外　部	任务的难度 "这很容易"成功 "这太难了"失败	运气 "我运气好"成功 "我运气不好"失败

韦纳认为，每一维度对动机都有重要的影响。在内外维度上，如果将成功归因于内部因素，会产生自豪感，从而动机提高；归因于外部因素，则会产生侥幸心理。将失败归因于内部因素，则会产生羞愧的感觉；归因于外部因素，则会生气。在稳定性维度上，如果将成功归因于稳定因素，会产生自豪感，从而动机提高；归因于不稳定因素，则会产生侥幸心理。将失败归因于稳定因素，将会产生绝望的感觉。将失败归因于不稳定因素，则会生气。在控制性维度上，如果将成功归因于可控因素，则会积极地去争取成功，归因于不可控因素，则不会产生多大的动力。将失败归因于可控因素，则会继续努力，归因于不可控因素，则会绝望。

韦纳通过一系列的研究，得出一些关于归因的最基本的结论：① 个人将成功归因于能力和努力等内部因素时，他会感到骄傲、满意、信心十足，而将成功归因于任务容易和运气好等外部原因时，产生的满意感则较少。相反，如果一个人将失败归因于缺少能力或努力，则会产生羞愧和内疚，而将失败归因于任务太难或运气不好时，产生的羞愧感则较少。而归因于努力相对归因于能力，无论成功或失败都会产生更强烈的情绪体验。努力而成功，体验到愉快；不努力而失败，体验到羞愧；努力而失败，也应受到鼓励。这种看法与我国传统的看法一致。② 在付出同样努力时，能力低的应得到更多的奖励。③ 能力低而努力的人受到最高评价，而能力高却不努力的人则受到最低评价。因此，韦纳总是强调内部的、稳定的和可控的维度。

---

[1] Atkinson J W. Towards experimental analysis of human motivation in terms. Of motives, expectancies and incentives. In: Atkinson J W. Ed. Motives infantasy, action, and society. Princeton: Van Nostrand, 1958: 288-305.

由此可见，归因理论的研究有助于了解心理活动发生的因果关系，有助于根据学习行为及其结果推断出个体的稳定的心理特征和个性差异，有助于从特定的学习行为及其结果预测个体在某种情况下可能产生的学习行为。因此，作为教师，我们有责任帮助学生正确归因，并有针对性地对不同类型的学生进行个别化的差异性教育。

（三）成就动机理论

最早集中研究成就动机的心理学家有默里（Murray）、麦克里兰（David McClelland）（如图10-6所示）、阿特金森（Atkinson）等人。默里将成就需要定义为：克服障碍，施展才能，力求尽快尽好地解决某一难题。20世纪40—50年代，麦克里兰在他的基础上进一步发展了成就动机理论。个人的成就动机可以分成两部分：其一是力求成功的意向；其二是避免失败的意向。也就是说，成就行为体现了趋向成功或避免失败两种倾向的冲突。一个人不可能不考虑失败的后果去追求成功。因而一个人趋近目标的行为最终要受到这两种动机的综合作用而决定。如果一个人追求成功的动机高于避免失败的动机，那么这个人便将努力去追求特定的目标。如果一个人避免失败的动机强于追求成功的动机，那么这个人就尽可能选择减少失败机会的目标。这种理论指出，一般的人特别是有成就的人，都有如下一些特征：① 能全力以赴地完成某种困难的工作，看重声誉并获得成功；② 有明确的目标和较高的抱负水平，对自己有足够的信心；③ 精力充沛、好奇探新、求异开拓；④ 选择伙伴以能力为标准，而不是以交往的疏密为标准。

图10-6　戴维·麦克里兰

戴维·麦克里兰（David McCleland，1917—1998），美国社会心理学家，1987年美国心理学会杰出科学贡献奖得主。1941年获耶鲁大学心理学哲学博士学位。曾先后任康涅狄格女子大学讲师、韦斯利昂大学教授及布林莫尔学院教授，1956年开始在哈佛大学担任心理学教授，1987年后转任波士顿大学教授直到退休。麦克利兰从心理学和企业管理的角度入手，把激励理论广泛地推演到整个人类社会的层面，并用以观察、分析和改造社会，提出"成就动机理论"。其主要著作有《渴求成就》《权利的两面性》《取得成就的社会》《权利：内省经验》《成就动机是可以培养的》等。

专栏10-3

学会获得成就

戴维·麦克里兰（David McClelland），哈佛大学的一位心理学家，二十多年来一直致力于他的"成就需要"研究。他利用主题统觉测验的一种变式，来测量这种动机的强度,在测验中要求被试对特地制备的图画编说故事(例如,一张图画是一个男孩在学习,另一张表示体育运动竞赛)。

麦克里兰和其同事用这种方法做了许多研究。一个主要的研究问题是美国和其他国家的各社会文化阶层在成就需要上的差别。他们的发现之一是各个国家内各社会阶级,在对儿童将来的期望上有所不同。下层阶级的成就需要是低的,而中产阶级的却是高的。中产阶级家庭的家长一般抱负水平较高,他们在子女幼小时就鼓励其独立完成活动,接触新事物,掌握学习的知识和技能。在这样的家庭里,父母本身的成就和成就动机既可以为其子女的抱负水平提供榜样,又可提供一种有利于高抱负水平形成的气氛。而那些抱负水平低的父母,则多限制其子女的独立自主行为,爱插手处理他们的事务,不关心他们的学业,这些很不利于儿童抱负水平的提高。

麦克里兰认为这种过程不可听其自然。他编制与应用了一套训练计划,企图提高穷人的成就需要,并相应地改变他们的行为,提高进取心争取更大的成就。这些计划至少在短期内已有一定的成就。

——克雷奇(Krech D.),等.心理学纲要[M].周先庚,等,译.北京:文化教育出版社,1981:364.

成就动机理论应用于指导学生的学习时要注意以下几点:① 要根据学生个人的能力安排学习、工作,并创造一定条件放手让他们去独立完成,让他们体验强烈的成就感。② 给学生的学习任务的难度要适中。过易不能激发他们完成学习任务的意念;过难则因不能完成任务而使他们心灰意冷。成就动机高的学生,要安排他们去完成难度比较高的学习任务,使之竭尽全力去完成。③ 对学生的进步要有明确的、及时的反馈。如对他们的工作给予正确评价,给予一定的奖励。

心理学家认为,成就需要和成就动机的存在是希望的永恒来源。教师在课堂设计时要密切关注学生的能力和潜力,要满足学生的进步要求、成就需要,给他们提供适当的任务和条件,使他们感到满足和愉悦。要坚信每一个学生都是渴望成功的。

四、学习动机的培养和激发

学习动机的培养与激发既有区别,又有联系。学习动机的培养是指学生把社会和教育的客观要求变为自己的内在学习需要的过程,而激发是利用一定的诱因使已形成的学习动机由潜伏状态转入活动状态,使它成为推动学生学习的内部动力。

(一)学习动机的培养

1.帮助学生建立起明确适当的学习目标

学习目标是学生对学习结果的期待,达到学习目标,学生会受到各种强化。可以从时间上把学习目标划分为长远目标和近期目标。在学习的各个环节,教师要向学生提出明确而具体的学习目标,同时注意将近期目标与长远目标相结合。同时还要帮助学生建立与自己能力一致的个人目标。目标过高,与学生本身的能力差距太大,学生可望而不可求,对学生不仅没有激励作用,而且还易使学生产生无力感;目标过低,缺乏挑战性,即使成功,强化作用也不大。只有在学生能力范围之内,具有适当难度的目标才具有激发动机的作用。

2. 培养学习兴趣,增强求知欲

学习兴趣是学习动机的重要心理成分。具有学习兴趣的学生,会把学习看成是内心的满足,而不是把学习当成一种负担。因此,培养学生积极的学习兴趣和强烈的求知欲望,是学校教育工作的主要任务之一。教师的教学应使学生感到"有趣、有味、有奇、有惑"。所谓有趣,就是指学生对教师所教的内容兴致勃勃地去学;所谓有味,就是指学生觉得所学的知识内容精深,值得品味,甚至回味无穷;所谓有奇,是指教师的教学新颖有创见,每每使学生感到新奇,觉得出乎意外,体验到学习是一种乐趣;所谓有惑,就是教师的讲解既有启迪又留有余地,使学生听讲之后,自己提出问题,从而产生继续探索的求知欲望。教学中的启发性,不只是提一些简单的问题,还要给学生提出一定的课题,使他们不能单纯利用已有的知识和习惯的方法去解决面前的问题,以进一步激发他们的学习需要。

3. 利用原有动机的迁移,使学生产生新的学习需要

有的学生或学生有的时候学习目的不明确,缺乏学习的动力。有经验的教师会将这类学生身上的积极因素迁移到学习活动中,从而使学生产生学习的需要。例如,苏联的莫洛佐娃在针对六年级某班男生们想当海员但又缺乏学习动力的情况,组织有关的主题活动。在海军活动的游戏中,要求孩子们学习各种有关的知识,如历史、地理、航海、摄影、制模以及音乐等,有效地激发了学生的认识兴趣,这是培养学生学习动机的重要经验。因此,教师要用极大的爱心去发现学生身上的闪光点,并采取有效措施将闪光点发扬光大,使之顺利地迁移到学习上。

(二)学习动机的激发

1. 创设问题情境,激发学生的求知欲望

所谓问题情境,就是指具有一定难度,不能直接用已有的知识处理,但可以间接用已有知识处理的情境。通过设置问题情境,引起学生的好奇心和思考的欲望。例如,当学生知道植物生长必须依靠光合作用的道理后,再提出深海里一些见不到阳光、叶绿素含量极少的植物的生长问题,通常能唤起他们对植物生长和种类的兴趣,使之产生学习动机。

2. 及时反馈

让学生及时了解学习的结果,看到自己的进步和所学知识的意义,这种信息反馈能够提高学生的学习兴趣,增强信心,增加努力程度。同时,通过反馈,学生知道自己的缺点和不足,可以及时改进学习方法,加强薄弱环节,并激起加倍努力,迎头赶上的决心。因此,日常教学中教师应注意及时批改和发还学生的作业、测验和试卷等,利用学生刚刚留下的鲜明记忆表象,满足其进一步提高学习的愿望,增强学习信心。评语要写得具体、有针对性、启发性和教育性,使学生受到鼓舞和激励。

> **专栏10-4**
>
> ### 反馈的作用
>
> 心理学家罗西和亨利（C. C. Ross & L. K. Henry）曾做过一个著名的实验：他们把一个班的学生分成三组，每天学习后就接受测验，测验后分别给予不同的反馈方式：第一组每天告知其学习结果；第二组每周告知一次学习结果；第三组只测验不告知其学习结果。如此进行8周，结果是第一组的学习成绩最好，第三组最差。8周以后改换条件，将第一组和第三组的反馈方式对调，第二组的反馈方式不变，实验也进行8周。反馈方式改变后，除第二组成绩稳步上升外，第一与第三两组的情况则有很大的变化，即第一组的成绩逐步下降，而第三组的成绩则有突出的进步。
>
> 这则实验说明，反馈在学习上的效果是很显著的。尤其是每天及时反馈，较之每周的反馈效率更高；不知道自己的学习结果，缺少学习的激励，则很少有进步。
>
> ——章志光.心理学［M］.北京：人民教育出版社，1992：86—87.

3. 科学使用表扬与批评、奖励与惩罚

正确运用表扬与批评、奖励与惩罚是利用反馈的另一方面。表扬与批评、奖励与惩罚运用得当都可以对学生的学习起推动作用。但一般来讲，表扬比批评、鼓励比惩罚可以更好地激起学生的积极学习动机，而适当的批评与惩罚也能提高注意水平。然而无论表扬还是批评、奖励还是惩罚，都必须客观和公正。表扬若被滥用或言过其实，会失去效力或使人骄傲自满、狂妄自大；批评过于严厉，反而会使他们产生恐惧心理与不安全感，从而对学习起阻碍作用。此外，表扬和批评还应注意学生的个性特点。对自信心不足的学生应多表扬鼓励，对过于自信的学生，则应更多地提出要求。

4. 适当开展学习竞赛活动

一般认为，竞赛是激发学生学习积极性和提高学习成绩的一种有效手段。因为竞赛可以向人们证明自己的能力和成就，满足自尊的需要并获得一定的名誉、地位和奖励，所以多数人在竞赛情况下学习和工作的效率会有很大的提高。但是，对于能否运用竞赛方式来激发学生学习动机的问题，国内外学者进行过长期的争论。大量研究表明，在学生学习知识的过程中，适当开展合理的学习竞赛活动是必要，也是有益的。竞赛虽有学习动机的效果，但各种形式的竞赛如果被频繁地使用，则不仅会失去其激励作用，反而会加重学生负担，增加学生的心理紧张度，产生一定的心理压力，具有一定的消极作用。因此，要适当运用这种手段。

第四节
兴趣

一、兴趣的概念

兴趣（interest）是指一个人积极认识探究某种事物、从事某种活动的心理倾向。兴趣是动机的重要表现形式，也是动机中最活跃的成分，反映了人对客观事物的选择性态度。例如，有的人对音乐感兴趣，不仅积极地去学习音乐知识，参加音乐活动，而且在学习和活动中感到了愉悦。

兴趣是在需要的基础上通过实践活动而形成和发展起来的。一个人只有对某种客观事物产生了需要，才有可能对这种事物发生兴趣。而且，他在满足某种需要的基础上又会产生新的需要，就使原来的兴趣也得到丰富和发展。但是需要不一定都表现为兴趣。如人有睡眠需要，不等于对睡眠有兴趣。

兴趣和动机既有联系，又有区别，它们都起源于需要，都是需要的表现形式，都是行为的动力因素。但是，兴趣是动机的进一步发展。对某一事物产生了动机，还不一定能发展为兴趣，若一旦成为兴趣，则必然有与之相伴随的动机。

二、兴趣的分类

从兴趣的内容看，有物质兴趣和精神兴趣之分。物质兴趣包括对衣、食、电视机、汽车等的兴趣，是由物质需要所引起的兴趣；精神兴趣是由精神需要所引起的兴趣，具体表现为人对科学、文艺和社会活动等的兴趣。

从兴趣的起因看，有直接兴趣和间接兴趣之分。直接兴趣是人对活动过程本身感兴趣，如幼儿对游戏的兴趣；间接兴趣是人对活动的结果感兴趣，如有的人之所以进行体育锻炼，是由于认识到这样做有利于增强体质、健康长寿，是为了这个结果才对这种活动感兴趣。直接兴趣和间接兴趣在一定条件下是可以相互转化的。

从兴趣发展的水平和深刻性看，有有趣、乐趣和志趣之分。有趣，是指人容易被一时的新异现象和新颖对象所吸引，从而对它们发生兴趣，这是兴趣的低水平阶段。乐趣是在有趣的基础上发展起来的，向专一的、深入的方向发展，即对某一事物或某一项研究产生了比较持久、稳定的兴趣。乐趣具有专一性、自发性和坚持性的特点。志趣是由乐趣经过实践和锻炼发展而来，是发展到高水平的兴趣。它与人的崇高理想和远大志向相联系，和坚强的意志分不开。人的志趣具有社会性、自觉性和方向性等三个特点。这是一种高尚的兴趣，对人的学习和工作有巨大的推动力。

从兴趣维持时间的久暂看，有短暂的兴趣和稳定的兴趣之分。短暂的兴趣一般指随着某种事物或活动而产生，又随着某种事物或活动的结束而消失；稳定的兴趣是指长期的、稳定的对一个人起积极作用的兴趣,不因某种活动的结束而消失。对学习、事业有了稳定的兴趣,才能专心致志、持之以恒、热情充沛地投入到学习和工作中去。

三、兴趣的品质

兴趣的品质是人在认识事物的过程中形成和表现出来的稳定的心理特征。

一般说来,兴趣的品质可以概括为以下四个方面。

(一)兴趣的倾向性

兴趣的倾向性是指人的兴趣是指向一定的事物的。每个人的兴趣指向具有很大的个别差异。如有的人对科学感兴趣,有的人对音乐感兴趣。兴趣不是天生的,兴趣的差异性主要是由于人的生活实践不同而造成的。

(二)兴趣的广阔性

兴趣的广阔性是针对人的兴趣范围的大小而言。有的学生兴趣范围很广,多才多艺;有的学生只知读书,兴趣范围狭窄。人的兴趣越广泛,知识也就越丰富,工作、学习上的造诣也会越深。一个在任何一个方面、一个领域有所成就的人,必然是在兴趣广泛的基础上有一个中心兴趣。如祖冲之对数学、天文、历法、哲学、文学、音乐都有兴趣,但他的中心兴趣是数学。

(三)兴趣的持久性

兴趣的持久性是指人对事物的兴趣维持时间的久暂。有的人对感兴趣的事物长期保持稳定,数年乃至数十年如一日,经过刻苦努力,最终取得成就。如居里夫人的科学研究就是她终生的兴趣。相反,有的人缺乏稳定的兴趣,见异思迁,朝三暮四,这种人是很难在工作和学习上取得成绩的。

(四)兴趣的效能性

兴趣的效能性是指兴趣对人的活动的推动作用的大小。有的人由于兴趣对某种事物"情有独钟",从而产生接近它、了解它的行为倾向,这种人的兴趣对他的活动的推动作用大;但有的人对事物的兴趣只停留在观望状态,并不曾实际参与,他们是"临渊羡鱼""心向往之",这种人的兴趣对他们的活动的推动力量小,是低效能的兴趣。高效能的兴趣才能促使人参与某项实际活动,从而获得知识,增长才干。

四、学习兴趣的培养

学习兴趣是学习动机中最活跃的心理成分。具有学习兴趣的学生,会把学习看成是内心的满足,而不是把学习当成负担,从而取得好的学习效果。学习兴趣不是与生俱来的,它是通过多种教育机制加以培养形成的。

(一)通过教学培养和发展学生的兴趣

首先,教学内容的"适度难易"和教学方法的"适度新颖"是激发学生学习兴趣的重要手段。心理学研究和教学实践证明,凡是过浅过易或过深过难的教学内容,都会降低学生的学习兴趣;凡是方法单调死板的教学,都会使学生感到枯燥乏味;而方法变化过多的教学,又会使学生穷于应付,因而降低兴趣。所以,在教学中为了引起学生的兴趣,调动学生学习的积极性,教学内容应当深浅得当、难易适度,必须是学生经过一定努力所能掌握的。在教学方法上必须适当变化并富于启发性。其次,需要是兴趣产生的基础,因此在教学中应当经常对学生进行学习目的教育,引导他们将社会的要求内化为自己的学习需要,从而激发其高尚的学习兴趣。最后,培养兴趣的最终目标,就是要使学生的兴趣由有趣、乐趣向志趣发展。因此,教学中培养学生的兴趣必须与帮助学生树立远大理想和正确的人生观、世界观结合起来。只有这样,才能使学生形成强烈稳固的学习兴趣并最终成为推动学生不断进步的强大动力。

(二)通过活动培养和发展学生的兴趣

人的兴趣是在实践活动中形成与发展起来的,并在活动中得到体现。没有活动,就不能产生人对客观事物的认知需要,也就不能产生与之相应的兴趣。正是实践活动,使人们更多地接触客观事物,加深对它们的认识,从而形成对该事物的特殊的认识倾向。因此,发展与培养学生的兴趣,就必须引导他们参加到各种有益的活动中去,不能因担心影响学习而限制学生的活动范围。

(三)增强学生积极的情绪体验——成功感

实践中的成功,对于巩固、发展人们的认知兴趣,提高对客观事物认识的积极性具有特殊的作用。苏联教育心理实践家苏霍姆林斯基指出:"只有在因学习获得成功而产生鼓舞力的地方,才会出现学习兴趣。"可见培养与巩固学生的学习兴趣,关键在于帮助与引导学生不断在学习上取得成绩,获得成功,感受到学习的欢乐,从而越学越感到不足,越学越爱学。当然,经常性的成功并不意味着没有困难,恰恰相反,学生在克服了困难而获得成功的情况下,会产生更大的满足感,从而更加巩固和发展已有的兴趣。

图 10-7 苏霍姆林斯基

苏霍姆林斯基(Suchomlinsky Vasyl Olexandrovych, 1918—1970),苏联著名教育实践家和教育理论家,提出把青少年培养成为"全面和谐发展的人,社会进步的积极参与者"。全面发展即:智育、体育、德育、劳动教育和审美教育。主要著作有《给教师的一百条建议》《把整个心灵献给孩子》《教育的艺术》《教育的艺术》等。

此外,教师对学生的热情关心,教师的治学严谨认真,教师的诲人不倦和循循善诱等,也都会对学生的学习情绪和兴趣产生重要作用。

本章小结

本章介绍了个性的概念、特点及结构；需要，动机，兴趣的概念、分类和相关理论，同时对如何培养和激发动机与兴趣提出了相应的策略。需要、动机、兴趣等是个性结构中的活跃因素，是心理活动的基本动力，决定着人对现实的态度，决定着人对认识活动的对象的趋向和选择。因此，掌握并恰当运用这些理论指导实践，正确培养和激发学生的学习动机与兴趣，是师范生从事教育教学工作的基础知识储备。

关键术语

需要　动机　兴趣　学习动机　兴趣品质

讨论与应用

1. 试思考，这句话反映出了什么观点？

古人讲"仓廪实而知礼节，衣食足则知荣辱"。

2. 思考下面的问题，分析动机强度与学习成绩存在什么关系？

在重大的考试面前，我们越想考好，考试的结果是否就越好？

3. 阅读下面的材料，请结合本章所学谈谈自己的看法。

达尔文对爬藤植物如何攀援爬高有兴趣，他曾专门找了一种叫蛇麻草的藤本植物放在家里，整日整夜不睡觉，看着它爬藤，终于弄清了其中的秘密。

本章讨论与应用答题思路与要点
（扫描二维码）

本章复习思考题
（扫描二维码）

本章进一步阅读书目
（扫描二维码）

本章测量量表
（扫描二维码）

第十一章
能 力
NENGLI

纵横捭阖的历史长河穿越千古,娓娓道来,我们看到了神机妙算的诸葛亮,看到了弯弓射大雕的成吉思汗,看到了诗成泣鬼神的李白……当然,有人一生成就非凡,也有人碌碌无为。那么,他们的能力是从哪里来的?能力又是什么?能力可以提高吗?让我们带着这些问题,开始本章的学习吧。

通过本章的学习,你能够:
- 掌握能力的含义及能力与知识和技能的关系
- 了解能力的种类和能力的结构
- 理解能力理论以及对能力理论的评价
- 了解智力测验
- 掌握能力发展的影响因素及能力的培养

【本章结构】

能力概述	能力理论	能力测量
◎ 能力的概念 ◎ 能力与知识、技能的关系 ◎ 能力的分类	◎ 能力的因素说 ◎ 能力的结构理论 ◎ 能力的信息加工理论	◎ 一般能力测量 ◎ 特殊能力测量 ◎ 能力测量的功用 ◎ 能力测验应具备的条件

能力的个别差异	能力的影响因素及培养
◎ 能力类型的差异 ◎ 能力发展水平的差异 ◎ 能力表现早晚的差异	◎ 影响能力发展的因素 ◎ 学生能力的培养

本章主要回答"什么是能力""能力的种类和结构"以及"如何进行能力的测量和培养"的问题。通过本章的学习,你可以对能力有更深入和明确的认识,能够采用适宜的方式和途径进行能力的培养并取得有效的成果。

第一节 能力概述

一、能力的概念

能力（ability）是人们顺利地完成某种活动所必备的个性心理特征。对此定义可作如下理解：

能力总是与活动密切相联。一方面，个人的能力总是在活动中形成和发展起来，也在活动中得到表现。如学生的口头表达能力和组织能力总是在言语交流与群体活动中锻炼出来和表现出来。另一方面，从事任何活动，都必须以一定的能力为条件。例如，教师要想很好地完成教学任务，除了要有明确的立场、观点和专业知识之外，还需要有驾驭教材的能力与较好的口头语言表达能力等。

但是，人在活动中表现出来的心理特征并不都是能力。如人在活动中的镇定自若与焦躁不安、谦虚谨慎与骄横傲慢等，虽然都是心理特征，也对人的活动有一定的影响，但它们不是成功地完成某种活动所必备的因素，也不会直接影响活动的效率，因而不能称之为能力。只有那些从事某种活动所必须的，缺了它们就不能顺利地、成功地完成活动的心理特征，才属于能力的范畴。

在实际生活中，人所从事的活动都比较复杂，仅凭一种能力是难以胜任的，有赖于多种能力的有机结合。这种在完成某种活动中，各种能力的独特结合称为才能。例如，完成教学活动需要有敏锐的观察力，流畅的言语表达能力，比较严谨的逻辑思维能力，以及有效的组织管理能力和合理的注意分配能力等，这些能力在教学中独特的结合就形成了教学的才能。高度发展的多种能力，在活动中最完备的结合，就称为天才。它使人能顺利地、独立地、创新性地完成某些复杂的活动，但它不是天生的，它离不开个人的勤奋，也离不开特定的社会历史环境。

二、能力与知识、技能的关系

我们都知道，人的能力有大有小，知识有多有少，技能有高有低。那么知识、技能与能力的关系究竟是什么，知识是否等于能力？了解这个问题对于做好教育工作和其他工作具有特别重要的意义。

知识（knowledge）是人脑对客观事物的主观表征。知识有不同的形式，一种是陈述性知识，即"是什么"的知识，如北京是中国的首都，艾菲尔铁塔在法国巴黎等；另一种是程序性知识，即"如何做"的知识，如骑马的知识、开车的知识、组装计算机的知识等。人一旦有了知识，就会运用这些知识指导自己的活动。从这个意义上来说，知识是活动的自我调节机制中不可缺少的构成要素，也是能力的基本结构中一个不可缺少的组成成分。

技能(skill)是指人们通过练习而获得的动作方式和动作系统。技能也是一种个体经验,但主要表现为动作执行的经验,因而与知识有区别。技能作为活动的方式,有时表现为一种操作活动方式,有时表现为一种心智活动方式。因此,按活动方式的不同,技能可分为操作技能和心智技能(智力活动)。操作技能的动作是由外显的机体运动来实现的,其动作的对象为物质性的客体,即物体。心智技能通常是借助于内在的智力操作来实现的,其动作对象为事物的信息,即观念。操作技能的形成,依赖于机体运动的反馈信息;而心智技能则是通过操作活动模式的内化形成的。由于技能直接控制活动的动作程序的执行,因此是活动的自我调节机制中的又一个组成要素,也是能力结构的基本组成成分。

知识、技能和能力是不同的三个概念,不能用知识的多少,技能的多寡,来代替能力的高低。只有那些能够广泛应用和迁移的知识和技能,才能转化为才能。能力不仅包含了一个人现在已经达到的知识的储备、技能的水平,而且还包含了一个人具有的潜力。例如,一个读书很多的人可能有较丰富的知识,但在解决实际问题时却显得能力低下,说明他的知识只停留在书本上,既不能广泛迁移,也不能用来解决实际问题。可见,三者是有区别的。

知识、技能与能力又有密切的关系。第一,能力的形成与发展依赖于知识、技能的获得。随着人的知识、技能的积累,人的能力也会不断提高。第二,能力的高低又会影响到掌握知识、技能的水平。一个能力强的人往往付出较小的代价就能获得知识和技能;而一个能力较弱的人可能要付出较大的努力才能掌握同样的知识和技能。所以,从一个人掌握知识、技能的速度与质量上,可以看出其能力的大小。

正确理解能力与知识、技能的关系,对教育工作具有重要意义。首先,我们不应该仅仅根据一个人知识的多寡去简单地断定这个人能力的高低。一个人的能力可能已经表现出来,也可能没有表现出来。仅仅根据知识的多少来断定能力的强弱,常常会做出错误的判断。其次,在教育工作中,我们不仅要关心学生知识与技能的掌握,而且要关心他们的能力发展,并促使其将知识与技能转化为能力。如果认为知识、技能等于能力,就可能导致只关心知识掌握而忽视能力发展的错误倾向。最后,由于能力不等于知识,人们才有必要研究评定能力的特殊方法,而不能用对知识的评定来代替对能力的鉴定。

综上所述,能力是掌握知识、技能的前提,又是掌握知识、技能的结果。两者是互相转化、互相促进的。正确理解能力与知识、技能的关系,有助于科学地传授知识、培养技能、发展能力,这对社会进步和个人发展具有重要意义。

三、能力的分类

心理学家从不同的角度对能力进行分类:

(一)一般能力和特殊能力

能力按照它的倾向性可划分为一般能力和特殊能力。

一般能力(general ability)指大多数活动所共同需要的能力。它又称普通能力,是人所共有的最基本的能力,适用于广泛的活动范围。它和认识活动紧密地联系着,观察力、记忆力、思维力、想象力、注意力都是一般能力。一般能力也就是通常所说的智力(intelligence)。

特殊能力（special ability）指为某项专门活动所必需的能力，它又称专门能力。它只在特殊活动领域内发生作用，是完成有关活动必不可少的能力。一般认为，数学能力、音乐能力、绘画能力、体育能力、写作能力等都是特殊能力。一个人可以具有多种特殊能力，但其中有1—2种占优势。同一种特殊能力，包含有多种成分，其中各种成分对活动的作用是不同的。例如，音乐能力包括音乐感知能力、音乐记忆和想象能力、音乐情感能力和音乐动作能力。这些能力使人们成功地完成音乐活动，但有些人可能在音乐情感能力方面占优势，有些人可能在音乐感知能力方面占优势等。这些要素的不同组合，就构成了各种独特的音乐才能。

在活动中，一般能力和特殊能力共同起作用，要成功地完成一项活动，既需要一般能力参加，也必须依靠特殊能力。而且，一般能力和特殊能力有机的联系着，一般能力是各种特殊能力形成和发展的基础，一般能力越是发展，就为特殊能力的发展创造了有利的条件；在各种活动中，特殊能力的发展同时也会促进一般能力的提高。

（二）认知能力、操作能力和社交能力

根据能力的特殊功能可将能力划分为认知能力（cognitive ability）、操作能力（operation ability）和社交能力（social ability）。认知能力是接收、加工、储存与应用信息的能力，它反映在人的认识活动中，是获取各种知识的心理潜能。操作能力指操纵、制作能力，该类能力以具体的操作实践为基础，又成为顺利掌握操作技能的重要条件。社交能力反映在人际交往中，它是加强人际沟通、正确处理人际关系的能力。言语表达能力、组织管理能力、判断决策能力等都是社交能力的重要组成部分。

（三）模仿能力和创造能力

能力按创造性大小可分为模仿能力（imitative ability）和创造能力（creative ability）。模仿能力是指仿效他人的言行举止而引起与之相类似的行为活动的能力。班杜拉认为，模仿是人们彼此之间相互影响的重要方式，是实现个体行为社会化的基本历程之一。他指出，通过模仿，能使原有的行为得到巩固或改变，习得新的行为。在行为举止方面，子女模仿父母，学生模仿教师，影迷模仿演员等，这都是模仿能力的体现。创造能力，是指在创造活动中能产生出具有社会价值的、独特的、新颖的思想和事物的能力。如作家、科学家、教育家的活动经常表现出创造能力。心理学家认为，创造能力的基本特征是独特性和有价值性。人们正是由于有了创造能力，才能在模仿的基础上有所突破、有所发展，社会才可能得以进步。模仿能力和创造能力是相互联系的。模仿能力一般都含有创造性因素，而创造能力的发展又需要以模仿能力为基础。

（四）流体能力与晶体能力

美国心理学家雷蒙德·卡特尔（Raymond Cattell）在1971年根据能力在人一生中的发展趋势以及能力对先天禀赋与社会文化因素的依赖关系，提出了流体能力和晶体能力理论，将能力划分为流体能力（或流体智力）（fluid intelligence）和晶体能力（或晶体智力）（crystallized intelligence）。流体能力是在信息加工和问题解决过程中所表现出来的能力。比如，对事物关系的认识能力和逻辑推理能力，对形成事物抽象概念的能力等。这种能力较少地依赖于文化和知识的内容，更多地取决于个人的禀赋。流体能力的发展与

年龄有密切关系,人一般在20岁以后,流体能力的发展达到顶峰。30岁以后,流体能力将随着年龄的增长而降低。流体能力属于人类的基本能力,其个别差异受教育文化的影响较少。晶体能力是指获得语言、数学知识的能力,它决定于后天的学习,与社会文化有密切关系。晶体能力在人的一生中是持续发展的,只是到25岁后,发展的速度渐趋平缓。晶体能力依赖于流体能力,如果两个人具有相同的经历,其中一个有较强的流体能力,那么他将发展出较强的晶体能力。然而一个有较高流体能力的人,如果生活在贫乏的智力环境中,那么他的晶体能力的发展将是低下的或平平的。

(五)认知能力与元认知能力

元认知能力(meta-cognition ability)是相对于认知能力而言的。一个人头脑里储存着某种知识是一回事,这些知识能否被他在需要的时候加以利用却是另一回事;具有技能和应用该技能是两回事;改进某种作业和对该作业改进的了解也是两回事。对于这类差异,心理学家用元认知能力这一术语加以说明。所谓元认知能力是指个人对自己的记忆、理解和其他认知活动的评价和监控能力。人们的元认知能力是有很大差别的。专家和新手的明显区别不仅在于前者对本领域知识知道得较多,而且还在于善于应用和组织所知道的知识,也就是说,二者在元认知能力上有着明显的区别。

元认知活动是很复杂的。弗拉维尔认为,元认知是通过元认知知识、元认知体验、目标(或任务)和行动(或策略)这四类现象相互作用而发生的。元认知知识即有关认知的知识,其中最重要的是关于人的思维过程的能量和限度的知识,即关于人(特别是自己)作为认知者的主体特征的知识。元认知体验是指与认知活动相伴随的感情体验。目标(或任务)指认知活动的目标。行动(或策略)指用来达到这些目标的认知或其他行为。元认知能力的差异就表现在上述四种因素相互作用的不同方式上。据林传鼎的分析,元认知能力包括个人怎样评价自己的认知活动,怎样从各种已知的可能性中选择出解决问题的确切方法(策略),怎样集中精力注意待解决的问题,怎样决定何时对一种难以对付的问题停止工作,怎样判断到底个人是否理解他所听到或看到的事,怎样将从一种情境中所学到的原则或方法转用到另一种情境中去,怎样判断目标是否和自己的能力相一致等。

第二节

能力理论

现代心理学研究已摆脱了思辨性猜测,对能力开始进行具体的"结构分析",这有助于对能力做形象描述,也有助于对能力做客观测量。当前,有代表性的能力理论有以下几种。

一、能力的因素说

（一）独立因素说

能力的"独立因素说"是由现代教育心理学的创始人桑代克（E. L. Thorndike）提出的。该学说认为，人的能力由许多独立的成分（或因素）组合而成。如抽象能力、对社会关系的适应能力、对机械问题的适应能力等都是构成能力的主要成分（因素）。各成分或因素之间无任何内在联系，完全是独立自主的。换言之，能力仅是诸多成分（或因素）机械组合而成的心理特征，能力发展只是单个成分独立的发展。后来，这一学说被大量的认知作业所证伪。完成不同认知作业所取得成绩的相关性表明，能力各组成部分（因素）不是完全独立的，而是相互联系的。

图 11-1 桑代克

桑代克（Edward Lee Thorndike，1874—1949），美国心理学家，动物心理学的开创者，心理学联结主义的建立者和教育心理学体系的创始人。他提出了一系列学习的定律，包括练习律和效果律等。1912年当选为美国心理学会主席，1917年当选为美国国家科学院院士。

（二）二因素说

二因素说是由英国心理学家、统计学家斯皮尔曼（C. E. Spearman）于20世纪初提出。该学说认为，人的能力由两个因素即一般因素和特殊因素构成（如图11-3所示）。一般因素（general factor，简称G因素）在相当程度上是遗传的，它是人完成各项活动所需的主要因素，是人基本的心理潜能，决定一个人的能力高低。特殊因素（special factor，简称S因素）是完成特定活动所必需的智力因素。按斯皮尔曼的理解，主要的特殊因素包括口语表达能力、数学计算能力、机械能力等。作为特定个体的能力都由一般因素和特殊因素组合而成，不同个体所具有的一般因素和特殊因素不尽相同，即使是同一种特殊因素，其程度也各有差异。人在认识与改造客观事物的实践活动中，凭借自己特有的G因素和S因素，表现出相应的智能水平，以适应各种实践活动的需要。

图 11-2 斯皮尔曼

斯皮尔曼（Charles Edward Spearman，1863—1945），英国心理学家。1906年在德国莱比锡获博士学位。回国后，1911年任伦敦大学心理学、逻辑学教授。1924年当选为英国皇家学会院士。斯皮尔曼根据智力测验相关的研究提出著名的二因素论，认为智力可被分析为G因素（一般因素）和S因素（特殊因素）。他反对联想理论，著有《智力的性质和认知的原理》《人的能力》《创造的心》等。

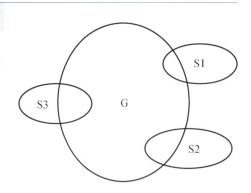

图 11-3 能力二因素理论模型图

斯皮尔曼将能力加以分解，并从中分辨出决定能力的主次因素，这无疑把人类对能力的认识推进了一大步。但"二因素说"仍将能力看做由孤立部分拼合而成的，是机械的镶嵌组合而无融合性的内在联系，这种观点显然有明显缺陷。事实表明，尽管具体活动的性质与要求不同，所需的能力的成分会有所区别，但能力本质上是一种整体机能，是其各组成成分有机结合的表现，从整体上决定人在活动中可能达到的成就水平。所以，作为能力结构成分的一般因素与特殊因素，二者之间是相互联系、相互渗透、彼此促进、共同发展的。

（三）群因素说

美国心理学家瑟斯顿（L. L. Thurstone）于20世纪30年代提出"群因素说"。他认为，能力是由一群彼此无关的特殊因素构成的。他从56种不同测验中，概括出7种重要因素：① 计算（简称N）；② 语词流畅（简称W）；③ 归纳推理（简称R）；④ 记忆（简称M）；⑤ 空间关系（简称S）；⑥ 知觉速度（简称P）；⑦ 语词理解（简称V）。他为每种因素都设计了测验，叫"瑟斯顿首要心理能力的测验"。但测验结果与他开始的设想相反，各能力因素之间有一定的相关量。例如，推理（R）与语词流畅（W）的相关为0.48；数字运算（N）与语词理解（V）的相关为0.38；语词流畅（W）与语词理解（V）的相关为0.51。这似乎说明在群因素之外还存在着一般因素。瑟斯顿修改了关于各因素之间独立性的看法，提出二阶因素（second order factor）的概念，即在彼此相关的第一阶因素的基础上，再度进行因素分析，提取高阶的共同因素，这样群因素理论就与二因素论趋于融合了。

（四）智力多元论

美国哈佛大学心理学家加德纳（H. Gardner）通过对脑损伤病人的研究和对智力特殊群体的分析，于1983年提出多元智力理论（multiple-intelligence theory）。他认为，智力应该是指在某种社会或文化环境的价值标准下，个体用以解决自己遇到的真正的难题或生产及创造出有效产品所需要的能力。智力的内涵是多元的，它由八种相对独立的智力成分所构成。每种智力都是一个单独的功能系统，这些系统可以相互作用，产生外显的智力行为。这八种智力成分是：① 言语智力，包括阅读、写文章或小说以及日常会话的能力；② 逻辑—数学智力，包括数学运算与逻辑思考的能力；③ 空间智力，包括

图 11-4 霍华德·加德纳

霍华德·加德纳（Howard Gardner, 1943—   ），世界著名发展和认知心理学家，多元智能理论创始人。现任美国哈佛大学教育研究生院认知和教育学教授、心理学教授，波士顿大学医学院精神病学教授和哈佛大学《零点项目》研究所两位所长之一。

认识环境、辨别方向的能力;④ 音乐智力,包括对声音的辨别与韵律表达的能力;⑤ 身体运动智力,包括支配肢体完成精密作业的能力;⑥ 社交智力,包括与人交往且能和睦相处的能力;⑦ 自知智力,包括认识自己并选择自己生活方向的能力;⑧ 自然智力。第八种是1995年加德纳在原有七种智力成分基础上新增加的。所谓自然智力是指能辨别动植物,对自然万物进行分门别类的智力,即认识、感知自然界事物的各种能力。

我国有的学者认为,加德纳的多元智力理论给我国的课程改革提供了一个重要启示,我们一定要把培养学生创造能力和实践能力放在重要的位置,重视智力的多种领域,让学生的智力得到全面发展。每一个学生都有其优势智力。我们的教育就是要培养学生的优势智力,成为发现差异、承认差异的教育,注重特长教育、平等教育和创造教育。

二、能力的结构理论

(一)层次结构说

英国心理学家弗侬(P. E. Vernon)1960年提出能力层次结构论,将能力概括为一种由上到下四个层面组合而成的结构(如图11-5所示)。最高层次为"普遍因素"(一般因素);第二层次为两个大因素群,包括语言和教育、机械和操作因素;第三层次为小因素群,包括言语、数量及机械信息、操作信息、空间信息等方面的能力;第四层次为各种特殊因素。四个层次自上而下形成完整的能力结构。能力"层次结构说"是弗侬以人工智能机为原型的一种建构,即以当代计算机的信息存储方式为模板的一种构思。他把大因素群分为言语和教育、机械和操作因素,在一定程度上得到了近年来脑科学研究成果的支持,即左右脑两半球功能的分工合作。

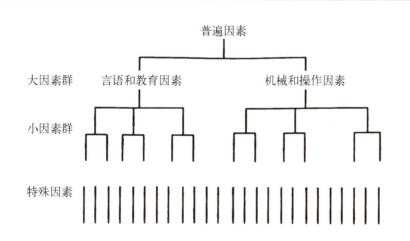

图11-5
弗侬能力层次结构图

(二)三维结构模型说

1967年,吉尔福特(J. P. Guilford)冲破智力结构探索中的常规思路,考察点从平面板块组合转向三维立体,从静态转向动态,从而形成了智力结构的"三维模型"。他认为,智力应当包括内容、操作和产物三个维度(如图11-6所示)。

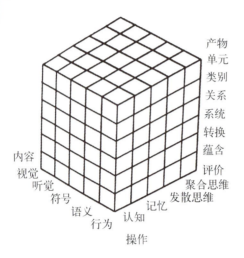

图 11-6
吉尔福特智力结构的三维模型

智力活动的内容(contents)维度,包括听觉、视觉(我们所听到、看到的具体材料,例如声调大小、形状、位置、颜色)、符号(字母数字及其他符号)、语义(语言的意义及概念)、行为(本人及别人的行为),它们是智力活动的对象或材料。

智力操作(operations)维度,指由上述种种对象或材料引起的智力活动的过程。其中包括认知(理解、再认)、记忆(保持)、发散思维(对一个问题寻找多种答案或思想)、聚合思维(对一个问题寻找最好、最适当、最普通的答案)、评价(对一个人的思维品质作出某种决定)。

智力活动的产物(products)维度,是指运用上述智力操作所得到的结果。这些结果可以按单元计算,可以按类别处理,也可以表现为关系、系统、转换和应用。由于三个维度和多种形式的存在,人的智力可以在理论上区分为 $5 \times 5 \times 6 = 150$(种)。这些不同的智力可以分别通过不同的测验来检验。例如,呈现一系列的四字母组合,如 PANL、CEIV、EMOC,要求被试把它们重新组合为熟悉的单词,如 PLAN、VICE、COME 等。在这项测验中,智力活动的内容为符号,操作为认知,产物为单元,其成绩可以按重新组合的字词数量来计算。根据产物的数量即可度量一个人对符号的认知能力。

吉尔福特的三维智力结构模型同时考虑到智力活动的内容、过程和结果,这对推动智力测验工作起到了重要的作用。1971年,吉尔福特宣布,经过测验,已经证明了三维智力模型中的近百种能力。这一成就对智力测验的理论与实践无疑是一个巨大的鼓舞。

三、能力的信息加工理论

(一)智力的三元理论

美国耶鲁大学的心理学家斯腾伯格(R. J. Sternberg)于1985提出了智力的三元理论(triarchic theory of intelligence),试图说明更为广泛的智力行为。斯腾伯格认为,大多数的智力理论是不完备的,它们只从某个特定的角度解释智力。一个完备的智力理论必须说明智力的三个方面,即智力的内在成分,这些智力成分与经验的关系,以及智力成分的外部作用。这三个方面构成了智力成分亚理论、智力经验亚理论和智力情境亚理论。

智力成分亚理论(component subtheory of intelligence)认为,智力包括三种成分

图 11-7 罗伯特·斯腾伯格

罗伯特·斯腾伯格（Robert J. Sternberg, 1949— ），美国心理学家，迄今为止，他的最大贡献是提出了人类智力的三元理论，为我们对智力的认识提供了一种新的角度和框架。此外，他还致力于人类的创作型、思维方式和学习方式等领域的研究，提出了大量富有创造性的理论与概念。他是耶鲁大学心理学和教育学IBM教授。他的研究领域包括爱情和人际关系，人类智慧和创造性等。斯腾伯格最近的著述有《思维方式》和《爱情心理学》，并与他人合作编著了《亲密关系中的满足感》和《性别心理学》（与安·比尔合编）。

及相应的三种过程，即元成分、操作成分和知识获得成分。元成分是用于计划、控制和决策的高级执行过程，如确定问题的性质，选择解题步骤，调整解题思路，分配心理资源等；操作成分表现在任务的执行过程，指接收刺激，将信息保持在短时记忆中并进行比较，负责执行元成分的决策；知识获得成分是指获取和保存新信息的过程，负责接收新刺激，做出判断与反应以及对新信息进行编码与存贮。在智力成分中，元成分起着核心作用，它决定人们解决问题时所使用的策略。

智力经验亚理论（experienced subtheory of intelligence）提出，智力包括两种能力，一种是处理新任务和新环境时所要求的能力；另一种是信息加工过程自动化的能力。新任务是个体以前从未遇到过的问题，新情境是一种新异的、富于挑战性的环境。当遇到新问题时，有的人就能够运用已有的知识和经验来解决它，有的人则束手无策；在面临新的情境时，有的人能应对自如，有的人则手足无措。在任务、情境和个体三者间存在相互作用。信息加工过程自动化的能力也是智力的重要成分。人们在完成复杂任务时，需要运用多种操作化的过程。只有许多操作自动化后，复杂任务才容易完成。如果个体不能有效地将一些自动化的操作运用于复杂问题的解决中，就会导致信息加工的中断，甚至使问题解决失败。斯腾伯格认为，应对新异性的能力和自动化的能力是完成复杂任务时两个紧密相连的方面。当个体初次遇到某个任务或某一情境时，应对新异性的能力开始发挥作用，在多次实践后，人们积累了对任务或情境的经验，自动化的能力才开始起作用。

智力情境亚理论（contextual subtheory of intelligence）认为，智力是指获得与情境拟合的心理活动。在日常生活中，智力表现为有目的地适应环境、塑造环境和选择新环境的能力，此能力统称作情境智力（contextual intelligence）。一般来说，个体总是努力适应他所处的环境，力图在个体及其所处环境之间达到一种和谐。当和谐的程度低于个体的满意度时，就是不适应。当个体在某种情境中感到不能适应或不愿意适应时，他会选择能够达到的另一种和谐环境。在另一些情况下，人们会重新塑造环境以提高个体与环境之间的和谐程度，而不只是适应或选择现存的环境。

在三元智力理论中，成分亚理论是最早形成和最为完善的部分，它揭示了智力活动的内在机制。根据这种理论编制的能力测验，能测量出人们是怎样解决问题的，因而对深入了解能力的实质，促进能力的训练与培养，都有重要意义。

专栏11-1

成 功 智 力

在学校中,艾丽丝学习成绩优异,老师认为她是最好的学生,同学们也认为她是最聪明的人。艾丽丝虽然在学业中出类拔萃,可在之后的职业生涯中却一直表现平平,同班同学里70%—80%在工作中都表现得比她出色。这样的例子在许多国家、许多学校都不难发现。中国也开始关注"第10名现象",即学习最好的学生不一定是工作最出色的人,而学习排名在第10名左右的学生,可能会在以后的职业中游刃有余。

这一现象说明了学业成就的高低并不能百分百地决定一个人是否成功,这涉及成功智力的问题。成功智力(successful intelligence)是一种用以达到人生中主要目标的智力,对现实生活的影响举足轻重。因此,成功智力与传统IQ测验中所测量和体现的学业智力有本质的区别。学业智力是一种"惰性化智力"(inert intelligence),它只能对学生在学业上的成绩和分数做出部分预测,而与现实生活中的成败较少发生联系。在现实生活中真正起作用的不是稳固不变的智力,而是可以不断修正和发展的成功智力。

成功智力包括分析性智力、创造性智力和实践性智力三个方面。分析性智力涉及解决问题和制定思维成果的质量,强调比较、判断、评估等分析思维能力;创造性智力涉及发现、创造、想象和假设等创造思维的能力;实践性智力涉及解决实际生活中问题的能力,包括使用、运用及应用知识的能力。

成功智力是一个有机整体,用分析性智力发现好的解决办法,用创造性智力找对问题,用实践性智力来解决实际问题,只有这三个方面协调、平衡时才最为有效。一个人知道什么时候以何种方式来运用成功智力的三个方面,要比仅仅是具有这三个方面的素质更为重要。具有成功智力的人不仅具有这些能力,而且还会思考在什么时候、以何种方式来有效地使用这些能力。在各个领域中,这三种智力都发挥着作用。在自然科学领域中,分析性智力可以将假设的理论与其他理论进行比较,创造性智力可以形成一种理论观点或设计出一个实验,实践性智力可以将科学原理应用于日常生活或实践领域中;在文学领域中,分析性智力用于分析剧情、主题或人物,创造性智力用来写作诗歌或小说,实践性智力将从文学中汲取的知识与教训应用于每天的生活中;在艺术领域中,分析性智力用来分析一位艺术家的风格和想传递的信息,创造性智力可以创作艺术作品,实践性智力则可以确定什么样的作品受欢迎;在体育领域中,分析性智力可以分析出对手的策略战术,创造性智力可以用来形成自己的战术,实践性智力可以运用心理战术来赢得比赛。

——R. J. 斯腾伯格. 成功智力[M]. 吴国宏,钱文,译. 上海:华东师范大学出版社,1999:111—145.

（二）智力的PASS模型

PASS模型是由纳格利尔里（J. A. Naglieri）和戴斯（J. P. Das）提出的关于智力的信息加工理论，PASS是指"计划—注意—同时性加工—继时性加工"（planning-arousal-simultaneous-successive，简称PASS）。它包含了三层认知系统和四种认知过程，其中注意系统又称注意—唤醒系统，它是整个系统的基础；同时性加工和继时性加工统称为信息加工系统，处于中间层次；计划系统处于最高层次。三个系统之间有动态的联系，它们协调合作，保证了一切智力活动的运行。也就是说，注意、信息加工和计划之间是相互作用和相互影响的。计划过程需要一个充分的唤醒状态，以使注意能够集中，进而促使计划的产生。个体如何加工信息也是计划的功能，同时性或继时性加工要受到计划功能的影响。

第三节 能力测量

> 在心理测量领域，19世纪80年代是高尔顿的十年，90年代是卡特尔的十年，20世纪头十年则是比奈的十年。
>
> ——波林

一、一般能力测量

（一）智力测验的由来

和许多科学理论与科学发明均起源于古代中国一样，中国也是心理测量的故乡。

中国古代的能力测量可上溯到2500年前的思想家和教育家孔子，他在教育实践中凭借自己的经验观察首先评定学生能力的个体差异，并将人的智力分成三个等级，即中上之人、中人和中下之人。这实际上相当于现代测量学中的称名量表和顺序量表。汉代学者董仲舒曾最早论及注意测验，他说："一手画方，一手画圆，莫能成。"（《春秋繁露·天无二道》）。三国时期刘劭的《人物志》可以说是一部研究能力的专门著作，20世纪30年代，美国学者将其译为《人类能力的研究》并在美国出版。而出现于清代的益智图（俗称"七巧板"）和九连环则可以认为是最早出现的创造力测验。

19世纪末，英国生物学家高尔顿设计了高尔顿音笛和高尔顿棒，分别测量人的听觉和视觉辨别力，试图通过感觉辨别力来评估人们智力的高低。到19世纪末心理学兴起之后，心理学家们放弃了高尔顿的生理功能取向，转而从心理取向来鉴别人类的智力。

（二）比奈—西蒙智力量表

系统采用测验方法来测量人的智力，是在20世纪初由法国心理学家比奈（A. Binet，1857—1911）和医生西蒙（T. Simon, 1873—1961）提出来的。比奈早年就从事测验的研究，曾花三年时间测验了自己的两个女儿，并于1903年出版了《智力的实验研究》一书。1904年，比奈受法国教育部的委托，参与筹建智障儿童研究委员会，并承担任务，开发一套鉴定智力落后儿童的程序，以便将其从普通儿童中区分出来。1905年，比奈在西蒙的帮助下，编制了一个包括30个项目的正式测验，每个项目的难度逐渐上升。根据儿童通过项目的多少来评定他们智力的高低。这就是第一个正式的心理测验：比奈—西蒙智力量表（Binet-Simon Scale）。

（三）斯坦福—比奈智力量表

比奈—西蒙智力量表问世后，尤其是在美国的改进使其更为适用。当中以推孟（Terman）在斯坦福大学先后四次修订而成的斯坦福—比奈智力量表（Stanford-Binet Intelligence Scale）最为有名。该量表包括一系列的分测验，每一个分测验适合一个特定的心理年龄。比奈—西蒙智力量表修订为斯坦福—比奈智力量表后，最大的改变是将原来表示智力高低的心理年龄改用智力商数来表示。智商（intelligence quotient，简称IQ）是一个人的心理年龄（MA）与其实足年龄（CA）的比值，因而也称为比率智商（ratio IQ）。智商的计算公式如下：

$$智商 = 心理年龄（MA）/实足年龄（CA）\times 100$$

举例来说，某儿童实足年龄为8岁2个月，如以月数表示，他的实足年龄即为98个月，即CA=98。设该童接受斯坦福——比奈智力量表后的成绩是：通过8岁组的全部题目，其基本心理年龄是96个月；通过9岁组的4个题目，再加8个月；通过10岁组的2个题目，再加4个月；11岁组（及以后）的题目全未通过。总计该儿童的成绩，其心理年龄计为108个月，即MA=108。按智商公式计算，得出其智商为110。

智商是心理年龄除以实足年龄的得数，所以智商为100者，其智力相当于他的同年龄人的一般水平，属于中等智力。智商高于100表明智力较佳，低于100则表明智力较差。在一般人口中，智商呈正态分布（normal distribution），即中等水平的居多数，两极端的为少数。

比率智商有一个明显的缺点。人的实际年龄逐年在增加，但其智力发展到一定阶段却基本稳定在一个水平上。这样，采用比率智商来表示人的智力水平，智商将逐渐下降。这和智力发展的实际情况是不相符的。

（四）韦克斯勒智力量表

斯坦福—比奈量表是对个体智力状况的综合测量，只能给人一个相当笼统的概念。但是智力并不是一种单一的能力，它包含着各种结构成分。在同一个人身上，智力的各个成分可能有不同的发展水平。为了更真实地反应出一个人的智力状况，韦克斯勒（D.

Wechsler）编制了若干套智力量表。1949年编制的韦氏儿童智力量表（Wechsler Intelligence Scale for Children，简称WISC），适用于6—16岁的儿童；1955年编制的韦氏成人智力量表（Wechsler Adult Intelligence Scale，简称WAIS），适用于16岁以上的成人；1963年编制的韦氏学前儿童智力量表（Wechsler Preschool and Primary Scale of Intelligence，简称WPPSI），适用于4—6.5岁的儿童。这些量表测量的能力范围较广。

图 11-8　大卫·韦克斯勒

大卫·韦克斯勒（David Wechsler, 1896—1981），美国医学心理学家，韦氏智力测验的编制者。韦克斯勒是继法国比奈之后对智力测验研究贡献最大的人，其所编的多种智力量表，是当今世界最具权威的智力测验。

以1981年《韦克斯勒成人智力量表》修订版（WAIS-R）为例，该量表包括11个分量表，既可以用于计算全量表智商分数，也可以测得言语智商和操作智商分数。所以，应用韦氏量表，不仅可以测量出智力的一般水平（综合智力），而且可以测量出智力的不同侧面，即分别得到言语智商和操作智商。言语智商和操作智商虽然有很高的正相关（0.77—0.81），但用这两种量表测得的却是不同的能力。

韦氏智力量表的另一个重要特点是采用了离差智商（deviation IQ）。所谓离差智商就是用标准分数来表示智商，即让每一个被试和他同年龄的人相比。提出离差智商的根据是：人的智力水平符合正态分布，大多数人的智力处于中等水平，其平均值IQ=100；离平均数越远，获得该分数的人数就越少；人的智商从最低到最高，变化范围很大。智商分布的标准差为15。这样，一个人的智力水平就可以用其测验分数在同龄人的测验分数分布中的相对位置来表示。公式为：

$$IQ = 100 + 15(X - \bar{X})/S$$

（五）智力分布以及分类标准

大量研究表明，人类的智力水平呈正态分布，即两头小、中间大。著名心理测量学家推孟认为：智商为100左右的人约占全部被试的46%，130以上的人少于3%，70以下的人也少于3%。

专栏 11-2

智力测量的公平性问题

虽然多年来心理学家们致力于用智力测验这个工具来鉴别个体间或团体间的智力差异，但问题成堆。文化公平就是其中一个突出的问题。不同文化中的人甚至连什么是聪明都有着不同的看法。例如，有人曾进行了一项很有趣的智力的跨文化研究（Cole et al, 1971）。研究者要求非洲格贝列部落的成人完成概念分类任务。在西方文化中，要求成人在智力测试中完成分类任务时，智商越高的人一般都以上下等级的方式分类。例如，他们可能把各种鱼的名称放在一起，然后把"鱼"这个词标在上面，而把"动物"标在"鱼"和"鸟"之上。智商较低的会按照功能分类。例如，他们可能把"鱼"和"吃"归为一类，因为我们吃鱼，把"衣服"与"穿戴"归为一类，因为我们穿衣服。研究人员试图让格贝列人学会自然地按等级分类，但没有成功，格贝列人仍然只能按功能分类。失望之余，其中一位实验者要求一个格贝列人像傻子那样去分类，结果这个格贝列人很快轻而易举地按照等级进行了分类。格贝列人始终都是按功能分类，他们不按照等级分类只是因为他们认为那样做很愚蠢，他们多半也会认为提出按等级分类的研究人员很愚蠢。

虽说智力确实是有高低之分的，但仅靠文字和数字编制的测验就能揭示出智力的高低吗？文字和数字大都偏于习得的知识，这对不同文化或不同社会阶层的人来说，显然是不公平的。因此，一些心理学家尝试编制不受文化影响的测验来解决上述问题。免文化影响测验（culture free test）的构想是试图不用文字，而以图形等材料作为测题，以此来排除习得知识的影响。然而，智力本身就是遗传与环境交互作用的结果，而文化是环境中的重要因素。完全排除了与文化有关的题目，智力的高低根本就无从测量。以圆圈为例，它只是一个简单圆形，但会有不同的联想：太阳，月亮，轮子，风车，洞口……不同的联想显然受到不同文化的影响。因此，研究者们现在一般已不再使用"免文化影响"的提法，转而提出文化公平测验（culture fair test）。

文化公平的尝试在智力测验编制的取向上是很有价值的。但是，即使测量工具能够编制得更加公平，仍然会存在种族间的差别。有研究表明，实际的测验情境比测验的内容有更多的文化不公平问题。人们在能力测验中的成绩会受刻板印象威胁（stereotype threat）的影响，即一部分人（少数族群）在负面定势信念的支配下完成测验时会做得更差，影响他们的成绩表现（Steele，1997，Steele & Aronson，1998）。在美国的一项研究中，黑人和白人大学生都努力回答研究生入学考试中很难的语词问题，当黑人大学生相信实验成绩会用来检验他们的智力时，他们确实表现得更差，影响了测量的成绩（Steele & Aronson，1995）。那么怎样才能消除刻板印象威胁，以达成文化公平的智力测验呢？这个问题仍在探讨之中。

——黄希庭.心理学导论［M］.北京：人民教育出版社，2007：536—537.

二、特殊能力测量

（一）特殊能力的测量

要测定从事某种专业活动的能力，需要对某种专业进行分析，找出它所需要的心理特征，然后根据这些心理特征列出测验项目，设计测验，以便进行特殊能力的测验。例如，美国心理学家西肖尔（Seashore）等人于1939年编制了最早的音乐能力测验，适用于高中生和大学生。该测验用唱片（每分钟转数为33.33）和磁带呈现听觉刺激，主要是测量听觉辨别力的六个方面：音高、响度、节拍、音色、节奏和音调记忆。西肖尔测验中的所有题目都由一对刺激组成，在音调的测量中，被试必须判断第二个刺激声音与第一个相比是高了还是低了；音色的测量要求被试判断两个音的音质是否相同；音程分测验要求判断两个音程哪一个更长；在音序记忆测验中，被试需要指出两个音序是否相同。西肖尔认为这些能力是音乐能力全面发展的基础。每个分测验都提供了常模。

特殊能力的测验具有较强的针对性，因而对职业定向指导、安置和选拔从业人员、发现和培养具有特殊能力的儿童有重要意义。但这种测验发展较晚，因而测验的标准化问题尚未得到较满意的解决。

（二）创造力的测量

创造力即产生新思想，发现和创造新事物的能力。它与一般能力的区别主要在于它具有独创性与新颖性，其中最重要的是发散思维。测定发散思维能力，在一定程度上可知创造力的高低。因而许多创造力的测验都是设法测量被试的发散思维水平。20世纪60年代初，美国芝加哥大学首创了一套创造力测量表，这套测验由下列五个项目构成：词汇的联想、物体的用途、隐藏的图形、寓言的解释与问题的解答。这些项目要求被试作出大量而富有创造性的回答，在一定程度上反映了一个人的创造力。

三、能力测量的功用

能力测量对发展生产、增进人民健康、促进教育进步起着积极的作用。第一，能力测量作为一种方法，在诊断大脑机能障碍和精神疾病方面具有重要作用。第二，能力测量在选拔人才、帮助学生正确择业方面也有重要作用。如可以通过各种能力测量预测人们从事某种职业的适应性。第三，能力测量有助于教师辨别学生的能力特点，正确组织教育教学过程，并有利于发现学生的特殊才能，因材施教，促进早出人才、出好人才。

但是，能力测量也有其局限性，绝大多数能力测验所评量的仅仅是一个人的逻辑—数学能力和语言能力，其他能力我们不能测试到，或者说其他的能力我们无法给予定量化。所以说仅以这些靠纸和笔来完成的能力测验来判断学生的智能，并预测他们的长久发展，显然是片面的、不正确的。现代社会的智能观应是多元化的，并且是相互独立的。每个人都有不同的认知能力和认知方法。所以，上述的一些能力测验在我们的实际工作中只能作为一种参考数据，绝不能用它来判定学生的终身。

四、能力测验应具备的条件

能力测验是用来鉴别能力的科学工具，它必须精确、可靠、便于操纵。能力测验应当具备以下四个条件：

（一）标准化和常模

一个良好的能力测验在编制时必须经过标准化的过程。所谓标准化，就是指测验编

Unit 3 Division and Classification

by their companies on generous expat packages, which can include housing, expensive international schooling for their kids and perks like a personal driver.

[4] The Package Exec tends to live in a big house in far flung parts of the city, and is particularly vulnerable to the "expat bubble", containing him or herself to a world composed mostly of fellow Package Execs and overpriced Western food.

[5] The upside, though, includes getting paid a Western salary in a place where, if you want, you can live for 1/10th that price! The downside usually involves living in China without actually living in China, which is a huge waste of opportunity.

[6] Habitat: Gubei, Jinqiao, and other places miles from anything that could be considered an interesting part of the city

[7] Camouflage: Suit and tie

[8] Watering Holes: Element Fresh and any club with a number in its name

The Language Enthusiast

[9] The Language Enthusiast studied Mandarin or East Asian Studies in college/grad school and arrives in China to soak up more of the language.

[10] The problem they tend to encounter, as many people who have studied Chinese before coming here can attest, is that learning Chinese and living in China are two entirely different animals.

[11] Real Chinese comes at you hard, with non-standard Mandarin, weird accents, and that scary feeling you get when you realize that if you mess up something linguistically, there are consequences more substantive than just your grades.

[12] However, I've found that Language Enthusiast types tend to eventually do really well in China, if only because obtaining good Chinese skills requires a genuine passion and curiosity for the language.

[13] Habitat: Former French Concession walk-ups or a Beijing *hutong*

[14] Camouflage: Traditional Mao suit, but only for formal occasions

[15] Watering Holes: 5rmb "home cooking" dishes restaurants with no English menus

The Conquering Entrepreneur

[16] Brought here by the promises of an ever-expanding market, the Conquering

63

Entrepreneur can be found with a business card in-hand, perpetually excited about new opportunities in China.

[17] Shanghai is home to a seemingly unlimited number of these types, who are always cornering you in bars/subway stations/late-night street food stands to pitch their latest "disruptive" idea to you.

[18] I will admit that it is great to have that sort of entrepreneurial energy running through a country, but it can get annoying at times. The Conquering Entrepreneur tends to have poor Chinese skills, I've found, which doesn't make a lot of sense since they're trying to gain a foothold in the Chinese market.

[19] Entrepreneurs range from the impressively magnanimous to unspeakable levels of awfulness, but one thing's for sure: they're here to stay as long as China's economy keeps expanding.

[20] Habitat: Sleeping secretly in his shared office space in Jing'an because rent is just too damn high

[21] Camouflage: Various iterations of business casual

[22] Watering Holes: Foreigner-heavy sports bars and every conceivable happy hour

The Wandering Teacher

[23] Probably the most commonly-found foreigner in China, the Wandering Teacher comes in two distinct varieties: the no-jobs-at-home-might-as-well-teach-in-China type and the career teacher gaining experience.

[24] Fact is, English teaching jobs are very easy to come by in China, and it lures some seriously interesting characters here. I've met teachers who literally have warrants out for their arrest back home, as well as trustafarians traveling the world, one year and one place at time.

[25] The education market in China continues to boom, but in the last 5 years I've noticed a definite reduction in the deadbeat teacher numbers and a significant uptick among serious career teachers, which is great news for Chinese students!

[26] Habitat: Multiple roommates above an inexpensive bar with Filipina waitresses

[27] Camouflage: Cargo shorts and carpenter jeans

[28] Watering Holes: Any place with 10rmb Qingdaos on draft and 15rmb quesadillas on the menu

Unit 3 Division and Classification

The ABC (American-Born Chinese)

[29] One of the most interesting foreigner archetypes you'll meet in China is the ABC (or CBC ... or BBC ... etc.), who has often come to China seeking a reconnection with his or her culture, as well as for many of the same reasons as the types listed above.

[30] The China experience for ABCs is wildly different than it is for foreigners of other ethnicities, and they are usually held to a different standard by locals. I've heard ABC friends complain, for instance, that people from the Chinese mainland will consider their Mandarin skills less than perfect, and sometimes they can be turned down for jobs because some employers don't believe they truly have native-level English skills.

[31] Culturally, ABCs often have to make an extra effort to stand out from the locals, which leads to things like excessive partying and other abrasive behavior in an attempt to distance themselves from Chinese stereotypes — a huge portion of bar fights I've seen have involved ABCs in some capacity, for example.

[32] Habitat: Small but well-appointed apartment somewhere near the Bund

[33] Camouflage: Designer gear and the occasional flatbrim hat

[34] Watering Holes: M1NT, Bar Rouge and any club where people take black and white pictures and post them on social networking sites.

(https://www.yoyochinese.com/blog/learn-mandarin-chinese-5-types-of-foreigners-in-china)

1. Write down the thesis statement of the passage.

2. Five headings are used to present the five kinds of foreigners in China. How do you present them with topic sentences rather than headings?

3. Besides the obvious use of the writing pattern of classification or division, what other pattern(s) of writing is/are used in the passage?

4. What beginning method is used in the passage?

5. Besides the five types of foreigners mentioned in the text, are there any other types of foreigners in China?

• **Vocabulary Highlights**

Study the words and phrases in the passage with the help of a dictionary. Write down the definitions as they are used in the context.

far flung

be vulnerable to

upside

soak up

mess up

Unit 3 Division and Classification

substantive

perpetually

seemingly

disruptive

lure

deadbeat

archetype

Task 2

● **Writing Your First Draft**

> With the globalization of the world, more and more foreigners flock to China for all kinds of reasons. However, they have different attitudes toward immersion to Chinese culture or society and thus get soaked up in Chinese culture or society to different degrees. Write an essay to classify the foreigners in China according to their attitudes toward or situations of immersion in Chinese culture.

In-class Activities

▶ *What Are Division and Classification?*

Division is a method of dividing, separating, or breaking down one subject or topic (often a large or complex or unfamiliar one) into its component parts so that it may be better understood or used by readers. For example, the writer of this writing textbook divides the book into eight units so that you can understand and acquire the basic writing skills bit by bit. Another example is that a pair of glasses can be divided into frameworks and lens. The components and the topic form a part-to-whole relationship.

Classification is a method of developing an essay by arranging people, objects, or ideas with shared characteristics into particular categories to make the information easier to grasp. Without proper classification, the information can be a messy mingling of facts and figures. For example, in your university library, the books may be grouped and shelved into different fields like "Education", "Literature", "Engineering", "Psychology", etc. for the convenience of readers' choices. Another example is the garbage sorting, in which we classify different kinds of garbage into "Hazardous Waste", "Recyclable Waste", "Household Food Waste" and "Residual Waste", etc.

Both division and classification are useful strategies of organization in writing. Division stresses the distinction between different parts or components while classification emphasizes the similarities between the categories.

• Activity 1

In Task 2 of Pre-class Work, you are required to write the first draft of an essay to classify the foreigners in China according to their attitudes toward or situations of immersion in Chinese culture. Now work in groups to present the outline of your essay about the immersion situations of foreigners in China.

Unit 3 Division and Classification

• Activity 2

Read the topics below to see whether they suggest classification or division. Write down "C" beside a topic if it suggests classification. Write down "D" if it suggests division.

___ The components of a thesis

___ Kinds of scholarships in our university

___ A typical day in your winter holiday

___ Stages of grief

___ The characteristics of a good anchorman

___ Dishes on the table

• Activity 3

List three to five items that can be included in each of the following topics. Share your results with the rest of the class.

Games for children: _____

_____

The components of an ecosystem: _____

_____

Types of vegetables: _____

_____

The stages of a person's education: _____

_____

▶ Division or Classification in Paragraph Development

Division or classification can sometimes be used in a paragraph to present the different categories or parts of things clearly and logically. Parallelism is essential to good division or classification writing. That is, the categories or parts should be parallel to each other rather than overlap each other. For example, it's not proper if we classify the university majors into psychology, sciences, politics, law, mathematics, statistics, humanities because sciences and humanities are the names of schools rather than majors.

• Activity 4

Read the paragraphs below and answer the questions.

Paragraph 1

There are three kinds of book owners. The first has all the standard sets and best sellers — unread, untouched. (This deluded individual owns wood pulp and ink, not books.) The second has a great many books — a few of them read through, most of them dipped into, but all of them as clean and shiny as the day they were bought. (This person would probably like to make books his own, but is restrained by a false respect for their physical appearance.) The third has a few books or many — every one of them dog-eared and dilapidated, shaken and loosened by continual use, marked and scribbled from front to back. (This man owns books.)

—*Mortimer J. Adler*

1. What is the topic sentence in the paragraph?

_____

2. What method does the writer use to develop the topic, classification or division?

Unit 3 Division and Classification

3. What unifying principle does the writer use to classify book owners?

4. Besides classification, what other method(s) of development is/are used to classify book owners?

Paragraph 2

Every educated person has <u>at least</u> two ways of speaking his mother tongue. The first is that which he employs in his family, among his familiar friends, and on ordinary occasions. The second is that which he uses in discoursing on more complicated subjects, and in addressing persons with whom he is less intimately acquainted. It is, in short, the language which he employs when he is "on his dignity", as he puts on evening dress when he is going to dine.

—— *J. B. Green & G. L. Kittredge*

1. What is the topic sentence of this paragraph?

2. What method do the writers employ to develop the topic, classification or division?

3. What unifying principle do the writers use to develop the paragraph?

4. What does the underlined phrase "at least" in the first sentence imply?

• **Activity 5**

Discuss in pairs how you are going to develop the following topic sentences by division or classification.

University students are always faced with three kinds of pressures in their life.

A. _____

B. _____

C. _____

Several components contribute to a successful evening party.

A. _____

B. _____

C. _____

There are 4 types of blood in humans.

A. _____

B. _____

C. _____

D. _____

My family expenses mainly go to the following parts.

A. _____

B. _____

C. _____

Unit 3 Division and Classification

▶ *Determine the Purpose and Audience for Division or Classification Essays*

The purpose of division or classification essays is to inform the readers of the information by dividing or classifying a particular topic by a unifying principle. For example, if your principle is to emphasize the origin of English speakers, you may classify them into native English speakers and non-native English speakers. If you want to stress their English proficiency, then you can classify them into fluent and broken English speakers. If you want to present their different stages of English learning, you can also classify them into preliminary, intermediate or advanced English speakers.

When deciding on your principle of division or classification, the audience should also be taken into consideration. For example, when you write an essay about the different kinds of part-time jobs in a university, or the different ways to get financial help from the university, you may actually inform the needy students of the relevant information.

• Activity 6

We have numerous great leaders in all walks of life. What necessary qualities should a leader possess? The following essay unveils some of the qualities of different kinds of leaders who create the future. Read it to see whether you identify with the writer's opinions.

The 4 Kinds of Leaders Who Create the Future

Bill Taylor

[1] Alan Kay, the educator and computer designer, famously declared, "The best way to predict the future is to invent it." But what does it take to invent the future in such a turbulent and uncertain world? How do successful organizations build on their history, even as they craft a new point of view about what comes next? How do established brands stay true to their original promise, while also making themselves relevant to new customers with different values and preferences? How can accomplished executives be sure that all they know — their hard-earned wisdom and expertise — doesn't limit what they can imagine?

[2] These are the questions that separate organizations and leaders whose best years are ahead of them from those stuck in the past. I've made it a point, in research for my books and my HBR (*Harvard Business Review*) contributions, to pay close attention to leaders who seem energized by these questions rather than paralyzed by them. As I reflect on those leaders, on the habits of mind that drive them, I've realized that most could be sorted into one of four categories:

The Learning Zealot

[3] One of the great satisfactions of being a leader is that you get to be a teacher, sharing the wisdom you've acquired over the course of a career with young colleagues hungry for time-tested advice. But when it comes to inventing the future, the most effective leaders are the most insatiable learners. Creative leaders are always asking themselves, "Am I learning as fast as the world is changing?"

[4] Garry Ridge, CEO of WD-40, may be the most learning-obsessed executive I know. He's unleashed huge innovations and presided over unprecedented growth. The secret of WD-40's success? Ridge's devotion to building an organization of "learning maniacs" who are zealous about engaging with new technologies and business models. He empowered a group of executives and engineers, called Team Tomorrow, to turbocharge learning throughout the company. His favorite question to colleagues, a test of their zeal for learning, is, "When's the last time you did something for the first time?" Leaders who are fit for the future are determined to keep learning as fast as the world is changing.

The Personal Disruptor

[5] The longer you've worked in an industry, the more success you've achieved, the harder it can be to see new patterns and possibilities, new paths to what's next. All too often, senior leaders allow what they know to limit what they can imagine. That's a big problem: You can't invent the future if you cling to out-of-date ideas, even if they've worked in the past.

[6] Rosanne Haggerty, one of the country's great social activists, has made a huge impact in the fight against homelessness. But her biggest (and most revolutionary) achievement, the 100,000 Homes Campaign, required her to challenge everything she knew about her cause. "I concluded, to my horror, that we had developed a way of attacking the problem that was inherently limited," she says. "We had to blow ourselves up." That act of personal reinvention was

brutally difficult — and absolutely necessary. "Too often," she warns, "pride in your most recent idea becomes a barrier to seeing your next idea." Leaders who are fit for the future understand when it's time to disrupt themselves.

The Tough-Minded Optimist

[7] Leadership is emotional as well as intellectual. How we present ourselves, the attitude and outlook we exude, sets a tone about what's required to make deep-seated change in turbulent times. John Gardner, the legendary scholar of organizational life, argues that great leaders exude "tough-minded optimism". The future, he says, "is not shaped by people who don't really believe in the future. It is created by highly motivated people, by enthusiasts, by men and women who want something very much or believe very much."

[8] Vernon Hill, an entrepreneur whose young company, Metro Bank, is reshaping the future of financial services in the UK, exudes a spirit of energy and confidence that is infectious. Sure, his high-touch business model is reinventing a field notorious for lousy service. But it's the mindset he personifies that defines the fast-growing bank. "If we don't maintain a sense of energy," he says, "we are hurting the message." This is why the company looks for leaders with "zest", personal enthusiasm for the bank's mission. You can't invent a prosperous future for your company unless you are excited about what the future holds.

The Eager Experimenter

[9] There's a dirty secret about the future that many of us don't want to face: Even the most exciting breakthroughs are built on the backs of projects that fizzled, products that bombed, initiatives that failed. That's why leaders who are fit for the future are supporting lots of ideas, knowing that most of them won't deliver as planned, to discover the few that will deliver bigger than anyone imagined.

[10] Does any executive personify the spirit of experimentation better than Jeff Bezos? The Amazon CEO is the richest person in the world based on his willingness to embrace ideas that don't work out. "If you're going to take bold bets, they're going to be experiments," Bezos explained. "And if they're experiments, you don't know ahead of time if they're going to work." Leaders who are fit for the future understand that there is no success without setbacks, no progress without pitfalls.

[11] Of course, like all frameworks, this is a simplification. And many of us wouldn't fall into just one, clear-cut category. But for most of us, more fully embracing any of these traits would help with the hard work of big change. There is no guarantee that one particular attitude will help you invent a more prosperous future for your organization or yourself. But if each of us can figure out which of these habits of mind best suits who we are, we may become more fit for the future.

[12] In any field, leaders who move their organizations forward are the ones who can reimagine what they've always done, refresh and reinterpret the products and services they offer, and unleash bold experiments about what comes next. Are you that kind of leader?

(https://hbr.org/2017/12/the-4-kinds-of-leaders-who-create-the-future)

1. The organization of the preceding essay is rather clear, resembling the traditional one-three-one essay model. Fill in the missing paragraph numbers.

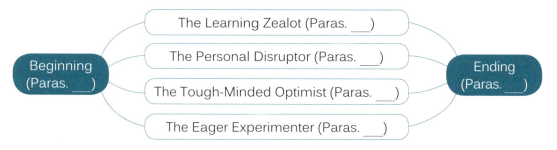

2. Besides the obvious use of the writing pattern of classification or division, what other writing method(s) is/are used in the passage?

_____

_____

3. What example is used to elaborate on each category?

Category	Quality	Example
The Learning Zealot		

(continued)

Unit 3 Division and Classification

Category	Quality	Example
The Personal Disruptor		
The Tough-Minded Optimist		
The Eager Experimenter		

4. What methods of beginning and ending are used in the essay?

Beginning: _____

Ending: _____

_____

5. Identify the words or phrases in Paragraph 2 which signal division or classification.

_____

6. What unifying principle of classification does the writer employ to organize the paragraphs?

_____

7. Are there any other types of leaders who create the future besides the four types mentioned in the text?

_____

_____

77

• Vocabulary Highlights

Study the words and phrases in the passage with the help of a dictionary. Write down the definitions as they are used in the context.

turbulent _____

energize _____

paralyze _____

insatiable _____

unleash _____

cling to _____

disrupt _____

exude _____

embrace _____

clear-cut _____

▶ *Organizing Division or Classification Essays by Different Means*

► Using headings

Many division or classification essays, especially longer ones, always use headings to present several categories or parts of things. Both of the two essays, "The 5 Types of Foreigners in China" and "The 4 Kinds of Leaders Who Create the Future", use headings to present the categories.

► Using words, expressions or sentence patterns indicating division or classification

As you can see, in the second paragraph of "The 4 Kinds of Leaders Who Create the Future", the writer uses the expressions "separate ... from ..." and "be sorted into

Unit 3 Division and Classification

one of four categories" to present the four kinds of leaders who create the future.

Some other words, expressions or sentence patterns indicating division or classification can be found in the following table.

Verbs/Verbal phrases	Nouns	Sentence patterns
fall into ... categories	categories	According to ..., there are principally two kinds of ...
fit into ...	subcategories	The division is based on ...
be divided into ...	groups	There are, broadly speaking, two basic types of ..., depending on ...
be classified into ...	subgroups	... fall into three kinds on the basis of ...
be grouped into ...	classes	...can be subdivided into...
be categorized into ...	subclasses	
consist of ...	divisions	
comprise ...	subdivisions	
be composed of ...	types	
be made up of ...	sorts	
	kinds	
	species	

▶ Some Guidelines for Developing a Classification or Division Essay

To compose a good division or classification essay, due attention should be paid to the following guidelines.

► **Sticking to the same unifying principle, and avoiding overlapping**

Each category should be unique. There should be no overlap among categories. If you say "In the past two years our university has admitted many foreign students:

African students, British students, American students, Egyptian students, Arab students, and Japanese students", then this classification is faulty because several principles (by continents or countries?) are used simultaneously and they overlap each other.

▸ Avoiding leaving out any critical category

If you say water sports of Hawaii include snorkeling and sailing, but you leave out surfing, your essay would be incomplete because surfing is one of Hawaii's most famous water sports. When sometimes there are too many categories to be included in your essay, you can use expressions like "and other …" or "etc." to indicate that you are aware that your division or classification is not complete, and that you don't feel it necessary to present them all.

▸ Arranging the categories by order

Arrange your body paragraphs in whatever clear and logical order, and make sure that the order of your body paragraphs matches the arrangement promised in your thesis sentence. So it's problematic and illogical to divide the audience in a theatre into little kids, adults and teenagers. Rather, we should divide them as "little kids, teenagers and adults" according to their age.

▸ Fully developing each category

Each category should include adequate specific details to make it recognizable and interesting. To that end, you can draw on some other methods of development to further support each category, like exemplification, comparison and contrast, and definition. Try to use the same method for each category to make the essay clear and logical. For example, the "4 Kinds of Leaders" essay uses one example in each category to illustrate the four kinds of leaders who create the future.

• Activity 7

Decide whether the following thesis statements are good ones or not for a division or classification essay.

Dogs can be classified into spaniels, terriers, long-haired, hounds and retrievers.

Unit 3 Division and Classification

There are four parenting styles: authoritarian, authoritative, permissive and uninvolved.

_____

Music can be divided into Chinese and Western music or into that of piano, violin and folk songs.

_____

In the Olympic Games were athletes from every continent of the world — Asia, Europe, Africa, North America, and South America.

_____

> Suppose you are going to develop the following topics into full-length essays of classification or division, what categories or parts will you come up with?

The Three Ox Spirit

_____

_____

_____

_____

The Four Matters of Confidence

_____

_____

_____

_____

The Essence of Chinese Dream

_____

_____

_____

_____

Below is a student essay on friendship. Read it and do the exercises.

Three Kinds of Friendships

[1] A question often asked is: "What kind of friendship should people value?" The answers may be variously described with complicated classifications of friendship. According to the level of intimacy, however, friendship can be simply classified into three kinds.

[2] The first kind of friendship is the acquaintanceship, the lowest intimacy between friends. When friends are on this level, they're just on speaking terms, most likely to ignore the names of each other. They know each other by sight and don't keep in touch.

[3] The friendship between ordinary friends comes second. Ordinary friends are those who are less intimate than close friends, but closer than acquaintances. People make such friends with colleagues, schoolmates simply because they meet each other very often. People do not usually contact their ordinary friends unless they need help from such kind of friends.

[4] The highest degree of intimacy exists between bosom friends who share extremely strong interpersonal ties with each other. This type of friendship is a much stronger bond than acquaintanceship. The acquaintances just know each other on a shallow level such as the name, appearance or something else. Yet best friends share everything. They love and respect each other, tolerant of all hateful defects of their friends. Furthermore, bosom friends always encourage and stand by each other under any circumstances.

[5] R. L. Stevenson once said, "A friend is a present which you give yourself." Therefore, no matter what kind of friends people have, they should cherish them.

(https://wenku.baidu.com/view/a7fd7172650e52ea5418982f.html)

1. Make an outline for the essay by filling the following blanks.

Thesis statement	
Topic sentence 1	

(continued)

Unit 3 Division and Classification

Topic sentence 2	
Topic sentence 3	

2. What unifying principle does the writer use to classify friendship into three kinds?

   _____

3. Is the essay well-organized? What words and expressions of classification or division does the writer use to make the essay coherent?

   _____
   _____
   _____
   _____

4. What do you think is the writer's purpose in writing this essay?

   _____
   _____

• Activity 8

Write a second draft of the essay in Task 2 of Pre-class Work about foreigners' different immersion situations in China. Then, work in pairs and review each other's writing according to the four bases of essay writing: unity, support, coherence and sentence skills. Make sure that you check the following aspects: (1) The whole essay has only one central idea according to one unifying principle; (2) There is adequate and specific evidence for each category or part; (3) The essay presents the categories or parts by using some transitional words; (4) All the sentences in the essay are error-free.

After-class Practice

Task 1

Suppose you are to develop the following topics into essays of classification or division, how are you going to state the topic sentences? Make sure that the paragraphs are connected.

Topic	Topic sentences of developmental paragraphs
Three friends in cold weather in Chinese culture	
The quintessence of Chinese culture	
The Belt and Road Initiative	

Task 2

The essays we have covered so far are mainly classification articles. The next one will be a typical division essay. Read it carefully to get a better understanding of how to write division essays, and then compose a division essay by yourself.

4 Basic Components of an Online Course

Devon Haynie

[1] When Weishuang Liu, 27, started her online degree two years ago, she had no idea what to expect.

[2] Would she have to log in to watch lectures in real time, she wondered? How would she access her readings? And what was up with discussion boards? What if she had nothing to say?

[3] "It's a learning experience," says Liu, who is slated to graduate from Indiana

Unit 3 Division and Classification

University's Kelley School of Business with an MBA in June. "But everybody is trying to learn the systems just like you."

[4] As Americans increasingly turn to online courses, many wonder just exactly what they're getting into. But there's good news for those who seem overwhelmed by digital learning: Experts say it's fairly easy to adapt to the virtual classroom.

[5] "The learning curve is very low," says Todd Hitchcock, senior vice president of online solutions for Pearson, an education services company. "For the most part, 95 percent of people logging on have been on the Web."

[6] Although distance learning can vary from institution to institution, most online courses have similarities, experts say. Below are what experts consider the four basic components of a typical online course.

[7] **The learning management system.** Shortly after students enroll in a course, they'll be asked to log in to a learning management system, or LMS. Hitchcock calls this "the infrastructure that enables the learning to happen."

[8] The LMS is the platform where students can view their syllabus, learn how to contact their professor and access most course materials, including online readings, videos, audio files and other resources. This is also where students go to participate in discussion boards — written exchanges with fellow classmates. In some systems, students can also email and instant message their classmates and instructors.

[9] Although some schools design their own learning management systems, most colleges use Blackboard, Moodle and Desire2Learn, says Peter Shea, an education professor at the University at Albany-SUNY. Most of these systems are similar and fairly intuitive, he says.

[10] **Course materials.** Online learners can be exposed to course material in a range of different ways. Some instructors ask that students read e-books, while others suggest ordering textbooks. Other possible resources include podcasts, PowerPoint presentations, webcasts featuring lectures and instructional videos on sites such as TeacherTube.

[11] Typically, students are free to listen, read or watch assignments on their own schedule.

[12] "An instructor doesn't mandate a time," Pearson's Hitchcock says. "You have

to have strong time management skills. If you don't, then you'll be in trouble."

[13] **Assignments and group projects.** Once students log in to the LMS, they should find a list of assignments and due dates. Most students will be required to submit papers as well as participate in and moderate discussion boards.

[14] Kathleen Ives, an online professor and associate executive director and chief operating officer of Sloan Consortium, a nonprofit dedicated to promoting online learning, says students often make the mistake of underestimating the amount of time they will need to spend on the discussions. She gives her students a word count for their responses.

[15] "You have to say something more than, 'I agree,'" she says. "A substantive post is something that is at least 100 words and furthers the discussion."

[16] In addition to papers and discussion boards, students are often asked to create blogs or projects demonstrating their subject knowledge.

[17] And just because online programs require little face-to-face interaction, that doesn't mean instructors don't require group projects. In those cases, students say they are apt to contact each other through Skype, conference calls or Google Hangouts.

[18] Liu, the Indiana student, says she was surprised by how often she actually heard the voices of her classmates.

[19] "We would email back and forth and then get on a call and I'd think, 'I didn't think you sounded like that,'" she says.

[20] **Grading.** Although some students might wish otherwise, testing and assessments play a significant role in the virtual classroom. The way instructors grade students varies, experts say. Some will give multiple choice tests graded by the computer, while others will rely more on papers or major projects.

[21] To make sure students don't cheat on exams, Albany's Shea says it's increasingly common for schools to use proctored tests. In some cases, students need to report to a physical location where they will be monitored. On other occasions, students are asked to use a webcam and take a proctored exam at their desk. To make sure the right person is taking the test, students can be asked to flash their photo identification into the camera.

[22] In general, Shea says, instructors familiar with their students' work product are quick to notice when someone might be taking advantage of the system.

Unit 3 Division and Classification

[23] "It's actually easy to get to know your students from the quality of work they submit," he says. "In some ways that inhibits breaches of academic integrity."

(https://www.usnews.com/education/online-education/articles/2013/04/24/4-basic-components-of-an-online-course)

1. Suppose you are required to compose an essay of division with the same title "4 Basic Components of an Online Course", will the four components you come up with be identical to the ones presented in the above essay?

2. What method of beginning is used in this essay?

3. During the COVID-19 pandemic, online courses have become increasingly familiar to us. Do you think online courses will replace traditional courses one day? Why or Why not?

4. Write an essay of division, presenting the basic components of an offline course.

Expansion

Passage 1

1. The following essay is a classic classification writing by the British philosopher and writer Francis Bacon 400 years ago. Locate the sentences of classification or division in the essay, and give a unifying principle for each of them.
2. Suppose you have to compose an essay entitled "Of Thinking Abilities", what ideas would you include in your essay?

Of Studies

Francis Bacon

[1] Studies serve for delight, for ornament, and for ability. Their chief use for

delight, is in privateness and retiring; for ornament, is in discourse; and for ability, is in the judgment and disposition of business. For expert men can execute, and perhaps judge of particulars, one by one; but the general counsels, and the plots and marshalling of affairs come best from those that are learned.

[2] To spend too much time in studies is sloth; to use them too much for ornament is affectation; to make judgment wholly by their rules is the humor of a scholar. They perfect nature and are perfected by experience: for natural abilities are like natural plants, that need pruning by study, and studies themselves do give forth directions too much at large, except they be bounded in by experience.

[3] Crafty men condemn studies, simple men admire them, and wise men use them, for they teach not their own use; but that is a wisdom without them and above them, won by observation. Read not to contradict and confute; nor to believe and take for granted; nor to find talk and discourse; but to weigh and consider. Some books are to be tasted, others to be swallowed, and some few to be chewed and digested; that is, some books are to be read only in parts; others to be read, but not curiously; and some few to be read wholly, and with diligence and attention. Some books also may be read by deputy and extracts made of them by others; but that would be only in the less important arguments, and the meaner sort of books; else distilled books are, like common distilled waters, flashy things.

[4] Reading maketh a full man; conference a ready man; and writing an exact man. And therefore, if a man write little, he had need have a great memory; if he confer little, he had need have a present wit; and if he read little, he had need have much cunning to seem to know that he doth not.

[5] Histories make men wise; poets witty; the mathematics subtle; natural philosophy deep; moral grave; logic and rhetoric able to contend. *Abeunt studia in mores.* Nay, there is no stond or impediment in the wit, but may be wrought out by fit studies: like as diseases of the body may have appropriate exercises. Bowling is good for the stone and reins; shooting for the lungs and breast; gentle walking for the stomach; riding for the head; and the like. So if a man's wit be wandering, let him study the mathematics; for in demonstrations, if his wit be called away never so little, he must begin again. If his wit be not apt to distinguish or find differences, let him study the Schoolmen; for they are *cymini sectores.* If he be not apt to beat over matters, and to call up one thing to prove

and illustrate another, let him study the lawyers' cases. So every defect of the mind may have a special receipt.

Notes:

Abeunt studia in mores: studies pass into character

cymini sectores: dividers of cumin seeds, or hair-splitters

(https://wenku.baidu.com/view/5adfe1923968011ca200918a.html)

Passage 2

We are all storytellers, storytellers about the world, about other people, and about ourselves. Stories about ourselves, however, may fall into different categories. The essay below may shed light on the stories you are always telling, and what kind of people you are.

The Two Kinds of Stories We Tell About Ourselves

Emily Esfahani Smith

[1] We are all storytellers — all engaged, as the anthropologist Mary Catherine Bateson puts it, in an "act of creation" of the "composition of our lives." Yet unlike most stories we've heard, our lives don't follow a predefined arc. Our identities and experiences are constantly shifting, and storytelling is how we make sense of it. By taking the disparate pieces of our lives and placing them together into a narrative, we create a unified whole that allows us to understand our lives as coherent — and coherence, psychologists say, is a key source of meaning.

[2] Northwestern University psychologist Dan McAdams is an expert on a concept he calls "narrative identity". McAdams describes narrative identity as an internalized story you create about yourself — your own personal myth. Like myths, our narrative identity contains heroes and villains that help us or hold us back, major events that determine the plot, challenges overcome and suffering we have endured. When we want people to understand us, we share our story or parts of it with them; when we want to know who another person is, we ask them to share part of their story.

[3] An individual's life story is not an exhaustive history of everything that has

happened. Rather, we make what McAdams calls "narrative choices". Our stories tend to focus on the most extraordinary events, good and bad, because those are the experiences we need to make sense of and that shape us. But our interpretations may differ. For one person, for example, a childhood experience like learning how to swim by being thrown into the water by a parent might explain his sense of himself today as a hardy entrepreneur who learns by taking risks. For another, that experience might explain why he hates boats and does not trust authority figures. A third might leave the experience out of his story altogether, deeming it unimportant.

[4] McAdams has been studying narrative identity for over 30 years. In his interviews, he asks research subjects to divide their lives into chapters and to recount key scenes, such as a high point, a low point, a turning point or an early memory. He encourages participants to think about their personal beliefs and values. Finally, he asks them to reflect on their story's central theme. He has discovered interesting patterns in how people living meaningful lives understand and interpret their experiences. People who are driven to contribute to society and to future generations, he found, are more likely to tell redemptive stories about their lives, or stories that transition from bad to good. There was the man who grew up in dire poverty but told McAdams that his hard circumstances brought him and his family closer together. There was the woman who told him that caring for a close friend as the friend was dying was a harrowing experience, but one that ultimately renewed her commitment to being a nurse, a career she'd abandoned. These people rate their lives as more meaningful than those who tell stories that have either no or fewer redemptive sequences.

[5] The opposite of a redemptive story is what McAdams calls a "contamination story", in which people interpret their lives as going from good to bad. One woman told him the story of the birth of her child, a high point, but she ended the story with the death of the baby's father, who was murdered three years later. The joy over the birth of her child was tainted by that tragedy. People who tell contamination stories, McAdams has found, are less "generative", or less driven to contribute to society and younger generations. They also tend to be more anxious and depressed, and to feel that their lives are less coherent compared to those who tell redemptive stories.

Unit 3 Division and Classification

[6] Redemption and contamination stories are just two kinds of tales we spin. McAdams has found that beyond stories of redemption, people who believe their lives are meaningful tend to tell stories defined by growth, communion and agency. These stories allow individuals to craft a positive identity: they are in control of their lives, they are loved, they are progressing through life and whatever obstacles they have encountered have been redeemed by good outcomes.

[7] One of the great contributions of psychology and psychotherapy research is the idea that we can edit, revise and interpret the stories we tell about our lives even as we are constrained by the facts. A psychotherapist's job is to work with patients to rewrite their stories in a more positive way. Through editing and reinterpreting his story with his therapist, the patient may come to realize that he is in control of his life and that some meaning can be gleaned from his hardships. A review of the scientific literature finds that this form of therapy is as effective as antidepressants or cognitive behavioral therapy.

[8] Even making smaller story edits can have a big impact on our lives. So found Adam Grant and Jane Dutton in a study published in 2012. The researchers asked university call-center fundraisers to keep a journal for four consecutive days. In one condition, the beneficiary condition, the researchers asked the fundraisers to write about the last time a colleague did something for them that inspired gratitude. In the second condition, the benefactor condition, the participants wrote about a time they contributed to others at work.

[9] The researchers wanted to know which type of story would lead the research subjects to be more generous. To find out, they monitored the fundraisers' call records. Since the fundraisers were paid a fixed hourly rate to call alumni and solicit donations, the researchers reasoned, then the number of calls they made during their shift was a good indicator of prosocial, helping behavior.

[10] After Grant and Dutton analyzed the stories, they found that fundraisers who told a story of themselves as benefactors ultimately made 30 percent more calls to alumni after the experiment than they had before. Those who told stories about being the beneficiary of generosity showed no changes in their behavior.

[11] Grant and Dutton's study suggests that the ability of a story to create meaning does not end with the crafting of the tale. The stories the benefactors told about

themselves ultimately led to meaningful behaviors — giving their time in the service of a larger cause. Even though the fundraisers knew they were only telling their stories as part of a study, they ultimately "lived by" those stories, as McAdams would put it. By subtly reframing their narrative, they adopted a positive identity that led them to live more purposefully.

(https://ideas.ted.com/the-two-kinds-of-stories-we-tell-about-ourselves.)

Unit 4
Cause and Effect

Objectives

At the end of this unit, you should be able to

- ✓ understand the role of cause-and-effect in paragraph and essay development;
- ✓ structure in block or chain, avoid logical fallacies, keep the causal chain complete, and use causal expressions;
- ✓ write an essay with skills of cause-and-effect after thinking critically about a virtue.

Pre-class Work

Task 1

• Reading for Writing

Will you report a fortune-teller to the police for fraud? Would you rather believe in sincere assurance of a businessman than cold numbers in the account books? Should a politician feel ashamed of his unfounded claim even though it is sincerely held and conveyed? Read the passage below and see if you would have different answers.

Sincerity: An Overrated Virtue

Lewis Jones

[1] Today, if suppliers of the paranormal say that they can produce an apport, they are immediately classified as deliberate frauds, as the public are well aware that no amount of faith could produce physical objects out of nowhere. Consequently, these frauds have mostly moved into safer and more fashionable areas: astrology, tarot card reading or faith healing.

[2] This kind of move has made it more difficult to decide whether your local aura-reader is a conscious fake, or just a sincere but confused would-be benefactor. All too often if he/she is sincere, everything is going to be all right. However, I submit that sincerity is not enough. I am not concerned here with

legal definitions, because these can differ from country to country, and I am not concerned with whether there is a deliberate intent to defraud. But I am concerned with the way in which "sincerity" is being used as an excuse for malpractice.

[3] E. Haldeman-Julius, in *The Outline of Bunk*, spotted the danger back in 1929: "It is well to stress early this point about sincerity. It is a much-overrated virtue. Sincerity, joined with ill thought and ill will — sincerity that has no intelligence to guide it — is one of the most dangerous things in this world. ... When in other days a heretic was burned at the stake, it mattered not to the victim that those who lit the fagots were sincere. ... When Voltaire was forced into exile, when his writings were destroyed, when he was assailed by all the forces of intolerance, it signified really nothing to him whether the bigots were sincere men. ... Sincerity can be cruel, unscrupulous, outrageous, and fraught with the peril of passionate abuse."

[4] I sincerely believe that by praying over your child I can cure her of a ruptured spleen. You are at liberty to write me off as an idiot. But if my claims manage to divert you from seeking the simple surgery the child needs, "she's dead in a day", and I stand revealed as a public menace. The trouble with naked sincerity is that it sees its beliefs as above the need for testing. This is fatal to any attempt to discover whether or not those beliefs are true. As Antony Flew puts it in *Thinking about Social Thinking*: "Suppose someone claims to be in business, no doubt among other things, to turn a profit; or suppose that the captain of a cricket team says that he is playing, no doubt again among other things, in order to win. Then what trust could we give to these professions if there is no care to keep, in the one case, accounts and, in the other case, the score."

[5] As Aaron Wildavsky points out in *But Is It True?*, in a world ruled by sincere but unfounded beliefs, "science as a search for universal truths would be replaced by personal testimony. 'What is true' would be replaced by 'what is personally authentic'. Science, in a word, would be replaced by sincerity".

[6] Acting on sincerity alone is a sure sign of the amateur thinker. In philosopher Paul Feyerabend's terms: "The distinction between the crank and the respectable thinker lies in the research that is done once a certain point of view is adopted. The crank usually is content with defending the point of view in its original, undeveloped, metaphysical form, and he is not at all prepared to test its

usefulness in all those cases which seem to favor the opponent, or even to admit that there exists a problem."

[7] Or, as John F. Kennedy put it more simply in his inaugural address: "Sincerity is always subject to proof."

[8] If you still harbor warm feelings towards the purely sincere, imagine yourself in a jumbo jet just before take-off, hearing the following words over the intercom: "Good morning, ladies and gentlemen. This is not your captain speaking. But I've just slipped into the captain's seat, and I'm all set for take-off. I haven't had any training for this, and I have no idea what all these little flashing lights mean, but I've always felt I was cut out for flying. You don't need to worry, though, because I really, really believe most sincerely that I can do this. Here we go."

[9] Your first reaction might well be to see in a new light Oscar Wilde's assertion: "A little sincerity is a dangerous thing, and a great deal of it is absolutely fatal." There is a common view that if a man's sincere but groundless belief should turn out to be true after all, this means he is off the hook. But not so: "It is an established maxim and moral that he who makes an assertion without knowing whether it is true or false is guilty of falsehood, and the accidental truth of the assertion does not justify or excuse him." So said Abraham Lincoln. Politicians don't always get it wrong.

(*Skeptical Briefs*, 1997)

1. How does the writer give restrictions to sincerity? Why does he do it?

   _____
   _____
   _____
   _____

2. At sight of the expression "naked sincerity", readers may think of a very similar one, "naked truth". What do you know about it? Why does "naked sincerity" mean in the passage?

   _____

Unit 4 Cause and Effect

3. What does the writer imply in the last sentence "Politicians don't always get it wrong"?

• Vocabulary Highlights

Study the words and phrases in the passage with the help of a dictionary. Write down the definitions as they are used in the context.

paranormal

heretic

assail

divert ... from

menace

testimony

metaphysical

be subject to

off the hook

justify

Task 2

• Thinking Critically on a Virtue

1. Match the virtues in the table with their definitions or interpretations.

Virtues	Definitions
(_) Courtesy	A. The quality of being humble, modesty.
(_) Diligence	B. Behavior marked by polished manners or respect for others.
(_) Prudence	C. Continued effort despite difficulties, failure, or opposition.
(_) Generosity	D. Discretion in practical affairs.
(_) Humility	E. Giving good things to others freely and abundantly.

Virtues	Interpretations
(_) Patience	A. It means you do not let fear stop you.
(_) Forgiveness	B. Integrity, choosing what's right rather than what's convenient.
(_) Courage	C. It's not the ability to wait, but the one to be calm while waiting.
(_) Honesty	D. Being accountable for your results.
(_) Responsibility	E. Bearing with the faults of others as you'd have them bear with yours.

2. Examine the virtues including but not limited to the ones mentioned above, consider the following questions and pick one that you consider least valuable and most vulnerable as the topic of your essay.

- Does it keep up with the times? Is it too old-fashioned to practice?
- Does it stand true in all nations, genders, races, or religions?
- Does it apply to contingencies like a critical moment or even a war?
- Does it harm a particular group to benefit another?
- Does it contain a part that can be used as an excuse to evade responsibility?
- Does it violate other virtues, regulations or laws in a particular case?
- Does too much of it backfire?

Unit 4 Cause and Effect

- Does it lure people to act recklessly to be morally good?

Your topic: _____ : An Overrated Virtue

Tips on Developing Your Essay

3. Study the following example and write down your own outline in the next table.

Example:

Humility: An Overrated Virtue			
Who	Where/When	Reason/Result	Evidence
Celebrity	News reports	Resemblance to hypocrisy and dishonesty. People get mocked at.	Liu Bei declared himself Emperor of Han.
Player Negotiator	Game Negotiation	Bluffing is no longer an option in bargaining. Signs of weakness and non-aggressiveness.	Texas Poker Game. The Cuban Missile Crisis.
Genius	Talent selection and evaluation	The public may hugely underestimate geniuses who may also have little clue as to what they are capable of.	What if Mao Sui did not recommend himself? Few minds could understand Einstein's ideas at first. What if he were modest?
Thesis statement: In a culture where one is educated to keep a low profile, humility is most likely overrated because it makes a celebrity easily misinterpreted as a hypocrite, a participant shackled with fewer strategies to use in a competition, and a talent less likely to be scouted and his work harder to be acknowledged.			

Your outline:

_____ : An Overrated Virtue			
Who	Where/When	Reason/Result	Evidence

(continued)

Who	Where/When	Reason/Result	Evidence

Your thesis statement:

⸻

- **Writing Your First Draft**

    Develop your outline into a 500-word first draft.

In-class Activities

▶ What Is Cause-and-effect Writing?

In the popular puzzle game *Angry Birds*, you start by placing a bird on the slingshot, take a careful aim, pull the strings back, and fire it off. Then the bird, tailed by a white long-dotted line, soars into the air, flutters across the sky, and plummets toward the target, until it thumps against the wooden structure. The collapse of buildings. The screeches of pigs. The retrieval of eggs. A winner is born! In fact, with the same bird, the same firing power, the same shooting angle, you will see the same trajectory, get the same pig killed and retrieve the same eggs anytime you wish. This is cause and effect, the shooting being the cause and the victory the result.

Cause-and-effect is a method of paragraph or essay development that analyzes the reasons for — and/or the results of — an action, event, or decision. In cause-and-effect writing, "cause" is something that brings about a result while "effect" inevitably follows

Unit 4 Cause and Effect

an antecedent. That is why it is sometimes referred to as reason-and-result writing.

But in a sentence, use "effect" as a noun to mean "consequence, outcome or result", and "affect" as a verb to mean "have an influence on", or "have an effect on".

▶ Why Do You Write a Cause-and-effect Essay?

Amusing as those angry birds are, cause-and-effect writing is a serious, painstaking process not only because of its popularity in examinations like TOEFL, IELTS and GRE, but because a main goal of research is to identify that a particular independent variable influences the dependent variable of interest. Therefore, cause-and-effect writing aims at a clear understanding of connections between events, actions, or conditions. Although this type of writing is not exclusively used to address an issue, it often includes a proposal to solve a problem at the end of an essay.

• Activity 1

In the following exercises, you are going to identify causes and effects.

1. Fill in the blanks in the following summary of the essay "Sincerity: An Overrated Virtue."

In the article, "Sincerity: An Overrated Virtue" printed in the September 1997 issue of *Skeptical Briefs*, Lewis Jones centers on negative _____ of sincerity and his belief that acting on sincerity alone cannot justify malpractice. He starts the article by reporting that _____ often go unnoticed and unpunished because sincerity is cunningly and shamelessly exploited. He then cites E. Haldeman-Julius to illustrate how ill-intended, passionately-abused _____ has harmed heretics. He goes on to demonstrate that the harm can extend from a sick child to all trades and professions, because "naked sincerity" has surpassed the need for _____ and has taken the place of _____. He then cites sources to argue that the difference between a _____ and a respectable thinker lies in whether one acts on sincerity alone. He further constructs a scenario in which an airplane is about to be _____ by an enthusiastic but inexperienced passenger. He _____ by proposing that no one is supposed to use sincerity as an excuse to walk away from a groundless assertion delivered at will.

2. Read the following paragraph and answer the questions.

When a solar-powered water pump was provided for a well in India, the village headman took it over and sold the water, until stopped. The new liquid abundance attracted unwanted nomads. Village boys who had drawn water in buckets had nothing to do, and some became criminals. The gap between rich and poor widened

101

since the poor had no land to benefit from irrigation. Finally, Indian village women broke the pump, so they could gather again around center of their social lives.

(1) Can this paragraph be used to support that charity is an overrated virtue?

_____

(2) The effects of a solar-powered water pump do NOT include _____.

A. the sales of the well water   B. the arrival of unwanted nomads

C. boys' stealing well water   D. the widened gap between rich and poor

(3) Why is the paragraph coherent although only one transitional word is used?

_____

3. Discuss in pairs for a list of causes of the given phenomenon and write them down in key words.

In *mukbang*, or "eating broadcasts", millions watch a stranger swallow food. This is because of _____.

_____

_____

4. Discuss in pairs for a list of causes of the given phenomenon and write them down in clauses.

Millions of Chinese medical workers, hospital builders, community volunteers battled in the frontline to contain the COVID-19 epidemic. This is because _____.

_____

_____

_____

_____

▶ For Whom Do You Write?

To make your proposal twice effective, it is necessary to consider prior knowledge and major concerns of your audience, just as Stephen Keague, author of *The Little*

Unit 4 Cause and Effect

Red Handbook of Public Speaking and Presenting, once said, "Proper planning and preparation prevent poor performance."

Here is an example. Rather concerned with your child's school lunch, you decide to address the issue in a formal letter to authorities. You first point out to the Board of Directors the cause of your discontent — students do not take in sufficient protein, vitamins and minerals owing to the miscalculation of nutrients in lunch recipes. You go on to note that this is likely to undermine concentration of students and undercut their research capability. You then demonstrate to the Parent Committee the negligence of caterers in that beverages and meat have been repeatedly reported stale. You warn them of an imminent outbreak of diarrhea, hepatitis, and botulism as a result of an ill-managed cafeteria. You then make a pledge that you will not rat it on to the local media if they take precautions. You conclude with a proposal of a tightened inspection and an immediate dismissal of a few managers. Then rest assured. No one cares productivity more than school administrators. No one cares children's health more than parents. Their remedy will soon live up to your consideration.

To sum up, carefully selected messages delivered to target readers with a keen awareness of their concerns can maximize the effect of your writing.

▶ *Which One Do You Focus On?*

The complaint letter exemplifies one typical writing pattern: an introduction to a problem, examination on causes, description of effects and a proposal of solution. All in one. This is common, as the relation of cause to effect is often too close to be considered independently of the other.

However, a writer can also focus on either of them, depending on the purpose. Take researching the causes of a devastating fire as an example. A police officer may size up the situation and assess whether it is arson, negligence or a pure accident. A retired firefighter, however, may attribute the big fire to the aging firefighting pipes, insufficient manpower and absence of a contingency plan, pointing fingers at the director of fire department. An anti-smoking activist, however, may jump at the opportunity to publicize the harm of smoking, which he believes to be "definitely" a culprit. Whatever they intend to do, causes are important and thus emphasized. In contrast, a short paragraph, emphasizing effects, may appear on the blackboard of a kindergarten classroom where a teacher kindly responds to curious kids — if people do not stop at red lights, they are likely to be bumped off by speeding cars, busted by the police or haunted with a guilty conscience.

All in all, your purpose of writing determines the focus on causes, effects or both. In the following exam prompts for cause-and-effect writing, some topic suggestions emphasize causes while others highlight effects.

Topics emphasizing causes	Topics emphasizing effects
• Causes of Sibling Rivalry • Why College Mathematics Is So Difficult • Why Adults Enjoy Halloween More than Kids	• Effects of "Winners Take It All" • Effects of Information Cocoons • Effects of Labels on Students

• Activity 2

Your purpose of writing determines the focus on causes, effects or both. In the following exercises, put yourselves in the shoes of the readers, consider the information gap, their major interests and concerns.

1. Suppose you are part of a team dispatched to a key high school shortly after the National College Entrance Examination with a mission to encourage straight-A students to apply for your university. In the brochure, you first inform them of a new municipal policy that Hukou will be offered to graduates from four elite universities located in Shanghai, including yours. Then among the effects, which TWO should stay out of your brochure? Why?

A. Increased competitiveness of Shanghai.

B. Drain of talents from second-tier cities.

C. Configuration of China's human capital.

D. Honor and welfare that students may enjoy.

E. Loneliness of parents as empty nesters.

_____

_____

2. In your brochure, in which order are you going to arrange the effects? Why?

_____

_____

_____

Unit 4 Cause and Effect

3. Read the following paragraph and answer the questions.

Regarded as an element of success by Bill Gates, patience has long been accredited as a virtue, often preached to children, who are expected to accept that things happen in a different order, at a different rate than what they have in their mind. It is true that patience plays a role in child-rearing and courting a loved one; however, it can also be an idler's lame excuse, a talent's worst nightmare, and a manipulator's most valued tool.

(1) Write down some other scenarios in which patience plays a good part.

___

(2) Why are the merits of patience included?

___

___

(3) Is it necessary to add "as far as I am concerned" or "in my opinion" in the thesis statement?

___

___

How Do You Structure Cause-and-effect Writing?

▶ Use the phenomenon–cause/effect–proposal pattern

A clear structure guides a reader out of a maze of inferences and a mountain of statistics. Typically, cause-and-effect writing starts with a phenomenon, or most often, a problem. It is then followed by detailed demonstration of causes and/or effects and ends up in speculation about how to solve the dilemma.

To illustrate, let us wind the clock back to the first time when you read the article "Sincerity: An Overrated Virtue". You must be impressed by the exquisitely designed structure. Lewis Jones starts his essay with a phenomenon that people often let frauds go unpunished before presenting the claim that he is "concerned with the way in which 'sincerity' is being used as an excuse for malpractice". Then the effects are illustrated. The burning of heretics. The exile of Voltaire. A girl of a ruptured spleen "is dead in a day". What underlies these tragedies, imaginary or real, is the main cause: science being replaced by a sincere yet groundless belief.

Then the return of the effects. Distrust for all trades and professions. Danger of letting a greenhand pilot a plane. In the end, he proposes that politicians ought to be guilty of making speculative claims.

The well-structured article is well worth a second reading, through which you can learn how the effect-cause-effect shift flows as seamlessly as running water.

▶ Use the chain or block structure

To craft a body part that a reader can breeze through, a writer is advised to organize either in a block or chain structure. In the **block structure**, all causes are stated first before all effects debut. This organization is often found in shorter essays and enjoys the merit of a clearer structure.

A **chain structure**, on the other hand, ensures that any effect a writer presents relates directly to the cause he has given. In this structure, packed together is a bundle of a cause and its effect. Does the complaint letter to school authorities still ring a bell? Irresponsible caterers miscalculate the nutrients to cause malnutrition of students whose academic capacity are soon to be curbed. Cause-effect. Furthermore, their health is being threatened due to an ill-managed cafeteria that serves expired milk and tainted meat, which sooner or later, will trigger food poisoning on campus. Cause-effect.

Block structure	Chain structure
Cause 1 Cause 2 Cause 3 Transition sentence or paragraph Effect 1 Effect 2 Effect 3	Cause 1 & Effect of Cause 1 Cause 2 & Effect of Cause 2 Cause 3 & Effect of Cause 3

Either structure a writer sees fit, causes and effects should be presented in consistency with the plan of development in the thesis statement, with the same content and in the same order.

▶ Use categorization

Block or chain, the body paragraphs can still be finetuned. Just like a carpenter's chisel to wood, categorization of causes and/or effects can help readers better

Unit 4 Cause and Effect

sketch relationships of paragraphs. In addition, if skillfully used, it punches more credibility and memorability to the writing.

A writer may classify according to how important a cause or an effect is, and thus applies the emphatic order. One typical way is to start with the main cause or the primary effect. Readers thus can make better judgments about the worth of causes or effects, just in the same way triage is routinely practiced in hospitals, where dozens of patients are sorted according to three tiers of injury: serious, moderate and light, with serious patients receiving care first.

Alternatively, a writer may classify the causes and effects according to a certain criterion such as time, group, gender, location, or subject. For example, he may first discuss the proximate causes of China's modernization and then the ultimate one. Or he can predict the impacts of deglobalization in such aspects as economy, diplomacy, and culture.

Discipline	Time	Visibility	Range
• economically speaking • culturally speaking	• long-term • short-term	• physical • psychological	• individual • community

• Activity 3

To craft a body part that a reader can breeze through, a writer is advised to organize either in a block or chain structure with categorization. Now finish the following exercises and try to structure cause-and-effect writing.

1. Note the structure of the article and the function of each part. Fill in each blank with a word.

Topic	The Increase of Women in Workplace
Structure	_____
Main idea	Women's liberation and feminism have meant that the precious situation has been transformed and in contemporary society women are playing an almost equal role to men in terms of work. This has had significant consequences, both in terms of the family, for example by improving quality of life and increasing children's sense of independence, and also for society itself with greater gender equality.

(continued)

Topic	The Increase of Women in Workplace
_____	The reasons behind the increase of women in workplace are women's liberation and feminism. ...
_____ paragraph	They have brought huge changes, both to family life and to society as a whole.
Categorized _____	• A woman can make a significant contribution to the family income. ... • Another effect on the family is more independence in children. ... • In terms of society, the most remarkable impact is greater gender equality. ...
Summary	In conclusion, the increasing number of women at work has brought about some important changes to family life, including improved quality of life and increased independence for children, as well as affecting the society itself. ...

2. Note the consistency between the thesis and paragraphs. Fill in each blank with a word.

Topic	Teen Obesity
Thesis statement	In today's world, unhealthy diets and _____ pursuits have led to teen obesity, which is not only a threat to the health of individuals but a burden for national health services.
Cause 1	Firstly, a person gains weight if his diet is rich in salt, sugar and fat. ...
Cause 2	When imbalanced _____ meet sedentary pursuits, obesity follows inevitably. ...
Transition paragraph	_____, obesity easily develops into health problems for individuals and creates heavy burden for medical system.
Effect 1	For _____, chronic diseases, traditionally correlated with a much older population, are increasingly common in teenagers, mainly in the form of diabetes and hypertension. ...
Effect 2	For _____ health services, the cost of treatment has surged as recently as 15 to 20 years, as hospitals are seeing an increased demand to care for obese patients, which further causes a drain of national fiscal fund. ...
Suggestion	For less _____ obesity, individuals should be better-informed of nutrition, and encouraged to engage in more outdoor activities. ...

Unit 4 Cause and Effect

3. In the article, "The Asian Advantage", Nicholas Kcristof makes a list of uncategorized reasons why Asian-Americans succeed in school education. Reorganize them by belief and effort.

Belief: _____   Effort: _____

A. East Asia's long Confucian emphasis on education.

B. Getting kids into good school districts and making sacrifices.

C. Belief in hard work and no acceptance for A-.

D. Expectation from teachers.

E. Stereotype Promise from others.

F. Individuals' efforts to break the bamboo ceiling.

Steer Clear of Logical Fallacies in Paragraph Development

▸ Slippery slope

Lectures concerning cause-and-effect are often heard, not only in university auditoriums, but in families where parents preach at pre-school kids that good marks will qualify them for a distinct primary school, then a key high school, and eventually an elite university, where, upon graduation, decent job offers will come in handy, a proper marriage will be awaiting, and a life-long journey of happiness is ready to embark on. Otherwise, one might end up living alone on a poorly-paid job in a rented basement for his whole life.

Well-intentioned as the preach is, what underlies the monotonous monologue is an errant application of essentialism that boils down academic, career and marital successes to a single factor – marks. What is worse, there is also a logical fallacy in which all inferences are based on possible results rather than established facts. This error, often referred to as **slippery slope**, or the **domino fallacy**, means that the initial step taken is a precursor to a chain of events that eventually lead to undesirable or disastrous results.

The slippery slope is a fallacy, says Jacob E. Van Fleet, "precisely because we can never know if a whole series of events and/or a certain result is determined to follow one event or action in particular. Usually, but not always, the slippery slope argument is used as a fear tactic." To illustrate, in the lecture to kids, parents mistake a **necessary or contributary cause** for a **sufficient cause**, and reduce other possibilities into one speculation which is later used as the cause to the next effect.

It easily ruins the credibility and often backfires.

To stay away from the slope, one has to realize that there can be multiple causes for a single effect and multiple effects for a single cause. For instance, the increase in pork prices may result from growing global population, a shift to a meat diet, and shrinking agricultural workforce, all of which have **long-term effects** on supply and demand, but none should be held responsible for a sudden surge of prices in a week or two.

Similarly, the increased pork prices may give rise to a drastic fall in domestic pork consumption and a temporary price control. Both of these **short-term effects** are predictable, but one can't go so far as to rule out other possibilities and take it for granted that the amount of imported pork is bound to be up. Such a far and wild inference makes little sense, because other factors may play a part. For example, a tightened inspection on the package for coronavirus may cause huge delay in shipping, disrupt the supply chains and eventually affect the amount of import.

Looking back, one can easily trace along the footprints of an occurrence and rationalize the inevitability; however, looking ahead, discretion is highly necessary in a world so intricated, interlinked and interacted. Therefore, it is essential to give a second thought to the **main cause** or the **primary effect**.

▸ Post hoc

Just as damaging as the previous one, **post hoc** is another trap that a careless writer easily walks into. Condensed from "post hoc, ergo propter hoc," which literally means "after this, therefore because of this", it is a fallacy in which one event is said to be the cause of a later incident simply because the event occurred earlier.

This fallacy is best exemplified with the discourtesy of a legendary football superstar, Pelé, who retrieved a jersey that he gave away to a fan of his, because he stubbornly matched his "no goal" in the next several games with the giving of that gift. Why did the reasoning go in the wrong direction? It is because **causality** involves more than sequence. It should be able to explain why something happened and predict what might happen again.

Nonetheless, Pelé isn't the only victim to the faulty causality. The long search for the cause of malaria was fraught with post hoc fallacies, too. Stuart Chase notes in *Guides to Straight Thinking* that night air was first assumed to be the cause of malaria, because people who went out at night often got caught with the disease. However, experiments eventually proved that malaria was a result of bites of mosquitoes that often attack in the dark.

Underlying the misjudgment is an upgraded version of **post hoc**, in which sequence, compounded by correlation, makes the trap even more inconspicuous. Look at the beautiful correlation in the chart below. How absurd it is to conclude that just because a person ate more cheese, he would be more likely to die of a bed sheet!

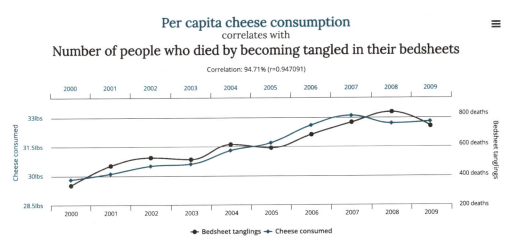

The same pattern can be discovered in the case of malaria — the number of people who took night tours correlated with the number of infection. One can use the correlation to make an informed decision: stay indoors. But doing so does not make going out a cause. As a matter of fact, correlations are everywhere. The number of lighters, for example, correlates with how frequently its owner coughs, but it is not the lighter but lighting a cigarette that contributes to a subsequent cough.

Part of the reason why people constantly fall into such a trap is that humans are evolutionarily predisposed to see patterns and psychologically prone to gather information that supports pre-existing views, a trait known as **confirmation bias**.

Therefore, a decent writer tries hard not to confuse correlation with causality. It is true that cause-and-effect writing, like narration, links situations and events together in time, with causes preceding effects. But on the other hand, the most obvious correlation may not be the main cause and sometimes not even a cause at all.

In conclusion, when a factor linked to an effect is identified, the job of a responsible writer planning cause-and-effect paragraph is to take a close examination on whether it is a cause, and then reason with discretion whether it is the main cause. That is also why cause-and-effect writing needs the support of abundant evidence, plentiful explanation and delicate connection.

• **Activity 4**

Read the following table and match each paragraph with a logical fallacy.

Paragraphs	Fallacies
1. Tong Xiangyu, a female character of *My Own Swordsman*, often makes such complaint. "I had been wrong since the beginning. If I had not married my husband, he would not have died. If he had not died, I would not have ended up here. …"	A. Correlation is causality.
2. In 1974, Massachusetts passed the Bartley-Fox Law, which requires a special license to carry a handgun outside the home. Studies by Glenn Pierce and William Bowers of Northeastern University documented that after the law was passed, handgun homicides in Massachusetts fell 50% and the number of armed robberies dropped 35%. This is why we should outlaw gun carrying in public.	B. Slippery slope.
3. In the U.S., violent crime rose in 2005 and 2006, just as America's streets filled with millions of people visibly wearing, and being distracted by, expensive electronic gear. Therefore, the rise in violent offending and the explosion in the sales of iPods and other portable media devices is more than coincidental.	C. Post hoc.

Keeping the Causal Chain Complete in Paragraph Development

Back to the case of malaria, the tragic death of the victims can be traced back from high fevers and shaking chills, then a bite of mosquitoes that feed on humans, till in the end, the malaria parasite living inside a mosquito. This route of how malaria is transmitted showcases the concept of a **causal chain**, a path of influence running from one end to the other. A **root cause**, as in the parasite, stays at the farthest end from effects. The one that is closest to effects is an **immediate cause**, or a **proximate cause**, as in fevers and chills that torture the infected to death. The link in-between is a bite of a mosquito, known as the **intermediate cause**. Likewise, the **immediate effect**, and the **ultimate effect** can be observed in cause-and-effect writing, too.

If one intermediate link is omitted or misplaced, readers will cast doubt on the validity of the chain. To avoid jumping to a conclusion, a good writer is expected

Unit 4 Cause and Effect

to fully develop all important links along the timeline. In the following example, drinking alcohol is linked through ADH and dried cells to the symptoms of a hangover in chronological order.

> Drinking alcohol turns off your ADH, which is designed to stop your urinating. Then your body passes all the liquid you drink right through. Your cells slowly dry up, particularly your brain cells, as the night wears on. In the morning, you have a headache, and a dry mouth, which are caused by thirsty cells: a hangover.

Therefore, keep the chain complete, and the emphasis on causal connections.

• Activity 5

The demonstration of a causal chain will be much easier for a reader to understand if all important links in the chain are fully developed. Finish the following exercises and try to keep the causal chain complete.

1. Identify the causal chain, make an educated guess and fill in the blanks.

For over twenty years, from the 1960s to the 1980s, the college board scores of high school seniors steadily declined. This decline began soon after television became popular, and therefore many people concluded that the two events were connected. The idea is plausible because children did seem to be reading less in order to watch television more and because _____ is one of the chief skills the tests evaluate.

2. Read the following paragraph and answer the questions.

To get to see your whales, you have to travel, by car, coach or plane. Each time you do so you're effectively setting fire to a small reservoir of gasoline — and releasing several roomfuls of carbon dioxide into the atmosphere. Leisure travel accounts for half of all transport; and Americans are responsible for giving off more than five tons of carbon each into the atmosphere every year. That's nearly 107.4 times the rate of the stay-at-home Bangladeshis. The cumulative result of such activity is one of the biggest disruptions in the Earth's history — global warming, climate change and rising seas.

(1) Which writing skill is NOT used in the paragraph? _____
A. Exemplification. B. Comparison.
C. Classification. D. Cause-and-effect.

(2) What is the causal chain in the paragraph?

_____

3. Complete the intermediate links in the causal chain.

A. aging society → _____ → _____ → more pet stores

B. city expansion → _____ → _____ → people's loneliness

4. Compare the sentences that both illustrate the claim that "excessive meat consumption leads to pollution". Are they jumping to conclusions? Which writing is better? Why?

[A] Fueled by excessive demand for meat, the rise in livestock production has led to the growing demand for grain, fertilizer, and herbicide, all of which require more energy in manufacturing. During the process, large amounts of toxic gases are released. That is why excessive meat consumption is one of the culprits of air pollution.

[B] Excessive meat consumption means more production of pigs, ducks, and chickens whose feces, if improperly disposed, bring about pollution to land and water.

_____

_____

_____

▶ How Do you Bind Cause-and-effect Elements?

▸ Use causal conjunctions

Once a causal chain and supportive evidence set, it is time for causal conjunctions to play. They are responsible for gluing the scattered pieces into a whole. Among them are the famous four: because, since, as, and for.

Among them, "because" indicates the strongest causal relationship, and is a conjunction that gets the most use. For example, as for reasons why China's 9-9-6 work culture makes sense, Rebecca Fannin responds in a paralleled structure, "because the tech economy is growing too fast, the competition is too brutal, and the opportunities are too vast in China to take a laid-back approach".

Carrying a strong causality as well, the word "since", however, is often a trigger

Unit 4 Cause and Effect

of heated debates among lexicographers, as in the sentence "Since Reagan became president, the Soviets have come to the bargaining table." Ed Good humorously explains and suggests:

> If you're a Republican, you'll read "since" to mean "because". If you're a Democrat, you'll read "since" to mean "after". Thus, if you mean "because" and want to avoid the possible ambiguity, then use "because", not "since".

The same ambiguity is also embedded in a rather formal word, "as", which has more usual meaning "while". Unlike the three conjunctions mentioned above, "for" is a **coordinating conjunction**, often used to join two elements of equal grammatical rank and syntactic importance. Therefore, it does not often show up in a thesis statement where the claim stays in the main clause, followed by subordinate clauses of less important ideas.

In an article "Which Conjunction Should You Use to Show Cause?", Merriam-Webster experts cleverly advise:

> "Since", as a causal conjunction, is sometimes preferable when you want the cause to be less directly linked to the effect. "As" will garner more criticism if you use it as a causal conjunction, but if you need the formality of "as", make sure that the sentence can't be misconstrued at all by substituting in both "because" and "while" in your sentence. When in doubt, you can always default to "because", since no one finds fault with it.

In conclusion, you might consider yourself a director of a musical. Think of "because" as a leading singer, and she rightfully gets her attention. It matters little to turn a blind eye to the glee of the three: since, as, and for.

▸ **Use other causal expressions**

Despite what mentioned above, do not make the understudies sit on the bench for too long, because an overuse of "because" makes audience bored. Give other causal expressions a shot from time to time. They might as well play a nice role, just as the following underlined ones do.

- Compared with dramatic rise of college tuition in America, the remarkably lower growth rate in Chinese tuition fees can be attributed to an emphasis on equal learning opportunities, and multi-sourced supports from the society.

- She starts with an account of a pleasant trip to a vast lake where she went water-skiing alone, <u>so</u> thrilled at the splendid view <u>as to</u> speed a motorboat away from her company, deep into the lake.
- To start with, the problem is claimed to <u>result from</u> mismanagement and greed of administrators, who counter that evaluation effective for profit-making enterprises does not apply to higher education and that the rise <u>comes from</u> growing academic salaries, boom in technology and higher proportion of student aid.

In the following table, X is used to indicate a cause, while Y the effect.

Verbs and verbal phrases	
(X) adversely affects (Y) (X) impacts (Y) (X) influences (Y) (X) leads to (Y) (X) brings about (Y) (X) gives rise to (Y) (X) is responsible for (Y) (X) causes (Y) (X) results **in** (Y) (X) **contributes to** (Y)	(Y) derives from (X) (Y) originates in (X) (Y) springs from (X) (Y) flows from (X) (Y) arises from (X) (Y) stems from (X) (Y) is related to (X) (Y) is caused by (X) (Y) results **from** (X) (Y) **can be attributed to** (X)
Other transitions	
Because of (X), Due to (X), Owing to (X), Thanks to (X), On account of (X), On the ground of (X), For one thing, ... For another, ... (X) has effects on (Y) (X) has an influence on (Y) (X) has an impact on (Y) (X) is a leading cause of (Y) (X) is the primary reason why (Y)	Therefore, (Y) Thus, (Y) Hence, (Y) Accordingly, (Y) Consequently, (Y) As a result, (Y) As a consequence, (Y) For this reason, (Y) The primary effect is (Y) (Y) is a result of (X) (Y) often occurs as a consequence of (X) The main reason why (Y) is that (X)

▶ **Use other connectors**

Apart from the solo of "because" and the chorus of causal expressions, other connectors can contribute in the background. Just as musical notes can be grouped

Unit 4 Cause and Effect

into a chord, causal sentences, too, can be put together for coherence. This can be done when a writer uses repeated words, pronouns, and synonyms.

> When our class was assigned to **Mr. Fleagle** for third-year English, I anticipated another cheerless year in that most tedious of subjects. **Mr. Fleagle** had a reputation among students for dullness and inability to inspire. **He** was said to be very formal, rigid and hopelessly out of date. To me he looked to be sixty or seventy and excessively prim. **He** wore primly severe eyeglasses, **his** wavy hair was primly cut and primly combed. **He** wore prim suits with neckties set primly against the collar buttons of his white shirts. **He** had a primly pointed jaw, a primly straight nose, and a prim manner of speaking that was so correct, so gentlemanly, that **he** seemed a comic antique.

In the excerpt from *Writing for Myself*, Russel Baker skillfully sketches out an old-fashioned teacher with just a few lines. The repetitive use of "Mr. Fleagle" and "he" puts the old man under the spotlight from beginning to end. No wonder his class is "cheerless, tedious, dull, and uninspiring", because synonyms such as "formal, rigid, and out-of-date", echo beautifully with "correct and gentlemanly", not to mention the eye-catching repetition of the word "prim". In the end, a life-like portrait of a comic antique is pieced together by these connectors.

Note in the following paragraph how repeated words and synonyms tightly lock the logic flow and produce the continuity of a causal chain that impresses readers.

> Beginning in 1946, as American soldiers returned home, the United States birth rate began to rise dramatically. As the numbers of births increased, the creation of goods and services designed to meet the needs of this growing new population also increased. As **advertisers** competed to attract this group's attention to these products, the so-called "baby boom generation" became more and more **visible**. Consequently, baby boomers were perceived as more and more powerful — as voters as well as **consumers**. As a result, this group's emergence has been a major factor in shaping American political, social, cultural, and **economic** life.

• Activity 6

Finish the following exercises and pay attention to various connectors in cause-and-effect writing.

1. Fill in the blanks with causal expressions from the table.

cause	consequences	result	result in
resulting from	contributes to	attribute ... to	

(1) Is personality the _____ of conditioning from parents and society, or are we born with it?

(2) Greed has been cited as a major _____ for the dramatic rise of corruption.

(3) The _____ are so severe that teeth decay much faster than they are supposed to.

(4) Little exercise primarily _____ _____ child obesity, and adult obesity can be largely attributed to slower metabolic rate and consumption of sugar, both of which further _____ _____ a host of problems.

(5) Two major factors lead to devastating summer flooding along the Yangtze River. First, erosion _____ _____ deforestation in the upper reaches of the river and, second, heavy silting which raises the riverbed in the main channel.

(6) The explanation for the rising teenage suicide rate involves complicated factors. Some _____ it _____ an overemphasis on early success, others point it to mounting peer pressure, and still others to confusion over changing social values.

2. Fill in the blanks with conjunctions and prepositions. The first letter has been given.

Filial piety is an overrated virtue, b_____ it easily brings disappointment to parents and distress to children. The tragedy usually starts w_____ anyone's awareness. I_____ the name of love and deference, some parents first pry i_____ children's private affairs, then meddle w_____ their life choices, take further charge u_____ they get to dominate children's decision-making, s_____ as which university to apply for, which job offer to turn down, and which person to have a date with. Meanwhile, obedient children respectfully give in t_____ their authoritarian parents, afraid to react or rebel. S_____ parental interference replaces children's motivation and accountability w_____ compliance and low desire, it is just a matter of time b_____ the dislocation of roles backfires. Regretfully, what begins a_____ moral excellence often ends u_____ in disappointed parents and painful children.

3. Read the following paragraphs and answer the questions.

[A] Many of today's kids are engaged in sedentary pursuits made possible by a level

Unit 4 Cause and Effect

of technology unthinkable as recently as 25 to 30 years ago. Computer, video, and other virtual games, the availability of feature films and games on DVD, plus high-tech advancements in music-listening technology have come down into the range of affordability for parents and even for the kids themselves. These passive pursuits have produced a downside of reduced physical activity for the kids, often with the explicit or implicit consent of the parents.

[B] Other fairly recent developments have also contributed to the alarming rise in child obesity rates. Fast food outlets offering consumables that are both low in price and low in nutritional content have exploded all over the American landscape since the 1960s, especially in suburban areas close to major highway interchanges. Kids on their lunch breaks or after school often congregate in these fast food outlets, consuming food and soft drinks that are high in sugar, carbohydrates, and fat. Many parents, themselves, frequently take their children to these fast food places, thus setting an example the kids can find justification to emulate.

(1) Which words are repeatedly used in Paragraph A for better coherence?

_____

(2) Which words are used to connect the two paragraphs?

_____

(3) Which words in Paragraph B correspond with the underlined expression?

_____

● Activity 7

Do you usually take a walk? Do you think that being inside means being uncreative? Read the passage for more insight.

Your Brain Was Made for Walking:
Creative inspiration is only a short stroll away

Jeffrey Davis

[1] If a president, a legendary philosopher, and one of the bestselling authors of all time credited the same secret for their success, would you try to follow it too? In fact, you probably do it every day. Here's what Friedrich Nietzsche wrote:

"It is only ideas gained from walking that have any worth." Thomas Jefferson: "Walking is the best possible exercise. Habituate yourself to walk very far." And Charles Dickens made his point with uncharacteristic brevity: "If I could not walk far and fast, I think I should just explode and perish."

[2] Are you still sitting there reading this? Get walking! It's not just these three great minds who made a case for it as a prime creativity booster. Researchers have traced numerous connections between walking and generating ideas. A Stanford University study found that participants were 81 percent more creative when walking as opposed to sitting. Another famous-person example: As part of his daily writing routine, Kurt Vonnegut would take a midmorning break from his office to walk and then swim before eventually returning to work. I would argue that this habit wasn't just a habit but an intentional, necessary element of his creative process.

[3] The movement aspect of walking is obviously key. You've probably heard the phrase "exercise your creativity", which refers to the brain as muscle. Our creative mindset is triggered by physical movement, which is exactly why walking — with your dog, a friend, or alone — feeds creative thinking.

[4] But the scenery is almost as important as the sweat. The National Human Activity Pattern Survey reveals that Americans spend 87 percent of their time indoors. Being inside, you're more prone to stagnation, the antithesis of energy. Without energy, you can't wonder or create. Disrupting your routine with a walk can be a catalyst for garnering fresh insights into problems or projects. Just by going outside, you are stepping out of your habitual surroundings and your comfort zone, which is necessary if you want to open your mind to new possibilities. You can walk through a tree-filled neighborhood. You can walk through a park and observe people sauntering or birds singing. Even when you walk down a busy street, you can't help but get distracted by the sweet cinnamon smells wafting from a food cart or the child pointing to a building you hadn't even noticed before.

[5] Our brains work harder to process in different environments, so walking outside fosters our ability to glean new ideas, to take in new sights, sounds, smells, and flavors. *Shinrin-yoku*, or "forest bathing", is a common form of relaxation and medicine in Japan. It was developed in 1982, and recent studies demonstrate that being in the forest and walking among the trees lowers your

Unit 4 Cause and Effect

stress levels. The effects are so powerful that *shinrin-yoku* is now a government-endorsed policy in Japan. But you don't have to live near a forest to receive the psychological benefits. Research has shown that immersion in nature, and the corresponding disconnection from multimedia and technology, increased performance on a creative problem-solving task by a full 50 percent in a group of hikers.

[6] So instead of setting a fitness goal, why not set a creativity goal that starts with walking? Engage more closely with your surroundings for the next four weeks. Turn off your phone and give yourself the chance to be present in the world, to hear conversations and natural sounds, to notice the way people move, the way the sun reflects in a puddle. Walk not just for exercise. Walk for wonder.

(Reader's Digest, 2020)

1. Fill in the blanks in the outline. The first letter has been given.

The passage is written in b____ structure. The writer starts the essay by citing q____ from three great minds, and then lists the reasons why walking b____ creativity as follows:

(1) Researchers have t____ numerous connections between walking and generating ideas.

(2) The movement during walking stimulates our brain to generate creative ideas.

(3) The scenery along walking can be a c____ for our brain to garner fresh insights.

(4) Our brains work harder to process in different environments.

In the body part, the sentence "but the scenery is almost as important as the s____" serves as a t____. He ends the passage with a p____ for walking.

2. What evidence is given in each part to support the claim? Fill in each blank with one word or one number.

Categories	Evidence
Great minds	• A president: Thomas _____ • A legendary philosopher: Friedrich _____ • One of the bestselling authors: Charles _____
Physical _____	• A Stanford University study found that participants were _____ percent more creative when walking as opposed to sitting. • Kurt Vonnegut would take a _____ break from his office to walk and then swim before eventually returning to work.

(continued)

121

Categories	Evidence
_____ benefits	• The National Human Activity Pattern Survey reveals that Americans spend _____ percent of their time indoors. • As a government-endorsed policy in Japan, *shinrin-yoku*, or "forest _____", was confirmed to be able to lower your stress levels. • Research has shown that immersion in nature, and the corresponding disconnection from multimedia and technology, increased creativity by a full _____ percent in a group of hikers.

3. "It is only ideas gained from walking that have any worth." Do you agree with the statement? Will you change your mind if you know Friedrich Nietzsche said so? What if you are a fan of his?

_____

_____

_____

_____

_____

_____

4. "Researchers have traced numerous connections between walking and generating ideas." Is it causality or correlation between walking and generating ideas?

_____

5. Does the writer give specific instructions about walking? What can be included?

_____

_____

• Vocabulary Highlights

Study the words and phrases below with the help of a dictionary. Write down the definitions.

credit _____

Unit 4 Cause and Effect

brevity	
make a case for	
booster	
intentional	
trigger	
be prone to	
stagnation	
antithesis	
catalyst	
garner	
glean	
endorse	
immersion	

Below is a rebuttal essay written by a student. Read and see how rebuttal is done.

Being Inside Is Being Creative

[1] In the article "Your Brain Was Made For Walking: Creative Inspiration Is Only a Short Stroll Away", Jeffrey Davis writes that "Being inside, you're more prone to stagnation, the antithesis of energy. Without energy, you can't wonder or create". He seems to suggest a causal chain that links being inside to being

uncreative. That sounds plausible at first glance; however, I insist that staying indoors stands opposite to stagnation; rather, human beings are prone to being inquisitive and exploratory, whether indoors or outdoors, and that ordinary people create history in their ways.

[2] For starters, a great many minds are not trapped in stagnation when they think, write and create indoors. For example, curled up on a sofa, Sherlock Holmes does hours' pipe-smoking for a new lead, still and speechless, in his head and in the living room. What's more, Thomas Jefferson drafted the Declaration of Independence in a rented room in the home of a Philadelphia bricklayer, where he efficiently finished his jobs in under three weeks, in addition to three drafts of the Virginia Constitution, committee reports, and a position paper. The great names in the list of indoor wonders extend to superwomen as well. Emily Dickinson, a great American lyric poet of nearly 1,800 poems, spent a considerable part of her adult life in what people call self-imposed confinement, rarely venturing outside the family in Amherst. Similarly, Nobel Prize Winner Tu Youyou created a cure for malaria in a secret military program, known as "Mission 523".

[3] Following the footsteps of these titans, the less known make miracles indoors as well. The inspirational stories of garage wonders in Silicon Valley surely ring a bell. Besides, Taylor Wilson, at 14, became the youngest person to achieve fusion — with a reactor born in the family backyard. Another teenager, Sara Volz, at 17, set up a groundbreaking algae biofuel lab under the bed in her home and won the Intel Science Talent Search with a $100,000 award. These geeks have made a case for the point: what matters indeed is not where they are but what they are determined to do.

[4] How about the less talented? Well, ordinary people are not trapped in stagnation, either. It is true that they spend 87% of time indoors; rather, they do not sit idle. They sit exams. They do interviews. They run simulations. Office hours. Staff meetings. Television debating. Video Conferencing. Brainstorming. You name it. Diligent students crowd on library benches and burn the midnight oil against ticking clocks. Chefs pore over online cuisine videos, after a day's smell and sweat in ill-equipped kitchens, as noisy as bar, as hot as oven, and as messy as a schoolboy's answer sheet. Abroad, over 1,000 minds in *Deep Mind* still toil ahead in front of computers despite a decisive victory with AlphaGo

Unit 4 Cause and Effect

that dethroned humans five years earlier. At home, engineers in cubicles risk ending up in an ICU but hold on to the 9-9-6 work schedule.

[5] As a result, every spark of inspiration, every birth of a new idea, and every jigsaw of a blueprint, pieced together, amount to huge torrents of creation that allow us to "see" gravitational waves, to "hear" cosmic murmurs, to "touch" the DNA, to "smell" artificial meat, and to "feel" the pulse of plants. Indoors, we devise medicine in labs and use laser scalpels on operation tables. We manufacture probers in dust-free workshops to send them beyond the Solar System. We create artificial intelligences that can not only read poems, sing songs, and copy paintings but compose new ones as beautiful as ours.

[6] Underlying these marvels is a trend of human integration into "The One", first put forward by a world-renowned futurist, Alvin Toffler. It is an entity of combined computing power that features ubiquitous connectivity, algorithm-based iteration, and full access to unprecedented numbers of knowledge bases. We stay foolish, hungry, and mainly indoors, to observe with Google glass, to learn on Wikipedia, to think via Mind Mapping, to predict with Big Data, and to create through 3D printers. Underpinned by mobile technologies, searchable databases, virtual reality, and wearable gadgets, "The One" has congregated experiences, methodologies, doctrines, and philosophies, East and West, past and present. It has become a mail pigeon to give instant feedback, a test ground to verify new theses, and an amusement park to take stress away. The time has already changed: we are no longer short of stimuli; rather, hooked up to "The One", we are more inspired.

[7] I am not denying the benefits of an afternoon walk. But if energy is defined as being physically active, it will at best be a contributary cause of being creative, and not a necessary or sufficient one, let alone the main cause, because without expertise, know-hows, and hands-on experience, no matter how much vigor a person possesses, he may not be able to make something as simple as a wooden stool. In addition, if energy is key to creativity, the honor of being most creative will surely be crowned to robust athletes, rather than scientists, inventors, and researchers. Perhaps creative inspiration is a short stroll away; however, brilliant ideas may also spring up before, during and after a delicious meal, a soothing bath, a pleasant nap, or nice Cuban cigars in the house of chain smokers such as Winston Churchill, Lu Xun, and Sherlock Holmes.

[8] To sum up, living in an information age, masters, talents, and ordinary people are working wonders in their fields, by their means and at their paces, because human beings are fundamentally inquisitive and exploratory, indoors and outdoors.

1. Why does the writer mention Winston Churchill, Lu Xun, and Sherlock Holmes?

_____

_____

2. Think critically about the content of the essay. Write down your thoughts.

Doubts	Rebuttals
Are the two writers talking about the same stagnation?	
Examples of Sherlock Holmes and Thomas Jefferson	
Other doubts	

Unit 4 Cause and Effect

3. Think critically about the language. Write down your answers.

Original sentences	Problems	Improved sentences
... however, I insist that staying indoors stands opposite to stagnation; rather, human beings are more prone to being inquisitive and exploratory, whether indoors or outdoors, and that ordinary people create history in their ways.		
How about the less talented? Well, ordinary people are not trapped in stagnation, either.		
Chefs pore over online cuisine videos, after a day's smell and sweat in ill-equipped kitchens, as noisy as bar, as hot as oven, and as messy as a schoolboy's answer sheet.		
I am not denying the benefits of an afternoon walk.		
But if energy is defined as being physically active, it will at best be a contributary cause of being creative, and not a necessary or sufficient one, let alone the main cause, ...		

• Activity 8

Write a second draft of the essay in Task 2 of Pre-class Work about an overrated virtue. Then, work in pairs and review each other's writing. Be a critical thinker. Try hard to find faults with the content, structure, and language of your peer's essay just as you have done to yours. Swap the essay, complete the checklist and write comments or suggestions on the margins of your peer's essay.

Items	Questions	Y/N	Points
Opening remarks	Is the lead attractive?		
Thesis statement	Are there any restrictions?		
	Does it have a plan of development?		
	Does it agree with the topic sentences?		
	Are the ideas original and sound?		
Structure	Is block or chain structure used to organize the body paragraphs?		
	Is there categorization on causes or effects?		
Topic sentences	Does each one sum up its paragraph?		
	Is there transition between one and another?		
Logic	Is there slippery slope?		
	Is there post hoc?		
	Is correlation causality?		
Paragraph	Is the causal chain short and complete?		
	Is it evidence-based?		
	Is evidence adequate, specific, relevant, and credible?		
	Are there ambiguous causal conjunctions?		
	Are the sentences well connected?		
Summary sentence	Is it a paraphrased thesis statement?		
Sentence skills	Is there parallelism, or other rhetorical devices?		
	Are there grammar mistakes, redundancy, or ambiguity?		
Overall evaluation	A thumb of rule: Each question is worth 5 points, but you may adjust on your own.	Overall score	

Unit 4 Cause and Effect

After-class Practice

Task 1

List at least three reasons in sentences.

Why on the one hand are people aware that "Practice is the sole criterion for testing truth", but on the other, tend to believe in an assertion conveyed sincerely, repeatedly, and authoritatively?

Write a paragraph to be announced in a media press focusing on effects.

China has provided 166 regions, countries, and international organizations with nearly RMB 400 billion in aid.

Task 2

Is it morally justified to help one and ignore some others? Read the rebuttal essay concerning how empathy is viewed in a dialectical way.

The Most Overrated Virtue

Rabbi Shai Held

[1] Empathy is having a moment. The primatologist Frans de Waal has heralded our time as an "age of empathy", which he sees as the key ingredient for a kinder, more just society. The linguist-cum-political advocate George Lakoff insists that "behind every progressive policy lies a single moral value: empathy". And advocating for what he calls "global empathic consciousness", the social theorist Jeremy Rifkin maintains that only "global empathy" can prevent "global collapse". Paul Bloom, a professor of psychology at Yale, will have none of it. Not only is empathy a "poor moral guide", he argues in his provocative book, *Against Empathy: The Case for Rational Compassion*, but it is actually "morally corrosive". He calls upon individuals of all political persuasions to "join hands and work together in the fight against empathy".

[2] What justifies this all-out assault on an ostensible virtue? In a metaphor he returns to time and again, Mr. Bloom suggests that empathy, which he defines as "the act of feeling what you believe other people feel — experiencing what they experience", is like a spotlight. A spotlight can direct attention and assistance to where it is needed, but its focus is necessarily narrow. Thus empathy always focuses exclusively on what is captured by its glow.

[3] While we concentrate on the few whose suffering has become salient for us, we forget the many others who also need our help. Worse, since it is easier to empathize with those who are similar to us, empathy all too often reflects our biases. "Intellectually, a white American might believe that a black person matters just as much as a white person, but he or she will typically find it a lot easier to empathize with the plight of the latter than the former," Mr. Bloom writes. Thus, "empathy distorts our moral judgments in pretty much the same way that prejudice does". Try as we may, Mr. Bloom insists, we are simply incapable of empathizing with more than a handful of people at a time because

Unit 4 Cause and Effect

we have limited emotional capacity; accordingly, empathy necessarily constricts our vision and entrenches our prejudices.

[4] Empathy is also innumerate. As many studies have demonstrated, if you show someone a picture of an individual starving child, she will likely open her wallet. But if you tell her about hundreds of faceless, nameless children in need in some far away place, she will remain unmoved. "If our concern is driven by thoughts of the suffering of specific individuals," Mr. Bloom writes, "then it sets up a perverse situation in which the suffering of one can matter more than the suffering of a thousand."

[5] What, then, is the proper alternative to all this empathy-induced immorality? Championing the role of "deliberative reasoning" in everyday life, Mr. Bloom argues that "we should strive to use our heads rather than our hearts". Human goodness depends, he says, on an "escape from empathy" and a turn towards rules and principles which alone make fairness possible and will lead to a far greater alleviation of suffering. Mr. Bloom does see a place — albeit a limited one — for emotions in the moral life. He advocates for compassion, which he insists is "a more diffuse concern for the fates of others" than empathy. Because such concern is less intensely focused, it can presumably be more widely directed and more thoughtfully applied.

[6] It is fine and good to argue for a greater emphasis on reason in moral decision-making — a long line of distinguished philosophers past and present would agree — but one wonders whether it is really fair to assail empathy as ferociously as Mr. Bloom does. He writes that "the problems we face as a society and as individuals ... are often due to too much [empathy]". Really? More than bigotry, bias or entrenched hatreds? And there is something downright bizarre about Mr. Bloom's insistence that "we should aspire to a world in which a politician appealing to someone's empathy would be seen in the same way as one appealing to people's racist bias".

[7] Empathy can indeed limit and distort our moral vision, but Mr. Bloom fails to seriously engage with the fact that reason can also be marshaled for nefarious ends. Gesturing towards troubling research on how Nazi doctors "used their intelligence to talk themselves into doing terrible things", he acknowledges that those doctors "would have been better off listening to their hearts". Mr. Bloom opens this door but refuses to walk through it. If emotions can sometimes serve

as a corrective to wayward reason, then why the glorification of the latter and the unrelenting suspicion of the former? Neither reason nor emotion guarantees moral goodness.

[8] Mr. Bloom is undoubtedly right that empathy alone makes for bad policy: While it can motivate us to care, we need reason to help us design and implement policies aimed at reducing suffering. And I am extremely sympathetic to Mr. Bloom's worry that our moral lives are too tribal (my word, not his). But like many other human emotions, empathy is double-edged. It can limit our horizons, but perhaps it can also expand them. We see the enemy as less than human, until we notice her crying over the death of her child, just as we would. Frans de Waal reaches a conclusion antithetical to Mr. Bloom's: Empathy, he writes "is the one weapon in the human repertoire that can rid us of the curse of xenophobia ... Our best hope for transcending tribal differences is based on the moral emotions, because emotions defy ideology".

[9] It is naive to think that any one thing is "the one weapon" to cure what ails us. If we want to learn to care more deeply about others, especially about others who are distant from us, we will need both reason and emotion. But we ought to remember that neither reason nor emotion is static. We need not merely to deploy them but also to take responsibility for shaping and reshaping them.

(https://www.hadar.org/blog/most-overrated-virtue)

1. What are the effects of empathy, according to Mr. Bloom?

2. Why is concession made at the beginning in the 7th and 8th paragraphs?

3. In which paragraph do you find the two underlined words in Paragraph 3 again? Why does the writer reuse them?

4. To which extent do you agree with the following statement? The suffering of one thousand is more than the suffering of one. Why?

Expansion

Passage 1

1. Write down your doubt about the causal chain in the following paragraph.

   "Nonetheless, the weather intervened when a heavy fog rolled in, so the American forces were able to retreat, regroup, and survive to fight another day. Because of this fog, the United States was not defeated in its struggle for freedom. Consequently, today's United Kingdom of England, Wales, Scotland, and Northern Ireland does not include the United States."

2. For eight years, in the same weather, the ill-fed, ill-equipped, and ill-trained Chinese soldiers finally drove the Japanese invaders out of the country. Can this example be used against the writer's claim?

How Weather Has Changed World History

[1] It is tempting, and often comforting, to think that humans control their fates. The decisions that people make in their daily lives can affect many things, and the course of their lives cumulatively reflects these many small decisions. On the other hand, people cannot control every aspect of their environments, and forces beyond human control frequently intervene in human affairs. Notwithstanding many people's opinion that the weather has little influence in their lives besides determining what clothes they wear on a particular day, the weather has in fact caused world history to radically shift in important ways that are still felt today.

[2] Numerous examples from world history document the long-term effects of weather in the formation of cultures and nations. In the thirteenth century, Khubilai Khan ruled over the vast Mongol empire, which spanned from the Pacific Ocean in the east to the Black Sea in the west, from present-day Siberia in the north to Afghanistan in the south. To expand his reign further, Khubilai

Khan mounted two invasions of Japan. Two monsoons, however, caused him to end his attacks. Delgado (2008) describes legendary accounts of this event: "The legend, oft repeated in countless history books, speaks of gigantic ships, numbering into the thousands, crewed by indomitable Mongol warriors, and of casualties on a massive scale, with more than 100,000 lives lost in the final invasion attempt of 1281" (p. 4). Because of this unexpected defeat, Khubilai Khan decided to stage a third invasion of Japan, but he died before he could fulfill this ambition. Without these monsoons, Japan might have been defeated by the Mongols and thus lost its identity as a unique culture, with far-reaching consequences for Asian and world history.

[3] In the early years of America's Revolutionary War, which began in 1775, it appeared likely that the British would crush the armies of her colonial territory and incorporate it back into the empire. The British troops were a well-trained and disciplined army that was feared worldwide. In contrast, the American troops were newly trained, sometimes poorly organized, and lacked sufficient resources to fight effectively. General George Washington could have easily been defeated in the Battle of Long Island on August 22, 1776. Historical records show that Sir William Howe, the British commander, was clearly defeating Washington on Long Island and was actually winning handily (Seymour, 1995). Nonetheless, the weather intervened when a heavy fog rolled in, so the American forces were able to retreat, regroup, and survive to fight another day. Because of this fog, the United States was not defeated in its struggle for freedom. Consequently, today's United Kingdom of England, Wales, Scotland, and Northern Ireland does not include the United States. The United States is not a commonwealth of a mother country, as Canada and Australia are, though the United States still has strong ties to its colonial past.

[4] When Napoleon Bonaparte invaded Russia in the early nineteenth century, he met with early successes that appeared to guarantee that he might eventually rule the world as his personal domain. His soldiers captured Moscow and destroyed the city, which encouraged him to push farther in his military campaigns. However, because of his dreams of glory, Napoleon overlooked the simple fact that Russian winters are extremely cold. When the temperatures fell below freezing, many of his soldiers and their horses died in the brutal weather. As Belloc (1926) writes in his classic study of the Napoleonic wars,

Unit 4 Cause and Effect

"the cold was the abominable thing: The dreadful enemy against which men could not fight and which destroyed them" (p. 217). As a result of the failure of Napoleon's Russian campaigns, his own rule ended relatively soon after. His defeat led to a reorganization of power throughout the European nations, as well as to the rise of Russia as a major world power.

[5] As these three examples unambiguously demonstrate, the weather has caused numerous huge shifts in world history as well as in power balances among cultures and nations. Without the rainy storms of the monsoon season, Japan might be the eastern outpost of Mongolia; without the appearance of dense fog, the United States might still be a territory of the United Kingdom; and without winter snow, Muscovites might speak French. Today weather forecasters can usually predict with a high degree of accuracy when thunderstorms, hurricanes, tsunamis, and tornadoes will strike, but the course of history cannot be fully isolated from the effects of the weather.

(Keith, S., Folse. & Tison, P. *Great Writing*, 2020)

References

Belloc, H. *Napoleon's Campaign of 1812 and the Retreat from Moscow*. New York: Harper, 1926.

Delgado, J. *Khubilai Khan's Lost Fleet: In Search of a Legendary Armada*. Berkeley, CA: University of California Press, 2008.

Seymour, W. *The Price of Folly: British Blunders in the War of American Independence*. London: Brassey's, 1995.

Passage 2

1. Richard says, "I never learned hate at home, or shame. I had to go to school for that." Why?
2. In terms of cause-and-effect writing, how different is the short story from other passages?

Shame

Dick Gregory

[1] I never learned hate at home, or shame. I had to go to school for that. I was about seven years old when I got my first big lesson. I was in love with a little

135

girl named Helene Tucker, a light-complexioned little girl with pigtails and nice manners. She was always clean and she was smart in school. I think I went to school then mostly to look at her. I brushed my hair and even got me a little old handkerchief. It was a lady's handkerchief, but I didn't want Helene to see me wipe my nose on my hand.

[2] The pipes were frozen again, there was no water in the house, but I washed my socks and shirt every night. I'd get a pot, and go over to Mister Ben's grocery store, and stick my pot down into his soda machine and scoop out some chopped ice. By evening the ice melted to water for washing. I got sick a lot that winter because the fire would go out at night before the clothes were dry. In the morning I'd put them on, wet or dry, because they were the only clothes I had.

[3] Everybody's got a Helene Tucker, a symbol of everything you want. I loved her for her goodness, her cleanness, her popularity. She'd walk down my street and my brothers and sisters would yell, "Here comes Helene," and I'd rub my tennis sneakers on the back of my pants and wish my hair wasn't so nappy and the white folks' shirt fit me better. I'd run out on the street. If I knew my place and didn't come too close, she'd wink at me and say hello. That was a good feeling. Sometimes I'd follow her all the way home, and shovel the snow off her walk and try to make friends with her momma and her aunts. I'd drop money on her stoop late at night on my way back from shining shoes in the taverns. And she had a daddy, and he had a good job. He was a paperhanger.

[4] I guess I would have gotten over Helene by summertime, but something happened in that classroom that made her face hang in front of me for the next twenty-two years. When I played the drums in high school, it was for Helene, and when I broke track records in college, it was for Helene, and when I started standing behind microphones and heard applause, I wished Helene could hear it too. It wasn't until I was twenty-nine years old and married and making money that I finally got her out of my system. Helene was sitting in that classroom when I learned to be ashamed of myself.

[5] It was on a Thursday. I was sitting in the back of the room, in a seat with a chalk circle drawn around it. The idiot's seat, the troublemaker's seat.

[6] The teacher thought I was stupid. Couldn't spell, couldn't read, couldn't do

arithmetic. Just stupid. Teachers were never interested in finding out that you couldn't concentrate because you were so hungry, because you hadn't had any breakfast. All you could think about was noontime; would it ever come? Maybe you could sneak into the cloakroom and steal a bite of some kid's lunch out of a coat pocket. A bite of something. Paste. You can't really make a meal of paste, or put it on bread for a sandwich, but sometimes I'd scoop a few spoonfuls out of the big paste jar in the back of the room. Pregnant people get strange tastes. I was pregnant with poverty. Pregnant with dirt and pregnant with smells that made people turn away. Pregnant with cold and pregnant with shoes that were never bought for me. Pregnant with five other people in my bed and no daddy in the next room, and pregnant with hunger. Paste doesn't taste too bad when you're hungry.

[7] The teacher thought I was a troublemaker. All she saw from the front of the room was a little black boy who squirmed in his idiot's seat and made noises and poked the kids around him. I guess she couldn't see a kid who made noises because he wanted someone to know he was there.

[8] It was on a Thursday, the day before the payday. The eagle always flew on Friday. The teacher was asking each student how much his father would give to the Community Chest. On Friday night, each kid would get the money from his father, and on Monday he would bring it to the school. I decided I was going to buy a daddy right then. I had money in my pocket from shining shoes and selling papers, and whatever Helene Tucker pledged for her daddy I was going to top it. And I'd hand the money right in. I wasn't going to wait until Monday to buy me a daddy.

[9] I was shaking, scared to death. The teacher opened her book and started calling out names alphabetically: "Helene Tucker?" "My Daddy said he'd give two dollars and fifty cents." "That's very nice, Helene. Very, very nice indeed."

[10] That made me feel pretty good. It wouldn't take too much to top that. I had almost three dollars in dimes and quarters in my pocket. I stuck my hand in my pocket and held on to the money, waiting for her to call my name. But the teacher closed her book after she called everybody else in the class.

[11] I stood up and raised my hand. "What is it now?" "You forgot me?" She

turned toward the blackboard. "I don't have time to be playing with you, Richard."

[12] "My daddy said he'd ..." "Sit down, Richard, you're disturbing the class." "My daddy said he'd give ... fifteen dollars."

[13] She turned around and looked mad. "We are collecting this money for you and your kind, Richard Gregory. If your daddy can give fifteen dollars you have no business being on relief."

[14] "I got it right now, I got it right now, my Daddy gave it to me to turn in today, my daddy said."

[15] "And furthermore," she said, looking right at me, her nostrils getting big two and her lips getting thin and her eyes opening wide, "We know you don't have a daddy."

[16] Helene Tucker turned around, her eyes full of tears. She felt sorry for me. Then I couldn't see her too well because I was crying, too.

[17] "Sit down, Richard." And I always thought the teacher kind of liked me. She always picked me to wash the blackboard on Friday, after school. That was a big thrill; it made me feel important. If I didn't wash it, come Monday the school might not function right.

[18] "Where are you going, Richard!"

[19] I walked out of school that day, and for a long time I didn't go back very often.

[20] There was shame there. Now there was shame everywhere. It seemed like the whole world had been inside that classroom, everyone had heard what the teacher had said, everyone had turned around and felt sorry for me. There was shame in going to the Worthy Boys Annual Christmas Dinner for you and your kind, because everybody knew what a worthy boy was. Why couldn't they just call it the Boys Annual Dinner — why'd they have to give it a name? There was shame in wearing the brown and orange and white plaid mackinaw the welfare gave to three thousand boys. Why'd it have to be the same for everybody so when you walked down the street the people could see you were on relief? It was a nice warm mackinaw and it had a hood, and my momma beat me and called me a little rat when she found out I stuffed it in the bottom of a pail full of garbage way over on Cottage Street. There was

Unit 4 Cause and Effect

shame in running over to Mister Ben's at the end of the day and asking for his rotten peaches, there was shame in asking Mrs. Simmons for a spoonful of sugar, there was shame in running out to meet the relief truck. I hated that truck, full of food for you and your kind. I ran into the house and hid when it came. And then I started to sneak through alleys, to take the long way home so the people going into White's Eat Shop wouldn't see me. Yeah, the whole world heard the teacher that day — we all know you don't have a daddy.

[21] It lasted for a while, this kind of numbness. I spent a lot of time feeling sorry for myself. And then one day I met this wino in a restaurant. I'd been out hustling all day, shining shoes, selling newspapers, and I had googobs of money in my pocket. Bought me a bowl of chili for fifteen cents, and a cheeseburger for fifteen cents, and a Pepsi for five cents, and a piece of chocolate cake for ten cents. That was a good meal. I was eating when this old wino came in. I love winos because they never hurt anyone but themselves.

[22] The old wino sat down at the counter and ordered twenty-six cents worth of food. He ate it like he really enjoyed it. When the owner, Mister Williams, asked him to pay the check, the old wino didn't lie or go through his pocket like he suddenly found a hole.

[23] He just said: "Don't have no money." The owner yelled: "Why in hell did you come in here and eat my food if you don't have no money? That food cost me money."

[24] Mister Williams jumped over the counter and knocked the wino off his stool and beat him over the head with a pop bottle. Then he stepped back and watched the wino bleed. Then he kicked him. And he kicked him again.

[25] I looked at the wino with blood all over his face and I went over.

[26] "Leave him alone, Mister Williams. I'll pay the twenty-six cents."

[27] The wino got up, slowly, pulling himself up to the stool, then up to the counter, holding on for a minute until his legs stopped shaking so bad. He looked at me with pure hate. "Keep your twenty-six cents. You don't have to pay, not now. I just finished paying for it."

[28] He started to walk out, and as he passed me, he reached down and touched

my shoulder. "Thanks, sonny, but it's too late now. Why didn't you pay it before?" I was pretty sick about that. I waited too long to help another man.

(https://www.garlandisdschools.net/uploaded/high-schools/nghs/documents/ela/17-shame.pdf)

A Review Article for Reference

Unit 5
Comparison and Contrast

Objectives

At the end of this unit, you should be able to

- ☑ understand the role of comparison and contrast in paragraph and essay development;
- ☑ compare and contrast the subjects in paragraphs and essays by using appropriate transitional words and expressions;
- ☑ write a comparison and contrast essay about core socialist values such as equality, dedication and friendship.

Pre-class Work

Task 1

• Reading for Writing

Do you think females and males are born different? Read the essay below and discuss the way the writer uses to make comparison and contrast between men and women.

How Men's Brains Are Wired Differently than Women's

Tanya Lewis

[1] Men aren't from Mars and women aren't from Venus, but their brains really are wired differently, a new study suggests.

[2] The research, which involved imaging the brains of nearly 1,000 adolescents, found that male brains had more connections within hemispheres, whereas female brains were more connected between hemispheres. The results, which apply to the population as a whole and not individuals, suggest that male brains may be optimized for motor skills, and female brains may be optimized for combining analytical and intuitive thinking.

[3] "On average, men connect front to back [parts of the brain] more strongly than

Unit 5 Comparison and Contrast

women," whereas "women have stronger connections left to right," said study leader Ragini Verma, an associate professor of radiology at the University of Pennsylvania medical school. But Verma cautioned against making sweeping generalizations about men and women based on the results.

[4] Previous studies have found behavioral differences between men and women. For example, women may have better verbal memory and social cognition, whereas men may have better motor and spatial skills, on average. Brain imaging studies have shown that women have a higher percentage of gray matter, the computational tissue of the brain, while men have a higher percentage of white matter, the connective cables of the brain. But few studies have shown that men's and women's brains are connected differently.

[5] In the study, researchers scanned the brains of 949 young people aged 8 to 22 (428 males and 521 females), using a form of magnetic resonance imaging (MRI) known as diffusion tensor imaging, which maps the diffusion of water molecules within brain tissue. The researchers analyzed the participants as a single group, and as three separate groups split up by age.

[6] As a whole, the young men had stronger connections within cerebral hemispheres while the young women had stronger connections between hemispheres, the study, detailed today (Dec. 2) in the journal *Proceedings of the National Academy of Sciences*, found. However, the cerebellum, a part of the brain below the cerebrum that plays a role in coordinating muscle movement, showed the opposite pattern, with males having stronger connections between hemispheres.

[7] Roughly speaking, the back of the brain handles perception and the front of the brain handles action; the left hemisphere of the brain is the seat of logical thinking, while the right side of the brain begets intuitive thinking. The findings lend support to the view that males may excel at motor skills, while women may be better at integrating analysis and intuitive thinking.

[8] "It is fascinating that we can see some of functional differences in men and women structurally," Verma told *LiveScience*. However, the results do not apply to individual men and women, she said. "Every individual could have part of both men and women in them," she said, referring to the connectivity patterns her team observed.

[9] When the researchers compared the young people by age group, they saw the most pronounced brain differences among adolescents (13.4 to 17 years old), suggesting the sexes begin to diverge in the teen years. Males and females showed the greatest differences in inter-hemisphere brain connectivity during this time, with females having more connections between hemispheres primarily in the frontal lobe. These differences got smaller with age, with older females showing more widely distributed connections throughout the brain rather than just in the frontal lobe.

[10] Currently, scientists can't quantify how much an individual has male- or female-like patterns of brain connectivity. Another lingering question is whether the structural differences result in differences in brain function, or whether differences in function result in structural changes. The findings could also help scientists understand why certain diseases, such as autism, are more prevalent in males, Verma said.

(*LiveScience*, 2013)

1. Write down the thesis statement of the essay.

   _____

2. Which sentence do you think should be the topic sentence of Paragraph 4?

   _____

3. With which common method of conclusion does the essay end? _____
A. A summary and final thought.
B. Questions that prompt the readers to think further about what's been written.
C. A prediction.

4. Can you find more research findings which indicate differences between males and females?

   _____

   _____

   _____

Unit 5 Comparison and Contrast

• Vocabulary Highlights

Find words and expressions making comparison or contrast in the passage.

Study the words and phrases in the passage with the help of a dictionary. Write down the definitions as they are used in the context.

optimize

caution

computational

beget

intuitive

pronounced

diverge

lingering

Task 2

• Writing Your First Draft

The way a father or mother treats a child affects greatly for the child's future growth both physically and mentally. Who makes a better parent and has a greater role of caring children, men or women? Write a comparison and contrast essay of about 250 words.

In-class Activities

▶ What Is Comparison and Contrast Writing?

Comparison and contrast writing is used to show readers the similarities and/or differences between two subjects. Comparison writing focuses on similarities (ways things are alike), while contrast writing focuses on differences or ways they are not alike.

In order to do this, the subjects chosen have to be related or share at least some characteristics. You may have heard that it's impossible to compare apples and oranges. This isn't true, of course: an apple can easily be compared to an orange, since they both share many characteristics (both fruit, both vaguely round, both on sale at the store, both considered nutritious, etc.). However, some items would be very difficult to compare: writing a short essay comparing a Fuji apple to an Apple MacBook might result in no meaningful similarities. That paper would, likely, be a waste of readers' (and the writer's) time.

Meaningful comparison, however, can enlighten an audience toward unknown similarities or differences between subjects. The more informative or surprising a comparative is, the more likely an audience is to be engaged. For example, writing a paper that compares two well-known superheroes and discusses their similarities might not be that interesting. Showing how alike a superhero and a villain are, though, might subvert the audience's expectation (that heroes and villains have nothing in common), which could lead to a more interesting paper.

What Are the Purposes of Comparison and Contrast?

The purpose of a comparison and contrast paper seems obvious — we're talking about similarities and/or differences between two subjects to better inform our readers. However, there's sometimes a secondary purpose to these papers: Comparison papers are often written to convince readers that one subject is superior to the other.

A subjective comparison includes factual information about both subjects but may also include the writer's opinions. It may also work to convince readers to consider one subject to be better than the other. Subjective comparisons also include the writer's evaluation of the information. In addition, a subjective comparison will lead toward a conclusion at the end, deciding between the subjects being compared.

By contrast, an objective comparison paper does not automatically seek to decide between options when it begins. It may list the categories for comparison that the subjects will be judged against, but it will build toward its conclusion through presenting facts, evidence, and analysis, not through subjective evaluation.

Comparison in writing discusses elements that are similar, while contrast in writing

Unit 5 Comparison and Contrast

discusses elements that are different. A comparison and contrast essay, then, analyzes two subjects by comparing them, contrasting them, or both.

The key to a good comparison and contrast essay is to choose two or more subjects that connect in a meaningful way. The purpose of conducting the comparison or contrast is not to state the obvious but rather to illuminate subtle differences or unexpected similarities. Drawing distinctions between elements in a similar category will increase the audience's understanding of that category, which is the purpose of the comparison and contrast essay. Similarly, to focus on comparison, choose two subjects that seem at first to be unrelated. The more divergent the two subjects initially seem, the more interesting a comparison essay will be.

Patterns of Development in Comparison and Contrast Writing

When you compare two items, there are two ways you can organize the evidence. You can say all you want to about one subject, then the other. This is called a subject-by-subject comparison, and it works best if you are doing a brief comparison of two subjects. You can also organize your essay by points of comparison. Under each point, you discuss one subject, then the other. This is called a point-by-point comparison, and it works best if you have a great deal to say about both your subjects.

Which Pattern Should You Use?

As you prepare to compose your first draft, you might ask yourself, "Which pattern of organization should I choose — subject by subject or point by point?" Indeed, this is not your simple "paper or plastic" supermarket choice. It's an important question — to which there is no single, easy answer.

For most writers, choosing the appropriate pattern of organization involves thinking time in the pre-writing stage, before beginning a draft. Many times, your essay's subject matter itself will suggest the most effective method of development. The subject-by-subject method might be the better choice when a complete, overall picture of each subject is desirable. On the other hand, your essay topic might best be discussed by presenting a number of distinct points for readers to consider one by one. Essays that evaluate, that argue the superiority or advantage of one thing over another ("A cat is a better pet for students than a dog because ..."), often lend themselves to the point-by-point method because each of the writer's claims may be clearly supported by the side-by-side details. However, none of the preceding advice always holds true. There are no hard-and-fast rules governing this rhetorical choice. Each writer must decide which method of organization works best in any particular comparison and contrast essay. Before drafting begins, therefore, writers are wise to sketch out an informal outline or rough plan using one method and then the other to see which is more effective for their topic, their purpose, and their audience.

- ## Activity 1

    What is the thesis statement of the essay "How Men's Brains Are Wired Differently than Women's"? According to the writer of the essay, what are the major differences between men and women? What are the purposes of writing? In what aspects do you contrast these two genders about taking a better role of taking care of children? Work in groups to share your outlines and discuss what evidence you want to cite to support your ideas.

- ## Activity 2

    Read the following paragraphs and answer the questions.

Paragraph 1

There are some differences between academic and professional writing. Academic paper usually includes traditional, well-developed paragraphs. Additionally, academic writing uses the more objective third-person point-of-view, such as the use of "he, she, or it". On the other hand, professional writing often contains short direct paragraphs with bullet point to highlight key ideas. And professional writing uses the first-person point of view, or uses "I", so that the communication comes directly from the author.

1. What is the topic sentence of this paragraph?

_____

2. How does the writer develop the topic sentence?

_____

Unit 5 Comparison and Contrast

3. What do you think is the effect of contrast on the explanation of the two ideas?

___

4. How does the writer show the differences and build up relations between them?

___

Paragraph 2

Teachers and actors, if compared with each other carefully, you'll find that they share many similarities. Firstly, they both have audience and both must be clear speakers, with a pleasing voice — loud and nice enough to attract the audience at the very beginning of the performance. Secondly, they both have to improve their acting skills for the sake of audience. A good teacher must pour all his knowledge to his students and get them well prepared for their latter career, while a good actor can catch the audience's attention and be famous by acting vividly and emotionally and make themselves a part of the play.

1. What is the topic sentence of this paragraph?

___

2. How does the writer develop the topic? How is it different from Paragraph 1?

___

3. How does the writer show the similarities and build the connection with the two ideas?

___

Comparison and Contrast in Essay Development

There are two principal patterns of organization for comparison and contrast essays. For most short papers you should choose one of the patterns and stick with it throughout the essay. If you are assigned a longer essay, you may want to mix the patterns for variety as some professional writers do, but do so only if you can maintain clarity and logical organization.

• Activity 3

Discuss in pairs how you are going to compare or contrast the topics below. You can turn to the subject-by-subject and point-by-point outline examples below.

1. Confucius thought of education and that of Socrates
2. Fast food chains and fine dining restaurants
3. Chinese dream and American dream
4. Dragons in Chinese and Western cultures

A subject-by-subject outline example:

I.	Introduction	
II.	High school	
	a. cost	
	b. workload	
	c. social aspects	
III.	University	
	a. cost	
	b. workload	
	c. social aspects	
IV.	Conclusion	

A point-by-point outline example:

I.	Introduction
II.	Cost

(continued)

Unit 5 Comparison and Contrast

II.	a. high school	
	b. university	
III.	Workload	
	a. high school	
	b. university	
IV.	Social aspects	
	a. high school	
	b. university	
V.	Conclusion	

Suppose you are going to compare or contrast the following topics into a full-length essay, how are you going to develop the essay? Discuss in pairs and list them on the lines below.

1. Different views on working while studying

_____
_____
_____
_____

2. An opinion you held before coming to college that has changed

_____
_____
_____
_____

3. Different consumption views in China and America

___

4. High context culture and low context culture

___

- ## Activity 4

What's your understanding of the difference between a worker or a laborer? Discuss in pairs to what extent do you agree with the quotes below.

1. People rarely succeed unless they have fun in what they are doing. —— *Dale Carnegie*
2. Work is the grand cure for all the maladies and miseries that ever beset mankind. —— *Thomas Carlyle*

Read the essay below and answer the questions that follow.

Will You Be a Worker or a Laborer?

[1] So far as I know, Miss Hannah Arendt was the first person to define the essential difference between work and labor. To be happy, a man must feel, firstly, free and, secondly, important. He cannot be really happy if he is compelled by society to do what he does not enjoy doing, or if what he enjoys

Unit 5 Comparison and Contrast

doing is ignored by society as of no value or importance. In a society where slavery in the strict sense has been abolished, the sign that what a man does is of social value is that he is paid money to do it, but a laborer today can rightly be called a wage slave. A man is a laborer if the job society offers him is of no interest to himself but he is compelled to take it by the necessity of earning a living and supporting his family.

[2] The antithesis to labor is play. When we play a game, we enjoy what we are doing, otherwise we should not play it, but it is a purely private activity; society could not care less whether we play it or not.

[3] Between labor and play stands work. A man is a worker if he is personally interested in the job which society pays him to do; what from the point of view of society is necessary labor is from his own point of view voluntary play. Whether a job is to be classified as labor or work depends, not on the job itself, but on the tastes of the individual who undertakes it. The difference does not, for example, coincide with the difference between a manual and a mental job; a gardener or a cobbler may be a worker, a bank clerk a laborer.

[4] People's attitude toward their work determines everything. To a worker, leisure means simply the hours he needs to relax and rest in order to work efficiently. He is therefore more likely to take too little leisure than too much; workers die of coronaries and forget their wives' birthdays. To the laborer, on the other hand, leisure means freedom from compulsion, so that it is natural for him to imagine that the fewer hours he has to spend laboring, and the more hours he is free to play, the better.

[5] Besides, the mere hours spent in leisure workers and laborers differ in the amount of personal satisfaction they derive from their jobs. Workers who enjoy their jobs will be happier less stressed and generally more satisfied with their lives. They will also work with more diligence and precision because they have fostered a sense of personal pride in their jobs. On the other hand, laborers whose sole incentive is earning their livelihood feel that the time they spend on the daily grind is wasted and doesn't contribute to their happiness. Instead of valuing all 24 hours of their day as enjoyable and productive hours, they gauge only the time spent in leisure and play as meaningful. Unfortunately, laborers are all too commonplace and only a small percentage of the population is in the

lucky position of being workers.

[6] In recent decades, technological innovation and the division of labor have caused major economic changes by eliminating the need for special strength or skill in many fields and have turned many paid occupations with enjoyable work into boring labor. Increasing productivity with automated machines such as robots has reduced the number of necessary laboring hours. It is possible to imagine an upcoming society in which the majority of the population will have almost as much leisure time as in earlier times was enjoyed by the medieval aristocracy. The medieval aristocrats had an abundance of leisure time but often wasted it in trivial pursuit of games and fashion. Likewise, modern-day laborers with too much leisure time may find it difficult to refrain from the addictive and trivial pursuits of celebrity gossip extravagant fashion and excessive video games and TV, similar bad habits that waste valuable time.

[7] However it's not necessary to take such a toxic attitude toward such a positive thing as leisure time. In fact, in many countries people now use their leisure time to improve their minds and their working conditions to create a happier, more contented life. Lifelong learning can make the difference between being bored, unhappy laborers and workers who find meaning and joy in their employment and life. "Continuing education" or "experiential learning" can offer an array of classes from pleasant diversions such as sports art classes or music to leadership development advanced accounting skills or CAD (computer-aided design), to name only a few.

[8] Whatever the job, people who enjoy their work find time passes quickly. They hurl their passion into their work, be it physical like the work of a smith or more mental like that of a scientist or an artist. Even purely mental work can suffice as an outlet as aptly expressed by the phrase "sinking one's teeth into a problem".

[9] Eventually, everyone has to find a job and earn a living. Laborers are slaving away at a job they don't enjoy for a small monetary reward waiting all day until they go home and play. But while laborers are counting down the hours, workers are energized and focused taking optimum pleasure in the task at hand. By choosing a job that is both useful to society and personally fulfilling workers maintain a simultaneous sense of purpose and enthusiasm that

Unit 5 Comparison and Contrast

improves their whole lives. So in the end, whatever job you choose you must contend with this essential question: Will you be a laborer or a worker?

(New Horizon College English, Book III, 2011)

1. Find the words and expressions showing comparison and contrast in the passage.

   _____

2. How does the writer define labor and work?

   _____

   _____

   _____

3. Why does the writer make a comparison between a gardener and a bank clerk?

   _____

   _____

4. According to the writer, what are the differences between laborers and workers?

   _____

   _____

   _____

   _____

5. Fill in the blanks in the summary. Note how information is organized.

The text argues, by differentiating among work, labor, and play, that interest and _____ in work are important for the benefit of both _____ and society.

There are three major differences between workers and laborers. Firstly, workers and laborers are different in their _____ toward their work. Workers will dedicate more time to _____ and spend less time on leisure, whereas laborers will regard leisure as _____ from compulsion and the more hours they have free for play, the better. Secondly, workers and laborers differ in the amount of _____ they derive from their jobs. Workers will achieve greater _____ than laborers. Thirdly, in modern times, workers and laborers spend their _____ in different ways. While social development has created

155

much more leisure time than ever before, modern laborers spend their leisure time in fostering _____. Considering this phenomenon, _____ can make the difference between being bored, unhappy laborers and workers who find meaning and joy in their _____ and life. Moreover, workers, unlike laborers, hurl their _____ into their work, be it physical or mental.

Everyone has to find a job and _____, and that whatever job you choose, you must _____ this essential question: Will you be a laborer or worker?

• Vocabulary Highlights

Study the words and phrases in the passage with the help of a dictionary. Write down the definitions as they are used in the context.

compel _____

coincide _____

compulsion _____

aristocracy _____

toxic _____

hurl _____

suffice _____

simultaneous _____

▶ The Structure of a Comparison and Contrast Essay

When you compare two subjects, you examine their similarities, the characteristics that make them alike. When you contrast two subjects, you examine their differences, the characteristics that set them apart. Since it is difficult to do one without the other, you usually examine both the similarities and the differences between subjects when you are comparing them.

As an organizational pattern, comparison and contrast is also useful for examining

Unit 5 Comparison and Contrast

the advantages and disadvantages of choosing one object, idea, or action over another. To use the pattern effectively, follow these steps:

1. Choose an appropriate topic;
2. Determine your purpose;
3. Write a good thesis statement.

▶ **Choose an Appropriate Topic**

Your topic should consist of two subjects for comparison that have something in common. Choose subjects that belong to the same category or class of things. For example, suppose the topic is "communication tools", you may approach it in a number of ways. For example, you could begin it by narrowing your topic to "letter", "telephone", "instant message", or "video call". You can select two ways of communication you want to compare. How you limit the topic is your choice, but the subjects of your comparison should be of the same class.

▶ **Determine Your Purpose**

Suppose the topic you have chosen is "two restaurants". Why do you want to compare two different restaurants? What do you want to say about them? Was one make you more comfortable than the other? Did you like one more than the other? Perhaps you just want to explain the similarities and differences between the two restaurants without making judgment about either of them. Maybe you decide the restaurant where you will celebrate your approaching birthday. Generally speaking, there are two major purposes of comparing and contrasting subjects:

1. To identify and explain the similarities and/or differences that clearly distinguish between one subject and another of its class;
2. To identify and explain the similarities and/or differences between two subjects to show that one has advantages over the other or to make some other value judgment.

The first purpose is informational. You simply want readers to know how the two subjects compare. You are not making a judgment about the subjects; you leave that for your readers. The second purpose contains an element of persuasion. You want readers to understand or react to your own views or values about one or both subjects. For example, if you want to explain all the way in which two restaurants are different or similar, you may select the first purpose. If you want to explain why you consider one restaurant better than the other, you may select the second purpose.

▶ **Write a Good Thesis Statement**

The thesis statement should make clear to your readers why you are writing about the two subjects you have chosen (purpose) and how you plan to compare and contrast them (parts). For example, you are considering to adopt a pet. The purpose of your writing is to find better pets between cats and dogs. You should:

1. State your topic and purpose: to contrast cats and dogs to find out better pets;
2. State the aspects of contrast: lifestyles; finance; household accommodation;
3. Combine topic, purpose, and aspects of contrast into one complete sentence that is free of grammatical errors.

Then, you may write a thesis statement like:

> Indoor cats make better pets than indoor dogs because cats make less of an impact on an owner's lifestyle, they are less expensive to care for, and they need few special household accommodations.

There are other effective ways to write a thesis statement, but combining topic, purpose, and points of contrast into one sentence is a reliable method.

• Activity 5

Judge whether the following statements are true or false.

1. ___ A comparison and contrast essay is used to describe differences or similarities.
2. ___ The introduction serves three main functions: to identify the general topic, catch readers' attention, and state the thesis.
3. ___ A thesis statement is the stand you take, an opinion you must support.
4. ___ In the introductory paragraph of a comparison and contrast essay, your thesis should identify the two items being compared or contrasted and your opinion about them should be presented.
5. ___ The thesis statement is just like the title of the essay.
6. ___ The parallel structures in your thesis statement must present the points and the sequence they will follow in the body paragraphs.

Unit 5 Comparison and Contrast

7. ___ In a comparison and contrast essay, the conclusion must do the same job that it does in all essays: it sums up the main points and reinforces the thesis.

• Activity 6

In English, there are a number of words and expressions to indicate comparison and contrast. Below are some examples.

For comparison	For contrast
like	unlike
similar	different
similarities	differences
similarly	on the contrary
in comparison	in contrast
both	neither
in common	differs from
also	however
share	instead of
too	on the other hand

Fill in the blank with proper words or phrases in the following paragraph of subject-by-subject contrast.

Modern cities with skyscrapers like New York do provide busy urban residents with feelings of prosperity. Flashing billboards at night almost illuminates the city proper, presenting a spectacular view even from outer space. _____, living near the countryside, one can breathe the clean atmosphere, experience the closeness to nature and enjoy the quiet, peaceful landscape as if wandering in the paradise.

Fill in the blanks with proper words or phrases in the following paragraph of point-by-point contrast.

It is true that television news can vividly bring into our living rooms dramatic events of singular importance, such as space launchings, natural disasters, wars and so on,

_____ it cannot cover important stories in the depth they may deserve because of its time limitation. _____, print news excels in its ability to devote as much space to a story as it sees fit, _____ it cannot compete with television visually.

Fill in the blanks with the expressions from the table.

differ	in contrast	both	likewise
similar	on the other hand	unlike	

1. The climate in the spring is _____ in San Francisco and New Orleans.
2. Regular cardio exercise does wonder for your overall heart health. _____, it contributes to the betterment of your mental health.
3. _____ Leonardo da Vinci and Francisco Goya were renowned painters in their respective eras.
4. People who play basketball are generally quite tall. _____, gymnasts and jockeys are typically short.
5. On the one hand, a career in the military earns one a lot of respect from everyone. _____, soldiers tend to experience severe depression fairly commonly.
6. _____ aerobics, walking entails no expensive fees for classes or clubs.
7. The present and previous means of communication _____ in regard to their speed and the range of tools available.

• Activity 7

Below is a student essay. Using a point-by-point analysis, she explains her choice of workplace after college graduation.

A Vote for Bigger Cities

[1] Nowadays, many young employees and college graduates are facing with a tough choice: should they flee big cities or live their dreams there? The opponents of living in big cities are always complaining a lot. However, when I compare big cities with small ones, the advantages of living in big cities are clear.

[2] First of all, people in big cities enjoy educational and medical benefits of better quality. Children in big cities are entitled to better education opportunities.

Unit 5 Comparison and Contrast

The schools have more teachers with university degree and are equipped with modern teaching devices like multi-media and projectors. What's more, people in big cities are more likely to receive good medical care. There are famous medical experts in big cities. However, if we live in small cities, the situation changes a lot. In small cities, teachers are not as professional as those in big cities and the educational devices aren't advanced. And there are almost no professional specialists in small cities. And people living in towns will have to travel dozens of miles to visit doctors in well-renowned hospitals in bigger cities if the diseases are serious.

[3] Secondly, big cities offer more working experiences and job opportunities. For instance, for a college student majoring in finance, staying in economically-developed cities like Shanghai and Guangzhou after graduation is a good choice for his career development. A large number of transnational corporations and private enterprises offer positions and create a positive employment environment. On the contrary, there are fewer working chances in small cities. Take my sister, a graduate from a key university of finance and economics, as an example. She tried hard but failed to find a suitable job in my hometown, a third-tier city. Then she took the civil service exam and is now working as a secretary in a public institution, which is not relevant to her major at all. Luckily, the job allows her to devote more time to her family.

[4] Last but not least, people in big cities have more access to rich cultural lives. They usually visit museums, attend concerts or go to exhibitions at weekends, which can broaden their horizons. In addition, in some international metropolises, individuals can have a better understanding of the world by communicating with those from different countries face to face. However, in small cities, the cultural life is much duller because there are few museums, concerts and exhibitions. To watch a favorite band or see a live concert is never easy. And local people seldom build social relationships with people from different backgrounds, which prevent them from growing into open-minded individuals.

[5] In short, big cities are superior to small ones for they provide better educational and medical resources, a variety of job opportunities and colorful cultural activities. I will choose to live in a big city after graduation to make a promising future.

1. Make an outline of the essay.

Thesis statement	
Topic sentence 1	
Topic sentence 2	
Topic sentence 3	
Conclusion	

2. In Paragraph 2, what "change of direction" signal does the writer use to indicate that he/she has finished discussing the big cities and is now going to discuss small cities?

3. Can you provide one example that logically support the point that there are famous medical experts in bigger cities?

4. Which sentence in Paragraph 3 should be omitted in the interest of paragraph unity?

5. Write the word or the phrase in Paragraph 4 that indicate the writer has used emphatic order in organizing his or her supporting points.

Unit 5 Comparison and Contrast

• Activity 8

Write a second draft of the essay in Task 2 of Pre-class Work about whether men or women make a better parent. Then, work in pairs and peer-review your partner's essay and answer the following Yes or No questions. You should also recommend three specific changes from the first draft to the second one.

Items	Questions	Yes/No
Unity	Does the essay have a clearly stated thesis?	
	Does the essay include irrelevant materials?	
Support	Does the essay provide enough details about the advantages of men's and women's taking care of their children?	
	Does the essay describe how men and women are different in making a parent?	
Coherence	Does the essay use a single method of development in each supporting paragraph?	
	Are transitional words and expressions used appropriately to make the points of comparison and contrast clear?	
	Does the conclusion include a paraphrased thesis statement and a final thought?	
Sentence skills	Has the writer used a consistent point of view through the essay?	
	Does the essay include specific rather than general words?	
	Has the writer avoided wordiness and used concise wording?	
	Are the sentences varied?	

If you could recommend three specific changes from the first draft to the second one, what would they be?

After-class Practice

Task 1

Suppose you are to develop the following topics into a comparison and contrast essay, how are you going to state the topic sentences? Make sure that the paragraphs are connected.

Topics	Topic sentences of developmental paragraphs
Study alone or study with a group of students	
Watch a movie in a theatre or watch a movie at home	
Differences between English and Chinese	
Graduate schools home and abroad	
Two subjects of your choice	

Unit 5 Comparison and Contrast

Task 2

Read the essay below and answer the questions that follow.

What Social Distancing Reveals about East-West Differences
The pandemic could spur psychological changes in both the U.S. and China

Gish Jen & Qi Wang

[1] Social distancing worries Americans. Yale professor Nicholas Christakis warns that it asks us "to suppress our profoundly human and evolutionarily hard-wired impulses for connection", for example. And journalist Greg Miller and others cite possible ramifications that include "heart disease, depression, dementia, and even death". In striking contrast, there has been little talk along these lines in Chinese mainland. A search of Chinese social media yields almost no posts on the subject: shutdown-related concerns expressed by Chinese are primarily about the safety of themselves, family and friends; change of lifestyle; boredom; physical confinement; and the resulting social conflict due to close and extended interaction time while simultaneously managing work, childcare and household tasks. A review of China's academic literature likewise yields no articles.

[2] This may seem counterintuitive. Shouldn't the group-oriented Chinese have more social-distancing anxiety than Americans, not less? To give a little background: Individuals in both Western and Eastern societies have social needs, which we meet in a variety of ways. However, our "go-to" strategies do tend to differ. In the more individualistic West, we love our families, of course, but tend to rely heavily on friendship as well — on elective ties reflective of "who we really are". Conducive to personal growth, these friendships can coalesce into "chosen families".

[3] But these relationships depend on nuanced in-person interaction, which, unfortunately, is made difficult by social distancing. Cornell researchers Duyen Nguyen and Susan Fussel have shown that compared with the Chinese, Americans rely more on nonverbal behavioral cues such as head turns, facial

expressions and eye contact to support communication. We can also be more skittish — more likely, for example, to attribute a lack of affirmative body language to a lack of interest or involvement. As these sorts of subtle behavioral cues are poorly conveyed by electronic media, Americans now reliant on Zoom or FaceTime can find it hard to maintain a sense of connection with others.

[4] In contrast, people in more collectivistic societies like China tend to meet their social needs with given or blood ties — with family or schoolmates, for example. Less personalized though they may be, these relationships also require less upkeep. Indeed, the lab run by one of us (Qi Wang) recently found that Asians can derive a sense of closeness from almost any kind of social exchange, including talking about the weather. A sense of connection is thus easily maintained even during long periods of social distancing.

[5] That's not to say that epidemics don't distress the Chinese. They absolutely do, in both the short term and the long term. A study of the survivors of the 2003 SARS outbreak in Hong Kong, China, for example, found not only that survivors were traumatized, but that even a year later, they had "alarmingly high levels of depression, anxiety, and posttraumatic symptoms". This distress, though, was interestingly linked only to the illness itself. Though social distancing was practiced in Hong Kong in 2003, the possible ill effects of this elicited little Chinese concern. Interestingly, research found that during the SARS pandemic, residents in Hong Kong in fact experienced increased social connectedness through their communities.

[6] Might Americans ever be as little distressed by social distancing as the Chinese? Possibly. Cultural phenomena like individualism and collectivism are, of course, hugely complex and dynamic. No one can make predictions about them with certainty. Still, we might ask: could the current pandemic and its ensuing economic fallout prove large enough a shock to temper the extreme American individualism — an individualism which has arguably reached not only the highest levels in the world but in human history? Perhaps. Already many college students have moved back in with their parents, altering their relationships in ways that could have ongoing effects. If nothing else, these adult children may become more keenly aware of the safety net that blood ties afford in a crisis.

Unit 5 Comparison and Contrast

[7] What's more, a severe recession, should one set in, might draw various and sundry unemployed family members into active child-raising. The nuclear family could become less nuclear; multigenerational households could proliferate; and the very young could emerge with a more collectivistic orientation — an orientation that has laid latent in many parts of America, overwhelmed by a dominant discourse that paints America as a nation of cowboys.

[8] Ironically, the pandemic may have the opposite effect in China. A number of Chinese cities saw a sharp uptick in divorces — a long-accepted marker of individualism — following the lifting of their lockdown. Such is the demand for divorces in the southern city of Shenzhen that, according to the Chinese website *Sixth Tone*, "couples are having to make reservations a month in advance before they can get a divorce", and in a small city in Hunan, divorce-related administrators have been so busy they don't "even have time to drink water".

[9] Of course, the stress of confinement contributed to some of these breakups. As in the U.S., there has been a surge in domestic violence. But some breakups appear traceable to the surfacing of individualistic thinking that, for example, stresses choice and voluntary effort, and downplays duty and obligation. Thus when 34-year-old Zhang Ning found herself stuck taking care of her son and in-laws alone in Wuhan for months on end, she was outraged by her husband. "When I called him wanting to release my emotions, at first he comforted me a bit, but then he became impatient," she told *Sixth Tone*. Then one day, he snapped at her: "Aren't you supposed to do all this?" — a classic collectivistic reaction. And that, she reported, was that.

[10] In short, while the Chinese may not experience social-distancing anxiety as Americans do, the pandemic seems to have brought out individualistic ways of thinking in some. Of course, divorce rates and rationales can only tell a small part of the sprawling story that is China. Still, might the globalization that has drawn East and West so much closer together physically also, via the pandemic, draw us ever so slightly closer together psychologically as well? It's possible.

(https://blogs.scientificamerican.com/observations/
what-social-distancing-reveals-about-east-west-differences)

 Background Information on the Writers of the Essay

1. What is the writers' purpose of writing this passage?

2. According to the passage, in what ways do the East-West people differ?

3. What method do the writers adopt to organize the passage?

4. What do you think are the reasons for the increasing divorce rate in China during the pandemic?

5. What do you think are the other distress Chinese people experience during the pandemic?

6. Write an effective comparison and contrast essay emphasizing the differences between Chinese and American approaches to education.

Unit 5 Comparison and Contrast

Expansion

Passage 1

1. Read the essay below and summarize the writer's view on Chinese humanism.
2. Why does the writer cite the Western philosophers' interpretations of the meaning of life in the article?

Chinese Humanism

Lin Yutang

[1] To understand the Chinese ideal of life one must try to understand Chinese humanism. The term "humanism" is ambiguous. Chinese humanism, however, has a very definite meaning. It implies, first a just conception of the ends of human life; secondly, a complete devotion to these ends; and thirdly, the attainment of these ends by the spirit of human reasonableness or the Doctrine of the Golden Mean, which may also be called the Religion of Common Sense.

[2] The question of the meaning of life has perplexed Western philosophers, and it has never been solved — naturally, when one starts out from the teleological point of view, according to which all things, including mosquitoes and typhoid germs, are created for the good of this cocksure humanity. As there is usually too much pain and misery in this life to allow a perfect answer to satisfy man's pride, teleology is therefore carried over to the next life, and this earthly life is then looked upon as a preparation for the life hereafter, in conformity with the logic of Socrates, which looked upon a ferocious wife as a natural provision for the training of the husband's character. This way of dodging the horns of the dilemma sometimes gives peace of mind for a moment, but then the eternal question, "What is the meaning of life?" comes back. Others, like Nietzsche, take the bull by the horns, and refuse to assume that life must have a meaning and believe that progress is in a circle, and human achievements are a savage dance, instead of a trip to the market, but still the question comes back eternally, like the sea waves lapping upon the shore: "What is the meaning of life?"

[3] The Chinese humanists believe they have found the true end of life and are conscious of it. For the Chinese the end of life lies not in life after death, for the idea that we live in order to die, as taught by Christianity, is incomprehensible;

nor in Nirvana, for that is too metaphysical; nor in the satisfaction of accomplishment, for that is too vainglorious; nor yet in progress for progress' sake, for that is meaningless. The true end, the Chinese have decided in a singularly clear manner, lies in the enjoyment of a simple life, especially the family life, and in harmonious social relationships.

[4] The first poem that a child learns in school runs:

> While soft clouds by warm breezes are wafted in the morn,
> Lured by flowers, past the river I roam on and on.
> They'll say, "Look at that old man on a spree!"
> And know not that my spirit's on happiness borne.

[5] That represents to the Chinese, not just a pleasant poetic mood but the *summum bonum* of life. The Chinese ideal of life is drunk through with this sentiment. It is an ideal of life that is neither particularly ambitious nor metaphysical, but nevertheless immensely real. It is, I must say, a brilliantly simple ideal, so brilliantly simple that only the matter-of-fact Chinese mind could have conceived it, and yet one often wonders how the West could have failed to see that the meaning of life lies in the sane and healthy enjoyment of it. The difference between China and the West seems to be that the Westerners have a greater capacity for getting and making more things and a lesser ability to enjoy them, while the Chinese have a greater determination and capacity to enjoy the few things they have. This trait, our concentration on earthly happiness, is as much a result as a cause of the absence of religion. For if one cannot believe in the life hereafter as the consummation of the present life, one is forced to make the most of this life before the farce is over. The absence of religion makes this concentration possible.

[6] From this a humanism has developed which frankly proclaims a man-centered universe, and lays down the rule that the end of all knowledge is to serve human happiness. The humanizing of knowledge is not an easy thing, for the moment man swerves he is carried away by his logic and becomes a tool of his own knowledge. Only by a sharp and steadfast holding to the true end of human life as one sees it can humanism maintain itself. Humanism occupies, for instance, a mean position between the other-worldliness of religion and the materialism of the modem world. Buddhism may have captured popular fancy

in China, but against its influence the true Confucianist was always inwardly resentful, for it was, in the eyes of humanism, only an escape from life, or a negation of the truly human life.

[7] On the other hand, the modem world, with its over-development of machinery, has not taken time to ensure that man enjoys what he makes. The glorification of the plumber in America has made man forget that one can live a very happy life without hot and cold running water, and that in France and Germany many men have lived to comfortable old age and made important scientific discoveries and written masterpieces with their water jug and old-fashioned basin. There needs to be a religion which will transcribe Jesus' famous dictum about the Sabbath and constantly preach that the machine is made for man and not man made for the machine. For after all, the sum of all human wisdom and the problem of all human knowledge is how man shall remain a man and how he shall best enjoy his life.

(*My Country and My People*, 1936)

Passage 2

1. How does the writer manage to grab readers' interest immediately at the beginning of the text? What is the thesis of the article?
2. According to the writer, what are the three main differences between sloppy and neat people? Which contrast pattern is adopted?

Neat People vs. Sloppy People

Suzanne Britt

[1] I've finally figured out the difference between neat people and sloppy people. The distinction is, as always, moral. Neat people are lazier and meaner than sloppy people. Sloppy people, you see, are not really sloppy. Their sloppiness is merely the unfortunate consequence of their extreme moral rectitude. Sloppy people carry in their mind's eye a heavenly vision, a precise plan, that is so stupendous, so perfect, it can't be achieved in this world or the next.

[2] Sloppy people live in Never-Never Land. Someday is their métier. Someday they are planning to alphabetize all their books and set up home catalogues. Someday they will go through their wardrobes and mark certain items for

tentative mending and certain items for passing on to relatives of similar shape and size. Someday sloppy people will make family scrapbooks into which they will put newspaper clippings, postcards, locks of hair, and dried corsage from their senior prom. Someday they will file everything on the surface of their desks, including the cash receipts from coffee purchases at the snack shop. Someday they will sit down and read all the back issues of *The New Yorker*.

[3] For all these noble reasons and more, sloppy people never get neat. They aim too high and wide. They save everything, planning someday to file, order, and straighten out the world. But while these ambitious plans take clearer and clearer shape in their heads, the books spill from the shelves onto the floor, the clothes pile up in the hamper and closet, the family mementos accumulate in every drawer, the surface of the desk is buried under mounds of paper and the unread magazines threaten to reach the ceiling.

[4] Sloppy people can't bear to part with anything. They give loving attention to every detail. When sloppy people say they're going to tackle the surface of the desk, they really mean it. Not a paper will go unturned; not a rubber-band will go unboxed. Four hours or two weeks into the excavation, the desk looks exactly the same, primarily because the sloppy person is meticulously creating new piles of papers with new headings and scrupulously stopping to read all the old book catalog before he throws them away. A neat person would just bulldoze the desk.

[5] Neat people are bums and clods at heart. They have cavalier attitudes toward possessions, including family heirlooms. Everything is just another dust-catcher to them. If anything collects dust, it's got to go and that's that. Neat people will toy with the idea of throwing the children out of the house just to cut down on the clutter.

[6] Neat people don't care about process. They like results. What they want to do is to get the whole thing over with so they can sit down and watch the wrestling on TV. Neat people operate on two unvarying principles: Never handle any item twice, and throw everything away. The only thing messy in a neat person's house is the trash can. The minute something comes to a neat person's hand, he will look at it, try to decide if it has immediate use and, finding none, throw it in the trash.

Unit 5 Comparison and Contrast

[7] Neat people are especially vicious with mail. They never go through their mail unless they are standing directly over a trash can. If the trash can is beside the mailbox, even better. All ads, catalogs, pleas for charitable contributions, church bulletins and money-saving coupons go straight into the trash can without being opened. All letters from home, postcards from Europe, bills and paychecks are opened, immediately responded to, then dropped in the trash can. Neat people keep their receipts only for tax purposes. That's it. No sentimental salvaging of birthday cards or the last letter a dying relative ever wrote. Into the trash it goes.

[8] Neat people place neatness above everything, even economics. They are incredibly wasteful. Neat people throw away several toys every time they walk through the den. I knew a neat person once who threw away a perfectly good dish drainer because it had mold on it. The drainer was too much trouble to wash. And neat people sell their furniture when they move. They will sell a La-Z-Boy recliner while you are reclining in it.

[9] Neat people are no good to borrow from. Neat people buy everything in expensive little single portions. They get their flour and sugar in two-pound bags. They wouldn't consider clipping a coupon, saving a leftover, reusing plastic non-dairy whipped cream containers or rinsing off tin foil and draping it over the unmoldy dish drainer. You can never borrow a neat person's newspaper to see what's playing at the movies. Neat people have the paper all wadded up and in the trash by 7:05 a.m.

[10] Neat people cut a clean swath through the organic as well as the inorganic world. People, animals, and things are all one to them. They are so insensitive. After they have finished with the pantry, the medicine cabinet, and the attic, they will throw out the red geranium (too many leaves), sell the dog (too many fleas), and send the children off to boarding school (too many scuffmarks on the hardwood floors).

(https://www.ccboe.com/schools/stone/images/pdfs/Composition--Rhetoric-NEAT_PEOPLE_VS._SLOPPY_PEOPLE_-_Suzanne_Britt-1.pdf)

Unit 6
Definition

Objectives

At the end of this unit, you should be able to

- ☑ understand the role of definition in paragraph and essay development;
- ☑ define the key terms in essays with a clear logic;
- ☑ define the terms such as a hero in paragraphs and essays.

Pre-class Work

Task 1

• Reading for Writing

Have you ever thought of defining a university since you are in it? What is the purpose of defining it? Is the university the writer defines here exactly the one you think it to be?

What Is a University?

Todd Pettigrew

[1] As some philosopher said regarding time, I know what a university is — so long as nobody asks me, so I was curious as to what my own definition would look like if I tried to spell it out. The answer is not obvious, though, because a university has not always meant the same thing over the centuries, and it does not necessarily mean the same thing to everyone now. And it matters because very often the arguments we have about universities turn on our assumptions about what universities are and what they ought to be. What follows then is my initial, and admittedly provisional attempt to define what we ought to consider a university in this country. I hope it provides readers with some food for thought and some opportunity for debate.

[2] A university has two principal functions: providing instruction on matters of intellectual importance and conducting research on those same matters.

[3] These two functions, to the extent reasonably possible, should support one another. University teaching, therefore, is distinguished from other modes of

education not only by seeking the highest levels of sophistication, but also by deriving its vitality from the atmosphere of on-going discovery fostered at the institution. For this reason, most, if not all courses at a university should be taught by faculty who are active researchers in the disciplines in which they teach. Conversely, research ought not to be done in isolation from teaching. Researchers should be open to allowing issues that arise in teaching to suggest new research questions and, where feasible, students, both undergraduate and graduate, should be given opportunities to participate in research.

[4] Because strong intellectual work can only be done in an atmosphere where scholars feel free to take risks, challenge conventions, and change their minds, universities must foster an environment that prizes intellectual freedom.

[5] Though university education should provide the kind of intellectual enrichment that would serve any graduate well in the working world, university education should never be construed solely or even primarily as a path to employment. Even in disciplines with obvious professional connections such as education or law, the university should first aim to teach the history, theoretical underpinnings, crucial knowledge, and critical skills necessary to build a profound understanding of the discipline. A university law program, for example, should aim primarily to produce graduates with a profound understanding of law, rather than lawyers, per se.

[6] A university has one additional secondary function: to serve as a cultural touchstone in its community to encourage all members of the public to participate in the life of the mind. Universities should, within reasonable limits and without needlessly detracting from its primary missions, sponsor and host artistic performances and displays, public talks, open debates, and other events that excite interest in intellectual pursuits, broadly construed.

[7] This to me seems like a good starting point for a real, meaningful debate on what a university should be. Some readers might object and say that I have simply described Canadian universities as they are. To the extent that that is true, we should consider ourselves lucky, and seek to conserve and develop what we already have.

[8] In any case, what we mean by the term "university" is a debate that we have to continue to have in this country. Have at it.

(https://www.macleans.ca/education/university/what-is-a-university)

1. How does the writer define a university? What are the words the writer uses in defining the university?

   _____
   _____
   _____
   _____

2. Why does the writer say "university education should never be construed solely or even primarily as a path to employment" (Paragraph 5)? How does the writer prove his point?

   _____
   _____
   _____
   _____
   _____

3. Write down the key words, phrases and expressions that organize the whole essay.

   _____
   _____

- ## Vocabulary Highlights

  Study the words and phrases in the passage with the help of a dictionary. Write down the definitions as they are used in the context.

  assumption   _____

  provisional   _____

Unit 6 Definition

sophistication

construe

discipline

per se

detract from

Task 2

• Writing Your First Draft

We are taught by our parents and teachers to love our country. But what is one's love for one's country like? Write an essay on "What Is Patriotism?" with emphasis on definition.

In-class Activities

• Activity 1

Read the following paragraphs in "What is a university?" again and answer the questions.

Paragraphs 1–2

A university has two principal functions: providing instruction on matters of intellectual importance and conducting research on those same matters.

These two functions, to the extent reasonably possible, should support one another. University teaching, therefore, is distinguished from other modes of education not only by seeking the highest levels of sophistication, but also by deriving its vitality

179

from the atmosphere of on-going discovery fostered at the institution. For this reason, most, if not all courses at a university should be taught by faculty who are active researchers in the disciplines in which they teach. Conversely, research ought not to be done in isolation from teaching. Researchers should be open to allowing issues that arise in teaching to suggest new research questions and, where feasible, students, both undergraduate and graduate, should be given opportunities to participate in research.

1. How are the two functions related to each other?

___

2. How does the writer correlate the two functions in the second paragraph?

___

___

___

___

3. How does the correlation contribute to the definition of the university?

___

Paragraph 3

Because strong intellectual work can only be done in an atmosphere where scholars feel free to take risks, challenge conventions, and change their minds, universities must foster an environment that prizes intellectual freedom.

4. In this paragraph, the writer argues for the importance of the intellectual freedom by saying that in a university, "scholars feel free to take risks, challenge conventions, and change their minds". Please use some examples and facts to further support the writer's argument.

Argument One: Scholars need freedom to take risks to carry out strong intellectual work.

Support: ___

Unit 6 Definition

Argument Two: Scholars need freedom to challenge conventions to carry out strong intellectual work.

Support: _____

Argument Three: Scholars need freedom to change their minds to carry out strong intellectual work.

Support: _____

▶ How to Define a Term?

▸ By pointing out the class and the basic features of the term

In the simplest sense, to define a term is to show what class or group the term belongs to and then point out the basic features which distinguish it from other members of the same group. For example:

> A tornado is a violent storm with strong winds which move in a circle.
>
> Human rights in developing countries first mean the right to a decent life: sufficient food, clothing and a basic education.

Besides, some typical expressions as listed below are frequently used in definitions.

- ✓ mean
- ✓ is (be)
- ✓ signify
- ✓ refer to
- ✓ constitute
- ✓ involve
- ✓ is considered to be
- ✓ is defined as, can be defined as
- ✓ ... by definition ...
- ✓ state that ...
- ✓ namely
- ✓ that is (i.e.)
- ✓ The essence of the concept is ...
- ✓ The main/basic features included are ...

• Activity 2

Define the following terms in one sentence in this way by using the expressions suggested above.

An e-book _____

A tsunami _____

An elective course _____

• Activity 3

Definitions play an important part in our daily life and academic research. Some significant definitions will influence and even change people's understanding of things. Write down your topic sentences to prove the point in this definition and use the writing strategies you have learned in the previous units to support your point.

Writing Strategies	Thesis: Science and technology are the primary productive forces.	
Exemplification	Topic Sentence 1: Science and technology are making our transportation much faster and easier.	Example 1: high speed rail Example 2:
	Topic Sentence 2:	Example 1: Example 2:
Cause and effect	Topic Sentence 1: Science and technology enable our country to feed the increasing population.	Reason 1: Reason 2:
	Topic Sentence 2:	Result 1: Result 2:

(continued)

Unit 6 Definition

Writing Strategies	Thesis: Science and technology are the primary productive forces.	
Comparison and contrast	Topic Sentence 1: The contribution by the development of science and technology to GDP in the past and at present is different.	Differences:
	Topic Sentence 2:	Similarities:

▸ **By basing the definition on standard or authoritative statements**

In academic writing, the easiest and safest way to define a term is to base the definition on the standard or authoritative statements of the term.

● **Activity 4**

Read the essay below and answer the questions that follow.

What Is a Public Library?

[1] A public library is a library that is accessible by the general public and is usually funded from public sources, such as taxes. It is operated by librarians and library paraprofessionals, who are also civil servants.

[2] There are five fundamental characteristics shared by public libraries: they are generally supported by taxes (usually local, though any level of government can and may contribute); they are governed by a board to serve the public interest; they are open to all, and every community member can access the collection; they are entirely voluntary in that no one is ever forced to use the services provided; and they provide basic services without charge.

[3] Public libraries exist in many countries across the world and are often considered an essential part of having an educated and literate population. Public libraries are distinct from research libraries, school libraries, and other special libraries in that their mandate is to serve the general public's information needs rather than the needs of a particular school, institution, or research population. Public libraries also provide free services such as preschool story

times to encourage early literacy, quiet study and work areas for students and professionals, or book clubs to encourage appreciation of literature in adults. Public libraries typically allow users to borrow books and other materials, i.e., take off the premises temporarily; they also have non-circulating reference collections and provide computer and Internet access to patrons.

(https://en.wikipedia.org/wiki/Public_library)

1. How does each paragraph fulfill the writer's defining purpose?

2. What writing strategies does the writer use in defining a public library? And how do they work?

3. Locate the key words and phrases in each of the five characteristics of a public library. Is there a better logical order they can be arranged in? Why or why not?

4. How does Paragraph 2 help readers understand the public library?

Unit 6 Definition

• Activity 5

In defining a term, we are going to first find some important characteristics of it and organize them in a logical order. For example, some psychologists have discovered 12 central traits of a hero:

1. bravery;
2. conviction;
3. courage;
4. determination;
5. helpfulness;
6. honesty;
7. inspirational;
8. moral integrity;
9. protective;
10. self-sacrifice;
11. selflessness;
12. strength (Kinsella, Ritchie & Igou, 2015).

Pick up 3 from the 12 traits that you think to be most important or common in a hero. Write three topic sentences with each of the three traits as the point of the topic sentence, and then develop each of them into a paragraph with supporting details.

What Is a Hero?

Topic sentence 1: _____

Support 1: _____

Support 2: _____

Topic sentence 2: _____

Support 1: _____

Support 2: _____

Topic sentence 3: _____

Support 1: _____

Support 2: _____

▸ **By negation**

Another useful way to define a term is to define it by negation, that is, to tell what the term does not mean. To write a definition by negation, you have only a few rules to follow:

First, apply the definition by negation to either a term or a talking point.

Second, a definition by negation does not need to include everything that is not.

In the following paragraph, the writer is defining a young adult by what he/she is not.

> A young adult is not mentally and physically mature enough to be taken as an adult, and meanwhile, he/she is not young any more to be taken as a baby boy/girl. He/she is not able to be fully responsible for what he/she says or does as an adult does, and he/she is, in any way, not willing to live under the 24-hour supervision of the parents.

• Activity 6

Write a paragraph to define the following terms by negation, and think how negations can make your definition more definite and persuasive.

1. an Internet celebrity
2. a tablet PC
3. spaghetti

• Activity 7

Some terms have definite, concrete meanings, such as a donut, a book, or a tree. Terms such as honesty, honor, or love are abstract, and their meanings depend more on a person's point of view. Talk about the terms given below in pairs and write an outline of a definition essay on one of them.

Unit 6 Definition

1. a voluntary worker
2. academic writing
3. patriotism

Title: _____

Introduction: _____

Body: _____

Topic Sentence 1: _____

Topic Sentence 2: _____

Topic Sentence 3: _____

Conclusion: _____

Exchange your outline with your classmates and discuss what the hardest part in defining the term is and whether you found any new ways besides the ones you have learned in this unit to define the term.

● Activity 8

Write a second draft of the essay in Task 2 of Pre-class Work about "What Is Patriotism?". Then, work in pairs to review each other's writing according to the four bases of essay writing: unity, support, coherence and sentence skills. Make sure that you check the following aspects:

(1) The whole essay has only one central idea according to one unifying principle;
(2) There are adequate and specific evidence for each part;
(3) The essay presents the parts by using some transitional words;
(4) All the sentences in the essay are error-free.

After-class Practice

Task 1

Suppose you are to develop the following topics into an essay, how are you going to state the topic sentences? Make sure that the paragraphs are connected.

Topics	Topic sentences of developmental paragraphs
typhoon	
a professor	
depression as a mental disease	
a pet	

Unit 6 Definition

Task 2

Read the essay below and answer the questions that follow.

What Is Happiness?

John Ciardi

[1] The right to pursue happiness is issued to Americans with their birth certificates, but no one seems quite sure which way it ran. It may be we are issued a hunting license but offered no game. Jonathan Swift seemed to think so when he attacked the idea of happiness as "the possession of being well-deceived", the felicity of being "a fool among knaves". For Swift saw society as Vanity Fair, the land of false goals.

[2] It is, of course, un-American to think in terms of fools and knaves. We do, however, seem to be dedicated to the idea of buying our way to happiness. We shall all have made it to Heaven when we possess enough.

[3] And at the same time the forces of American commercialism are hugely dedicated to making us deliberately unhappy. Advertising is one of our major industries, and advertising exists not to satisfy desires but to create them — and to create them faster than any man's budget can satisfy them. For that matter, our whole economy is based on a dedicated insatiability. We are taught that to possess is to be happy, and then we are made to want. We are even told it is our duty to want. It was only a few years ago, to cite a single example, that car dealers across the country were flying banners that read "You Auto Buy Now". They were calling upon Americans, as an act approaching patriotism, to buy at once, with money they did not have, automobiles they did not really need, and which they would be required to grow tired of by the time the next year's models were released.

[4] Or look at any of the women's magazines. There, as Bernard DeVoto once pointed out, advertising begins as poetry in the front pages and ends as pharmacopoeia and therapy in the back pages. The poetry of the front matter is the dream of perfect beauty. This is the baby skin that must be hers. These, the flawless teeth. This, the perfumed breath she must exhale. This, the sixteen-

year-old figure she must display at forty, at fifty, at sixty, and forever.

[5] Once past the vaguely uplifting fiction and feature articles, the reader finds the other face of the dream in the back matter. This is the harness into which Mother must strap herself in order to display that perfect figure. These, the chin straps she must sleep in. This is the salve that restores all, this is her laxative, these are the tablets that melt away fat, these are the hormones of perpetual youth, these are the stockings that hide varicose veins.

[6] Obviously no half-sane person can be completely persuaded either by such poetry or by such pharmacopoeia and orthopedics. Yet someone is obviously trying to buy the dream as offered and spending billions every year in the attempt. Clearly the happiness-market is not running out of customers, but what is it trying to buy?

[7] The idea "happiness", to be sure, will not sit still for easy definition: the best one can do is to try to set some extremes to the idea and then work in toward the middle. To think of happiness as acquisitive and competitive will do to set the materialistic extreme. To think of it as the idea one senses in, say, a holy man of India will do to set the spiritual extreme. That holy man's idea of happiness is in needing nothing from outside himself. In wanting nothing, he lacks nothing. He sits immobile, rapt in contemplation, free even of his own body. Or nearly free of it. If devout admirers bring him food, he eats it; if not, he starves indifferently. Why be concerned? What is physical is an illusion to him. Contemplation is his joy and he achieves it through a fantastically demanding discipline, the accomplishment of which is itself a joy within him.

[8] Is he a happy man? Perhaps his happiness is only another sort of illusion. But who can take it from him? And who will dare say it is more illusory than happiness on the installment plan?

[9] But, perhaps because I am Western, I doubt such catatonic happiness, as I doubt the dreams of the happiness-market. What is certain is that his way of happiness would be torture to almost any Western man. Yet these extremes will still serve to frame the area within which all of us must find some sort of balance. Thoreau — a creature of both Eastern and Western thought — had his own firm sense of that balance. His aim was to save on the low levels in order to

Unit 6 Definition

spend on the high.

[10] Possession for its own sake or in competition with the rest of the neighborhood would have been Thoreau's idea of the low levels. The active discipline of heightening one's perceptions of what is enduring in nature would have been his idea of the high. What he saved from the low was time and effort he could spend on the high. Thoreau certainly disapproved of starvation, but he would put into feeding himself only as much effort as would keep him functioning for more important efforts.

[11] Effort is the gist of it. There is no happiness except as we take on life-engaging difficulties. Short of the impossible, as Yeats put it, the satisfactions we get from a lifetime depend on how high we choose our difficulties. Robert Frost was thinking in something like the same terms when he spoke of "the pleasure of taking pains". The mortal flaw in the advertised version of happiness is that it purports to be effortless.

[12] We demand difficulties even in our games. We demand it because without difficulty there can be no game. A game is a way of making something hard for the fun of it. The rules of the game are an arbitrary imposition of difficulty. When the spoilsport ruins the fun, he always does so by refusing to play by the rules. It is easier to win at chess if you are free, at your pleasure, to change the wholly arbitrary rules, but the fun is winning within the rules. No difficulty, no fun.

[13] The buyers and sellers at the happiness-market seem too often to have lost their sense of the pleasure of difficulty. Heaven knows what they are playing, but it seems a dull game. And the Indian holy man seems dull to us, I suppose, because he seems to be refusing to play anything at all. The Western weakness may be in the illusion that happiness can be bought. Perhaps the Eastern weakness is in the idea that there is such a thing as perfect (and therefore static) happiness.

[14] Happiness is never more than partial. There are no pure states of mankind. Whatever else happiness may be, it is neither in having nor in being, but in becoming. What the Founding Fathers declared for us as an inherent right, we should do well to remember, was not happiness but the pursuit of happiness.

What they might have underlined, could they have foreseen the happiness-market, is the cardinal fact that happiness is in the pursuit itself, in the meaningful pursuit of what is life-engaging and life-revealing, which is to say, in the idea of becoming. A nation is not measured by what it possesses or wants to possess, but by what it wants to become.

[15] By all means let the happiness-market sell us minor satisfactions and even minor follies so long as we keep them in scale and buy them out of spiritual change. I am no customer for either puritanism or asceticism. But drop any real spiritual capital at those bazaars, and what you come home to will be your own poorhouse.

(Harwell, C. W. & Dorrill, J. F., *Read and Write: A Guide to Effective Composition*, 1987)

1. Is there a thesis sentence for this essay? If so, identify it and justify its location.

2. What strategies of development does the writer use in Paragraphs 3, 7, and 12?

3. What does the writer mean by "having", "being" and "becoming" in Paragraph 14?

Unit 6 Definition

Expansion

Passage 1

1. What strategies does the writer of the essay below use in defining good taste in knowledge?
2. "We must give up the idea that a man's knowledge can be tested or measured in any form whatsoever." What is the writer's purpose in saying so when defining a good taste in knowledge?

Good Taste in Knowledge

Lin Yutang

[1] The aim of education or culture is merely the development of good taste in knowledge and good form in conduct. The cultured man or the ideal educated man is not necessarily one who is well-read or learned, but one who likes and dislikes the right things. To know what to love and what to hate is to have taste in knowledge. I have met such persons, and found that there was no topic that might come up in the course of the conversation concerning which they did not have some facts or figures to produce, but whose points of view were deplorable. Such persons have erudition, but no discernment, or taste. Erudition is a mere matter of cramming of facts or information, while taste or discernment is a matter of artistic judgment.

[2] In speaking of a scholar, the Chinese generally distinguish between a man's scholarship, conduct, and taste or discernment. This is particularly so with regard to historians; a book of history may be written with the most fastidious scholarship, yet be totally lacking in insight or discernment, and in the judgment or interpretation of persons and events in history, the author may show no originality or depth of understanding. Such a person, we say, has no taste in knowledge. To be well-informed, or to accumulate facts and details, is the easiest of all things. There are many facts in a given historical period that can be easily crammed into our mind, but discernment in the selection of significant facts is a vastly more difficult thing and depends upon one's point of view.

[3] An educated man, therefore, is one who has the right loves and hatreds. This

we call taste, and with taste comes charm. Now to have taste or discernment requires a capacity for thinking things through to the bottom, an independence of judgment, and an unwillingness to be bulldozed by any form of humbug, social, political, literary, artistic, or academic. There are various kinds of humbugs: fame humbugs, wealth humbugs, patriotic humbugs, political humbugs, religious humbugs and humbug poets, humbug artists, humbug dictators and humbug psychologists. When a psychoanalyst tells us that the performing of the functions of the bowels during childhood has a definite connection with ambition and aggressiveness and sense of duty in one's later life, or that constipation leads to stinginess of character, all that a man with taste can do is to feel amused. When a man is wrong, he is wrong, and there is no need for one to be impressed and overawed by a great name or by the number of books that he has read and we haven't.

[4] Taste then is closely associated with courage, as the Chinese always associate *shih* with *tan*, and courage or independence of judgment, as we know, is such a rare virtue among mankind. We see this intellectual courage or independence during the childhood of all thinkers and writers who in later life amount to anything. Such a person refuses to like a certain poet even if he has the greatest vogue during his time; then when he truly likes a poet, he is able to say why he likes him, and it is an appeal to his inner judgment. This is what we call taste in literature. He also refuses to give his approval to the current school of painting, if it jars upon his artistic instinct. This is taste in art. He also refuses to be impressed by a philosophic vogue or a fashionable theory, even though it were backed by the greatest name. He is unwilling to be convinced by any author until he is convinced at heart; if the author convinces him, then the author is right, but if the author cannot convince him, then he is right and the author wrong. This is taste in knowledge. No doubt such intellectual courage or independence of judgment requires a certain childish, naive confidence in oneself, but this self is the only thing that one can cling to, and the moment a student gives up his right of personal judgment, he is in for accepting all the humbugs of life.

[5] Confucius seemed to have felt that scholarship without thinking was more dangerous than thinking unbacked by scholarship; he said, "Thinking without learning makes one flighty, and learning without thinking is a disaster." He

Unit 6 Definition

must have seen enough students of the latter type in his days for him to utter this warning, a warning very much needed in the modern schools. It is well known that modern education and the modern school system in general tend to encourage scholarship at the expense of discernment and look upon the cramming of information as an end in itself, as if a great amount of scholarship could already make an educated man. But why is thought discouraged at school? Why has the educational system twisted and distorted the pleasant pursuit of knowledge into a mechanical, measured, uniform and passive cramming of information? Why do we place more importance on knowledge than on thought? How do we come to call a college graduate an educated man simply because he has made up the necessary units or week hours of psychology, medieval history, logic, and "religion"? Why are there school marks and diplomas, and how did it come about that the mark and the diploma have, in the student's mind, come to take the place of the true aim of education?

[6] The reason is simple. We have this system because we are educating people in masses, as if in a factory, and anything which happens inside a factory must go by a dead and mechanical system. In order to protect its name and standardize its products, a school must certify them with diplomas. With diplomas, then, comes the necessity of grading, and with the necessity of grading come school marks, and in order to have school marks, there must be recitations, examinations, and tests. The whole thing forms an entirely logical sequence and there is no escape from it. But the consequences of having mechanical examinations and tests are more fatal than we imagine. For it immediately throws the emphasis on memorization of facts rather than on the development of taste or judgment. I have been a teacher myself and know that it is easier to make a set of questions on historical dates than on vague opinions on vague questions. It is also easier to mark the papers.

[7] The danger is that after having instituted this system, we are liable to forget that we have already wavered, or are apt to waver from the true ideal of education, which as I say is the development of good taste in knowledge. It is still useful to remember what Confucius said: "That scholarship which consists in the memorization of facts does not qualify one to be a teacher." There are no such things as compulsory subjects, no books, even Shakespeare's, that one must read. The school seems to proceed on the foolish idea that we can delimit a

minimum stock of learning in history or geography which we can consider the absolute requisite of an educated man. I am pretty well educated, although I am in utter confusion about the capital of Spain, and at one time thought that Havana was the name of an island next to Cuba. The danger of prescribing a course of compulsory studies is that it implies that a man who has gone through the prescribed course *ipso facto* knows all there is to know for an educated man. It is therefore entirely logical that a graduate ceases to learn anything or to read books after he leaves school, because he has already learned all there is to know.

[8] We must give up the idea that a man's knowledge can be tested or measured in any form whatsoever. Chuangtse has well said, "Alas, my life is limited, while knowledge is limitless!" The pursuit of knowledge is, after all, only like the exploration of a new continent, or "an adventure of the soul", as Anatole France says, and it will remain a pleasure, instead of becoming a torture, if the spirit of exploration with an open, questioning, curious and adventurous mind is maintained. Instead of the measured, uniform and passive cramming of information, we have to place this ideal of a positive, growing individual pleasure. Once the diploma and the marks are abolished, or treated for what they are worth, the pursuit of knowledge becomes positive, for the student is at least forced to ask himself why he studies at all. At present, the question is already answered for the student, for there is no question in his mind that he studies as a freshman in order to become a sophomore, and studies as a sophomore in order to become a junior. All such extraneous considerations should be brushed aside, for the acquisition of knowledge is nobody else's business but one's own. At present, all students study for the registrar, and many of the good students study for their parents or teachers or their future wives, that they may not seem ungrateful to their parents who are spending so much money for their support at college, or because they wish to appear nice to a teacher who is nice and conscientious to them, or that they may go out of school and earn a higher salary to feed their families. I suggest that all such thoughts are immoral. The pursuit of knowledge should remain nobody else's business but one's own, and only then can education become a pleasure and become positive.

(The Importance of Living, 2004)

Unit 6 Definition

Passage 2

1. Why does the writer use personal feelings to define poverty?
2. What has made the writer's definition of poverty so impressive?

What Is Poverty?

Jo Goodwin Parker

[1] You ask me what is poverty? Listen to me. Here I am, dirty, smelly, and with no "proper" underwear on and with the stench of my rotting teeth near you. I will tell you. Listen to me. Listen without pity. I cannot use your pity. Listen with understanding. Put yourself in my dirty, worn out, ill-fitting shoes, and hear me.

[2] Poverty is getting up every morning from a dirt-and-illness-stained mattress. The sheets have long since been used for diapers. Poverty is living in a smell that never leaves. This is a smell of urine, sour milk, and spoiling food sometimes joined with the strong smell of long-cooked onions. Onions are cheap. If you have smelled this smell, you did not know how it came. It is the smell of the outdoor privy. It is the smell of young children who cannot walk the long dark way in the night. It is the smell of the mattresses where years of "accidents" have happened. It is the smell of the milk which has gone sour because the refrigerator long has not worked, and it costs money to get it fixed. It is the smell of rotting garbage. I could bury it, but where is the shovel? Shovels cost money.

[3] Poverty is being tired. I have always been tired. They told me at the hospital when the last baby came that I had chronic anemia caused from poor diet, a bad case of worms, and that I needed a corrective operation. I listened politely — the poor are always polite. The poor always listen. They don't say that there is no money for iron pills, or better food, or worm medicine. The idea of an operation is frightening and costs so much that, if I had dared, I would have laughed. Who takes care of my children? Recovery from an operation takes a long time. I have three children. When I left them with "Granny" the last time I had a job, I came home to find the baby covered with fly specks, and a diaper that had not been changed since I left. When the dried diaper came off, bits of my baby's flesh came with it. My other child was playing with a sharp bit of

broken glass, and my oldest was playing alone at the edge of a lake. I made twenty-two dollars a week, and a good nursery school costs twenty dollars a week for three children. I quit my job.

[4] Poverty is dirt. You can say in your clean clothes coming from your clean house, "Anybody can be clean." Let me explain about housekeeping with no money. For breakfast I give my children grits with no oleo or cornbread without eggs and oleo. This does not use up many dishes. What dishes there are, I wash in cold water and with no soap. Even the cheapest soap has to be saved for the baby's diapers. Look at my hands, so cracked and red. Once I saved for two months to buy a jar of Vaseline for my hands and the baby's diaper rash. When I had saved enough, I went to buy it and the price had gone up two cents. The baby and I suffered on. I have to decide every day if I can bear to put my cracked sore hands into the cold water and strong soap. But you ask, why not hot water? Fuel costs money. If you have a wood fire, it costs money. If you burn electricity, it costs money. Hot water is a luxury. I do not have luxuries. I know you will be surprised when I tell you how young I am. I look so much older. My back has been bent over the wash tubs every day for so long, I cannot remember when I ever did anything else. Every night I wash every stitch my school age child has on and just hope her clothes will be dry by morning.

[5] Poverty is staying up all night on cold nights to watch the fire knowing one spark on the newspaper covering the walls means your sleeping child dies in flames. In summer poverty is watching gnats and flies devour your baby's tears when he cries. The screens are torn and you pay so little rent you know they will never be fixed. Poverty means insects in your food, in your nose, in your eyes, and crawling over you when you sleep. Poverty is hoping it never rains because diapers won't dry when it rains and soon you are using newspapers. Poverty is seeing your children forever with runny noses. Paper handkerchiefs cost money and all your rags you need for other things. Even more costly are antihistamines. Poverty is cooking without food and cleaning without soap.

[6] Poverty is asking for help. Have you ever had to ask for help, knowing your children will suffer unless you get it? Think about asking for a loan from a relative, if this is the only way you can imagine asking for help. I will tell you how it feels. You find out where the office is that you are supposed to visit. You circle that block four or five times. Thinking of your children, you go in.

Unit 6 Definition

Everyone is very busy. Finally, someone comes out and you tell her that you need help. That never is the person you need to see. You go see another person, and after spilling the whole shame of your poverty all over the desk between you, you find that this isn't the right office after all — you must repeat the whole process, and it never is any easier at the next place.

[7] You have asked for help, and after all it has a cost. You are again told to wait. You are told why, but you don't really hear because of the red cloud of shame and the rising cloud of despair.

[8] Poverty is remembering. It is remembering quitting school in junior high because "nice" children had been so cruel about my clothes and my smell. The attendance officer came. My mother told him I was pregnant. I wasn't, but she thought that I could get a job and help out. I had jobs off and on, but never long enough to learn anything. Mostly I remember being married. I was so young then. I am still young. For a time, we had all the things you have. There was a little house in another town, with hot water and everything. Then my husband lost his job. There was unemployment insurance for a while and what few jobs I could get. Soon, all our nice things were repossessed and we moved back here. I was pregnant then. This house didn't look so bad when we first moved in. Every week it gets worse. Nothing is ever fixed. We now had no money. There were a few odd jobs for my husband, but everything went for food then, as it does now. I don't know how we lived through three years and three babies, but we did. I'll tell you something, after the last baby died I destroyed my marriage. It had been a good one, but could you keep on bringing children in this dirt? Did you ever think how much it costs for any kind of birth control? I knew my husband was leaving the day he left, but there were no goodbye between us. I hope he has been able to climb out of this mess somewhere. He never could hope with us to drag him down.

[9] That's when I asked for help. When I got it, you know how much it was? It was, and is, seventy-eight dollars a month for the four of us; that is all I ever can get. Now you know why there is no soap, no needles and thread, no hot water, no aspirin, no worm medicine, no hand cream, no shampoo. None of these things forever and ever and ever. So that you can see clearly, I pay twenty dollars a month rent, and most of the rest goes for food. For grits and cornmeal, and rice and milk and beans. I try my best to use only the minimum electricity. If I use

more, there is that much less for food.

[10] Poverty is looking into a black future. Your children won't play with my boys. They will turn to other boys who steal to get what they want. I can already see them behind the bars of their prison instead of behind the bars of my poverty. Or they will turn to the freedom of alcohol or drugs, and find themselves enslaved. And my daughter? At best, there is for her a life like mine.

[11] But you say to me, there are schools. Yes, there are schools. My children have no extra books, no magazines, no extra pencils, or crayons, or paper and most important of all, they do not have health. They have worms, they have infections, they have pink-eye all summer. They do not sleep well on the floor, or with me in my one bed. They do not suffer from hunger, my seventy-eight dollars keeps us alive, but they do suffer from malnutrition. Oh yes, I do remember what I was taught about health in school. It doesn't do much good.

[12] In some places there is a surplus commodities program. Not here. The country said it cost too much. There is a school lunch program. But I have two children who will already be damaged by the time they get to school.

[13] But, you say to me, there are health clinics. Yes, there are health clinics and they are in the town. I live out here eight miles from town. I can walk that far (even if it is sixteen miles both ways), but can my little children? My neighbor will take me when he goes; but he expects to get paid, one way or another. I bet you know my neighbor. He is that large man who spends his time at the gas station, the barbershop, and the corner store complaining about the government spending money on the immoral mothers of illegitimate children.

[14] Poverty is an acid that drips on pride until all pride is worn away. Poverty is a chisel that chips on honor until honor is worn away. Some of you say that you would do something in my situation, and maybe you would, for the first week or the first month, but for year after year after year?

[15] Even the poor can dream. A dream of a time when there is money. Money for the right kinds of food, for worm medicine, for iron pills, for toothbrushes, for hand cream, for a hammer and nails and a bit of screening, for a shovel, for a bit of paint, for some sheeting, for needles and thread. Money to pay in money for a trip to town. And, oh, money for hot water and money for soap. A dream of when asking for help does not eat away the last bit of pride. When the office

you visit is as nice as the offices of other governmental agencies, when there are enough workers to help you quickly, when workers do not quit in defeat and despair. When you have to tell your story to only one person, and that person can send you for other help and you don't have to prove your poverty over and over and over again.

[16] I have come out of my despair to tell you this. Remember I did not come from another place or another time. Others like me are all around you. Look at us with an angry heart, anger that will help you help me. Anger that will let you tell of me. The poor are always silent. Can you be silent too?

Note:

The essay was published in America's *Other Children: Public Schools Outside Suburbs*, by George Henderson in 1971 by the University of Oklahoma Press. The author has requested that no biographical information about her be distributed. The essay is a personal account, addressed directly to readers, about living in poverty.

(Henderson, G., *Other Children: Public Schools Outside Suburbs*, 1971)

Unit 7
Argumentation

Objectives

At the end of this unit, you should be able to

- ☑ understand the role of argumentation in paragraph and essay development;
- ☑ emphasize arguments in paragraphs and essays by using appropriate transitional words and expressions;
- ☑ write an argumentative essay with critical thinking and a positive voice encouraging core socialist values such as civility, freedom, harmony, and prosperity.

Pre-class Work

Task 1

● **Reading for Writing**

Do you use social media often? Some people are worried that social media will do harm to us. Do you agree? Why or why not?

The Dark Side of Social Media

Ntianu Obiora

[1] These day, social media is doing more harm than good with young men and women becoming increasingly insecure due to unrealistic beauty ideals. Social media is both the joy and the curse of the 21st century. In one way, the digital age has opened us up to another world, created jobs that we never knew could exist and connected people, the world over. On the other hand, the pressure to keep up with what we see online has become an unhealthy cycle, which is destroying lives one click at a time. In particular, men and women have found themselves battling identity issues because of the unrealistic beauty standards set by what they see on social media. Many have developed serious mental issues, identity issues and even body abnormality trying to follow the beauty standards that are simply unattainable.

Unit 7 Argumentation

[2] The first thing most of us do when we wake up in the morning is to instinctively reach for our phones. From the very minute we open our eyes, we are immersing ourselves in an alternate reality. Just as most of us use social media to promote ourselves, tons of celebrities, influencers, models and brands, also use it to sell themselves by creating an image of perfection. It's hard not to see a multitude of perfectly toned beauties. Thousands of social media accounts promote images of perfectly sculpted men and women. Whilst we may believe we are mindlessly scrolling through such content, our subconscious is soaking it all up and before we know it, those perfectly formed bodies have become the standard by which we measure everything else. There is an apparent problem within this false world of idealism. Thousands of famous people and models on social media document their workout routines, eating habits, and other aspects of their lifestyle that contribute to the way they look. There is only one problem with this industry; it's all fake.

[3] A social media model can post a picture of herself in a bikini, showing off her taut stomach, holding up a weight loss tea supplement. Her caption reveals that said supplement is the secret to her honed physique. This alone, sends a very dangerous message to millions of her followers, the majority of whom are impressionable young adults. It is spreading the idea that supplements, diet spills and detox teas are the best way to achieve her body type, when in reality, it could not be further from the truth. More often than not, their looks are a combination of gym, plastic surgery and a generous amount of retouching. Her job is to look perfect and promote merchandise. This creates an unrealistic beauty standard for all of her followers who believe that this product is their ticket to a perfect body.

[4] In reality, a perfect body does not exist. An immense amount of planning, makeup and photo editing went into the final picture she posted online. It's designed to sell a product, not support a healthy lifestyle. This leads to low self-esteem and negative thinking towards food. It is incredibly important to teach young women and men that social media is not real life. Every day, we see the hashtag "body goals" or "thinspo", which is supposed to serve as inspiration to acquire a thin body. In essence, social media tells us that we need to be a beautiful person in order to be worthy which could not be further from the truth.

[5] According to eating disorders statistics estimated by the National Eating Disorders Association, in the USA up to 30 million people suffer from an eating disorder such as anorexia nervosa, bulimia nervosa or binge eating disorder. Worldwide the figure is more like 70 million sufferers. There is a positive correlation between the rise of social media and the rise in eating disorders among young men and women. Many desperately trying to emulate the types of bodies they see and ending up doing more physical and psychological damage to themselves.

[6] In a kickback against the devastating effects of social media on, in particular on young people already struggling to understand themselves and where they fit in, a bunch of accounts have popped up revealing the truth behind those "perfect" pictures. Accounts such as @celebface may seem like they are picking on people but in reality, they are created to remind us that social media is nothing but smoke and mirrors and that those we hold in such high self-esteem are nothing but mere mortals.

[7] Celeb Face will make you feel better about yourself and realize that "celebs they're just like us!!!". You can see their pores and fine lines, and they too use FaceTune. The account also reveals before and after surgery shots of celebrities and influencers so that we can see that some of these "ideal" bodies are man-made. Overall, it reminds us not to be so hard on ourselves.

(*The World of English*, 2020)

1. Write down the thesis statement of the passage.

_____

_____

2. All the evidence below is used by the writer to support the main point except that _____.

A. social media creates an unrealistic industry in which people cannot distinguish reality from the fake

B. social media provides an unrealistic beauty standard for the followers of some celebrities and leads to low self-esteem, for it tells us that we need to be a beautiful person in order to be worthy

C. social media causes people to suffer from eating disorders while they emulate the types of bodies they see

Unit 7 Argumentation

D. Celeb Face will not make you feel better about yourself and realize that "celebs they're always perfect!!!"

3. What does the last paragraph mean? What does the writer want to tell readers?

_____

_____

4. Why do you think the writer uses statistics from the US National Eating Disorders Association?

_____

_____

_____

5. Do you agree that many people have developed serious mental issues, identity issues and even body abnormality because of the beauty standards set by what they see on social media? Why or why not?

_____

_____

• Vocabulary Highlights

Study the words and phrases in the passage with the help of a dictionary. Write down the definitions as they are used in the context.

dysmorphia   _____

                   _____

supplement   _____

impressionable   _____

                   _____

retouch   _____

                   _____

207

anorexia nervosa

bulimia nervosa

binge eating
disorder

pick on

Task 2

● **Writing Your First Draft**

> Social media is both the joy and the curse of the 21st century. On the one hand, the digital age has opened us up to another world and connected people, the world ever. On the other hand, the pressure to keep up with what we see online has become an unhealthy cycle, which is destroying lives one click at a time. What do you think of social media? Write an essay with emphasis on argumentation to develop your ideas.

In-class Activities

▶ What Is Argument?

Argument refers to the process of reasoning which includes one or a set of claims with proper and sound support over a controversial point. It is frequently used as a strategy, not only to clarify something, but also to convince and persuade someone. Without argument, the claims you make are not strongly supported and less likely to influence your readers to your point of view. Thus, using argument is an important skill for EFL writers.

Unit 7 Argumentation

What Is Argument for?

Arguments are mainly used in argumentative writing. For example, when you argue for or against the use of cell phones in the classroom, your position can be clearly made and backed up by solid evidence. If you are for the use of cell phones in the classroom, your claim might be clearly supported by rebutting the opposite opinions and presenting advantages that using cell phones in the classroom have. With this argument, your position over the controversial issue is defended and your readers are made to agree with your point of view.

An awareness of the role of argument in writing can make efficient readers. While reading editorials of newspapers, articles on controversial political or theoretical issues, and various proposals, you should keep an eye for the writer's claim and his or her way to support the claim. With regard to the use of argument, you should notice what arguments are used, how they are used, and whether they are used properly. This process of exploration, becoming skilled in clear, logical reasoning, can enhance your ability to read and write.

What Is Argumentation?

Argumentation refers to the use of argumentative strategies in paragraph and essay development. Generally speaking, it serves the purposes of making claims, providing supporting arguments for the claims, rebutting the opposite opinions, and ultimately persuading readers. It is one of the most effective ways to convince readers to change their mind or behavior and agree with our thoughts, ideas, etc. We often need to use argument, i.e. an interactive activity which revolves around a claim supported by solid evidence, to target a specific population to persuade. Therefore, how to use argument effectively is essential to settle conflicts and promote communication.

The way you develop your topic largely depends on the topic and your intention. For example, if you are writing about whether plastic surgery is harmful to its patients, you would probably want to develop your topic with arguments that refute the practice of plastic surgery. But the length varies according to your intention: it could be a full-length essay or a single paragraph. In the former case, the essay may include a few paragraphs dealing with supporting arguments that show plastic surgery leads to serious physical, psychological and emotional problems. All these problems might be presented with supporting arguments, or even with the rebuttal of differing viewpoints. In the latter case, however, the paragraph might be a concessional one in an essay focusing on the benefits of plastic surgery, thus it suffices to list the possible problems encountered by the patients before switching back to the main theme of the article, namely the benefits.

Argumentation in Paragraph Development

Argumentation is an effective method to develop a paragraph, responding to an assertion, questioning something which is believed to be certain by a significant party, or even convincing someone that a certain view is correct or wrong. Arguments in paragraph development also vary considerably in length. In some cases, one or two short supporting arguments are enough as long as they can serve to defend your claim in the paragraph. In other cases, however, it may not be enough to simply acknowledge supporting arguments. When you are dealing with an issue that your readers feel strongly about, you may need to present the opposing argument and rebut that point, then present your counterargument.

• Activity 1

Read one of your classmates' first draft and try to find out how he or she developed the essay by argumentation.

(1) The controversial issue of the writing is focused on _____.

(2) The position of the writing is _____.

(3) The position is defended by the following arguments:

_____

_____

_____

(4) How are the opposing views acknowledged?

_____

(5) How is the writing ended?

_____

Unit 7 Argumentation

Read the following paragraphs and answer the questions.

Paragraph 1

Cooperating with popular live-streaming hosts to get a share of the Chinese market has certain branding advantages. "Live-streaming hosts have far better promotion skills than mainstream celebrities," says Xintong Liu, a young female professional working in Shanghai who watches live-streams regularly to purchase beauty products and clothing. "I followed many popular live-streaming hosts' live streaming because they could better explain the ingredients used in a powder, which situation each of the lipstick colors would be best in, and so on," she explained. Key opinion leaders (KOL) also have more time to interact with their viewers than celebrities, and their live-streaming practice usually takes around six or seven hours daily, which creates a sense of intimacy between KOL and viewers. And consumers are more likely to purchase a product once some trust is built.

(Yang, Q., Live-streaming KOL Meltdowns, The World of English, 2020)

1. What is the topic sentence of the paragraph?

___

2. How does the writer develop the topic sentence?

___

3. What do you think is the effect of argument on the support of the topic sentence?

___

211

4. How does the writer build up relations between the arguments?

___

Paragraph 2

More than anything, the Internet has brought big-city life to provincial backwaters. Some people claim that the Internet has brought country living to the town, fostering a new urban romance with rural China. The feeling is encapsulated in *xiangchou*, longing for one's hometown — a Chinese form of "cottagecore". As young tourists increasingly shun big resorts for rustic retreats, rural youths see urban enthusiasm for their lifestyle. Undoubtedly that can be true. However, now a small but growing counterflow of migrants has begun to go home. The rural young shop on their phones like the urban young, spending hours on the same social media and video apps. With a few taps, they can get almost anything delivered thanks to the sprawling logistics industry underpinning Chinese e-commerce. Returning youth often find jobs selling stuff from premium tea to *tofu*. Since mid-2019, over 100,000 livestreamers have tuned in from farms to shift goods on one of the giant e-shops.

(The Gap Between China's Rural and Urban Youth Is Closing, The Economist, 2021)

1. What is the topic sentence of this paragraph?

___

2. How does the writer develop the topic sentence? How is it different from Paragraph 1?

___

Unit 7 Argumentation

3. How does the writer build up relations between the differing arguments?

_____

_____

_____

_____

● **Activity 2**

Discuss in pairs how you are going to use argument to make a point. List the pros and cons according to the topic sentences below.

1. PE grades should be required for college admission.

PRO 1: _____

_____

PRO 2: _____

_____

PRO 3: _____

_____

CON 1: _____

_____

CON 2: _____

_____

CON 3: _____

_____

2. It is a waste for well-educated women to be housewives.

PRO 1: _____

PRO 2: _____

_____

PRO 3: _____

_____

CON 1: _____

_____

CON 2: _____

_____

CON 3: _____

_____

3. It is time to embrace a plant-based diet.

PRO 1: _____

_____

PRO 2: _____

_____

PRO 3: _____

_____

CON 1: _____

_____

CON 2: _____

_____

CON 3: _____

_____

Unit 7 Argumentation

▶ *Argument in Essay Development*

In the case that the topic is a broad one, you cannot adequately cover it in one single paragraph. You would need to write a longer essay to cover the topic effectively. Generally, the topic would be divided into subtopics which are then illustrated in turn in the supporting paragraphs.

• Activity 3

Suppose you are going to develop the following topics into a full-length essay, what argument will you use?

1. China's communal eating culture

Thesis statement: _____

_____

_____ (Transition) _____

_____ (Topic sentence 1)

_____ (Transition) _____

_____ (Topic sentence 2)

_____ (Transition) _____

_____ (Topic sentence 3)

2. Gig economy

Thesis statement: _____

_____

_____ (Transition) _____

_____ (Topic sentence 1)

_____ (Transition) _____

_____ (Topic sentence 2)

_____ (Transition) _____

_____ (Topic sentence 3)

3. Ride-hailing services

Thesis statement: _____

_____ _____
(Transition)

_____ (Topic sentence 1)

_____ _____
(Transition)

_____ (Topic sentence 2)

_____ _____
(Transition)

_____ (Topic sentence 3)

• Activity 4

To what extent do you agree "it is no use doing what you like; you have got to like what you do" and "work banishes those three great evils: boredom, vice, and poverty"? Read the following article and finish the exercises.

Teenagers and Jobs

[1] "The pressure for teenagers to work is great, and not just because of the economic plight in the world today. Much of it is peer pressure to have a little bit of freedom and independence, and to have their own spending money. The concern we have is when the part-time work becomes the primary focus." These are the words of Roxanne Bradshaw, educator and officer of the National Education Association of the US. Many people argue that working can be a valuable experience for the young. However, working more than about fifteen hours a week is harmful to adolescents because it reduces their involvement with school, encourages a materialistic and expensive lifestyle, and increases the chance of having problems with drugs and alcohol.

[2] The first problem lies in schoolwork and extracurricular activities. As more and more teens have filled the numerous part-time jobs offered by fast-food malls,

Unit 7 Argumentation

teachers have faced increasing difficulties. They must both keep the attention of tired pupils and give homework to students who simply don't have time to do it. In addition, educators have noticed less involvement in the extracurricular activities that many consider a healthy influence on young people. School bands and athletic teams are losing players to work, and sports events are poorly attended by working students. Those teens who try to do it all — homework, extracurricular activities, and work — may find themselves exhausted and prone to illness. A recent newspaper story, for example, describes a girl in Pennsylvania who came down with mononucleosis as a result of aiming for good grades, playing on two school athletic teams, and working thirty hours a week.

[3] Another drawback of too much work is that it may promote materialism and an unrealistic lifestyle. Some parents claim that working helps teach adolescents the value of a dollar. Undoubtedly that can be true. It's also true that some teens work to help out with the family budget or to save for college. However, surveys have shown that the majority of working teens use their earnings to buy luxuries — computers, video-game systems clothing, even cars. These young people, some of whom earn $500 or more a month, don't worry about spending wisely — they can just about have it all. In many cases, as experts point out, they are becoming accustomed to a lifestyle they won't be able to afford several years down road, when they no longer have parents paying for car insurance, food, lodging, and so on. At that point, they'll be hard-pressed to pay for necessities as well as luxuries.

[4] _____

Teens who put in hours may seek a quick release from stress, just like the adults who need to drink a couple of martinis after a hard day at work. Also, teens who have money are more likely to get involved with drugs.

[5] Teenagers can enjoy the benefits of work while avoiding its drawbacks, simply by limiting their work hours during the school year. As is often the case, a moderate approach will be the most healthy and rewarding.

(Langan, J., *College Writing Skills With Readings*, 2014)

1. What arguments are given by the writer in each category? What are the intended meanings of these arguments?

Categories	Arguments	Intended meanings
Involvement with school		
A materialistic and expensive lifestyle		
Problems with drugs and alcohol		

2. Write down the thesis statement of the essay.

_____

_____

3. What do you think should be the topic sentence of Paragraph 4? Write it down on the line in the essay.

4. The writer ends the essay by _____ .

5. What are Chinese people's attitudes toward whether teenagers should have part-time work? Ask people around and make a list of pros and cons according to this topic.

_____

_____

Unit 7 Argumentation

6. How does the writer organize the paragraphs? Are the arguments enough to support the writer's central claim? Why or why not?

___

• Vocabulary Highlights

Study the words and phrases below with the help of a dictionary. Write down the definitions.

plight

prone to

mononucleosis

drawback

luxury

hard-pressed

moderate

List the expressions giving arguments in the passage.

219

Using Argument

An outline of the preceding essay might look like this.

> **Thesis statement:** However, working more than about fifteen hours a week is harmful to adolescents because it reduces their involvement with school, encourages a materialistic and expensive lifestyle, and increases the chance of having problems with drugs and alcohol.
> **Topic Sentence 1:** The first problem lies in schoolwork and extracurricular activities.
> **Topic Sentence 2:** Another drawback of too much work is that it may promote materialism and an unrealistic lifestyle.
> **Topic Sentence 3:** Finally, teenagers who work a lot are more likely than others to get involved with alcohol and drugs.
> **Conclusion:** Teenagers can enjoy the benefits of work while avoiding its drawbacks, simply by limiting their work hours during the school year.

This is a typical essay developed by argumentation. In order to support the viewpoint that teenagers should not work long hours, the writer resorts to three supporting arguments, namely too much work reduces their involvement with school, promotes materialism, and increases the chance of having problems with alcohol and drugs. These arguments provide solid evidence for the writer's claim.

While we use argumentation as a writing strategy, we should bear in mind a few factors that help win over readers whose viewpoint may differ from ours. These factors are the number of arguments, the essence of good arguments, and the organization of arguments.

▶ Number of arguments

The number of arguments to include largely depends on your purpose, or specifically, on your thesis statement: if it is of a modest scope, three or four arguments will suffice; if it is broad enough, its adequate development calls for numerous arguments. For example, if you are writing about whether college students should do part-time jobs, you might first make a point before you support it with arguments. Your thesis statement will probably be: "College students should do part-time jobs." To persuade readers to support your opinion, your claim will then be supported by the benefits of doing part-time jobs, such as "good for developing money management skills", "learning to budget time for job, school, and social life", and "a chance to use the skills learned in school". In this way, you provide your readers with a clear main point about a controversial topic and plenty of logical evidence to back it up.

▶ Essence of good arguments

There are some shared features of good arguments. Firstly, the arguments you use to support the thesis statement should fairly support it. In other words, you should use appropriate arguments at proper places. For example, when arguing that the practice of martial arts is not useless, you should advance it with arguments related to the benefits of martial arts to our health, mind, and emotion. These arguments are to the point. However, those arguments only focusing on how we practice martial arts might be irrelevant.

Besides, good arguments are specific. Readers have a natural tendency to prefer specific reasons and supporting evidence instead of vague generalities. To provide concrete arguments, you may resort to effective methods of logic reasoning, such as giving examples, presenting a comparison or contrast, showing a cause-and-effect relationship, arguing by definition, etc. A specific argument can serve to explain a writer's points and easily engage and convince a reader.

More importantly, good arguments should be complete. That is to say, in order to effectively support your thesis, you must make sure that the information you give about each argument is complete. This means that you must not only emphasize arguments that are related to your topic, but also give some facts that relate to and support the controlling ideas. Suppose you are writing an essay with the thesis statement: "Online shopping at home has several advantages." If you supported this thesis with "such shopping is convenient", you haven't supported the controlling idea — that online shopping at home has advantages. A more complete example would be: "Such shopping is convenient, saves money, and saves time. It is not surprising that growing numbers of people are doing the majority of their shopping on the Internet for everything from turnip seeds to televisions." Now your argument shows one of the advantages of online shopping — saving money and saving time.

• Activity 5

Finish the following exercises and try to formulate good arguments.

1. Write down the arguments for the thesis statement "college students should do part-time jobs".

   _____
   _____
   _____
   _____
   _____

2. The arguments for the topic "the practice of martial arts is not useless" do NOT include _____.
A. the practice of martial arts varies from person to person
B. the benefit of martial arts to our mind
C. the benefit of martial arts to our emotion
D. the benefit of martial arts to our health

3. To provide concrete arguments, the writer of the following paragraph resorts to effective methods of logic reasoning, which do NOT include _____.

Local TV newscasters are as much the subject of the news as the stories they present. Nowhere is this more obvious than in weather reports. Weatherpersons spend valuable news time joking, drawing cartoons, chatting about weather fronts as "good guys" and "bad guys", and dispensing weather trivia such as statistics about relative humidity and record highs and lows for the date. Reporters, too, draw attention to themselves. Rather than just getting the story, the reporters are shown jumping into or getting out of helicopters to get the story. When reporters interview crime victims or the residents of poor neighborhoods, the camera angle typically includes them and their reaction as well as their subjects. When they report on a storm, they stand outside in the storm, their styled hair blowing, so we can admire how they "brave the elements." Then there are the anchorpersons, who are chosen as much for their looks as their skills. They, too, dilute the news by putting their personalities at center stage.

Unit 7 Argumentation

A. giving examples

B. presenting a comparison or contrast

C. showing a cause-and-effect relationship

D. arguing by definition

4. Suppose you are writing an essay with the thesis statement "online shopping at home has several advantages". If you supported this thesis with "such shopping is convenient", you haven't supported the controlling idea. What is a more complete argument?

_____

_____

_____

▸ Organization of arguments

The arguments in a supporting paragraph can be organized according to time, familiarity, and importance. In an argumentative essay, the principle of organization is essentially the same. Different as they are, these principles all underlie a fundamental rule: that is the writer's prediction of readers' response. You should judge your readers' familiarity with the arguments, their interest or other reader-related factors before you can organize your arguments in a reader-friendly way.

Besides the organizing principles, transitions between paragraphs also matter much. Developmental paragraphs in the argumentative essay must be connected so that they flow smoothly. This helps readers clearly understand the progression of thought. Just as a paragraph will be incoherent if the sentences can be switched around without significant change in meaning, an essay will be incoherent if the paragraphs can be switched around without significant change.

In an argumentative essay, there are also different transitional words and phrases that can be used in each developmental paragraph. They are signal words to remind readers of the use of arguments; they are also connectors to maintain close relations between paragraphs. Below is a list of commonly-used transitional words and phrases for emphasizing arguments.

Paragraphs	Arguments
First	✓ First, there is no doubt that … ✓ It is universally acknowledged that … ✓ To begin with, it is a common belief that … but …
Second	✓ Second, it seems obvious that … ✓ What's worse, … has a serious effect not only on … but also on … ✓ Some people assume that …, while others argue that …
Last	✓ Last but not least, it is reasonable to … ✓ Worst of all, there is no denying that … ✓ Most important of all, it is true that … but it doesn't follow that …

Transitional expressions are useful for making paragraphs connect logically; however, if these phrases are used all the time, they can become mechanical and repetitious. For variety and for even more smoothness, you are advised to pick up a key idea, word, or phrase from one paragraph and then use it in the sentence introducing the next paragraph.

• Activity 6

Complete the following sentences with expressions from the table.

| despite | although | however | admittedly |
| in favor of | on the contrary | against | |

1. _____, old people are unlikely to face physically challenging tasks. _____, there are many jobs that are especially suitable for them, such as jobs that call for more experience and wisdom than physical power.

2. _____ there are certainly gentle men and aggressive women, by and large, females are less likely to resort to violence in attempting to solve problem.

3. _____ its importance, there is no denying that every now and then, advertising leads consumers into an impulse purchase, thereby causing wasteful spending.

4. There are different opinions among London citizens in terms of home quarantine order. Over 70% citizens are _____ this order on account of the recent outbreak

Unit 7 Argumentation

of coronavirus. _____, others hold the view that home quarantine order is a threat to their freedom.

5. Supporters believe that considering the rapid spread of coronavirus among UK, the home quarantine order published by UK government is a wise decision. But those _____ it offer an explanation that home quarantine will lead to economic recession and employment decline.

Refer back to the reading "Teenagers and Jobs" and focus on the beginning sentence of each developmental paragraph. These sentences are replaced by sentences that repeat key words and phrases. Make a comparison of the original version and the improved version (see below) and understand how this helps achieve better flow of information and certainly better connections between paragraphs.

Original version	Improved version
The first problem lies in schoolwork and extracurricular activities.	Schoolwork and the benefits of extracurricular activities tend to go by the wayside when adolescents work long hours.
Another drawback of too much work is that it may promote materialism and an unrealistic lifestyle.	Apart from reducing teenagers' involvement with school, too much work promotes materialism and an unrealistic lifestyle.
Finally, teenagers who work a lot are more likely than others to get involved with alcohol and drugs.	The worst influence of working too much is that it is likely to cause teenagers' problems with alcohol and drugs.

• Activity 7

Read the student essay on whether modern technology is beneficial or not and do the exercises.

Modern Technology, Magical or Addictive?

[1] Nowadays in China, it is quite a common scene that people at all ages use their mobile phones to scan the QR code at almost any place, which a lot of my foreign friends are confused about. Then I tell them that's a mobile payment platform and what makes it so popular is the rapid growth of modern

technology. Some people may consider modern technology harmful and addictive. But we cannot deny the benefits modern technology has brought, for it has changed the way we live, the way we play and the way we receive medical care.

[2] To begin with, the way we live has been changed. First, it changes the way we pay in daily life. In China, there are few people going out with cash on their side these days thanks to the popularization of online payment, which brings us so much convenience. Over 90% shops and department stores are now using online payment as their main way of collection. Also, transportation in China has been shockingly changed with the use of sharing system. You now can use those online apps to ride a shared bike or drive a shared car without buying one. The only thing you have to do is to scan the QR code and pay by your phone.

[3] Besides, the way we play has also been greatly changed. In the past, things we played with were so limited that we sometimes felt bored in our spare time. Now there are countless new game devices such as sense games being invented thanks to modern technology. What's more, modern technology enables us to get into the magical world that we used to imagine and appreciate. For example, virtual reality, a newly-invented technology, has been widely used in the gaming areas. If you are a big fan of Harry Potter, with such technique you will feel like being in the Triwizard Tournament and fighting the Dark Lord with Harry, which will absolutely give you an unbelievable experience.

[4] Last but not least, the way we receive medical care has gone through a great reform as well. In my memory, queuing for registration in the hospital had always been a nightmare when I was a kid. Standing still for more than two hours, being crowded by all kinds of patients and suffering from the pain of illness made the experience in hospital terrible. But that was all in the past. Nowadays most of these things can be done automatically. You can register online first instead of queuing for hours. After the diagnosis and treatment, you can also get the medicine according to the order given automatically by computer, thus totally making things much easier and more convenient.

[5] In conclusion, modern technology seems to play an active role in people's daily life, entertainment, and healthcare. Though technology is a two-edged sword, I believe, if people take advantages of modern technology as above, they will benefit from it certainly.

Unit 7 Argumentation

1. Make an outline for the essay.

Thesis statement	
Topic sentence 1	
Topic sentence 2	
Topic sentence 3	
Conclusion	

2. Change the beginning sentence of each developmental paragraph by "repeating key words and phrases".

Original sentences	Revised sentences
Topic sentence 1	
Topic sentence 2	
Topic sentence 3	

Activity 8

Write a second draft of the essay in Task 2 of Pre-class Work about whether social media is the joy or the curse of the 21st century. Then, work in pairs to review each other's writing. Be a critical thinker. Find faults with the content, structure, and language of your peer's essay just as you have done to yours. Swap the essay, finish the checklist and write comments or suggestions on the margins of your peer's essay.

Items	Questions	Y/N	Points
Opening remarks	Is the lead attractive?		
Thesis statement	Does it have a plan of development?		
	Does it agree with the topic sentences?		
Topic sentences	Does each one sum up the corresponding paragraph?		
	Is there transition between one and another?		
Paragraphs	Has each one provided details to support its argument?		
	Is transitional words used within the paragraphs to help readers follow the writer's train of thought?		
Summary sentence	Is it a paraphrased thesis statement to summarize the writer's argument or add a final persuasive touch?		
Sentence skills	Is parallelism, or other rhetorical devices used in the essay?		
	Are there any spelling mistakes, grammar mistakes, redundancy, or ambiguity?		
Overall evaluation	A thumb of rule: Each question is worth 10 points, but you may adjust on your own.	Overall score	

Unit 7 Argumentation

After-class Practice

Task 1

Suppose you are going to develop the following topics into an argumentative essay, how are you going to state the topic sentences? Make sure that the paragraphs are connected.

Topics	Topic sentences of developmental paragraphs
Is the cashless era in China coming?	
Which do you prefer, home care or nursing home care?	
Does free Internet access help students study?	
Is it time to abandon the overwork culture?	
Does technology lower our creative abilities?	
Should we stop using plastic bags?	

Task 2

The technologies expected to dominate the new decade also seem to cast a dark shadow. Read the following passage and do the exercises.

Pessimism vs Progress

[1] Faster, cheaper, better — technology is one field many people rely upon to offer a vision of a brighter future. But as the 2020s dawn, optimism is in short supply. The new technologies that dominated the past decade seem to be making things worse. Social media were supposed to bring people together. In the Arab spring of 2011 they were hailed as a liberating force. Today they are better known for invading privacy, spreading propaganda and undermining democracy. E-commerce, ride-hailing and the gig economy may be convenient, but they are charged with underpaying workers, exacerbating inequality and clogging the streets with vehicles. Parents worry that smart phones have turned their children into screen-addicted zombies.

[2] The technologies expected to dominate the new decade also seem to cast a dark shadow. Artificial intelligence (AI) may well entrench bias and prejudice, threaten your job and shore up authoritarian rulers. Autonomous cars still do not work, but manage to kill people all the same. Polls show that Internet firms are now less trusted than the banking industry. At the very moment banks are striving to rebrand themselves as tech firms, Internet giants have become the new banks, morphing from talent magnets to pariahs. Even their employees are in revolt.

[3] The *New York Times* sums up the encroaching gloom. "A mood of pessimism", it writes, has displaced "the idea of inevitable progress born in the scientific and industrial revolutions". Except those words are from an article published in 1979. Back then the paper fretted that the anxiety was "fed by growing doubts about society's ability to rein in the seemingly runaway forces of technology".

[4] Today's gloomy mood is centred on smart phones and social media, which took off a decade ago. Yet concerns that humanity has taken a technological wrong turn, or that particular technologies might be doing more harm than good, have arisen before. In the 1970s the despondency was prompted by concerns

about overpopulation, environmental damage and the prospect of nuclear immolation. The 1920s witnessed a backlash against cars, which had earlier been seen as a miraculous answer to the affliction of horse-drawn vehicles — which filled the streets with noise and dung, and caused congestion and accidents. And the blight of industrialization was decried in the 19th century by Luddites and Romantics, who worried (with good reason) about the displacement of skilled artisans, the despoiling of the countryside and the suffering of factory hands toiling in smoke-belching mills.

[5] Stand back, and in each of these historical cases disappointment arose from a mix of unrealized hopes and unforeseen consequences. Technology unleashes the forces of creative destruction, so it is only natural that it leads to anxiety; for any given technology its drawbacks sometimes seem to outweigh its benefits. When this happen with several technologies at once, as today, the result is a wider sense of techno-pessimism.

[6] However, that pessimism can be overdone. Too often people focus on the drawbacks of a new technology while taking its benefits for granted. Worries about screen time should be weighed against the much more substantial benefits of ubiquitous communication and the instant access to information and entertainment that smart phones make possible. A further danger is that Luddite efforts to avoid the short-term costs associated with a new technology will end up denying access to its long-term benefits — something Carl Benedikt Frey, an Oxford academic, calls a "technology trap". Fears that robots will steal people's jobs may prompt politicians to tax them, for example, to discourage their use. Yet in the long run countries that wish to maintain their standard of living as their workforce ages and shrinks will need more robots, not fewer.

[7] That points to another lesson, which is that the remedy to technology-related problems very often involves more technology. Airbags and other improvements in safety features, for example, mean that in America deaths in car accidents per billion miles travelled have fallen from around 240 in the 1920s to around 12 today. AI is being applied as part of the effort to stem the flow of extremist material on social media. The ultimate example is climate change. It is hard to imagine any solution that does not depend in part on innovations in clean energy, carbon capture and energy storage.

[8] Technology itself has no agency: it is the choices people make about it that shape the world. Thus the techlash is a necessary step in the adoption of important new technologies. At its best, it helps frame how society comes to terms with innovations and imposes rules and policies that limit their destructive potential (seat belts, catalytic converters and traffic regulations), accommodate change (universal schooling as a response to industrialization) or strike a trade-off (between the convenience of ride-hailing and the protection of gig-workers). Healthy skepticism means that these questions are settled by a broad debate, not by a coterie of technologists.

Fire up the moral engine

[9] Perhaps the real source of anxiety is not technology itself, but growing doubt about the ability of societies to hold this debate, and come up with good answers. In that sense, techno-pessimism is a symptom of political pessimism. Yet there is something perversely reassuring about this: a gloomy debate is much better than no debate at all. And history still argues, on the whole, for optimism. The technological transformation since the Industrial Revolution has helped curb ancient evils, from child mortality to hunger and ignorance. Yes, the planet is warming and antibiotic resistance is spreading. But the solution to such problems calls for the deployment of more technology, not less. So as the decade turns, put aside the gloom for a moment. To be alive in the tech-obsessed 2020s is to be among the luckiest people who have ever lived.

(*The Economist*, 2019)

1. What is the writer's central claim in the passage?

_____

_____

2. How does the writer support his claim? Is it effective? Why?

_____

_____

_____

_____

Unit 7 Argumentation

3. According to the writer, the technologies expected to dominate the new decade also seem to cast a dark shadow. Which side of the technologies are you on?

4. Do people in China have the same worries? Why?

5. Write an argumentative essay stating your viewpoint of the technology.

Expansion

Passage 1

1. What is the writer's central idea and how does he support it with argument?
2. Do you agree with the writer's central claim? Why or why not? Defend your position with argument.

Hell Is Other People's Vacations

Ben Healy

[1] If you feel like you need a vacation, you're almost certainly right. Americans get far fewer paid days off than workers in pretty much any other industrialized democracy, and the time we actually take off has declined significantly, from 20.3 days in 1987 to 17.2 days in 2017.

[2] Beyond souvenirs and suntans, the best reason to take a break may be your own health. For the Helsinki Businessmen Study — a 40-year cardiovascular-health

study that also happens to be the working title of the solo album I'll probably never get around to recording — researchers treated men at risk of heart disease. From 1974 to 2004, those men who took at least three weeks of vacation were 37 percent less likely to die than those who took fewer weeks off.

[3] Even if we don't view time off as a matter of life and death, people who take more of their allotted vacation time tend to find their work more meaningful. Vacation can yield other benefits, too: People who took all or most of their paid vacation time to travel were more likely than others to report a recent raise or bonus. And time not taken depresses more than individual career prospects: In 2017, the average U.S. worker left six paid vacation days unused, which works out to 705 million days of travel nationally, enough to support 1.9 million travel-related jobs.

[4] For longevity to career growth to macroeconomic feats of strength, the case for vacation seems open-and-shut. Yet the picture's not entirely rosy. Tourism's carbon footprint grew four times as much as expected from 2009 to 2013, and accounted for 8 percent of all greenhouse-gas emissions in that period. What's more, the travel industry is expected to consume 92 percent more water in 2050 than it did in 2010, and 189 percent more land. In other environmental news, people are less likely to recycle while on vacation (both because they're unsure how to, and because getting away with things seems to be a key part of getting away from it all).

[5] The frisson of pitching plastic is not the only thrill tempting travelers. Interviews with tourists returning from various international destinations reveals that they used more drugs while on vacation than in everyday life. Other studies have found that people are more likely to engage in risky sexual behavior while traveling. We eat with abandon, too: On vacations of one to three weeks, tourists gain an average of 0.7 pounds, a significant portion of average annual weight gain. Finally, a 2015 study found that "travel and leisure" provoked envy — perhaps the single most toxic substance known to man — more than any other attribute examined (including "relationship and family", "appearance", and "money and material possessions"). The effect may be especially acute on social media: 62 percent of people who described Facebook-included bouts of jealousy said they'd been triggered by travel or leisure experiences — versus less than a quarter of people whose envy had

Unit 7 Argumentation

been piqued in person.

[6] So for your own health, book that vacation. But for everyone else's, please travel as sustainably as you can, and take it easy with the social media.

(*The Atlantic*, 2019)

Passage 2

1. What is the writer's central idea and how does he support it with argument?
2. Nibbling between meals has had bad press in recent years. Do you agree with it? Why or why not? Defend your position with argument.

Snack Your Way to Better Health

Dawn Yanek

[1] To snack or not to snack? That is the question ... for doctors, for nutritionists and for you, as you try to decide what to do about your grumbling stomach when it's nowhere close to mealtime. The short answer: Have the snack.

[2] Snacking has fallen out of favour in certain dieting circles, thanks in part to the popularity of intermittent fasting, in which you severely restrict your food intake on a periodic basis. Some folks interpret the Paleo diet, in which the diet-conscious attempt to imitate the food habits of our hunter-gatherer ancestors, as anti-snacking as well. But many modern-day studies have found that snacking can have positive effects on your health, both physical and mental. Like what? Grab a banana — or a handful of peanuts — and read on!

Weight Loss

[3] Can snacking help you drop a few kilos? Yes, but nutritionists' insight into what works has changed. They once thought that eating more frequently could boost your metabolism — your body would be working more often to burn calories. Alas, studies have been mixed when it comes to proving that theory. But a smart snack can prevent the kind of unhealthy binge eating that comes from hard-core hunger. "Your body is always talking to you — you just have to listen," says New York-based internal and functional medicine specialist Robert Graham, MD, MPH. "So if you're starting to feel a little hungry, don't wait." He recommends a simple approach: a three-meal plan interspersed with

two or three snacks.

[4] But you can't grab hold of any old snack. Chips, cookies, crackers and other simple carbohydrates boost your blood sugar quickly, which ultimately leads to the sugar crash we've all experienced. Instead, try nuts, complex carbs and fruits. "Toasted wholegrain bread with nut or seed butter with sliced tomato or cucumber is a great option and so are fruits such as pears, strawberries and oranges. Sprouted pulses such as moong, moth beans or chana can be made into a chaat by chopping in some tomatoes and onions with a sprinkling of lemon juice, salt and chopped coriander, for a delicious and nutritious mid-meal snack," says Naini Setalvad, a Mumbai-based obesity, lifestyle and disease consultant.

[5] Graham loves a fibre-rich apple because it's the perfect snacking size. Pair it with protein-rich nut butter and you'll feel fuller longer.

Overall Health

[6] Snacking is a way to sneak a variety of nutrients into your diet. Maya Feller, a registered dietician from New York, says you can't go wrong with a handful of mixed nuts. With polyunsaturated fats, fibre, protein, magnesium and calcium, nuts can help your heart. The *Journal of Nutrition* reported that eating almonds regularly can improve good HDL cholesterol levels and remove bad cholesterol from the body. Snacking on protein-rich foods helps preserve your muscle mass and stamina. The body can absorb only a finite amount of protein per meal, says Lisa Reed, CEO of Lisa Reed Fitness, citing research in the *Journal of the International Society of Sports Nutrition*. Distributing protein throughout the day via snacking can maximize protein intake. That's especially beneficial for people over 60. "When seniors don't get enough protein, they are more at risk for falls and fractures," she explains.

[7] Divvying up your calories and nutrients into smaller meals may also provide benefits for those worried about Type 2 diabetes. A small 2017 study from Greece showed that eating six smaller meals each day not only improved blood sugar levels but also reduced hunger in obese people with prediabetes or diabetes. "In my patients trying to control sugar levels," says Feller, "if they have a snack that's well balanced, they're more likely to have level blood sugar readings, as opposed to the highs and the lows." Other studies show that

blueberries may fight age-related memory decline and may even help ward off Alzheimer's, while yogurt and cheese can help protect bone health. Smart snacks with multiple health benefits include fresh vegetables with hummus, Greek yogurt with berries, hard-boiled eggs and avocado.

Mood and Mental Health

[8] If you've ever snapped at someone when you were hungry, you know that food — or lack thereof — can influence your mood. But when you're 'hangry', it's not just because your blood sugar has dropped. A study in the journal *Emotion* revealed that hunger has the ability to make unpleasant things seem even worse. Snacking helps you avoid that precarious position, resulting in fewer mood swings and better focus. This can have a positive ripple effect on your day and your food choices.

[9] Some studies have shown that healthy snacking may also improve memory and cognitive performance and help alleviate mental health issues such as anxiety and depression, says Ashwini Nadkarni, MD, an associate psychiatrist at Brigham and Women's Hospital and an instructor at Harvard Medical School. If you wait too long to eat between meals, your body thinks it's starving and releases the stress hormone cortisol to correct your glucose levels. "Cortisol will cause the release of inflammatory substances such as cytokines and leukotrienes, which can produce symptoms of depression and anxiety," Nadkarni explains. Again, snacking helps you sidestep this trap.

[10] Fasting and meal-skipping, along with dehydration, are also migraine triggers. As Graham explains, "When the brain is starved of both sugar and water, it will talk in the form of a headache." His prescription? In addition to drinking water, snacking on fresh fruit, with its natural sugars, can help. A small study published in the *Journal of Clinical Neuroscience* also found that snacking at night, rather than earlier in the day, reduces the odds of having a headache the next day by 40 per cent.

A Word of Caution

[11] Except in the case of preventing migraines, researchers generally advise skipping that midnight snack. People are more likely to make bad food choices late at night, which can contribute to weight gain. And studies show that night-time snacks increase problems with blood sugar regulation,

inflammation, cholesterol and triglyceride levels and cognitive ability.

[12] "For a quick fix, most people munch on high glycaemic index foods such as biscuits, chips and chocolate that are high in white sugar and white flour. These foods lead to fluctuation in blood sugar. The high and lows, in the long run, can lead to delayed recall. Sugar is the main cause of inflammation as well as elevated lipids," explains Setalvad. If you must have a snack at night, try cottage cheese. A 2018 study published in the *British Journal of Nutrition* found that eating 30 grams of it 30 to 60 minutes before bedtime can fill you up without making you gain weight. It can also improve your metabolism, muscle quality and overall health.

The Bottom Line

[13] There are different ways to go about this whole snacking thing. The one constant is to choose a healthy, filling option in an appropriate portion size. Do that, and the benefits don't stop at weight loss and improved health; your general approach to life might be affected. When you snack mindfully, says Nadkarni, "it's easier to take a deep breath, focus on exactly what you're eating at that moment and enjoy the day around you too."

(Reader's Digest, 2019)

Unit 8
Visual Description

Objectives

At the end of the unit, you should be able to

- ☑ understand how to describe various types of visuals and analyze their foci and purposes;
- ☑ master the writing skills and discourse patterns for describing the trend, ranking, comparison and contrast, or correlation in different visuals;
- ☑ write a coherent visual description essay to acknowledge and appreciate China's arduous efforts and great success in poverty alleviation.

Pre-class Work

Task 1

• Learning to Describe and Analyze Visuals

1. Match the following visuals with their corresponding names.

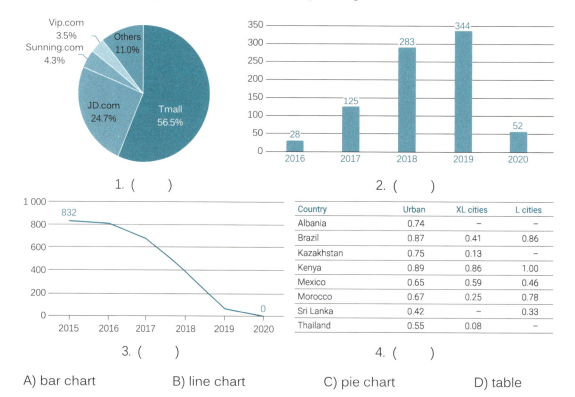

1. (　　)　　　2. (　　)　　　3. (　　)　　　4. (　　)

A) bar chart　　　B) line chart　　　C) pie chart　　　D) table

Unit 8 Visual Description

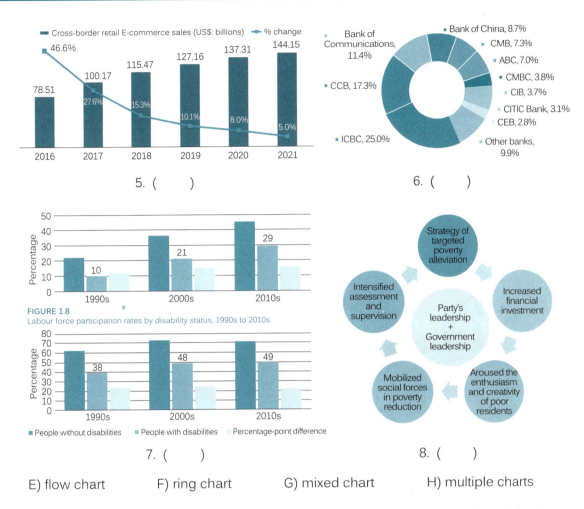

5. (　　)   6. (　　)

FIGURE 1.8
Labour force participation rates by disability status, 1990s to 2010s

7. (　　)   8. (　　)

E) flow chart   F) ring chart   G) mixed chart   H) multiple charts

2. Use the names from the box below to label the different components of the following bar chart.

| A) Illustrations | B) Note | C) Source | D) Title |

1. _____ : Annual Growth Rate of GDP and Consumption Level per Capita, Urban and Rural People

2. _____ :

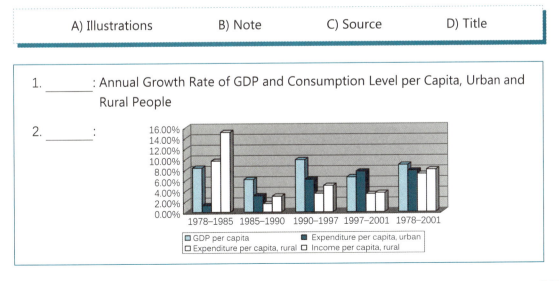

241

3. _____ : This figure is calculated at comparable price.

4. _____ of calculated data: Data of per capita consumption (1978–1999) are quoted from *A Collection of Statistical Data of New China's Fifty Years* edited by the Comprehensive Statistical Department of National Economy of National Statistical Bureau; the rest data are quoted from *China Statistical Yearbook* (2002).

3. Answer the following questions about the mixed chart.

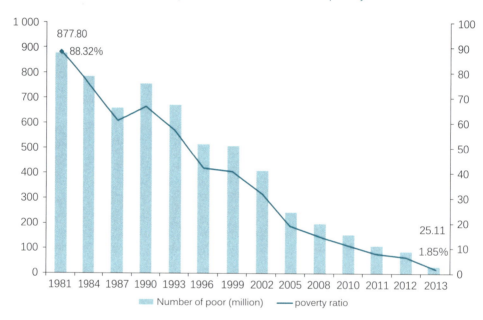

Poverty reduction in China: 1.9 dollar poverty line

(1) What is the unit of measurement for the X-axis in the mixed chart above?

_____

_____

(2) Which variable does the left Y-axis measure? What does "1000" on the left Y-axis mean?

_____

_____

Unit 8 Visual Description

(3) Which variable does the right Y-axis measure? What does "10" on the right Y-axis mean?

_____

_____

(4) What is the relationship between the bar chart and the line chart in this mixed chart?

_____

_____

_____

_____

(5) What is the core message of this mixed chart? How do the two Y-axes and the X-axis help to convey this message to the readers?

_____

_____

_____

_____

4. Fill out the following outline with information from the mixed chart below.

An Outline for the Mixed Chart Below
Target of Research: _____
Year of Conducting Research: _____
The left-sided bars represent _____ regions.
The right-sided bars represent _____ regions.
Number of Geographic Areas Under Survey: _____
Number of Countries and Areas in Total Under Survey: _____
Source of Calculated Data: _____

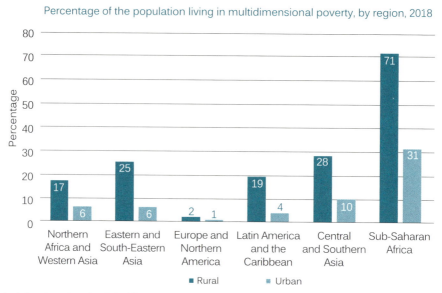

Source: Calculations based on the Oxford Poverty & Human Development Initiative's Global Multidimensional Poverty Index 2018, Tables 4.1–4.6. Available from https://ophi.org.uk/multidimensional-poverty-index/global-mpi-2018/. Accessed on 15 July 2019.

Note: Regional averages based on information for 13 countries and areas in Northern Africa and Western Asia, 10 countries in Eastern and South-Eastern Asia, 17 in Europe and Northern America, 20 in Latin America and the Caribbean, 12 in Central and Southern Asia, and 42 in sub-Saharan Africa. Results are not weighted by population size.

Task 2

• Focus and Purpose of Visuals

Read the following script with visuals and identify the purpose, focus, and illustrating power of visuals with the aid of discussion questions below.

Ending Poverty in China: Data Speak — China's Achievements in Poverty Alleviation

[1] China has seen one people shaking off poverty every 2.24 seconds since 2012, faster than global average and 10 million more than the population of Germany.

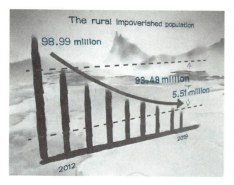
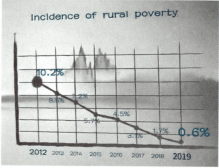

Unit 8 Visual Description

[2] The annual input of poverty alleviation funding from the central government increased by 100 billion yuan (US$14.3 billion).

[3] From 2013 to 2019, the disposable income of the rural poor increased by 19.7%, and 2.2 percentage points higher than the national average over the same period.

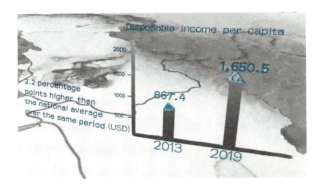

[4] Over 57 million rural people moved into safe houses; ten million poor people relocated to new communities; about 6,000 people moved out of the mountains every day; the rural per capita housing area expanded fivefold.

[5] All villages in impoverished areas can be accessed by paved roads; all villages within the coverage area of large power grids have access to electricity; almost all villages have broadband network coverage.

[6] Almost all are covered by universal health insurance. Over 95% of impoverished counties help maintain the school retention rate.

[7] All rural residents living below the current poverty line will be lifted out of poverty by 2020. China will achieve the Sustainable Development Goal on eradicating extreme poverty 10 years ahead of schedule.

(https://p.china.org.cn/2020-12/10/content-76997814.htm)

Discussion questions:

1. What overall topic does the above script focus on? How do the visuals support the presentation of the overall topic?

2. How many sub-topics are there in the above script? Try to match different sub-topics with the corresponding visuals.

3. Could you identify the name, components, units of measurement, and context for each of the visuals? How do these visuals facilitate the explanation of different sub-topics?

4. Does any of the visuals focus on comparison or trend? How do these visuals enhance the illustrating power of such comparison or trend?

5. What is the writer's purpose of using different visuals? How effective are these visuals in helping achieve the writing purpose?

Note:

The video for Task 2 can be accessed online. The complete video is of around 12 minutes on the topic of "Decoding World Poverty Reduction: China's Answer" at http://p.china.org.cn/2021-07/30/content_77662662.html.

In-class Activities

Paragraph Development in Diagram Writing

Writing about visuals, or diagram writing, is different from writing arguments or narratives. An essay of diagram writing usually consists of an introduction and a main-body paragraph. It is not necessary to write a conclusion for a diagram essay and you should refrain from offering your own opinion on the efficacy, reason or importance of the information and data in the diagram.

The introduction of a diagram writing essay consists of three parts. First, the introduction must first identify and describe the types of visual presented, such as a chart, a table, or a map. Second, the introduction should present the main message conveyed by the visual, i.e., the focus and the purpose of the chart or the table. Third, the introduction should provide contextual details shown in the visual, such as the units of measurement, time reference, and geographical area involved or given in the visual.

Unit 8 Visual Description

• Activity 1

Read the following sample carefully and then write introductions for the following charts and table respectively.

Sample introduction for the following line chart with notes:

The line chart illustrates the number of impoverished counties in China from 2015 to 2020.

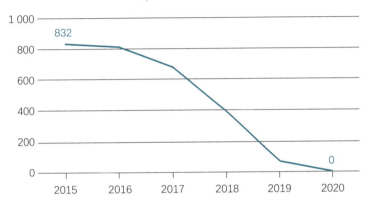

Source: The State Council Leading Group Office of Poverty Alleviation and Development

1. Write an introduction for the bar chart below.

_____

_____

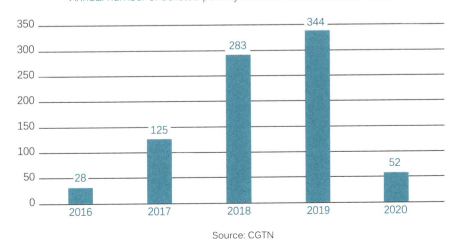

Source: CGTN

247

2. Write an introduction for the pie chart below.

_____

_____

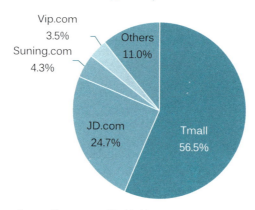

3. Write an introduction for the table below.

_____

_____

POVERTY SHARE OVER PROPORTION OF TOTAL POPULATION BY CITY SIZE

Country	Urban	XL cities	L cities	M cities	S cities	XS cities
Albania	0.74	–	–	0.73	0.69	0.79
Brazil	0.87	0.41	0.86	0.71	1.00	1.39
Kazakhstan	0.75	0.13	–	0.72	1.00	1.00
Kenya	0.89	0.86	1.00	1.00	7.00	1.00
Mexico	0.65	0.59	0.46	0.64	0.75	1.17
Morocco	0.67	0.25	0.78	0.74	1.00	1.00
Sri Lanka	0.42	–	0.33	0.33	0.50	0.50
Thailand	0.55	0.08	–	0.33	0.50	0.93

Calculations based on Ferré, Ferreira and Lanjouw (2012).

Notes:
1. Ferré, Ferreira and Lanjouw (2012) define city sizes as follows. XL for cities of more than 1 million inhabitants, L for cities between 500,000 and 1 million, M for cities between 100,000 and 500,000, S for cities between 50,000 and 100,000, and XS for cities of fewer than 50,000 people.
2. The eight countries shown were selected on the basis of their interest and the availability of data to construct detailed poverty maps (ibid.).

4. Discuss with your classmates to find out measures to help consolidate achievements of poverty alleviation.

Unit 8 Visual Description

• Activity 2

Finish the following exercises and try to write about trend in bar chart or line chart.

1. What is the focusing factor (i.e., the target of observation) in the bar chart below?

_____

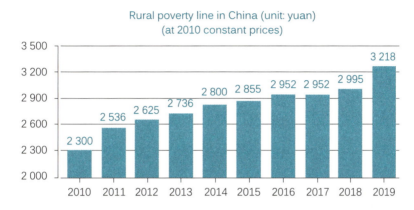

2. What is its unit of measurement? What is the context for this factor?

_____

_____

3. Is the target factor increasing at the same rate over the entire time span? If not, can you divide the increase into different stages?

_____

_____

4. What is the rate of increase for each stage according to your division? How does the increasing pattern differ among different stages?

_____

_____

_____

5. What was the initial value of this factor at 2010? When did it reach the peak value? What was the peak value?

_____

6. Now write about the trend in the above bar chart. Remember, do not divide the trend into too many stages and when describing the different stages, do not forget to provide the factor's values, i.e., you should mention the specific numbers in diagram writing.

Components	A paragraph on the trend in the above bar chart
An overview of the trend	
A description of the change in the 1st stage with key features	
A description of the change in the 2nd stage with key features	
...	
A description of Stage N with key features	

7. What factor does the line chart below represent? What factor does the bar chart indicate?

_____

_____

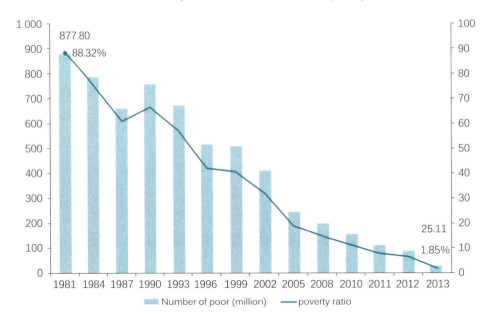

Poverty reduction in China: 1.9 dollar poverty line

Unit 8 Visual Description

8. What are the units of measurement respectively for the line chart and the bar chart?

   _____

   _____

9. How many stages can the line chart be divided into? And what about the bar chart?

   _____

   _____

10. What was the initial value, peak value, bottom value, respectively for the line chart and the bar chart?

    _____

    _____

    _____

    _____

11. How different are the decreasing rates for different stages in the line chart and the bar chart?

    _____

    _____

12. Now write two paragraphs on the trend in the above mixed chart.

Components	Paragraphs on the trend in the above mixed chart
An overview of the trend for the line chart	Paragraph 1 on the trend in the above line chart:
A description of all stages of the line chart with key features of change	

(continued)

251

Components	Paragraphs on the trend in the above mixed chart
An overview of the trend for the bar chart	Paragraph 2 on the trend in the above bar chart:
A description of all stages of the bar chart with key features of change	

13. Discuss and debate on what criteria and methods are suitable for deciding the exact poverty line for a specific region at a specific time point. Discuss what social and economic significance can be achieved by designating or adjusting poverty line.

• Activity 3

Finish the following exercises and try to write about ranking in pie chart or table.

  Writing About Ranking in Pie Chart or Table

1. Work in pairs or teams, observe the following pie chart and fill out the ranking table below.

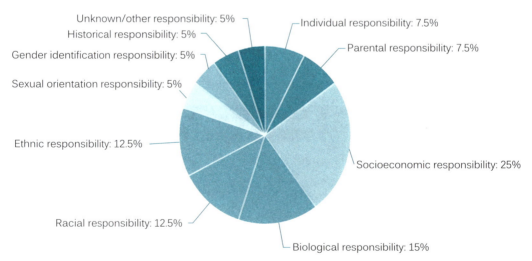

Note: The percentages in this chart are not research findings but just hypothetical speculations made by frugaling.org as supportive evidence to its claim. Do not take this pie chart as serious scientific research findings! This pie chart is only a product of frugaling.org's contemplation upon the possible external and internal causes of poverty, instead of blaming poverty solely on the individual, which is a common false assumption held by capitalist ideology. However, these categories can be thought-provoking by shedding light on the obstinate and systematic poverty in the Western world.

Unit 8 Visual Description

Placement in ranking	Name of category	Its share (in %)
No. 1 (the largest percentage)		
No. 2		
No. 3		
No. 4		
No. 5		

2. Now write a paragraph about the ranking in the above pie chart.

Components	A paragraph about the ranking in the above pie chart
An overview	
A description of prominent categories	
A description of other categories	
A description of similarity/contrast among different categories	

3. Work in pairs or teams, observe the following ring chart — a graphic variation of pie chart and discuss the questions below.

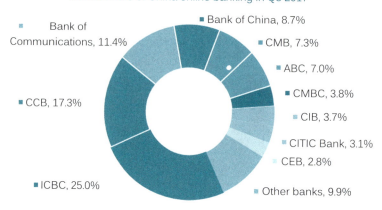

(1) How many categories are there in the above ring chart? What are the major players in China's online banking in the 3rd quarter of 2017?

_____
_____
_____
_____

(2) When there seem to be too many categories, what writing techniques can be adopted to present more data in a systematic way without rambling or redundancy?

_____
_____

(3) What is the core message conveyed by this chart? Discuss to identify the overall visual effect of this ring chart and write your overview at the beginning of the paragraph below.

_____
_____

Unit 8 Visual Description

4. Now write a paragraph about the ranking in the above ring chart.

Components	A paragraph about the ranking in the above ring chart
An overview	
A description of key details in either of the ranking patterns	
A description of similarity/contrast among different categories	

5. Discuss to find out the causes of poverty. Debate on who ought to shoulder the responsibility of poverty alleviation.

● Activity 4

Finish the following exercises and try to use comparison and contrast in visual description.

 Using Comparison and Contrast in Visual Description

1. Work in pairs or teams, observe the following two pie charts and discuss to choose a pattern of contrast.

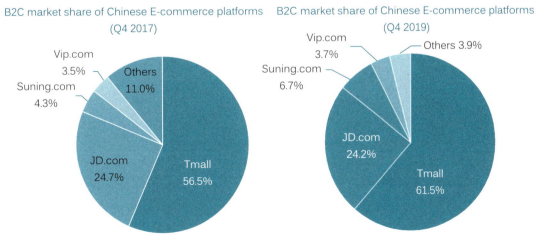

Source: Ecommerce Worldwide, Walkthechat Analysis

255

(1) How many platforms do the two pie charts present? What percentage did each of them account for in the 4th quarter of 2017 and the 4th quarter of 2019?

_____

_____

_____

_____

_____

_____

_____

(2) Which pattern of contrast would you like to use for describing these two pie charts?

(3) Among the various contrasts you would like to make and elaborate on, which contrast is more important, and thus worth more detailed coverage in your writing?

2. Now write a paragraph by using your chosen pattern of contrast for discussing the key information in these two charts. Stick to the same pattern of contrast in this paragraph, but you can also choose to write another version with the other pattern.

Components	A paragraph contrasting the above two pie charts
An overview of the two pie charts	
A description of key contrast with details	
A description of other contrasts with details	

Unit 8 Visual Description

3. Work in teams of four. Designate a team secretary and hold a review meeting with the help of the "Secretary's Memorandum on Group Review Meeting" table below. Observe the bar chart below and try to (1) find out all possible comparisons and contrasts that can be made from the data in this chart; (2) evaluate the importance or worth of each; and (3) reach a consensus on what to be included in your writings and what to be discarded, as well as the sequence for presenting different information.

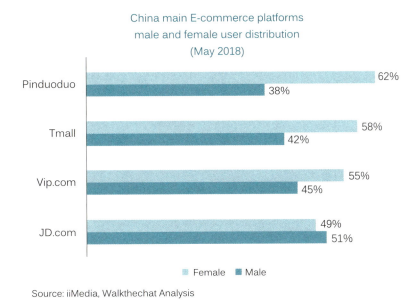

China main E-commerce platforms male and female user distribution (May 2018)

- Pinduoduo: Female 62%, Male 38%
- Tmall: Female 58%, Male 42%
- Vip.com: Female 55%, Male 45%
- JD.com: Female 49%, Male 51%

Source: iiMedia, Walkthechat Analysis

Secretary's Memorandum on Group Review Meeting	
Group secretary's name: _____	
Possible comparisons to be made	
Possible contrasts to be made	
What comparison(s) to be retained (evaluating the worth of each comparison)	
What contrast(s) to be retained (evaluating the worth of each contrast)	
How to sequence the comparisons	
How to sequence the contrasts	
Whether to discuss comparison first or contrast first?	

257

4. Now work with your teammates to co-write a paragraph by using both comparison and contrast with the aid of the above memorandum.

Components	A paragraph comparing & contrasting the above bar chart
An overview	
A description of the key comparison	
A description of the key contrast	
A description of other comparisons/ contrasts	

5. Discuss how to use E-commerce to facilitate poverty alleviation and to promote rural revitalization, industry upgrading and transformation. Discuss to find out the innovative measures to be taken via E-commerce in various regions and industries to help us achieve common prosperity.

• Activity 5

Finish the following exercises and try to discover correlations in mixed chart.

Discovering Correlations
in Mixed Chart

1. What is the focus and purpose of the mixed chart below?

_____

_____

_____

Unit 8 Visual Description

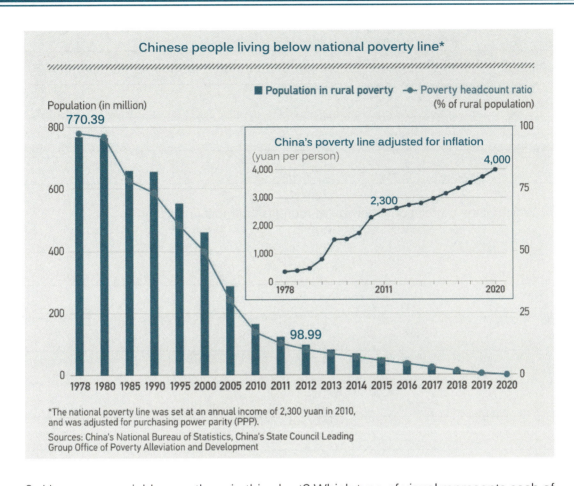

2. How many variables are there in this chart? Which type of visual represents each of them?

___

3. What correlation can you find between and among different variables in this chart?

___

259

4. Which of the correlations that you've found is the most important?

5. How are such correlations conducive to the illustration of the chart's core message?

6. How many correlations would you like to include in your essay? What are they?

Unit 8 Visual Description

7. In what order would you like to arrange all the key details in your main body paragraph?

8. Now convert your discussion results on the above questions into an essay on the mixed chart.

Components	An Essay Revealing Correlations in the Above Mixed Chart
An Introduction	
An Overview	
A description of the key details of the three charts	
A description of the key correlations	

After-class Practice

Task 1

Translate the following sentences into English.

1. 全国建档立卡贫困人口的人均纯收入由 2016 年的 4 124 元增加到了 2019 年的 9 057 元，年均增幅 30%。

2. 全国累计建成集中安置区 3.5 万个，安置住房 266 万套，960 万贫困搬迁民众乔迁新居，有效解决了"十三五"期间近五分之一贫困人口的脱贫问题。

3. 以现行农村贫困标准衡量，2012 年末我们农村贫困人口 9 899 万人，比 1985 年末减少 5.6 亿多人，下降了 85.0%

4. 过去四十年，我国贫困人口累计减少 7 亿多人，对全球减贫贡献率超过 70%。

5. 2018 年全国脱贫的 475 万贫困户中，得到产业扶贫帮扶的有 353 万户，占比达 74.2%。

Unit 8 Visual Description

Task 2

Fill out the following table that helps build your own verb reservoir for diagram writing, using a dictionary or thesaurus if necessary.

A Vocabulary Reservoir of Useful Verbs in Diagram Writing				
Verbs showing increase	Verbs showing decrease	Verbs for comparison	Verbs for ranking	Verbs for correlation

Task 3

Revise and edit the following sentences by eliminating redundancy or repetition.

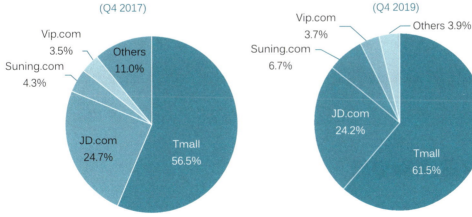

Source: Ecommerce Worldwide, Walkthechat Analysis

1. As can be seen in this pie chart, the pie chart depicts the B2C market share of Chinese e-commerce platforms.

263

2. The share of proportion taken up by Suning.com has undergone a much more faster increase than the share of proportion taken up by Vip.com.

3. In this pie chart, the pie slice representing Tmall was 56.5% in the fourth and last quarter of 2017, namely from October to December in 2017, and this pie slice had a significantly major rising increment to a percentage of 61.5% in the fourth quarter of 2019.

4. The fast-falling drop dive of percentage taken and accounted for by the others (meaning the other smaller platforms) suffered a rather much impressive and considerable plummeting decline-style with a fast pace of reduction, to a bottom minimum of 3.9% in the fourth quarter of 2019.

5. JD.com's share percentage is respectively in the separate number of 24.7% and 24.2% in both the fourth quarter of 2017 and 2019, which is equivalent of a stagnation of leveling off at 24.7% in 2017 and 24.2% in 2019.

Expansion

Passage 1

1. Read the passage below and summarize China's remarkable achievements in agriculture since the founding of the People's Republic of China in 1949.
2. How does the writer integrate the visuals effectively into illustrating the claim of this passage?

Unit 8 Visual Description

How China Feeds Its 1.4 Billion People

Hu Yiwei

[1] Chinese agricultural scientist Yuan Longping keeps talking about his dream of growing hybrid rice so huge that he could one day "hide in the shadow of the rice crops".

[2] It is not just about Yuan's ambition for a scientific breakthrough, but also his deep concern for food security in the world's most populous country — how to feed 20 percent of the world's population on merely nine percent of the world's farmland.

[3] China's food and agricultural system has undergone historic transformation to solve the problem.

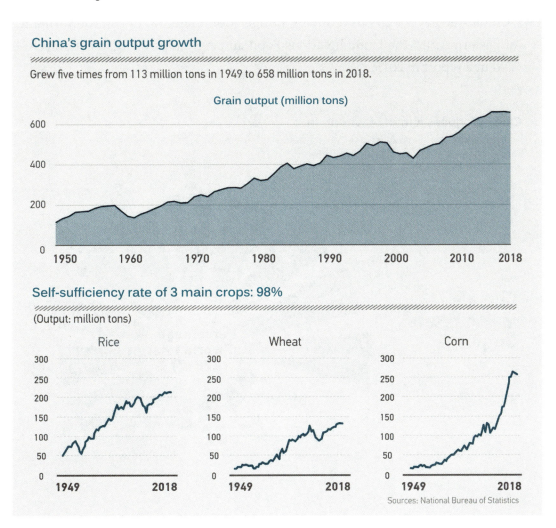

265

Path to self-sufficiency

[4] Back in 1949 when the People's Republic of China was founded, there were less than 600 grams of food available for each Chinese a day. The Chinese older generation can still recall the days when they had to buy meals with *liangpiao*, a food coupon issued by the government when food was scarce.

[5] Seventy years on, China's agriculture sector has seen rapid growth, with grain output expanding almost five times, reaching 658 million tons in 2018.

[6] The per capita output has more than doubled from 209 kg to over 470 kg, above the world average.

[7] The self-sufficient ratio of China's three staple crops — rice, wheat and corn — is now above 98 percent.

[8] "China's achievements in reducing hunger dominate the overall performance of Eastern Asia," the United Nations Food and Agriculture Organization (FAO) said in a report in 2015.

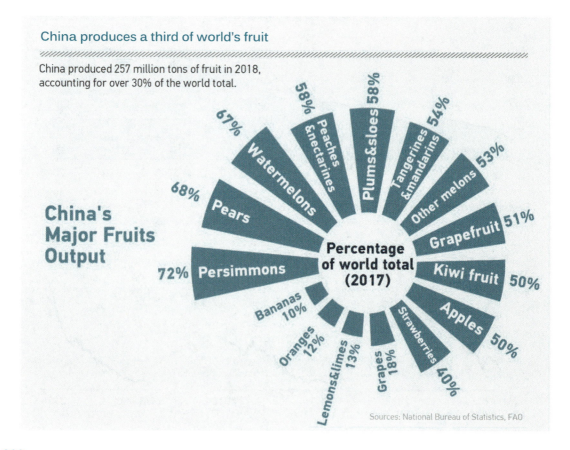

Unit 8 Visual Description

[9] This year China is also expecting a bumper harvest of crops from rice to corn and soybeans, according to officials.

Evolving diet

[10] China has now become both the world's largest producer and consumer of agricultural products. It is producing half the vegetables and 30 percent of fruit.

[11] Over a quarter of the global meat output also comes from China and its output of aquatic products has been ranked first in the world for 30 years.

[12] Today, the government's requirement for food production not only ensures that 1.4 billion Chinese people "have enough to eat", but also to "eat well".

[13] With many more food options for daily consumption, the Chinese diet has become healthier and more diversified.

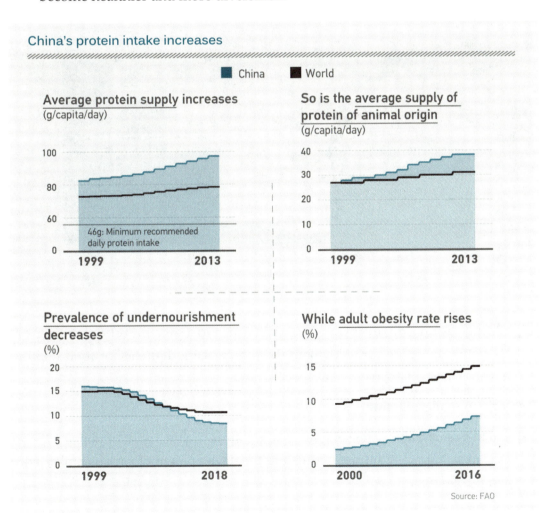

[14] The rate of the undernourished population fell from 23.9 percent in 1990 to 8.5 percent in 2018.

[15] The reduction coincided with China's economic rise and openness. The surging income stimulated the appetite of the country's burgeoning middle class, who tend to care more about food quality and nutrition and look for more food supplies overseas.

[16] The recent keenness for avocado is one of the most prominent examples. In 2017, China imported over 30,000 tons of the fruit, over 1,000 times the amount in 2011. It is also trying to grow avocado domestically.

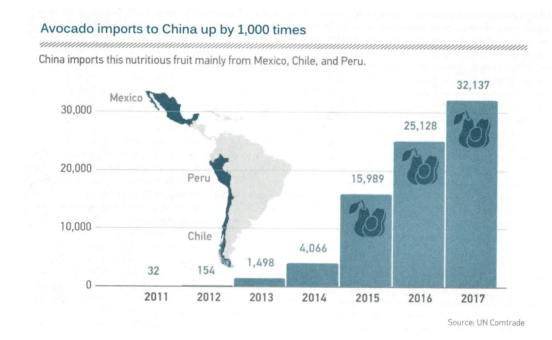

[17] China's food consumption has transformed from merely warding off starvation to eating for enjoyment, with increasing demand for food quality, nutrition and diversity.

Tech-driven modernization

[18] China's remarkable achievements in agriculture are the result of policy support as well as improved infrastructure and the development of agricultural science and technology.

Unit 8 Visual Description

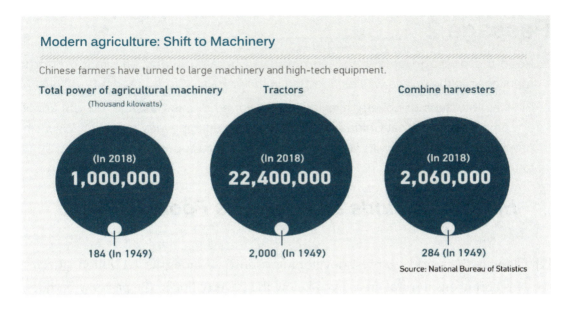

[19] Technological progress contributed to 58.5 percent of China's agricultural growth in 2018, over 30 percent above the figure of 40 years ago, according to official data.

[20] Large machinery and technology have been promoted. The overall rate of mechanization in major crop plowing, sowing and harvesting is more than 80 percent, revolutionizing the old way of heavy manual labor.

[21] Besides raising yield, China is also striving to improve the quality of its soil and to reducing water and fertilizer use.

[22] Further modernization of farm practices is underway, according to the Chinese Academy of Agricultural Sciences (CAAS).

[23] The academy has drawn up a five-year plan for developing key technologies in areas such as high-quality crop varieties, automated machines, agricultural product processing, modern food manufacturing, water efficiency, pollution control, agricultural waste recycling, and ecological restoration and protection.

[24] China aims to develop 800 million *mu* (53 million hectares) of high-standard farmland by 2020, and 1 billion by 2022.

[25] Starvation is no longer bothering China, while avoiding a food crisis has always been, and will continue to be among the nation's top priorities.

(https://news.cgtn.com/news/2019-09-23/Graphics-How-China-feeds-its-1-4-billion-people-KdLxOoA7x6/index.html)

Passage 2

1. Read the passage below and summarize China's poverty alleviation efforts mentioned in the text as well as depicted in the visuals.
2. Besides the steps of poverty alleviation mentioned in this passage, do you know any other measures that China has successfully taken in poverty reduction? Work in groups of 3–4. Discuss with your group members and report your group's findings to the whole class.

How China Finds and Helps Its Poorest People

Pan Zhaoyi

[1] China is the world's largest developing country. Among its 1.4 billion citizens, tens of millions in rural areas lived below the poverty line in the past few decades. But things have changed since the country's poverty alleviation campaign was rolled out.

[2] By the end of 2020, nearly 100 million people in rural areas had been lifted out of extreme poverty together with all the 832 designated poor counties, mostly in the central and western regions.

[3] Historically, identifying those truly in need is a challenging task for countries with such a large population in poverty.

It is imperative to know the impoverished so as to help them.

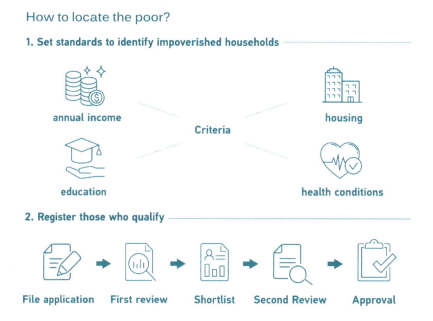

Unit 8 Visual Description

[4] China has developed a set of standards and procedures to accurately identify the poor, and grassroots officials have spent time in villages analyzing the distribution of the poor population, causes of their poverty and their actual needs.

[5] Poverty eradication covers a wide range of areas and is extremely complex, thus requiring rigorous investigation, organization, leadership and implementation.

After locating the poor, the next step is to determine who ought to offer help.

[6] China has established a management structure with the central government acting as coordinator, provincial governments formulating their own plans, and city and county-level governments overseeing implementation.

[7] The network covers all poor areas, and officials are sent to villages to help every needy household.

How to help?

[8] There are many different types of poverty, and the causes vary from case to case. Without the right remedies, the root cause cannot be fully addressed.

[9] China has adopted categorized and targeted measures to reduce poverty, based on the situation of individual households, local conditions and the causes for and types of poverty.

[10] These targeted measures include boosting the economy to provide more job opportunities, relocating poor people from inhospitable areas, improving education in impoverished areas, and providing subsistence allowances for those unable to shake off poverty solely on their own.

How to help?

Boost local economy, create jobs:

▶ Leverage local resources to establish

- **300,000** industrial bases
- **12,000** agricultural product brands
- **14,400** enterprises
- **719,000** rural cooperatives

▶ E-commerce

Geographic reach: **832** poor counties

Online retailers:
- 2016 — **1.32 million**
- 2020 — **3.11 million**

▶ Loans

Value: **710 billion** yuan
Beneficiaries: **150 million** households

Relocation programs:

▶ **9.6 million** relocated; **94.1%** employed

▶ Supporting policies

35,000 new houses **6,100** new schools **12,000** new hospitals

3,400 new nursing homes **40,000** new recreation venues

Ecological compensation for:

Protecting forests   Keeping waterways clean   Environmental restoration

1.1 million employed as forest rangers

(Each represent 10,000)

301,491 km² of farmland turned to forests and grasslands

Unit 8 Visual Description

Access to education:

▶ The numbers of teachers sent to

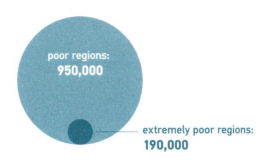

poor regions: **950,000**

extremely poor regions: **190,000**

▶ Financial aid for **640 million** students

Subsistence allowance:

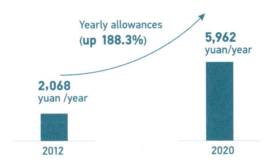

Yearly allowances (up **188.3%**)

2,068 yuan /year — 2012

5,962 yuan/year — 2020

[11] The governments have redoubled their efforts to boost employment for the poor through such means as offering free training on vocational skills, encouraging entrepreneurs to start businesses in those poor people's hometowns or villages, and creating public welfare jobs for the rest of the unemployed.

[12] Poor people who have the ability to work are encouraged to find employment locally or elsewhere, or start their own businesses.

(https://news.cgtn.com/news/2021-04-07/Graphics-How-China-finds-and-helps-its-poorest-people-ZgbSW5ByU0/index.html)

参考文献

Anonymous. Pessimism vs Progress. *The Economist*, December 18, 2019.

Anonymous. The Gap Between China's Rural and Urban Youth Is Closing, *The Economist*, January 21, 2021.

Anonymous. Three Kinds of Friendships. http://wenku.baidu.com/view/a7fd7172650e52ea5418982f.html.

Bacon, F. Of Studies. https://wenku.baidu.com/view/5adfe1923968011ca200918a.html.

Baker, R. Growing Up. New York, NY: Congdon & Weed, 1982.

Britt, S. Neat People vs. Sloppy People. https://rowenasworld.org/syllabi/ENGL1302/Britt-NeatVsSloppy.pdf.

Brulliard, K. The Surprise Thank-you. *Washington Post*, May 11, 2018.

Davis, J. Your Brain Was Made for Walking. Reader's Digest, November, 2020.

Dorrill, J. F. & Harwell, C. W. Read and Write: A Guide to Effective Composition. New York, NY: Harcourt Brace Jovanovich, 1987.

Folse, K. S. & Pugh, T, *Great Writing*, Fifth Edition, Washington, D.C.: National Geographic, 2019.

Gregory, D. Shame. https://www.garlandisdschools.net/uploaded/high-schools/nghs/documents/ela/17-shame.pdf.

Haynie, D. 4 Basic Components of an Online Course. https://www.usnews.com/education/online-education/articles/2013/04/24/4-basic-components-of-an-online-course.

Healy, B. Hell Is Other People's Vacations. *The Atlantic*, June, 2019.

Held, S. The Most Overrated Virtue. https://www.hadar.org/blog/most-overrated-virtue.

Henderson, G. *Other Children: Public Schools Outside Suburbs*. Norman, OK: University of Oklahoma Press, 1971.

Hu, Y. How China Feeds Its 1.4 Billion People. http://news.cgtn.com/news/2019-09-23/Graphics-How-China-feeds-its-1-4-billion-people-KdLxOoA7x6/index.html)

Hurwitz, M. The 5 Types of Foreigners in China. https://www.yoyochinese.com/blog/learn-mandarin-chinese-5-types-of-foreigners-in-china.

Jen, G. & Wang, Q. What Social Distancing Reveals About East-West Differences. https://blogs.scientificamerican.com/observations/what-social-distancing-reveals-about-east-west-differences.

Jones, L. Sincerity: An Overrated Virtue. *Skeptical Briefs*, December, 1997.

Kinsella, E. L, Ritchie, T. D, & Igou, E. R. Zeroing in on Heroes: A Prototype Analysis of Hero Features. *J Pers Soc Psychol, 108*(1), 2015.

Langan, J. *College Writing Skills with Readings*, Ninth Edition, Beijing: Foreign Language Teaching and Research Press, 2014.

Lewis, T. How Men's Brains Are Wired Differently than Women's. http://www.livescience.com/41619-male-female-brains-wired-differently.html.

Lin, Y. *My Country and My People*. London: William Heinemann Ltd., 1936.

Lin, Y. *The Importance of Living*. Beijing: Foreign Language Teaching and Research Press, 2009.

Lin, Y. *The Gay Genius: The Life and Times of Su Tungpo*. Omaha, NE: The John Day Company, 1947.

Miller, Q. *The Generation of Ideas: A Thematic Reader*. Boston, MA: Heinle Cengage Learning, 2004.

Obiora, N. The Dark Side of Social Media. The World of English, 2020 (6).

Pan, Z. How China Finds and Helps Its Poorest People. http://news.cgtn.com/news/2021-04-07/Graphics-How-China-finds-and-helps-its-poorest-people-ZgbSW5Byu0/index.html.

Pettigrew, T. What Is a University. https://www.macleans.ca/education/university/what-is-a-university.

Smalley, R. L., Ruetten, M. K. & Kozyrev, J. R. *Refining Composition Skills: Academic Writing and Grammar*. Boston, MA: Heinle Cengage Learning, 2011.

Smith, E. E. The Two Kinds of Stories We Tell about Ourselves. https://ideas.ted.com/the-two-kinds-of-stories-we-tell-about-ourselves.

Taylor, B. The 4 Kinds of Leaders Who Create the Future. https://hbr.org/2017/12/the-4-kinds-of-leaders-who-create-the-future.

Thompson, D. How Disaster Shaped the Modern City. *The Atlantic*, October, 2020.

Yanek, D. Snack Your Way to Better Health. *Reader's Digest India*, December, 2019.

Yang, Q. Live-streaming KOL Meltdowns. *The World of English*, 2020 (5).

Zinsser, W. On Writing Well. Harper Collins Publishers, 2016.

乔萍,瞿淑蓉,宋洪玮.散文佳作108篇[M].南京:译林出版社,2011.

王守仁.《大学英语教学指南》要点解读[J].外语界,2016(3).

郑树棠.新视野大学英语(第三版)[M].北京:外语教学与研究出版社,2011.

中华人民共和国教育部.教育部关于印发《高等学校课程思政建设指导纲要》的通知[EB/OL].http://www.gov.cn/zhengce/zhengceku/2020-06/06/content_5517606.htm.